Autocratization in Contemporary Uganda

Autocratization in Contemporary Uganda

Clientelism, Coercion and Social Control

Edited by
Moses Khisa

ZED

LONDON · NEW YORK · OXFORD · NEW DELHI · SYDNEY

ZED BOOKS
Bloomsbury Publishing Plc, 50 Bedford Square, London, WC1B 3DP, UK
Bloomsbury Publishing Inc, 1385 Broadway, New York, NY 10018, USA
Bloomsbury Publishing Ireland, 29 Earlsfort Terrace, Dublin 2, D02 AY28, Ireland

BLOOMSBURY and Zed Books are trademarks of Bloomsbury Publishing Plc

First published in Great Britain 2024
This paperback edition published 2025

Series design: Adriana Brioso
Cover image © Luke Dray/Getty Images

A catalogue record for this book is available from the British Library.

Library of Congress Cataloging-in-Publication Data
Names: Khisa, Moses, editor.
Title: Autocratization in contemporary Uganda : clientelism, coercion and social control /
edited by Moses Khisa. Other titles: Clientelism, coercion and social control
Description: London ; New York : Zed Books, 2024. |
Includes bibliographical references and index.
Identifiers: LCCN 2023031366 (print) | LCCN 2023031367 (ebook) |
ISBN 9781350323537 (hb) | ISBN 9781350323551 (ebook) |
ISBN 9781350323568 (epdf) | ISBN 9781350323575
Subjects: LCSH: Museveni, Yoweri, 1944- | Authoritarianism–Uganda. |
Uganda–Politics and government–1979-
Classification: LCC DT433.285 .A925 2024 (print) | LCC DT433.285 (ebook) |
DDC 967.61044–dc23/eng/20230711
LC record available at https://lccn.loc.gov/2023031366
LC ebook record available at https://lccn.loc.gov/2023031367

ISBN: HB: 978-1-3503-2353-7
PB: 978-1-3503-2354-4
ePDF: 978-1-3503-2356-8
eBook: 978-1-3503-2355-1

Typeset by Integra Software Services Pvt. Ltd.

For product safety related questions contact productsafety@bloomsbury.com.

To find out more about our authors and books visit www.bloomsbury.com
and sign up for our newsletters.

In Memorium: *Mzee Hassan Nangalama Wanyera, 1928–2018*

Contents

Preface and acknowledgements

The idea and inspiration for this book came out of the 'Uganda Politics' roundtable convened at the annual meetings of the African Studies Association (ASA) in the United States. Co-convened by Holger Bernt Hansen and Joshua B. Rubongoya, the roundtable served as an update and a quick-take reflection on major trends in Uganda's political direction under NRM rule. Along with Holger and Joshua, other equally senior scholars who studied politics in Uganda participated in the roundtable discussions, including Frederick Golooba-Mutebi, Ben Jones, Nelson Kasfir and Roger Tangri. While not anywhere close to the seniority of these colleagues, I was kindly invited to join the group in 2017 and have since regularly participated. After the 2019 ASA conference in Boston, I proposed bringing some of the conference presentations into a publication, perhaps a special journal issue.

The discussions at the ASA roundtable persuaded me that a comprehensive reassessment and rigorous explanation of Uganda's political trajectory under President Museveni were urgently needed. I started thinking about writing a broad-sweep monograph of Uganda's political development, writ large, covering as much empirical scope and theoretical ground as I could muster the wherewithal to. However, upon reflection and recognizing my limited intellectual bandwidth, I concluded that pulling together a wider pool of scholars for an edited volume would yield a better and more compelling study than I was capable of accomplishing in a monograph. The rich and engaging analyses by different authors in the current volume undoubtedly do greater justice to the issues at stake than I would have accomplished.

This book attempts to achieve two core goals. First, to provide a theoretical framework, laid out in the introductory chapter and given further treatment in the different chapters that follow, for explaining regime resilience and autocratic deepening in Uganda with comparative implications. The second goal is to survey a range of empirical domains and nodes that both descriptively illuminate Uganda's autocratic trajectory and account for why Museveni's rule has endured with all the attendant implications. Action-oriented and policy-interested actors may find some of our observations, analyses and conclusions worth taking up. In pursuing these interlinked goals, we have aimed to strike a balance between theoretical rigour and empirical detail, by situating our understanding of Uganda's political landscape in a wider theoretical and comparative compass without granting short shrift to the specificities of the Ugandan case study.

To be sure, a study of this magnitude is limited and invariably inexhaustive, so admittedly we could cover only so much within our institutional, intellectual and resource constraints. There is much more to do. With all the uncertainty in a fast-paced socio-economic environment, not to mention the ruptures that social scientists are woefully incapable of predicting, this book provides a modest endeavour in understanding where Uganda has come from and where it stands today, while saying very little about the future. Yet, ominous signs are so palpable that we would be remiss not to speculate about a possible perilous path ahead, considering the treacherous trajectory on which the incumbent party and president have placed the country. That said, the readers of this book may interpret events and happenings differently from us, the authors, perhaps discerning a positive outlook ahead or envisioning a silver lining to the rather dire portrait painted in the current volume. While much has gone wrong, hopeful Ugandans may see the possibility of a more progressive politics in the years ahead.

In completing this book, we have incurred numerous intellectual and institutional debts making this short acknowledgement note inadequate if somewhat perfunctory. Our deepest gratitude is to Joe Oloka-Onyango of Makerere University, Kampala, who read the entire manuscript at very short notice with an incredibly rapid turnaround. Joe provided critical and constructive comments on the whole manuscript and on each of the individual chapters. His observations and suggestions nudged us to rethink critical issues, correct glaring inaccuracies and reconsider many assertions, making the final manuscript significantly better. We are also grateful to an anonymous reviewer, whose comments especially on the introduction were greatly appreciated, and two other anonymous reviewers who provided thoughtful feedback and suggestions on the initial proposal for the book.

We presented early versions of some of the chapters in this book at the ASA annual meetings in 2020 and 2021. In addition, I presented iterations of the introduction at the Institute of African Studies of George Washington University, the Department of Political Science of Stellenbosch University and at the Department of Political Science writing group in the School of Public and International Affairs (SPIA) at North Carolina State University, my institutional home. Other contributors to this volume also presented drafts at platforms and spaces as acknowledged in their respective chapters. We are grateful to the audiences at these multiple institutions for their criticisms and feedback. I did part of the work of editing and chapter-writing during a fellowship at the Stellenbosch Institute for Advanced Study (STIAS), South Africa. I am grateful to STIAS staff especially the Director, Edward Kirumira, and Programme Manager, Christoff Pauw. I am equally grateful to the SPIA Director, Irwin Morris, my Department Chair, Michael Struett and my ever dependable intellectual home in Uganda, the Centre for Basic Research.

As the editor, it was a great privilege and pleasure to work with some of the very best scholars, young and old, bold and brilliant, who specialize in the politics of contemporary Uganda. I learnt a lot over the past three years working on this book. I was challenged in ways that were intellectually enriching and professionally invaluable. This book is the product of collective commitment, dedication and determination by all chapter authors. They made my job as editor less onerous and more enjoyable. Our commissioning editors at Bloomsbury, Olivia Dellow and Nick Wolterman, patiently responded to my incessant requests, inquiries and unmet deadlines. They shepherded the project with remarkable diligence and dedication. We are most grateful to them. We are equally grateful to the production team led by Shamli Priya Vijayan and Amy Brownbridge for helping get the project to the finish line.

A final note of acknowledgement is in memory of my late father, Mzee Hassan Nangalama Wanyera, who departed in 2018 at the ripe age of ninety. Mzee's fidelity to education was crucial for getting me to where I ended up professionally despite (or perhaps because) he had no more than five years of formal schooling. In his own inimitable way, he held political opinions he rarely expressed publicly, often insisting politics was so terrible that we, his children, should not talk about it! Nevertheless, he took his civic duties seriously. In late 2000 as the season for the 2001 elections heated up, I pressed him to comment on political developments underway in the country. He told me cryptically it was about time Museveni gave way! I was a 'small boy' then, in high school. Close to a quarter-century later, Museveni is still ruling Uganda! It is to Mzee Wanyera's memory that I dedicate this book.

Moses Khisa
Raleigh, North Carolina
October 2023

Abbreviations

ADF	Allied Democratic Forces
AES	Applied Energy Services
ANC	African National Congress
AU	African Union
CA	Constituent Assembly
CCM	Chama Cha Mapinduzi
CCEDU	Citizens' Coalition for Electoral Democracy in Uganda
CMI	Chieftaincy of Military Intelligence
CSOs	Civil Society Organizations
DfID	Department for International Development (UK)
DGF	Democratic Governance Facility
DNMC	District Non-Governmental Monitoring Committee
DP	Democratic Party
DRA	Descendants of Resistance Army
EAC	East Africa Community
EC	Electoral Commission
EPRDF	Ethiopian People's Revolutionary Democratic Front
ERA	Electricity Regulatory Authority
ESO	External Security Organization
FDC	Forum for Democratic Change
FEDEMU	Federal Democratic Movement
FOBA	Force Obote Back Again
FRONASA	Front for National Salvation
FUNA	Former Uganda National Army
GWOT	Global War on Terror

HRNJ	Human Rights Network for Journalists
HSM	Holy Spirits Movement
IDAHOT	International Day Against Homophobia, Transphobia and Biphobia
IGG	Inspector General of Government
IMF	International Monetary Fund
IPC	Inter-Party Cooperation
IPFC	Inter-Party Forces Cooperation
ISO	Internal Security Organization
JEEMA	Justice Forum
JIC	Joint Intelligence Committee
LRA	Lord's Resistance Army
MDAs	Ministries, Departments and Agencies
MP	Member of Parliament
MPLA	People's Movement for the Liberation of Angola
NDA	National Democratic Alliance
NEC	National Enterprise Corporation
NGO	Non-Governmental Organization
NRA	National Resistance Army
NRC	National Resistance Council
NRM/A	National Resistance Movement/Army
NSC	National Security Council
NUP	National Unity Platform
OAU	Organisation of African Unity
OWC	Operation Wealth Creation
PAP	People's Action Party
POMA	Public Order Management Act
PPAs	Power Purchase Agreements
PPP	People's Progressive Party
RC	Resistance Councils
RPF/A	Rwandese Patriotic Front/Army

SAPs	Structural Adjustment Programmes
SFC	Special Forces Command
SGBV	Sexual and Gender-Based Violence
SSR	Security Sector Reform
UAFU	Uganda African Farmers Union
UCC	Uganda Communications Commission
UCW	Uganda Council of Women
UEDCL	Uganda Electricity Distribution Company Limited
UETCL	Uganda Electricity Transmission Company Limited
UFF	Uganda Freedom Fighters
UFM	Uganda Freedom Movement
UHMG	Uganda Health Monitoring Group
UNC	Uganda National Congress
UNECL	Uganda National Electricity Company Limited
UNLF	Uganda National Liberation Front
UNRF	Uganda National Rescue Front
UPA	Uganda People's Army
UPDA	Uganda People's Democratic Army
UPC	Uganda People's Congress
UPDF	Uganda People's Defence Forces
UPM	Uganda Patriotic Movement
WNBF	West Nile Bank Front

Contributors

Gerald Bareebe is Assistant Professor in the Department of Politics at York University, Canada. He has a BA from Makerere University and a PhD from the University of Toronto. His work has been published in top international journals including *African Affairs*, *Journal of Democracy*, *Civil Wars*, *Commonwealth and Comparative Politics*, and book chapters by Lynne Rienner Publishers and the University of Antwerp Press.

Stephanie Cawood is Director of the Centre for Gender and Africa Studies at the University of the Free State, South Africa. She is interested in the interdisciplinary spaces between Africa and Gender Studies from a decolonial/postcolonial perspective with particular interest in matters of culture and heritage, rhetoric, the oral tradition and memory. She has taught in the Africa and Gender Studies programmes primarily in supervising postgraduate students, notably at PhD level, and has successfully graduated approximately thirty postgraduate students. She has held fellowships at the University of Bologna and the African Studies Centre Leiden, and was awarded a Newton Advanced Fellowship from the British Academy and Newton Fund to pursue research on the memorialization of struggle in post-liberation Africa.

Jonathan Fisher is Professor of Global Security at the University of Birmingham and a research fellow in the Centre for Gender and Africa Studies at the University of the Free State. He has a BA from University College London and a DPhil from University of Oxford. His current research is on authoritarianism and (in)security and the role of social media platforms and companies in African politics. More broadly, he has published on the international politics of aid, development and security with empirical focus on Eastern Africa, Nigeria and South Africa. He is the author of *East Africa after Liberation: Conflict, Security and the State since the 1980s* (Cambridge University Press, 2020) and (with Nina Wilen) *African Peacekeeping* (Cambridge University Press, 2022).

Frederick Golooba-Mutebi is currently a research associate at the Centre for African Studies, Uganda Martyrs University, and the Overseas Development Institute, UK. He has a BA from Makerere University, Uganda, and a PhD from the London School of Economics and Political Science (LSE). His research interests straddle politics of development, political economy, governance and political and governance, including post-war reconstruction and state building with focus on the Great Lakes region of Africa. He has taught and researched at Makerere University, the University of Witwatersrand, South Africa, and the LSE. He has worked on major research programmes by the Overseas Development Institute (Africa Power and Politics Programme; Developmental Regimes in Africa); the LSE (Crisis States Research

Programme); and the University of Manchester (Effective States in Development Programme).

Nelson Kasfir is Professor of Government Emeritus, Dartmouth College, USA. He has a BA from Yale University and a PhD from Harvard University. He is currently working on a book on rebel governance in Uganda and creating a worldwide dataset on rebel governance. He has published widely on Ugandan politics and society for more than fifty years. His recent articles were on Buganda Kingdom government in Ugandan politics; kingdom, state and civil society in Africa; multilayered government and armed groups. He also published 'Afterword-Explaining the 2016 elections: social structure or personal agency?' in Sam Wilkins and Richard Vokes, *Elections in Museveni's Uganda: Understanding the 2016 Polls* (Routledge, 2018).

Mesharch W. Katusiimeh is Associate Professor of Governance and Dean of Faculty of Arts and Social Sciences at Kabale University, Uganda. He has a BA from Makerere University, Uganda and a PhD from Wageningen University in The Netherlands. His research interests are in civil society and good governance, urban governance and the politics of development, among others. He has published widely on these themes and taught political science and public administration for over twenty years.

Moses Khisa is Associate Professor of Political Science (and Africana Studies) at North Carolina State University, and was recently a visiting fellow at the Stellenbosch Institute for Advanced Study, South Africa. He has a BA from Makerere University, Uganda, and a PhD from Northwestern University, USA. His research and teaching interests are in comparative politics, political economy of development and politics of institutional change in Africa. He is a columnist for *Daily Monitor* and a research associate with the Centre for Basic Research, both in Kampala. He is co-author of *Africa's New Global Politics* and co-editor of *Rethinking Civil-Military Relations in Africa*, both by Lynne Rienner Publishers, 2022.

Tabitha Mulyampiti is Associate Professor in the School of Women and Gender Studies at Makerere University, Uganda. She has a BA from Makerere University, Uganda and a PhD from the University of Vienna, Austria. She has over fifteen years of post-doctoral research, teaching, policy analysis and advocacy on gender and development, women's economic and political empowerment, gender and governance and feminist social movements, themes she has published on widely. She has worked on gender and development interventions in over twenty-two countries across Africa.

Andrew M. Mwenda is a journalist, an intellectual and a businessman. He has a BA from Makerere University, Uganda, and an M.Sc. from the School of Oriental and African Studies, University of London. He is founder and managing director of *The Independent* newspaper in Kampala, a platform for freewheeling debate of national, regional and international affairs. He has co-authored many articles for academic journals with Roger Tangri and they published a book together – *The Politics of Elite Corruption in Africa* (Routledge, 2013).

Sabastiano Rwengabo is a research fellow with the Centre for Basic Research in Kampala, Uganda, and specializes on fragility and resilience assessments, regionalism, political economy and security studies, among others, themes he has published on widely. He has a BA (first class) from Makerere University, Uganda, and a PhD from the National University of Singapore. He is the author of *Security Cooperation in the East African Community* (Africa World Press, 2018) and co-editor of *Peace, Democracy and Development in Africa* (Adonis & Abbey, 2020).

Anders Sjögren is Associate Professor in Political Science and Senior Lecturer in the Department of Government, Uppsala University, Sweden. He has a BA and PhD from Stockholm University, Sweden. His research interests are state formation, state-society relations, opposition parties and civil society in electoral autocracies, and democratization and autocratization. His empirical focus is Kenya and Uganda. His many publications include *Between Militarism and Technocratic Governance: State Formation in Contemporary Uganda* (Fountain Publishers, 2013).

Roger Tangri has taught at universities in nine African countries, including Makerere University in Uganda (1994–7). He has an MSc and PhD from the University of Edinburgh. Together with Andrew Mwenda, a former student and a friend of twenty-five years, he has co-authored a dozen articles as well as a book, *The Politics of Elite Corruption in Africa* (Routledge, 2013). He is now retired in the United States but continues to visit Uganda regularly.

Rebecca Tapscott is a lecturer in the Politics Department at the University of York, UK. She earned her BA at Georgetown University's School of Foreign Service, and PhD at the Fletcher School of Tufts University, USA. Her research interests include political violence and everyday authoritarianism, gender and militarized masculinities, and research ethics governance. She is the author of *Arbitrary States: Social Control and Modern Authoritarianism in Museveni's Uganda* (Oxford University Press, 2021), which was shortlisted for the African Studies Associations' Bethwell Ogot book prize. The book is open access and free to download on the publisher's website.

Introduction: Theory and trajectory of autocratization in Uganda

Moses Khisa

In March 2011, protests broke out in Uganda's capital, Kampala, soon spreading to other towns and urban centres across the country. The initial spark was the rising cost of living, unofficially blamed on excessive campaign spending in the February 2011 general elections and the possible printing of money, which may have fuelled an inflationary spiral.[1] The signature message of this nascent and novel protest movement was 'Walk-to-Work', ostensibly because people could not drive or afford public transport due to high gasoline prices and a corresponding spike in public transport fares.

In a rather dramatic turn, what started as a protest over economic hardships soon took on a political life, coming on the heels of a disputed general election in which the opposition, yet again, accused the ruling party of electoral fraud. It was not long before opposition leader, Kizza Besigye, emerged as the chief 'walker' and the main face of the protest movement.

This set up Museveni against a novel challenge, one that in all likelihood he had neither prepared for nor remotely anticipated. Heretofore, challenges to Museveni's otherwise durable rule had always been via elections and through armed rebel activities, the latter a turf on which he was always prepared to dare any enemy and readily willing to pick a fight without flinching. By sharp contrast, the Walk-to-Work protest movement came with an unprecedented and unconventional repertoire of contention. It presented a new nightmare for Museveni and his government.

The events in North Africa, in what became the Arab Spring,[2] provided a powerful inspiration and possible demonstration effect – President Ben Ali of Tunisia fled the country in the face of relentless street protests, and in Egypt after three decades in power, the military forced out President Hosni Mubarak in the face of a determined popular push from the streets. The spark in both cases was economic hardship. Worst of all, as the contagion of protest spread further afield, a violent and deadly crackdown on protestors in Libya prompted foreign intervention and an ignominious end to Muamar Gaddafi's four-decade rule.[3]

In Uganda, protests intensified in April and by early May 2011, the immediate goal appeared to have been to stop Museveni's swearing-in for a record fourth elective term (plus ten years unelected between 1986 and 1996), slated for 12 May. To ensure that the protestors did not disrupt the day's ceremonies that included visiting heads of state, on the morning of Museveni's swearing-in the state's coercive apparatus took decisive action against the 'chief walker', Kizza Besigye – the military and police violently arrested and airlifted him to Karamoja, the remotest part of the country where colonial authorities often banished anticolonial leaders.

In any event, for many weeks on, Kampala was in tumult. Museveni was on the back foot, fighting to put out a fire he was least prepared to fight given the unfamiliar terrain of street protests compared to the traditional rebel activity and armed violence, his familiar territory. However, by the end of May and early June, the protests had petered out. The situation returned to a semblance of normalcy but Kampala had become a city under military siege and Uganda came across as a country at war with itself. While not the first overt threat to Museveni's hold on power, it was the first unconventional and stern test, which he nevertheless successfully navigated and weathered. He went on to 'win' re-election in 2016 whose results, as always, were contested and rejected by the opposition.

Most recently, Museveni emerged from yet another contested and controversial re-election on 14 January 2021, after parliament had amended the constitution in 2017 and removed the 75-year age limit for eligibility to run for president. This time Museveni faced a different but nevertheless tough electoral challenge considering that his overall popularity and legitimacy have waned overtime, and given an unconventional main opposition challenger – a young populist popstar, Robert Kyagulanyi, whose arrest during the campaigns in November 2020 sparked deadly riots in and around Kampala resulting in more than fifty deaths.[4]

The above vignette suggests two key and interrelated empirical puzzles: the resilience of Museveni's rule and the deepening of a personalist, autocratic system. These two are not merely tangentially connected, one is arguably a consequence of the other – the longer Museveni has ruled Uganda, the more his rule has become personalist, institutionally fragmented and more autocratic. His longevity in power has entailed the weakening of constitutional checks on executive authority and the deepening of clientelist ties and networks, which feed off the extant system of spoils. In turn, the system depends on those ties and connections for its reproduction and survival.

Yet, it is not just that Museveni has undermined institutionalized rule, it is also that he has successfully instrumentalized critical institutional spaces, such as judicial, legislative and oversight institutions. Why and how has Museveni's dual-accomplishment of resilient and personalist autocratic rule been actualized? To successfully weather challenges to his rule and prolong his stay in power, Museveni has employed a range of strategies to produce a resilient system of personalist rule, placing Uganda on a firm path of autocracy.

This book is about autocratization – the gradual decline of democratic traits in already authoritarian situations.[5] In this introductory chapter, I provide an outline of the core theoretical levers and analytical pillars through which to make sense of Museveni's remarkably durable rule and the turn to a decidedly autocratic trajectory. Autocratization is the deepening of autocratic rule, which contrasts with democratization – the continuous process of strengthening and deepening systems of governing through predictable, accountable and responsive institutions. In practice, both autocracy and democracy are not pure types. They run on a continuum. It is possible to have democratic traits in authoritarian systems and autocratic practices in democratic settings. However, while autocratic tendencies may exist in both democratic and authoritarian systems, they tend to be far more prevalent in the latter.[6]

The primary focus of this book is Uganda under the rule of Yoweri Museveni, in power since 1986 and on course to rule for four decades, uninterrupted. This is a monumental feat. Why has he succeeded where others failed? What are the foundations of Museveni's regime's resilience? Why has his rule taken an increasingly personalist, more authoritarian drift and tenor?

Authoritarian resilience and deepening is not new to Uganda as the country's democratic trajectory took a turn for the worse only a few years after independence from Great Britain in 1962. The promise of democratic government in Uganda has remained elusive for most of the sixty years of independence. What is more, autocratization is not unique to Uganda; it is a worldwide phenomenon, with different stripes, types and trends. It ranges from sultanist-like forms (e.g. in Eritrea), post-totalitarian types as in North Korea, electoral autocracies, which is the predominant form, to state-party variants like China.

The causes of autocratization vary, and indeed so do the consequences diverge across countries and continents. Our primary objective in this book is to understand the growth and endurance of Uganda's autocratic system of rule under a single ruler, its causes, dimensions and implications. In so doing, we hope that our analyses, combining both the theoretical and empirical explorations in the different chapters, will yield insights and lessons beyond the single case study of Uganda.

The theme of autocratization or re-autocratization and democratic backsliding has recently generated substantial scholarly interest and policy debate across the world. But trends and dynamics on the African continent have not received ample, careful and comprehensive empirical analysis and theoretical engagement.[7] There is need to analyse the convergences and continuities in autocratic systems, and getting a proper grasp of country case studies is a useful way to arrive at broader cross-country and continental-level conclusions on trends and trajectories. In the case of Uganda, while there is a large corpus of scholarship on Museveni's rule, there is dearth of detailed and compelling explanations of why and how the trajectory of his rule has evolved in the direction it has, an explanatory framework that combines different analytical angles weaved under a unified theoretical frame. We hope to accomplish this task in the current book.

At the centre of the analysis is Museveni, by far the most important political actor of post-independent Uganda, one of the most influential rulers of his time in the broader context of regional and continental political developments. He has been a consequential figure and fixture in Ugandan politics since 1986. While he has faced fierce challenges and contests to his stay at the helm, he has proved adept at adapting and adjusting to changing circumstances. He has succeeded in constructing and perpetuating regime resilience, one that is at once autocratic and stable, characterized by, among other key features, a) political uncertainty, b) institutional fragmentation and c) elite co-optation. Adaptation has been at the core of Museveni's long rule. By adapting, he has had the legroom to rule for so long but also sustained the impetus to deepen an autocratic system of rule. To understand this trajectory, we need a dynamic theory and critical empirical investigation.

Uganda's autocratic trajectory

Uganda has been on a clear and decisive autocratic political trajectory, with possible downstream consequences for the present and future of the country. It is difficult to mark out the precise timing for the acceleration in Uganda's turn to a deepening of autocratic rule, but 2005 was a notable critical juncture when Museveni engineered the removal of presidential term limits from the constitution clearing the way for eligibility as a candidate, at the same allowing the re-adoption of multiparty politics through a national referendum.[8] Yet, ironically, the reintroduction of multiparty politics which meant, at least on the face of it, opening up space for political competition happened simultaneously with Museveni's tightening grip and a turn towards what has become a decidedly personalist system of rule. What some initially characterized as a 'third term' in 2005 in fact turned out to be a quest for life presidency, as one analyst perceptively observed at the time.[9]

While the gradual deepening of autocratic rule of a personalist and clientelist hue may have been long in the making and throughout Museveni's reign right from the onset, there has been an acceleration and deepening especially during the last two decades. A series of events and actions since 2005 constitute a set of puzzling empirical questions that deserve close, careful and critical investigation. Why did the return to multiparty politics not translate into true political pluralism and democratic praxis? How has Museveni successfully balanced the boat to maintain a firm grip on power even with declining legitimacy and a worsening environment for political freedoms and civic space?

Some of Museveni's close allies in 2005 who acquiesced to removing term limits, seeing it as a necessary stopgap measure, have since fallen out while the incumbent has managed to replenish the ranks of his ruling coalition and realigned the system to serve his stay at the helm. A great part of the realignment has happened in the military, the most important pillar of Museveni's rule. How has he navigated the effective use of military power in a country with a long history of coups and armed insurgency?

As with all major socio-political questions, there are no simple or quick answers that explain the deepening of NRM's and Museveni's autocratic rule especially in the last two decades. Numerous possible dimensions and recipes go into an explanatory framework considering the complex combination of factors and forces at play. Dissecting the above questions from different analytical and empirical angles can help yield a comprehensive and compelling framework that converges on a common theoretical thread. This book's goal is to bring together a set of analyses that examine Museveni's enduring hold on power and his autocratic trajectory, placing the outcomes in a broader comparative lens and theoretical compass.

Since the 2005 turning point, but especially during the 2010s, Uganda's socio-political landscape has had a series of unsettling developments and dramatic shifts.

For one, Museveni's determination to rule-for-life, simultaneous with a rumoured scheme of grooming his son, is a trend that complicates the state of Ugandan politics with implications for stability, security and succession dynamics. In a 2012 television interview with Uganda's NTV, Museveni stated categorically that he would not stay in power after seventy-five years, the constitutional age limit.[10] But in 2017 the age limit was deleted from the constitution. Earlier in 2015, the NRM party constitution was amended to give the party Chairman, Museveni, complete powers to appoint the Secretary General and other top party officials.[11]

What is more, fragmentation of opposition parties, the weakening of alternative centres of power and erosion of independent institutions are a feature of Uganda's political trajectory. These and other developments have combined to give Museveni's presidency an imperial grandeur and a deeper autocratic tenor arguably more pronounced than the period before 2005. In hindsight, the excitement of returning to multiparty politics in 2005 did not anticipate the rough winds ahead and Museveni's long-term power calculus. The expectations and excitement of returning to multiparty faded somewhat, giving way to frustration and disappointment in a political environment increasingly characterized by militarism, coercion and 'controlled consent'.[12]

In the early phases of his rule, both local and foreign analysts considered Museveni a reformist leader who had come with revolutionary promises and was presiding over a democratizing polity.[13] Despite the ban on political parties, instituted in 1986, which made Uganda a de facto one-party state but couched in the language of no-party democracy, a favourable assessment of Museveni and the NRM regime held up relatively well up to at least the early 2000s.[14] During the first two decades of NRM/Museveni's rule, Uganda's democratic credentials were modest, if tenuous, but the country's democratic institutional landscape during the 1990s and early 2000s held some promise for a stable and sustainable system of government, one that appeared to transcend individual preferences and idiosyncrasies including Museveni's.

Since the mid-2000s, however, especially during the 2010s and into the 2020s, the trend and tenor of Uganda's political landscape have decidedly and unequivocally pointed in the direction of a highly personalized autocratic system of rule, characterized by retrogression, repression, endemic political corruption and widespread uncertainty about both the present and future. A lot has gone wrong. From institutional malaise and rampant graft in the public sector, to contraction of space for political competition and civic engagement, the erosion of checks on executive authority and resort to unbridled patronage, Uganda sits at a particularly precarious intersection of state dysfunction and social tension. There has been an admixture of political twists and turns, stresses and strains, including fault lines in the ruling party, fragmentation of the opposition and social anxieties fuelled by a demographic drift of masses of unemployed and desperate young people. All these add up to tempestuous times in Ugandan politics and society.

There is so much at stake that requires rigorous scholarly investigation and a sharp-edged analytical exercise, which this book attempts to accomplish. While the issues at hand are expansive, the task ahead for this book is relatively circumscribed, focusing pointedly on the growth and resilience of a personalist autocracy but one that is situated within the broader terrain and chain of Uganda's recent political history. There is growing consensus that points to a resurgence in new forms of authoritarianism, including among previously relatively established democracies. There has especially been a turn to deeply personalist autocratic forms of rule in countries that have had latent and fledgling democratic institutions even when in practice falling short of meeting the minimum democratic threshold.[15] In that regard, some scholars have noted a 'third wave of autocratization',[16] suggesting that in the same way there were three major waves of democratization (pre, post-World War, and 1970s/80s) and two corresponding counter-waves (interwar period and late 1960s/70s), as argued by Samuel Huntington, a third counter-wave has been underway.[17]

In the next section, I propose a general theory of regime resilience and the bases of autocratization. While the theory addresses the Ugandan case study, its basic building blocks and underlying assumptions hold relevance beyond Uganda given that the deepening of autocratic regimes, of a highly personalist stripe, and the crisis of hitherto celebrated triumph of liberal democracy is now a worldwide phenomenon and the subject of considerable scholarly interest.

Autocratization: Theoretical and comparative overview

One of the most fascinating puzzles in comparative politics is why rulers and regimes that otherwise face legitimacy deficits, precisely because they came to power through illegitimate means or govern without popular mandate, are nevertheless able to keep a hold on power for so long with or without competitive elections. This puzzle and the attendant research programme have spawned a large body of literature that explains the surprising endurance of regimes and rulers that otherwise have questionable credibility and credentials. Such rulers maintain power in part through dubious elections that serve as legitimating devices, but they also engage in excesses and abuses of power that ordinarily further diminish their standing as to doom or at a minimum imperil their survivability. From Mexico's Institutional Revolutionary Party (PRI) and Malaysia's United Malays National Organisation (UMNO) to Africa's range of authoritarian hybrid regimes, the authoritarian research programme has analysed regime and incumbent durability as a function of both domestic and external forces.[18]

Externally, the key variable for a long time was the structure of global politics that pitted the United States and the Soviet Union in the Cold War confrontation, with both superpowers propping up regimes around the world as allies and proxies against their putative enemy. This overarching geostrategic calculus remained pivotal even after the Cold War disappeared from the global political stage. For example, in the post-Cold War era, authoritarian regimes and rulers that built close relations with the West benefitted from the latter's foreign aid patronage, often as rewards for their commitment to neoliberal economic policies and, in the wake of the 11 September 2001 terrorist attacks in the United States, as partners in the fight against global terrorism.

Internally, the most compelling comparative scholarship on authoritarian durability has accented the role of domestic political institutions – that is, robust political parties, strong militaries, electoral institutions as tools of regime legitimation and legislatures as instruments for intra-elite accommodation, among others. A large body of scholarship has underscored the persistence and perseverance of authoritarian regimes that relied heavily on different facets of strong and instrumentalized domestic political institutions.[19] Hosni Mubarak's Egypt epitomized the resilience of a regime that drew heavily on a robust political party and firm control over solid military apparatus.[20] So did Robert Mugabe's four-decade rule in Zimbabwe and the EPRDF under Meles Zenawi in Ethiopia.

However, the dramatic tumbling of the Mubarak regime in what became the 'Arab Spring', and more recently the toppling of Mugabe as well as Sudan's El-Bashir and Burkina Faso's Blaise Compaore, among others, showed that seemingly impregnable authoritarian regimes can collapse in quite unexpected and dramatic ways. These and other regimes relied heavily on the instrumental use of domestic political and military institutions, thus their rapid collapse slung wide open the puzzle of authoritarian survival and autocratic resilience. How are we to rethink the puzzle of regime endurance beyond authoritarian institutions as the definitive bulwark for durability and survivability? In Ethiopia, the ruling EPRDF (renamed the "Prosperity Party"), emblematic of an imposing and impregnable single-dominant party rule, found itself on the back-foot following the sudden death of its charismatic leader, Meles Zenawi.[21] In Tanzania, the CCM has often faced resurgent opposition challenges during the country's five-year electoral cycles even though it has maintained a firm grip relying heavily on commanding the power of coercive force and finance as well as the ruling party's unmatched rhizome-reach in Tanzanian society built over more than half-century in government.[22]

Within the wider scholarship on authoritarian politics, there is renewed focus on new forms and trends of democratic retrogression among established democracies and authoritarian resurgence in already nondemocratic states. In both, a common feature is the resurgence (in some cases the re-emergence) of more personalist forms of rule, a worldwide trend whereby incumbents exact oversized influence and override extant institutional checks and balances on the exercise of executive power. The phenomenon has played out among new democracies as well as authoritarian regime in Eastern Europe, South and Southeast Asia, Latin America, and Africa with remarkable growth in personalism as a dominant feature. At the end of the Cold War, for example, by one estimate, the more personalist authoritarian regime stripe accounted for only 23 per cent of all authoritarian regimes around the world. By 2017, however, the share had grown substantially to 40 per cent.[23]

President Yoweri Museveni's close to four decades' uninterrupted rule in Uganda is an incredible accomplishment in a socially complex country, and in an era where most long-surviving rulers find severe difficulty overcoming internal challenges or easily override legal and constitutional impediments to cling to power. Consider the fact that before Museveni took power in 1986, Uganda had eight different heads of state in only twenty-four years since attaining independence in 1962. By contrast, Museveni's long stay at the helm far outstrips all previous governments combined, a remarkable and striking feat when set in the social complexity of Uganda and situated in a broader and comparative African perspective.

Only two African incumbents today have continuously held power longer than Museveni: Theodore Obiang Nguema in Equatorial Guinea and Paul Biya in Cameron, the former in power since 1979 while the latter follows closely having ruled since 1982.[24] It is worth noting that Equatorial Guinea is a geographically tiny nation, a small population of just over a million people with enormous oil resources, and on paper is officially the richest African nation by per capita income, yet paradoxically one of the poorest on the Human Development Index. On his part, Biya maintains an inimitable reputation of ruling Cameroon practically in absentia, spending much of his time vacationing in Europe yet able to manipulate electoral outcomes,[25] able to sustain a system of loyal military hierarchy and political apparatchiks that feed off natural resource wealth and foreign aid rents.[26]

A common feature of long-surviving rulers and regimes is that longevity breeds personalization of power and institutional erosion. This can hold true in relatively democratic polities too, but it is arguably more pronounced under autocratic regimes precisely because sustaining an autocratic system necessarily requires the gradual weakening of key institutional checks and constraints on executive authority established by or predating the incumbent party and president. This goes along with weakening of alternative centres of power, and centralization of key decision-making processes. The erosion of institutional checks and contraction of alternative spaces for autonomous authority inevitably make the incumbent president the only truly consequential institution on crucial issues. This is where we place Uganda under Yoweri Museveni.

From the start, Museveni's reign was always short on meeting the minimum criteria for democratic governance; after all he came to power through force of arms and ruled for ten years without seeking the mandate of the people. But his rule has not been the same during the four decades of Museveni's firm hold on Ugandan society and politics. Instead, it has oscillated along a continuum that has included a popular and inclusive semi-democratic "no-party" experiment, a drift to a closed but participatory form approximating a one-party system, and later changed to a theoretically open multiparty arrangement but heavily influenced by Museveni's command of force and finance of seemingly competitive elections but whose outcomes are skewed in the incumbent's favour quite predictably.

Considering Uganda's complex social structure, the demographic dilemma of a budding and bulging youth population, a deep history of armed conflict and intense contestations for power, it is striking to count Yoweri Museveni along with Paul Biya and Theodore Obiang as the three current longest surviving African presidents. Museveni and his NRA rebel group captured power with a tenuous social base in a deeply plural country, a myriad of interest groups and social demands. The rebel group's core support was primarily in the central region and parts of western Uganda while much of the east and north were either indifferent or out rightly hostile to the new NRA government and its erstwhile rebel leader. It was a chequered start. Uganda's socio-political composition, with competing and variegated interest groups, ethnic cleavages, religious and regional divisions, political polarization and a deep history of instability all combined to present a herculean task to Museveni and his government when they captured state power in 1986.

Museveni had to secure regime legitimation and consolidation simultaneously with pursuing state building. Consider, for example, that shortly after capturing power, armed rebellions set off in earnest in the eastern and northern parts of the country with a proliferation of rebel groups that had disparate ambitions, goals and geographic reach. As of July 2008 at least sixteen rebel groups had fought Museveni's government at different times since 1986.[27] What is more, there were multiple demands for ceding power to sub-regional entities like the kingdom of Buganda more over at a time when the central government needed rugged state rebuilding and national cohesion. In all, the job of reconstituting a beaten down state, a nation torn apart and reviving a shattered economy was unmistakably daunting.

In the circumstances of 1986, if consolidating NRA/M rule was a truly tough task for Museveni and his new government, sustaining the government for more than three decades was arguably improbable. Perhaps even more intriguing, in hindsight, is the manner in which Museveni successfully negotiated his way around myriad practical, legal and normative hurdles in the course of his illustrious yet tainted long stay at the helm of Uganda. Today, Museveni has firmly clasped Uganda in a way no previous ruler has managed and to a magnitude far surpassing many of his continental contemporaries and peers. Why and how this has happened remain intriguing and puzzling. Understanding the underlying bases, foundation and overarching pillars of Museveni's autocratic rule is the task at hand for the chapters in this volume. In the next section I provide a general theoretical anchor for the book.

A theory of autocratic adaptation

To understand Museveni's autocratic trajectory and the NRM's regime survivability, along with the range of implications for political development in Uganda, we need a dynamic theory, informed by the specificities of Uganda but situated in a broader comparative frame. To get a good grip, the theoretical framing here should speak to general trends beyond Uganda even as the focus is on accounting for a specific Ugandan case study. In the post-Cold War era, with a near universal embrace of electoral politics and norms of human rights, regimes and rulers that stay in power for a long period are theoretically amenable to a variety of possible ousting. It could be through elections (Yahya Jemmah in The Gambia), popular protest (Blaise Compoare in Burkina Faso) or a carefully calibrated and disguised coup d'état despite the evolution of a global norm against coups (Robert Mugabe in Zimbabwe). To make sense of Uganda under Museveni, placed in a broad and generalizable framework, I propose a theory of *autocratic adaptability and resilience* to shed light on Museveni's remarkably long reign and his personal imprint on the country's political landscape.

Adapting to changing circumstances, adopting new tactics, exercising pragmatism and playing both hard and soft have been among the key defining hallmarks of Museveni's rule. At different times, Museveni has played hardball, when necessary, made tactical concessions where doing so did not hurt his long-term strategic objectives. In doing so, Museveni is able to mollify domestic contenders and appease external allies, satisfy local agitators and deflect foreign criticism. In some instances, he has deployed physical force, in others he has turned to the force of finance, relying as much on state coercion as crass patronage, employing persuasion and ideas in certain situations but also intimidation and violence. What all this adds up to is the art of skilfully striking a balance between clientelism and coercion, between money and military might, in order to achieve control and procure consent.

In practice, autocratic adaptability requires elite co-optation and flexibility in assembling a stable and credible ruling coalition. The ruling coalition has to strive to delicately balance-out different organized and unorganized interests and constituencies. Adapting includes successful accommodation of a range of contestations and clamouring for representation and voice. Equally important is sensitivity to the changing times and adapting to new demands as to shape the form, composition and iterations of the ruling coalition. This includes the steady adjustment to demographic shifts and technological changes which may present fresh dynamics and unprecedented demands even as they may provide opportunities (in the case of technological changes) for exercising sophisticated control and to extract consent. Consider, for example, that when Museveni captured power in 1986, the word internet had only a limited place in the vocabulary of the average Ugandan, young and old. Fast forward to 2023, and Museveni rules a country with a majority of the population that is not just in the youth age bracket but also heavily imbibed with a totally different approach to life in which the internet and other forms of technology occupy a central and commanding place.

To parse out the theory of autocratic adaptability, I propose three core components that underpin adaptability, resilience and survivability and form the basis for regime longevity simultaneous with propelling the wheels of autocratization and prolonging the incumbent's rule: 1) *institutional mosaic and manipulation*, 2) resource pool supply, and 3) coalitional replenishment and renewal. I will take up these three variables, seriatim, and demonstrate how in concert they serve as pillars for regime longevity and deepening of autocratic rule with a personalist tenor. Taken together, the three are both necessary and sufficient conditions for longevity and autocratization. The two outcomes – longevity and autocratization – are intertwined and somewhat inseparable. While the latter does not have to naturally follow the former, it is practically inconceivable to have a ruler who stays in power for too long and not end up trumping all government institutions and have an overriding influence on critical matters as to effectively personalize the state.

First, the idea of institutional mosaic and manipulation builds on but also transcends the extant literature on authoritarian institutions. The primary insight from the comparative politics literature on authoritarian institutions is that institutions matter for autocratic regimes and rulers. Institutions – defined as formal or informal rules of the game – constrain as much as they enable. They provide incentives and disincentives for both state elites and their opposition challengers. Whether electoral or legislative, institutions play crucial roles in social mobilization, in facilitating intra-elite accommodation, for purposes of monitoring and surveillance, in integrating and implicating a wider spectrum of society in the activities and actions of the extant regime and as tools for distributing patronage, etc. For example, for more than two decades Kenyan President Arap Moi relied heavily on the legislature and electoral processes as tools for soaking-in pressures and helping to weather opposition challenges.[28] Powerful political parties have also been critical in assuring the longevity of regimes and rulers in Southern Africa, Mexico and Southeast Asia, among others.[29]

However, institutions, whether formal or informal, can be double-edged swords. They can protect but also bring down rulers depending on how different institutional arrangements interact with other variables or when regimes and states experience exogenous shocks.[30] A strong and institutionally robust military can be crucial in sustaining a ruler in power, but that very institutional strength and autonomy can work against an incumbent especially in the face of dramatic popular uprisings as happened in Egypt against Hosni Mubarak in 2011, in Burkina Faso with Blaise Campaore in 2014 and most recently in Sudan against Omar el-Bashir in 2019. In all these cases, military institutions that had kept autocrats in power got to a point where they either sided with street protestors in pushing out the incumbent or deposed the ruler in the face of street pressure. What is more, formal institutions like constitutional term and age limits have in some contexts constrained incumbents and forced them out even if they did not want to.[31]

Elections too can prevent rulers from clinging to power by manipulating electoral outcomes or attempting to change constitutional and statutory rules. The examples of Jerry Rawlings in Ghana, Arap Moi in Kenya, Olusegun Obasanjo in Nigeria and most recently Yahya Jammeh in The Gambia, among others, are instructive. These rulers used electioneering to stay in power but were unable to manipulate constitutions in order to cling on to power, thus they failed where Uganda's Museveni and other peers have succeeded[32] – that is, the instrumental use of precisely those same institutional devices and avenues to hold onto state power in what, in the case of Museveni, has now approximated a life-presidency.

The instrumental use of formal institutions fails in many cases, but succeeds in others. Institutions provide latitude but also limits to incumbency manoeuvre and manipulation. If we reposition the analytical aperture on institutional mosaic and manipulation to view institutions not as mere instruments and mechanistic tools usable at will but as constituting a dynamic and complex process, we can make better sense of why some rulers successfully juggle institutional complexity and uncertainty to be able to overcome potential perils of institutionalized politics. In one sense, autocratic rulers need institutions as handy instruments for beating up opponents, for purposes of legitimation and to be used in co-optation, which means incumbents have to avoid being squeezed and constrained by the same institutional arrangements especially given how sticky and rigid certain institutional norms can be.

Museveni has been what Frederick Golooba-Mutebi and Sam Hickey characterized as the master of institutional multiplicity.[33] The institutional landscape in Uganda is a mosaic one, comprising a motely of agencies and bodies, legal and constitutional provisions, norms and practices, all of which are important sources of legitimation but also avenues for incumbent manoeuvre and manipulation. It is an arena at once characterized by institutional uncertainty, fragmentation and proliferation,[34] but also embodies centralized control and the decentralized distribution of spoils, making possible the widening of networks for patronage disbursement, creating openings for both bureaucratic and political corruption.[35] Uganda's institutional mosaic of fragmentation encourages a complex, contradictory and competitive environment where low-level authorities thrive, and allows the regime to outsource such tasks as security and governance provision without ceding authority to autonomous agents.[36]

In the broader scheme of sustaining autocratic rule, institutional spaces and processes provide a veneer of accountability, accommodation and responsiveness. They supply the appearance of 'good government' while serving as political malware for incumbency control and coercion. The irony here is that a ruler like Museveni rules by simultaneously promoting and eroding institutional processes, undermines but also relies on certain institutional resources to govern and procure legitimacy. Hence, there is a delicate balancing act, and how this happens in practice requires careful analysis, which the empirical chapters of this book will take up. For now, it suffices to underline that there are contradictory roles and ambiguous place for an institutional landscape in autocratic settings.

Institutional mosaic and manipulation entails constant reinventions and adjustments in the different facets of the extant institutional register. It is not that rulers can easily or freely turn-on and off the institutional switches, rather that autocratic sustenance and regime resilience entail navigating the institutional milieu in ways that simultaneously undermine and instrumentalize institutions, empower but also disempower. When it was convenient and prudent during the early phase of his rule, for example, Museveni insisted on a non-party legal and institutional framework, giving him and the NRM control of political processes that made possible power consolidation. Under the no-party system, which in practice was a single-party arrangement, agencies of the state – from those charged with security and defence to those tasked with political mobilization and election management – were concentrated and coalesced under direct control of the incumbent for two decades until 2006 when there was a shift to a de jure multiparty system.

In due course of time, however, with the façade of a 'no-party' arrangement untenable, and in the face of relentless internal denunciation by internal actors and external disapproval from foreign donors, Museveni tactfully conceded to a new legal, constitutional and institutional rearrangement – a 'turnaround' to multiparty politics.[37] The formal and legal return to multiparty politics was a tactical move that provided a much-needed safety valve to release pressure and relieve Museveni of political agitation especially from within his ruling group while carefully managing the transition in a way that did not jeopardize his ultimate hold on the levers of state power.[38]

Relatedly, within the realm of the institutional enablers of autocratization, are actors and groups operating outside the bounds of mainstream political spaces for power contestations but who are indirectly connected to the political status quo ante – the women's movement, business groups and civil society writ large, including the media. In one sense, activities of these groups can be a countervailing force against personalization of power and autocratic rule. In another sense, however, because these groups inhabit a legal and institutional landscape that grants them the latitude to engage certain activities, they contribute to legitimating the system, at least inadvertently. Their activities may not hurt the system or check the government as would ordinarily be expected of civil society under pluralism yet they contribute to the appearance of a veneer of democratic praxis. Added to this is the growth of religious movements – especially the evangelicals – who deliberately cultivate a relationship of patronage with the incumbent, and in turn depoliticize their flock under the guise of freedom of worship.

A second core component of the theory of autocratic adaptability is *resource-pool supply*. Autocratic resilience and deepening require a steady and sufficient supply of finance through internal revenue mobilization, external rewards and the pursuit of different sources of rents necessary to run a system of patronage. As an institutional mode of public management crucial to the sustenance of autocratic rule, patron-client relations and clientelism mediate the exchange of financial and material resources. This system is a critical institutional mechanism (largely informal) through which rulers procure support and legitimate their power.

In practice, clientelism becomes pervasive and ubiquitous with regime longevity because of the desperation to shore up support and secure a cushion against challengers, whether credible or otherwise, real or imagined. A steady supply of resources to oil the clientelist system and patronage networks is critical to survivability, particularly in the context where the targeted distribution of largesse to select groups and individuals is often a handy substitute for the more complicated and onerous task of providing general public goods and services. Without resources to fund clientelist ties and oil patronage networks, authoritarian rulers are vulnerable to elite defection, street protest or even electoral defeat.

Putting this in historical perspective, many African incumbents swept aside during the 'third wave' of democratization in the 1990s faced severe financial stress due to dwindling public revenues in part because of the collapse of global commodity prices, and the severe economic hardships citizens were forced to grapple with.[39] The paucity of public finances contributed to triggering economic crises, state failure and different stripes of state crises that compounded the fates of incumbents. In some countries there was near state collapse, in others economic distress propelled transitions that resulted in a combination of modestly stable democratic governments and tenuous quasi authoritarian systems – from Benin to Burundi, the Ivory Coast to Congo-Brazzaville, Zambia to Zaire.[40]

The contrasts were quite instructive. Consider for example that during the first three decades of independence, many African governments heavily relied on state revenue-returns from export of primary commodities (especially the three 'Cs' of coffee, cotton, copper). They also cashed in on Cold War superpower rent. However, the collapse of global commodity prices in the late 1970s and the freeze of Cold War financial flows doomed regimes that depended on domestic patronage distribution to secure a hold on power. When citizens' discontent intensified and the Eastern European democratization contagion arrived on the African continent at the end of the 1980s, single-party and military autocratic regimes fell on hard times unable to use revenues and rents for patronage. This became a crucial lesson that rulers like Museveni took very seriously from the events of the first half of the 1990s: keeping financial resources flowing is key; diversifying sources of revenue is critical for the long haul.

The survival of autocratic rule depends considerably on a steady supply of financial, diplomatic and ideational resources from both domestic and foreign sources, public and private. On the domestic scene, economic reform measures of the late 1980s and early 1990s, heavily influenced by Western donors and international financial institutions, placed Uganda on a steady path of economic recovery and modest GDP growth, sustained for more than two decades with three significant implications for Museveni's financial reservoir and political war chest.

First, it meant increased state revenue-yields particularly after undertaking key reforms in the area of revenue administration that included creation of a semi-autonomous revenue collection agency in 1991, the Uganda Revenue Authority. Second, economic reform measures opened up taps for Western aid, in part as rewards for Uganda's commitment to externally prescribed economic orthodoxy at the behest of the Washington Consensus and Bretton Woods institutions.

Third, the privatization of state parastatals under the broader economic reform programme brought into the fold local and foreign business actors wedded to the NRM, some with personal connections to Museveni, thus spawning a slew of large corruption scandals in the privatization processes and a key source of political finances including for campaign purposes.[41] These have served as Museveni's unassailable sources of financial resources, handing him the monetary wherewithal to beat back his opponents and literally pay his way out of innumerable political hurdles at different tough times throughout his long stay at the helm. In recent years, oil revenues and rents extracted from other natural resources have significantly augmented the resource base, providing the impetus for projecting a sanguine future under Museveni as president-for-life, thus his re-election campaign slogan for the 2020/1 cycle: 'securing the future'.

At the international level, Museveni has sustained substantial diplomatic support, from Brussels to London and Washington, Beijing to Moscow and Tehran in part for his perceived pivotal role in the sub-regional geopolitics and security dynamics of the Great Lakes region and the Horn of Africa. This has meant cashing in on Western diplomatic currency but also the flow of financial and military aid. Better still, foreign business dealings and activities of multinational corporations and powerful individuals are a key component of Uganda's political economy within the context of the neoliberal economic posture. Here, Museveni is able to draw from his connections to foreign business interests in his broader strategy of extracting rents from multinational capital and maintaining convivial relations with Western powers.

It is important though to emphasize that a steady flow of resources, whether domestic or foreign, in and of itself does not secure rulers in power nor does it propel autocratization. Libya's Muammar Gaddafi had enormous financial resources at his disposal, courtesy of massive oil deposits, enabling him to maintain a grip on the country but also engage in often brazen extra-territorial adventurism and foreign policy excesses that ultimately put him at loggerheads with Western powers. When the 'Arab Spring' wave arrived on Libyan soil, Western powers through the NATO alliance picked on the handy justification that Gaddafi was killing protestors to literally bomb him out of power. Would this have happened to Museveni who at that very time (of Gaddafi's ousting) faced similar protests in Kampala as noted at the start of this chapter? The point to underscore here is that resource-pool supply serves as a necessary but not sufficient condition for autocratic survival and endurance. Yet, to be sure, without steady resource flows, other aspects of autocratic adaptability sit rather precariously.

The third and final component in the theory of autocratic adaptability is *coalition replenishment and renewal*, largely overlooked in much of the literature on authoritarian resilience. Rulers and regimes that survive long, as of necessity, have to replenish their top ranks and renew the cadre of apparatchiks at different levels of the political system, both national and subnational, and in all the critical social spaces outside mainstream politics.

In authoritarian regimes that are prompted or compelled to transition from one ruler to another, the manner in which the incumbent party manages succession tends to have grave implications for electoral outcomes and the regime's survival fates. Daniel Arap Moi's move to handpick Uhuru Kenyatta in the 2001/02 transition in Kenya, for example, triggered a cascade of defections from the ruling Kenya African National Union (KANU), thus condemning Kenya's independence party to defeat at the hands of a united and resurgent multi-ethnic opposition coalition led by Mwai Kibaki. Similarly, Jerry Rawlings' (mis)handling of succession in Ghana created disquiet in the ruling National Democratic Congress (NDC) and in effect contributed to defeat of the incumbent party candidate, Professor Atta Mills in the crucial 2000 elections, at the hands of the New Patriotic Party (NPP) led by John Kufuor.

In the broader scheme of things, coalition-balancing and managing factional struggles are central to autocratic resilience and whether a regime takes a personalist texture or is more institutionally anchored and articulated. This is because fissures and fallouts in the core of the ruling coalition can produce at least two deleterious implications. First, defections and departures naturally weaken the incumbent president and party. Given the power of experience, retention is more critical than replenishment but also defections portent badly for public relations and popular perception. Second, and very crucial, defections can contribute to strengthening opposition ranks and ultimately emboldening the push for regime change.[42]

Defections can bring financial and human resources to opposition ranks while leaving destabilization and disarray in the incumbent party's camp. The problem of factional struggles and defections might be easier to manage for regimes that routinely change the topmost chief executive, for example the CCM in Tanzania and the ANC in South Africa, both with several leadership turnovers. By contrast, factionalism and defections tend to be a problem far more difficult to manage in the case of regimes presided over by one ruler without change. In Tanzania, for example, different factions often clash and jostle to keep ahead during moments of leadership transition, sometimes leading to fallouts and outright defections as happened with Prime Minister Edward Lowassa in 2015.[43]

Factionalism and defection is a dilemma far more difficult to manage for a personalist autocratic regime because the ruler has to deal with constant and changing demands and interests all requiring his/her direct or indirect attention. In a highly personalized system, key individuals personally intervene and mediate in just about everything that is remotely a possible flashpoint and threat to their power. This means the contours of coalition-balancing have to contend with absorbing different, often competing, factional interests and accommodating a range of actors, both new and old, who cut across ethnic, religious, regional and demographic lines. In dealing with possible intra-regime fallouts and internal disquiet or wrongdoing, the ruler has to tread carefully so as not to set off a possible cascade of defections. Reining in internal dissent and punishing errant factions may take a judicial approach rather than via extrajudicial measures, the latter reserved for external opponents.[44]

In autocratic regimes with a presidential system – the predominant form across African – three major centres of power are most critical and consequential for coalition replenishment and 'balancing the ship': in cabinet/executive, the national legislature and the military/security sector. Appointments to cabinet play crucial roles in appeasing and mollifying different constituencies and insulating the incumbent against possible intra-elite fallouts that may imperil the status quo. As the centre of executive authority, Cabinet holds a prized place in the public imagination, hence cabinet appointments – regardless of their substantive power – are nevertheless critical in assuaging opposition and delivering, at a minimum, symbolic satisfaction to key constituencies. Cabinet appointments are also an important coup-proofing tool, in some cases more important than, say, GDP growth.[45]

The military is a crucial component of coalition management and replenishment. Rulers who manage to hold power for long must necessarily undertake coup-proofing measures to ensure the military does not turn against the very regime it is meant to protect. One way of effecting this has been to build parallel structures and security outfits that are strictly loyal to the ruler as Blaise Compaore did in Burkina Faso and as Museveni has done in Uganda. Participation in foreign peacekeeping missions, engaging in lucrative business activities and exploiting avenues for elite corruption in military procurement are among the many other ways that rulers can employ to divert and appease officer corps away from proximity to the domestic political scene where they can launch coups or cause some form of political headache for the incumbent.[46]

For African rulers who captured power through guerrilla rebel organization, as part of their long-term strategy, they had to recruit, train and promote a new cohort of military commanders and heads of intelligence agencies who owed their loyalty to the appointing authority and were not beholden to the original founding ideals of the former rebel group before coming into government. With such a strategy of replenishing and renewing command and control positions in the military, incumbents can afford to take a trajectory that departs from the ostensible original set of ideals and not suffer pushback from the military leadership if the latter are not peers of the incumbent. This is precisely what Museveni has accomplished in what is, at least up to this point, a successful handling of the military question and the civil-military conundrum.[47]

These theoretical propositions, which in part draw from anecdotal trends and patterns, deserve systematic and comprehensive empirical treatment and exploration focusing on the Ugandan case study. This book positions Uganda as a mainspring for contributing to the broader comparative analyses of the contours and complexities of autocratization writ large. The primary proposition here is that autocratic resilience and the deepening of a system of personal rule, as seen in the Uganda case, are a function of adaptability to changing circumstances, conditions, contexts and contestations for power. How and in what ways this adaptability is fashioned, cultivated and reproduced constitute the primary empirical and analytical task for the chapters ahead.

How has Museveni managed to adapt to the shifts in Uganda's social and political landscape to rule for so long in a complex country whose demographical, sociological and technological contours have changed substantially since 1986? What are the social and institutional enablers of Museveni's long rule? How do we account for his gradual slide into a more personalist and perverse patronage-based autocratic system of rule? The chapters that follow dissect a range of factors and forces that underpin Museveni's autocratic adaptability and regime resilience that stands out in a continent where long-surviving rulers are often swept out of power by political currents and social forces often dramatic and unpredictable.

The three components of the theory of autocratic adaptability – institutions, resources and coalitions – add up to a comprehensive framework for understanding autocratization and autocratic resilience. They play a dual role of creating and perpetuating conditions of uncertainty and at the same time serve as tools for dealing with uncertainty. In one sense, institutions, resources and coalitions provide fertile ground for a flurry of contests and conflicts in the political arena and civic spaces. In another, they are precisely the means through which an autocratic ruler mediates and instrumentalizes conflicts and contestations. As the central pillars in the governing juggernaut, these three are critical in arming and empowering an autocrat to rule for life, hemming him; but are equally crucial in scattering opponents and demobilizing potential internal challengers.

Taking up the three variables outlined above makes possible building a comprehensive analysis justifiable on at least three grounds. First, they collectively speak to the core of how rulers fend off challenges to their power but also why their rule may turn more personalist and take on a deeper autocratic tenor. The three variables simultaneously account for resilience and retrogress. Institutions, resources and coalitions supply the fuel for regime resilience but also make possible the incentive structure and enabling environment for deepening autocratic rule. Second, the three cover both the formal terrain of politics and the informal contours where a lot of pertinent political processes take place. A robust theory of autocratic resilience and acceleration must encompass both formal institutions and informal norms and practices. Last, the three address the dual-problem of dealing with outsiders and insiders, the ins and outs that autocrat rulers have to contend with.

In sum, while a great deal of comparative politics scholarship has shown, in different ways, how institutions, patronage resources and coalitions have a bearing on regime politics, particularly survival and longevity, this book seeks to expand the debate by applying these factors to questions of how autocratization has deepened and why Uganda's ruling regime endures. We build on existing work to show how the interaction and intersection of the three variables discussed above play out in the Ugandan case and the broader comparative implications to be drawn. The theory of autocratic adaptability has important parallels with, and complements, comparative research on authoritarian learning about how regimes especially in North Africa, the Middle East and Eastern Europe have followed cues and appropriated templates from their peers in weathering challenges to their power.[48]

Subthemes and empirical focus

Taking autocratic adaptability as the central framing for understanding autocratization in Uganda, this book has four major subthemes which, taken together, illuminate the different nodes in the puzzle of Museveni's autocratic trajectory. In doing so, we throw light on the attendant theoretical and comparative implications for the African continent and beyond especially in the concluding chapter that synthesizes the core message of the book and the broader lessons.

The first subtheme that cuts across different chapters of this book revisits the institutional landscape as a mosaic with a range of roles. Here, for example, we examine the contours of negotiating the shift from no-party to multiparty politics in 2005, a critical turning point in the autocratization trajectory, which locked-in opposition parties. By embracing the return to multiparty competition, opposition parties and leaders legitimized the system and enabled Museveni and the NRM to strengthen dominance over the political playing field. It created an appearance of multiparty politics but grafted on an informal set of power practices and state control built in the preceding decades of no-party politics. Successfully navigation of this critical juncture handed Museveni a renewed grip and cemented his unmatched dominance of Uganda's politics.

Renegotiating the formal rules of the game at different critical junctures, as happened in 2005 and earlier in 1995, has been integral to the repertoires of adaptation and the survival strategies for Museveni and his NRM regime. The processes and mechanisms at play have been both formal and informal, entailing compromises in the formal legal realms but also an expansion of clientelist ties and patronage networks in the shadows of opaque political manoeuvres. Juggling the formal institutional terrain is tied to informal clientelist practices, often feeding off each other and playing complimentary roles.

Casting the spotlight on the formal and informal institutional landscape helps in making sense of the multiplicity of manoeuvres and machinations that continuously equip Museveni with the tools of control and coercion that both baits up and locks-in the opposition. This contributes to building the base for regime resilience and is part of the driving force in the acceleration of an autocratic trajectory with grave and long-term implications including the potential for future regime disintegration, state collapse and social disorder because the institutional landscape is compromised by short-term regime interests and power calculations of the incumbent.

The second line of inquiry is on the activities, actions and consequences of actors and groups operating outside the mainstream political system but which, directly or indirectly, deliberately or inadvertently, affect political processes and outcomes. In the past, the orthodox way of labelling this set of actors and activities was civil society, a conceptual aperture that became a catch-all and somewhat lost its analytical currency as the 'third wave' of democratization waned at the end of the last century. However, it is worth returning to and revisiting this theme to inquire into, for example, the anti-climax of the women's movement, its seeming demobilization and stasis, and how this dynamic feeds into the politics of autocratic deepening and resilience.

The third subtheme examines the security and defence sector, including law and order policies, practices and processes. Like most regimes and rulers with origins in armed movements, in the final analysis Museveni's lifeblood is control over the military might of the state. His rule is built around the military complex and securitization. While he participates in the rituals of routine electioneering and expresses a rhetorical belief in civil democratic processes, Museveni's ultimate primary source of power is the bullet not the ballot. His last redoubt, when all else fails and when push comes to shove is to revert to military might and the coercive arsenal of the state. Thus, command and control of the state's coercive apparatus and the full force of the military's core infrastructure is of utmost significance for regime survival but also is a key characteristic of the nature of the regime.

For regimes that capture power forcefully, keeping power necessarily requires maintaining a firm grip on the coercive apparatus and a careful management of intra-regime security challenges, factional struggles and external threats. The military is the primary gatekeeper, yet it is important for the ruler to guard against his guardians precisely because the same forces that keep him in power can just as easily turn against him; such has been the telling history in numerous countries, and in Uganda too but since 1986 Museveni has been adept at 'coup-proofing'.[49] While having a grip on military power has been a critical necessary condition in Museveni's long reign, such power in itself does not automatically translate into insulating him against challenges from within and without.

The fourth subtheme takes up the place and role of coalitional politics, institutions and electioneering in sustaining Museveni's rule and enabling his autocratic trajectory at both the national and subnational levels. Coalition compromises and concessions play critical roles in the dynamics of authoritarian regime politics. Internal coalition contests contribute to determining whether or not a regime fractures and fails or fights on and thrives even in the face of outside opposition threats; whether the ruler has to incessantly fight to put out fires in the backyard or is able to keep a firm control and unproblematic hold on the situation depends considerably on the composition and calibre of the governing coalition. Internal cohesion is critical.

The imperatives and calculations at play during specific moments of possible rupture and realignment have tremendous influence in shaping and forging coalition composition. It is instructive that since 2005, during successive electoral cycles Museveni has whipped into line every potential internal challenge and cemented his place as the 'sole candidate' for the NRM. There is never any attempt at pretending to have an open contest for the ruling party's Chairperson and presidential flagbearer – only one person is the candidate, unopposed: Museveni.

Summary of chapters

The eleven substantive chapters of this book are organized in three parts. The first part covers aspects of the material and nonmaterial bases of Museveni's rule. A key aspect here is clientelism as both a resource and an institution, both powerful and pervasive and through which autocratic political processes play out. In the same way that formal institutions like parties and parliaments can serve to sustain a regime or are tools for personalist exercises of power, clientelism as an informal institution plays equally crucial roles especially as a mechanism for mobilizing and distributing financial and other material resources that oil the extant political system.

Nelson Kafir's chapter analyses clientelism as both a feature of and an explanatory variable for Museveni's authoritarian rule. Clientelism describes but also explains Museveni's style of rule and his survival in power. In their chapter, Roger Tangri and Andrew Mwenda cast the spotlight on the mutually engaging and rewarding relationship between Museveni and foreign commercial interests focusing on the electricity sector where Museveni has personally presided over a great deal of big-money projects. Foreign business actors operating in Uganda have benefited from a relatively free and liberalized economic environment but one where Museveni plays a decisive role in navigating and overcoming costly red tape and bureaucratic corruption. Yet, the role Museveni played was detrimental to the energy sector and to his name as a reformist leader with largescale corruption and long delays in completing electricity dam projects.

In addition to material and financial resources, there is also the role of ideas in constructing and perpetuating Museveni's rule, specifically the rhetorical practices and language habits that inhabit a place in Uganda's public and political imagination. Money matters, but so do ideas. At different times and watershed moments, Museveni has articulated certain programmatic ideas and ideals, however self-serving, which have contributed to justifying his continued stay in power. A wide range of narratives of legitimation have dotted the evolution of Museveni's rule and provided succour to regime survival and autocratic trajectory. Here, the chapter by Jonathan Fisher and Stephanie Cawood reveals the ways in which harkening to historical memory of the 'bush war' reifies and reproduces a system of personalization that has augmented Museveni's stay at the helm.

These three chapters in part one of the book in various ways analyse the currency of resources, both material and ideational, that have underpinned the NRM regime but especially facilitated Museveni's long stay at the helm and the acceleration of a personalist brand of rulership. A system dependent on patronage needs a constant flow of material resources from domestic and foreign sources to provide state largesse to different constituencies and individual actors, but material resources alone are never enough to sustain a single regime of rule and enable one ruler to reign for so long.

The second part surveys the phenomenon of co-optation and coercion through a variety of institutional spaces and practices. Tabitha Mulyampiti's chapter takes up the women's movement, its contradictory roles in constraining but also enabling Museveni's long stay at the helm and the drive towards a decidedly personalist tenor of rule. Relatedly, Uganda is an interesting case of a vibrant and 'thick' milieu of civil society organizations, predominantly NGOs and fewer membership associations like professional bodies and trade unions. The status of civil society, the roles it plays in aiding autocratization and the state backlash against emboldened activism is the focus of Mesharch W. Katusiimeh's chapter. Beyond civil society, write large, there is the role of organized and unorganized business interests, both local and foreign, as well as religious movements and informal youth groups, which deserves more critical attention within the context of Uganda's political economy but are not addressed in this book.[50]

The chapters by Gerald Bareebe, Sabastiano Rwengabo and Rebecca Tapscott revisit Museveni's skilful use of the state's coercive apparatus in ways that have aided his firm grip on power but also simultaneously undermined the prospects of exorcising the historical ghosts of militarism and militarization in Ugandan politics. Rwengabo's chapter examines how the militarization of the state's otherwise civilian spaces is an integral part of Museveni's broader strategy and technology of embedding military control under the veneer of civilian rule, while Bareebe investigates the different ways that Museveni has instrumentalized the military by employing both co-optation and coercion. At the centre of autocratic adaptability, Tapscott's situates the notion of institutionalized arbitrariness characterized by unpredictable and uncertain exercise of coercive state power, fragmentation and simultaneous assertion and denial of social control.

These three chapters that focus on the military and coercive power speak to what for long was Museveni's primary *raison d'être,* predicated on his perceived (also self-proclaimed) distinctive capacity to assure security of person and property, projecting him as the definitive guarantor of national stability, security and prosperity. Indeed, his overarching political posture during successive electoral cycles since 1996 was one of a 'security president' – ostensibly a tried, tested and safe pair of gloves to entrust with superintending the country's immediate and long-term peace and prosperity. More recently, however, this narrative and branding ran its course and somewhat waned with the near disappearance of organized armed rebel groups challenging the central state.[51]

At any rate, to reinvent and recast himself, Museveni has had to repeatedly rearticulate and reposition the pivotal *raison d'être* for his stay in power because the traditional harkening to the security rationale increasingly has little appeal especially among the younger generations of Ugandans who have no direct experience with the widespread insecurity of the 1970s and 1980s. To continue making the case for being the 'security president', Museveni has to repackage this narrative in a fundamentally different light and sell his claim to being the guarantor of a stable and secure Uganda. His 2021 election slogan 'securing the future' was an attempt at projecting a hopeful message rather than painting a dark past, the latter having powerfully appealed to older Ugandans in the past but is now past its sell-by-date for younger generations.

The third and final part casts the aperture on different strands of the institutional landscape especially around coalitions, elections and political parties. Taking up the evolution of the NRM's/Museveni's ruling coalition, Moses Khisa's chapter shows that under certain conditions and circumstances, principled engagement and ideological predispositions have been the guiding basis for forging ruling coalitions; at other times, patronage, personal interests and crass pursuit of power are the drivers for weaving and sustaining Museveni's ruling coalition.

Whatever the actual specifics and conditions, the point to underline here is that the ruling coalition is never static, nor cast in stone. Rather, coalitions evolve and shift with time and in the light of the obtaining structural circumstances. They change both in form and substance. The form, shape and substance of the ruling coalition impinges upon regime sustainability and autocratic sustenance. Khisa's chapter analyses the transformation in Museveni's ruling coalition, showing how its shift from an initial orientation towards principled inclusivity in the days of 'broad-based' government to descent into a transactional, unprincipled politics.

Relatedly, Anders Sjögren analyses the role of electoral processes in regime legitimation and in propelling autocratization through the charade of contests against Museveni but in an environment where the levers of power are firmly under the incumbent's control. Frederick Golooba-Mutebi and Mesharch W. Katusiimeh put a spotlight on parties and their varied roles in the autocratization trajectory. This chapter focusses on the puzzle of why, despite their vocal presence and proliferation, political parties in Uganda remain largely ineffectual, enfeebled and unable to counter Museveni's dominance of the political scene and space or pushback against his personalization of power. Quite remarkably, even for the ruling NRM party itself, Museveni has successfully curtailed its autonomous and independent existence, which makes it unlikely that the party will outlive its founder in sharp contrast with continental peers such as the MPLA in Angola, the RPF in Rwanda, the ANC in South Africa and the CCM in Tanzania.

Implications and conclusions

Analysing the trajectory of regime politics in Uganda and the deepening autocratic rule of Museveni, seen from a wider comparative African perspective, yields implications that are theoretical, empirical and practical. Theoretically, approaching autocratization as a function of successful *adaptation* to changing circumstances and conditions accents both the purposive interventions of actors but also the role of contingency and structure – a combination of agency, contingency and structure. This approach casts the net wide enough as to speak to the varied roles played by actors including those who, strictly speaking, are situated outside the extant political system but inadvertently implicated in aiding the entrenchment of the system and attendant outcomes.

Empirically, studying Museveni's long and increasingly rusty regime opens up to grappling with one very consistent ramification of rulers who hang onto power in perpetuity in the manner Museveni has accomplished – longevity almost always means the end or the immediate aftermath is dire and disastrous. This is a practical dilemma with a consistent and notorious historical record. The end of Joseph Mobutu's three-decade reign set up the Congo for a tragedy of unimaginable proportions, including an African 'World War'.[52] Gaddafi's violent departure after four decades of personal rule in Libya left in its wake state implosion and sheer chaos in that country. In Egypt and Sudan, fragility and instability followed the violent deposing of Mubarak and El-Bashir. Considering Uganda's social complexity and a jinxed history of never having had a peaceful change of government and an orderly presidential turnover, the current trend points to ominous times ahead.

Arguably, the most important practical implication of Uganda's autocratic trajectory, the reproduction and the deepening of a system of personalist rule is the hollowing out of institutionalized politics and constraints on individual behaviour. The imperatives of autocratic survival inevitably sweep aside important institutional constraints on the ruler and members of the ruling core. Within the larger debate on global autocratization, Uganda stands out for many reasons but especially for the fact that just about everything that matters is now built around the power and performance of Museveni. This is not to say that Museveni rules alone or without the force of governmental institutions, rather it is that he has grown into the most important and consequential institution in the country. This is the more crucial given that Uganda occupies a pivotal position in the geopolitics of the great lakes region and the Horn of Africa.

To sum up, it is worth noting that over the past two decades, Ugandan politics has had dramatic twists and turns. Museveni has repeatedly defied predictions and crushed expectations, from a seeming idealist and progressive reformer to a pragmatic and somewhat retrogressive ruler. Understanding Uganda's political trajectory requires casting the spotlight on Museveni, but the analysis would be incomplete if it does not go beyond Museveni and the NRM.

Therefore, a close and comprehensive reassessment of Uganda's political development is timely and worthwhile. Recent major works have focused, rather narrowly, on electoral politics and other single-issue domains like land conflicts. By contrast, this book seeks to take a much broader focus by bringing together analytically deeper and empirically rich reflections on, on the one hand, Museveni's autocratic rule and resilience, and, on the other, the role played by shifts in Uganda's ruling coalition, the state of political parties, the civil society landscape, the military and security question and the state of (de)institutionalization of power, among others. The hope here is that the chapters in this book will enhance our scholarly grasp of Uganda's autocratic trajectory situating a set of empirical puzzles in a single analytical lens built around a unified theme and frame. But perhaps an even more important hope is that this book contributes to a practical reimagining and rebirth of new and promising Uganda.

Notes

1 Svein-Erik Helle and Lise Rakner, 'Grabbing an Election: Abuse of State Resources in the 2011 Elections in Uganda', in *Corruption, Grabbing and Development: Real World Challenges*, ed. Tina Søreide and Aled Williams (London: Edward Elgar Publishing, 2013), 164.

2 Asef Bayat, *Revolution without Revolutionaries: Making Sense of the Arab Spring* (Palo Alto: Stanford University Press, 2017).

3 Immanuel Wallerstein, 'The Contradictions of the Arab Spring', *Al Jazeera* (14 November 2011). https://www.aljazeera.com/opinions/2011/11/14/the-contradictions-of-the-arab-spring/

4 Sam Wilkins, Richard Vokes and Moses Khisa, 'Briefing: Contextualizing the Bobi Wine Factor in Uganda's 2021 Elections', *African Affairs* 120, no. 481 (2021): 639.

5 Anna Lührmann and Staffan I. Lindberg, 'A Third Wave of Autocratization Is Here: What Is New about It?', *Democratization* 26, no. 7 (2019): 1100.

6   Ibid.
7   A new book on Africa just came out as the current book is in advanced stages. See Leonardo R. Arriola, Lise Rakner and Nicolas van de Walle, *Democratic Backsliding in Africa? Autocratization, Resilience, and Contention* (Oxford: Oxford University Press, 2023).
8   It is debatable whether 2005 was indeed *the* turning point. There are varying interpretations of when Museveni and his regime showed outright signs of autocracy. For example, Joe Oloka-Onyango, who reviewed this book's manuscript and offered extensive and constructive comments, insisted that Museveni and NRM were never committed to democratic government right from 1986 and that 2005 was a continuation rather than a turning point. But it is also true that senior NRM figures like Eriya Kategaya, Amanya Mushega, Mugisha Muntu, among others, took 2005 and the removal of terms limits as a breaking point, resulting in a major split in part culminating in the founding a new opposition party, the Forum for Democratic Change (FDC).
9   Juma A. Okuku, 'Beyond "Third Term" Politics: Constitutional Reform and Democratic Governance in Uganda', *East African Journal of Peace and Human Rights* 11, no. 2 (2005): 182–219.
10 See https://www.youtube.com/watch?v=VfyhfgYGu_8
11 VOA, 'New Presidential Powers Lead to Political Shakeups in Uganda' (24 December 2014). https://www.voanews.com/a/new-presidential-powers-lead-to-political-shakeups-in-uganda/2572159.html
12 J. Oloka-Onyango and Josephine Ahikire, eds., *Controlling Consent: Uganda's 2016 Elections* (Trenton, NJ: Africa World Press, 2016).
13 Some of the earliest positive assessments of Museveni and the NRM included Greg Larkin, 'NRM and Uganda's Realities', *Ufahamu: A Journal of African Studies* 15, no. 3 (1987): 156–66. Later David Apter credited Museveni with a mode of 'consultative democracy'. See David E. Apter, 'Democracy for Uganda: A case for Comparison', *Daedalus* 124, no. 3 (1995): 155–90. Other relatively positive assessments of Uganda's rule in the 1990s included, Justus Mugaju and Petter Langseth, eds., *Post-Conflict Uganda: Towards an Effective Civil Service* (Kampala: Fountain Publishers, 1996); Dan Ottemoeller, 'Popular Perceptions of Democracy: Elections and Attitudes in Uganda', *Comparative Political Studies* 31, no. 1 (1998): 98–124; Sabiti Makara, Geoffrey B. Tukahebwa and Foster Byarugaba, eds., *Voting for Democracy in Uganda: Issues in Recent Elections* (Kampala: LDC Publishers, 2003); David Stasavage, 'The Role of Democracy in Uganda's Move to Universal Primary Education', *The Journal of Modern African Studies* 43, no. 1 (2005): 53–73. On the other hand, earliest critics included Daniel Wadada Nabudere, 'The Uganda Crisis: What Next?' *Ufahamu: A Journal of African Studies* 15, no. 3 (1987); J. Oloka-Onyango, 'Governance, Democracy and Development in Uganda Today: A Socio-Legal Examination', *African Study Monographs* 13, no. 2 (1992): 91–109 and J. Oloka- Onyango, 'Uganda's Benevolent Dictatorship', *Current History* 96, no. 610 (May 1997): 212–16. Also, Human Rights Watch, *Hostile to Democracy: The Movement System and Political Repression in Uganda* (New York: Human Rights Watch, 1999).
14 For a critique of the no-party experiment and its mostly one-party reality, see Giovanni Carbone, *No-party Democracy? Ugandan Politics in Comparative Perspective* (Boulder, CO: Lynne Rienner, 2008); Justus Mugaju and J. Oloka-Onyango, eds., *No-Party Democracy in Uganda: Myths and Realities* (Kampala: Fountain Publishers, 2000).

15 For a summary of this literature, see Lührmann and Lindberg, 'A Third Wave', especially pp. 1096–8.

16 Ibid., 1095.

17 Samuel P. Huntington, *The Third Wave: Democratization in the Late Twentieth Century* (Norman: University of Oklahoma Press, 1991).

18 Steven Levitsky and Lucan A. Way, *Competitive Authoritarianism: Hybrid Regimes after the Cold War* (Cambridge: Cambridge University Press, 2010).

19 For example, Beatriz Magaloni, *Voting for Autocracy: Hegemonic Party Survival and Its Demise in Mexico* (Cambridge: Cambridge University Press, 2006); Jennifer Gandhi, *Political Institutions under Dictatorship* (Cambridge: Cambridge University Press, 2008); Jennifer Gandhi and Adam Przeworski, 'Authoritarian Institutions and the Survival of Autocrats', *Comparative Political Studies* 40, no. 11 (2007): 1279–301; Dan Slater, *Ordering Power: Contentious Politics and Authoritarian Leviathans in Southeast Asia* (Cambridge: Cambridge University Press, 2010).

20 Jason Brownlee, *Authoritarianism in an Age of Democratization* (Cambridge: Cambridge University Press, 2007).

21 Ken Ochieng' Opalo and Lahra Smith, 'Ideology and Succession Politics in Ethiopia: Autocratic Leadership Turnover and Political Instability', *Democratization* 28, no. 8 (2021): 1463–82.

22 Melanie O'Gorman, 'Why the CCM Won't Lose: The Roots of Single-party Dominance in Tanzania', *Journal of Contemporary African Studies* 30, no. 2 (2012): 313–33.

23 Andrea Kendall-Taylor, Erica Frantz and Joseph Wright, 'The Global Rise of Personalized Politics: It's Not Just Dictators Anymore', *The Washington Quarterly* 40, no. 1 (2017): 8.

24 Obiang has surpassed the previous record by the late Muamar Gaddafi of Libya of forty-two years of uninterrupted rule.

25 Ericka A. Albaugh, 'An Autocrat Toolkit: Adaptation and Manipulation in "Democratic" Cameroon', in *Democratisation in Africa: Challenges and Prospects*, ed. Gordon Crawford and Gabriel Lynch (London: Routledge, 2012).

26 Nathan Jensen and Leonard Wantchekon, 'Resource Wealth and Political Regimes in Africa', *Comparative Political Studies* 37, no. 7 (2004): 816–41.

27 Janet I. Lewis, *How Insurgency Begins: Rebel Group Formation in Uganda and Beyond* (Cambridge: Cambridge University Press, 2020), 22.

28 Ken Ochieng' Opalo, *Legislative Development in Africa: Politics and Postcolonial Legacies* (Cambridge: Cambridge University Press, 2019), 133.

29 See Slater, *Ordering Power*; Magaloni, *Voting for Autocracy*.

30 For a survey of the different uses and abuses of formal institutions in Africa, See Nic Cheeseman, ed., *Institutions and Democracy in Africa: How the Rules of the Game Shape Political Developments* (Cambridge: Cambridge University Press, 2018).

31 Daniel N. Posner and Daniel J. Young, 'Term Limits: Leadership, Political Competition and the Transfer of Power', in Ibid.

32 Ibid.

33 Frederick Golooba-Mutebi and Sam Hickey, 'The Master of Institutional Multiplicity? The Shifting Politics of Regime Survival, State-Building and Democratisation in Museveni's Uganda', *Journal of Eastern African Studies* 10, no. 4 (2016): 601–18.

34 See Rebecca Tapscott, *Arbitrary States: Social Control and Modern Authoritarianism in Museveni's Uganda* (Oxford: Oxford University Press, 2021).

35 Moses Khisa, 'Inclusive Cooptation and Political Corruption in Uganda', in *Political Corruption in Africa. Extraction and Power Preservation*, ed. Inge Amundsen (Cheltenham/UK: Edward Elgar Publishing, 2019), 109.

36 Tapscott, *Arbitrary States*, 121.

37 Sabiti Makara, Lise Rakner and Lars Svåsand, 'Turnaround: The National Resistance Movement and the Reintroduction of a Multiparty System in Uganda', *International Political Science Review* 30, no. 2 (2009): 189.

38 Ibid., 194.

39 Robert H. Bates, *When Things Fell Apart: State Failure in Late Century Africa* (Cambridge: Cambridge University Press, 2008), 20.

40 Crawford Young, *The Postcolonial State in Africa: Fifty Years of Independence, 1960–2010* (Madison: The University of Wisconsin Press, 2012).

41 On official corruption tied to privatization and divestiture in Uganda, see, for example, Godfrey B. Asiimwe, 'Of Extensive and Elusive Corruption in Uganda: Neo-Patronage, Power, and Narrow Interests', *African Studies Review* 56, no. 2 (2013): 129–44; Roger Tangri and Andrew M. Mwenda, *The Politics of Elite Corruption in Africa: Uganda in Comparative African Perspective* (London: Routledge, 2013); Scott D. Taylor, *Globalization and the Cultures of Business in Africa: From Patrimonialism to Profit* (Bloemfontein: Indiana University Press, 2012); Roger Tangri and Andrew Mwenda, 'Corruption and Cronyism in Uganda's Privatization in the 1990s', *African Affairs* 100, no. 398 (2001): 117–33.

42 Moses Khisa, 'Managing Elite Defection in Museveni's Uganda: The 2016 Elections in Perspective', *Journal of Eastern African Studies* 10, no. 4 (2016): 729–48.

43 Dan Paget, 'Tanzania: Shrinking Space and Opposition Protest', *Journal of Democracy* 28, no. 3 (2017): 153–67.

44 Fiona Shen-Bayh, 'Strategies of Repression: Judicial and Extrajudicial Methods of Autocratic Survival', *World Politics* 70, no. 3 (2018): 323.

45 Leonardo R. Arriola, 'Patronage and Political Stability in Africa', *Comparative Political Studies* 42, no. 10 (2009): 1357.

46 Gerald Bareebe, 'Predators or Protectors? Military Corruption as a Pillar of Regime Survival in Uganda', *Civil Wars* 22, no. 2–3 (2020): 313–32.

47 See Moses Khisa, 'Politicisation and Professionalisation: The Progress and Perils of Civil-Military Transformation in Museveni's Uganda', *Civil Wars* 22, no. 2–3 (2020): 289–312.

48 For a general overview of authoritarian learning, see Stephen G. F. Hall and Thomas Ambrosio, 'Authoritarian Learning: A Conceptual Overview', *East European Politics* 33, no. 2 (2017): 143–61; Thomas Ambrosio, 'Constructing a Framework of Authoritarian Diffusion: Concepts, Dynamics, and Future Research', *International Studies Perspectives* 11, no. 4 (2010): 375–92. On Russia and Eastern Europe, See Stephen G. F Hall, 'Preventing a Colour Revolution: The Belarusian Example as an Illustration for the Kremlin'? *East European Politics* 33, no. 2 (2017): 162–83 and Thomas Ambrosio, 'Insulating Russia from a Colour Revolution: How the Kremlin Resists Regional Democratic Trends', *Democratisation* 14, no. 2 (2007): 232–52. On the Middle East and North Africa, see André Bank and Mirjam Edel, 'Authoritarian Regime Learning: Comparative Insights from the Arab Uprisings', *German Institute of Global and Area Studies*, Working Paper No. 274 (2015) and Marc Lynch, ed., *The Arab Uprisings Explained: New Contentious Politics in the Middle East* (New York: Columbia University Press, 2014).

49   Sabastiano Rwengabo, 'Regime Stability in Post-1986 Uganda: Counting the Benefits of Coup- Proofing', *Armed Forces & Society* 39, no. 3 (2013): 531–59.

50   See, for example, Tom Goodfellow, 'Taming the "Rogue" Sector: Studying State Effectiveness in Africa through Informal Transport Politics', *Comparative Politics* 47, no. 2 (2015): 127–47; Henni Alava and Jimmy Spire Ssentongo, 'Religious (de) Politicisation in Uganda's 2016 Elections', *Journal of Eastern African Studies* 10, no. 4 (2016): 677–92.

51   But Uganda still grapples with other national security problems including terrorism which has regional geopolitical dimensions as well as violent crime and mysterious assassinations.

52   See Gérard Prunier, *Africa's World War: Congo, the Rwandan Genocide, and the Making of a Continental Catastrophe* (Oxford: Oxford University Press, 2008).

Part One

Clientelism and resources

1

Political clientelism and Museveni's authoritarianism[1]

Nelson Kasfir

Yoweri Museveni became a more authoritarian president to successfully manage the structure of political clientelism he had created to ensure he stayed in power. Soon after he became president, his personal rule steadily grew in political importance. It was based on exchanges of jobs, opportunities for wealth, and cash payments for loyalty, votes and favours. This ancillary structure of influence eventually became as important to keeping him in power as the formal structures of government. It helped him remain president beyond the term limits and age limits envisioned in the 1995 Ugandan Constitution.

To create it, he dismantled many requirements for legal accountability, introduced extensive bureaucratic changes, and offered enticing prospects to followers and even opponents. He engaged, or countenanced others, engaging in various legal and illegal activities that greatly expanded his actions as president. The construction of this aspect of his regime did not occur all at once. Rather, it grew larger, more complex and far more expensive. To make it work, Museveni expanded his own authority at the expense of the state.

This intricate system is best labelled political clientelism. It has many moving parts essential to its operation. Though informal, it is directly related to formal institutions of government. It both competes with them and depends on them. It became a supplementary form of governance. To ensure he continued to control it, Museveni became more authoritarian over time, political clientelism became one of several factors in the growth of his authoritarianism.

In this chapter, I sketch Museveni's construction of political clientelism and its consequences for the changing nature of his regime. He often acts constitutionally within the rules and through the offices of the Ugandan government. However, the manner and timing through which they interconnect with political clientelism are unpredictable and opportunistic. That creates great uncertainty over the choice of policy and its implementation among officials, citizens and international donors.

The formation of Museveni's system of political clientelism began after he took power. To practise political clientelism, resources must be accumulated so they can be spent. Some of Museveni's transactions towards this end are illegal and therefore kept hidden. Consequently, applying the analytic frame laid out here is somewhat speculative; many of its elements can only be identified indirectly.

Nevertheless, writers on the Museveni regime have reported many instances of corrupt acquisition on the one hand and patronage expenditures on the other that together with additional organizational arrangements create a *prima facie* case for an intentional yet informal strategy that facilitates his preservation of power. Several of these writers recognize that Museveni uses these elements to support his regime.[2] We need to know more about this system. How did Museveni and his close allies organize it? What were its consequences for governance? Why did it cause him to become more authoritarian?

The next section discusses a model of political clientelism created over time by a national leader that serves as a supplementary form of governance. Then I propose a notion of authoritarianism appropriate to political clientelism. Following that, I outline the evolution of Museveni's political clientelism by examining four aspects of Museveni's political clientelism: positioning, funding, spending and protecting. Lastly, I suggest how the logic of the specific form of political clientelism Museveni has created became an important factor in the growth of his authoritarianism.

Rulers and political clientelism

Political clientelism is a leader's personal or official exchange of material resources for support, loyalty or services to gain, reinforce or extend political dominance through an informal hierarchy. Some of these exchanges conform to law, others are extra-legal. At its core, political clientelism concerns power not wealth, though pay-offs to achieve political ends are usually necessary.[3] 'The boss's control over patronage is a principal source of his authority.'[4]

Political clientelism can be centralized or decentralized.[5] That is, it can be monopolized by a single national leader or by several competing hierarchies, each separately funded. When undertaken by a national ruler, centralized political clientelism may become a symbiotic political system operating in conjunction with the state's conventional offices and playing a minor or major role in a leader's regulation of national affairs.[6] Contemporary political clientelism is always closely, though often paradoxically, tied to its legal order. The more a chief patron extracts resources from state offices, the more she and her sub-patrons need to protect themselves from state rules. The more a chief patron engages in personal rule, the more monopolistic political clientelism tends to become.

This concept avoids analytic difficulties engendered by various alternative concepts of corruption, patronage, prebendalism and neo-patrimonialism. These earlier notions made important advances in explaining rulers' political behaviour but ignored aspects essential to the concept. For example, prebendalism, appointing loyal followers to offices they use for personal and group benefit, leaves out various other corrupt and legal practices and, more importantly, fails to specify how leaders use it to strengthen their political domination.[7] Neo-patrimonialism, the most widely accepted approach, intrinsically relies on Weberian notions of patrimonialism which are often misleadingly entangled in cultural obligations rather than the straightforward material transactions actually at work.[8]

Many accounts of neopatrimonialism and political clientelism also fail to consider the funding mechanism that makes it effective at the national level. They look at demand, without recognizing how supply is organized.[9] The complexity involved in constructing a political clientelist system requires attention to other notions rarely analysed. The organizational activities that make it possible require consideration. The national patron, whether an individual or a group, must construct a multifaceted organization to manage funding clientelism, not just distributing resources. To accomplish both kinds of material transactions requires a political budget, however informal, to ensure its continuing operation.[10] 'The mechanics of patronage and therefore its stability are at the heart of a leader's political stability. The art of governing is not only the art of extracting resources, but also of redistribution.'[11]

While all national patrons exercise personal choice, they cannot do so directly with hundreds of thousands of clients throughout the country. National patrons must depend on others for the face-to-face relationships that occur beyond their immediate circle of associates.[12] Coordinating many clients requires establishing a hierarchy of agents. Its structure must ensure that the network of sub-patrons and their clients operates reliably. A national patron has to manage a complicated unstable hierarchy. National patrons engage diverse clients whom they must organize differently. For example, enriching legislators so they support a statute removing obstacles to the patron's capacity to act requires an entirely different type of clientelist organization from distributing money to voters in a presidential election.

Organizing mass expenditures works differently from elite expenditures. The influence of political clientelism on voting has received considerable attention throughout the world.[13] The literature suggests that national patrons develop this kind of system gradually. Kitschelt and Wilkerson observe that 'manag[ing] clientelistic relations is a drawn-out process'.[14] Building clientelism is an iterative process: 'Repeated interactions over time allow politicians to observe which voters keep their promises and which voters can be swayed, and to calibrate the size of an offer needed to sway those voters.'[15]

Organizing political clientelism includes managing protection of operatives against removal from their public positions or prosecution for patently illegal deeds. Protection enables trust. At the same time, political clientelism requires punishment of sub-patrons or clients who engage in disloyal acts – such as violating bargains or revealing illegal payments. To administer all these activities, the national patron needs 'societal management skills'.[16] In addition, assuming there is only one hierarchy of political clientelism, the patron must prevent challengers. That increases the likelihood that the patron will become a more authoritarian leader.

Despite its informal and personal character, political clientelism is inescapably conjoined to the formal and rational-legal principles of the government's bureaucracy for much of its resources.[17] Thus, it is generally a supplementary system of governance. A national patron typically has constitutional authority to use specific funds or appoint certain officers at personal discretion. However, that is insufficient to subsidize an extensive patronage network. For that, a national patron must also violate laws or regulations by giving positions to clients for kickbacks and acquiring material resources from administrative departments, donors or private citizens.

Consequently, operating its apparatus inevitably produces legal and political issues over misuse of bureaucratic resources and other irregularities. These conflicts must be resolved without impairing the apparatus – generally through further measures that violate either the letter or spirit of the law. Contemporary national patrons, whether or not they are authoritarian rulers, need to protect compliant operatives and punish defectors. Squabbling over shares between the national patron and the operatives who acquire resources illegally also creates political tensions. In addition, principled supporters of national patrons who oppose illicit behaviour also may cause them problems.

National patrons may be predatory or prudent.[18] The more rational among them will choose to insulate certain agencies, such as national banks and development bureaus, that produce wealth which could support predation later. Because of its frequent illegality and informality, the practice of political clientelism is unpredictable, even though both patrons and clients use it to satisfy their own goals. 'Clientelism clearly contributes to the reproduction of the institutional uncertainty that it is designed to overcome.'[19] This uncertainty reinforces the political dominance of the national ruler.

Centralized political clientelism is unstable. It depends partly on allies of the national patron who are likely to demand profits for taking risks of illegal action on the leader's behalf. It requires the national patron to protect them from the courts and to punish opponents who attempt to unmask the system. Furthermore, centralized political clientelism angers members of the public who receive neither selective nor collective rewards and recognize that their lives are not improving because beneficial policies are disrupted. To meet these threats, the manager of political clientelism may expand its reach, producing another round of popular anger. Finally, centralized political clientelism is unstable because it cannot outlive the complex informal relationships of trust its national patron has created.[20] Any aspirant to governing through clientelism must establish a new network.

Authoritarianism and political clientelism

Successful management of centralized political clientelism requires its patron and sub-patrons to engage in authoritarian practices. They intervene in offices of the government intermittently, depending on their current needs. In all regimes, some patronage appointments are constitutional. However, as clientelism grows, it will increasingly violate constitutional and statutory rules. The demands of centralized political clientelism have two unfortunate consequences. First, they de-institutionalize bureaucratic, legislative and judicial offices.[21] Second, they increase authoritarian rule by the national patron.

The conventional understanding of authoritarianism in political science is not adequate to analyse political clientelism because it is usually limited to the presence or absence of democracy. As Marlies Glasius points out the literature places 'an excessive focus on elections'.[22] Take, for example, Erica Frantz's suggestion that 'in the operational definition of an authoritarian regime this book uses, the distinguishing factor separating authoritarian regimes from democratic ones is whether government selection occurs via free and fair elections'.[23] Autocratization poses the same problem because political scientists have appropriated it to mean the opposite of democratization.[24]

Instead, we need a broader concept of authoritarianism. As her definition of authoritarianism, Glasius parsimoniously offers 'patterns of action that sabotage accountability to people over whom a political actor exerts control ... by means of secrecy, disinformation and disabling voice'.[25] The chief patron manages centralized political clientelism more effectively by removing or ignoring legal barriers. But that is not sufficient to cover centralized political clientelism because the notion must include the ruler's active penetration of executive, legislative and judicial offices as well as the loss of accountability. To fund, spend and protect themselves, personal rulers or ruling groups develop practices that undermine the legal order by establishing informal processes that obstruct rule-based activities throughout the government. Political clientelism is unstable because the national patron's subordinates are always hard to control, violations of law can be dangerous and underserving people's needs reduces legitimacy. Thus, the maintenance of political clientelism inevitably requires greater authoritarianism.

Formation and development of Museveni's political clientelism

During the National Resistance Movement (NRM) rebellion from 1981 to 1986, neither Museveni nor his inner circle provided any indication they intended to organize a political clientelist system after victory. At the time, it seems unlikely they even thought they would find it necessary. In their public statements throughout the civil war, they consistently rejected two of its core features – personal rule and corrupt officials.[26] Their ability to maintain support of the people among whom they fought depended appreciably on the future they insisted they would introduce after they won. They promised people would participate in decision-making by voting in free and fair elections and that constitutional restrictions would prevent rulers from acting in their own interests.[27] The NRM's decision to have villagers freely elect their own councils during its rebellion reflected the leadership's belief in democratic institutions.[28] This platform sharply distinguished NRM rebels from the politicians then controlling the state. It was vital to gaining popular support essential to their victory.

Immediately after taking power, the new government extended local elections throughout the country and to all levels of sub-national government. In the next few years, it held national legislative elections and appointed a commission to write a new constitutional draft that was debated and passed by an elected assembly. This constitution, promulgated in 1995, stressed institutional checks on personal rule, including term and age limits for the president, though ensuring that the 'Movement' would continue to rule for the following five years rather than permitting multiparty competition.[29] The new constitution also established several agencies to combat corruption and compel accountability. Thus, the constitution established significant legal obstacles to creating a structure of political clientelism. After its adoption, the willingness at first of parliament to check the president and even censure some of his ministers was a significant consequence of the new constitution's commitment to the rule of law.[30]

Nevertheless, soon after take-over, Museveni and other high officials in the NRM began to engage in practices that developed into a system of political clientelism. They did not justify it on traditional cultural patterns as some writers argue.[31] Instead, Museveni's political clientelism is basically a rational strategy to ensure he retains personal authority at the expense of formal rules. To identify it with neo-patrimonialism creates confusion about its analytic elements.

In its early years the NRM regime was militarily and politically insecure, confronting serious challenges to its control of government. When it took power, its social base was limited to central and western rural areas where it had fought. Elsewhere, its leaders were met with pervasive suspicion they would rule dictatorially. Uganda's colonial and post-colonial history had been driven by fears of ethnic domination. The new regime was viewed similarly. Since the national army, which it had just defeated, was largely identified with the northern and eastern regions, the NRM victory was met with great suspicion in those two regions. The new leaders were also suspect because so many of them came from one small ethnic group in the southwest.

Conservative politicians were wary of Museveni for his earlier pronouncements which they considered radical. The depth of these overlapping suspicions manifested in multiple rebellions that broke out within a year.[32] Defeating them, often brutally, created additional political fears. NRM leaders were so anxious about political opponents; they even arrested several of their own cabinet ministers for treason.[33] It cannot be surprising that NRM leaders began to look for additional means to keep themselves in power.

Furthermore, NRM officers and ordinary soldiers had suffered extraordinary hardships throughout the war. The domestic society they re-entered after victory had become increasingly corrupt as the result of misgovernment by the Amin and the second Obote regimes.[34] Scarcities in basic goods, rapid inflation and declining tax collections meant that public servants sold their services or official goods because they could not live on their salaries.[35] As well, the attractions of becoming rich overcame many soldiers' scruples. As Museveni put it after four years in power: 'Originally when we came into government, there was rampant corruption in the Civil Service. I am now, however, beginning to get persistent reports that there is corruption amongst our political leaders.'[36]

The huge infusion of funds by international donors that began only a year and a half after takeover created new and tempting possibilities for political clientelism. The amount of outside assistance was staggering compared to domestic funding available to the Ugandan government. In accepting this new source of finance, the NRM had to agree to World Bank requirements of structural adjustment. That meant reversing its rebel doctrine of a relatively autonomous pattern of self-sustained economic growth and replacing it with foreign-led development. Regime leaders were willing to diminish their dedication to their rebel principles. We cannot be sure whether the regime's willingness to exchange doctrine for outside assistance meant it regarded the new funds as a pragmatic route allowing the country to escape its economic quagmire or saw it as an opportunity for building regime political support. Most likely its leaders wanted both.

From 1987 forward, donor support to finance recovery and later development increased government coffers by more than half a billion US dollars in the first year that expanded annually to over 2 billion in 2019.[37] Every year from 1989 for the next two decades official development assistance received by the Ugandan government amounted to 10 per cent or more of the country's gross national income and reached an astonishing figure of more than 25 per cent of GNI in 1992.[38] Even as recently as 2019, official development assistance amounted to almost half the cost of central government spending.[39] While the amount received does not indicate how much regime leaders may have diverted to political clientelism, donors did little to prevent corrupt use of funds they contributed.[40] Nor were the anti-corruption agencies created by the 1995 Constitution successful in countering it.[41]

Museveni eventually emerged as the uncontested and unaccountable personal authority over much of the government, partly by becoming the chief patron of a national centralized form of political clientelism. By the early 2000s, political clientelism had become 'a central mechanism for regime maintenance'.[42] Museveni 'increasingly brought mainstream policy functions within State House and circumvented formal institutional mechanisms'.[43] His system was based on an opaque informal pyramidal apparatus that raised funds and then spent them for political support. Museveni managed it through an elaborate network of rebel military officers, ethnic associates and family members.[44] Ethnic favouritism, particularly for south-westerners in 'the more consequential positions in the inner core …. has remained a fairly constant phenomenon since the NRM took power'.[45] Over time Museveni steadily narrowed these elements in his clientelist apparatus to preserve tight personal control.[46] His frequently remarked 'growing tendency to micromanage' is an essential feature of successful political clientelism.[47]

Yet, there were obstacles to his exercise of political clientelism. At times, he acquiesced in growing demands and disputes over transactions from his sub-patrons. Maintaining this system became increasingly expensive. He had to overcome popular opposition and objections of formerly close allies. Nevertheless, he shielded from clientelism, though not consistently, the operations of certain government departments responsible for regulating the economy or promising future high value production – some fraction of which might become available to fund future clientelism.[48]

The regime's interest in hiding its illegal actions and the informal nature of its political clientelism make it difficult to demonstrate specifically how Museveni and his allies built their organization. Scholars who analyse the uses of corruption for governance despair of providing anything close to an exact description.[49] Nevertheless, several writers have provided accounts of specific legal and illegal acquisitions and distributions of resources involving Museveni directly or his close associates. They also show how he protected close allies accused of corruption and punished opponents who threatened either his objectives or exposed his methods. These practices are typical features of centralized political clientelism. As it grew, however, Museveni emerged from *primus inter pares* to establish a monopoly of control.

NRM doctrines positioning political clientelism

Ironically, two policies that had emerged from the NRM's rebel doctrine provided a unique foundation for building Museveni's centralized political clientelism. These civil war policies were its plan for a four-level hierarchy of elected local councils and its idea of 'no-party democracy' proposed to overcome ethnic antagonisms. Neither were originally intended to advance political clientelism. Both were borrowed to facilitate connections between national and local notables essential to create it. The NRM 'built its patronage machinery' through local 'political appointments ... budgetary control, and ... allocation of tenders'.[50] Its apparatus steadily expanded. 'Today, the NRM controls most of the rural local-level government structures in Uganda.'[51]

No-party democracy administered by the NRM government gave its leaders overwhelming advantages in constructing a system of political clientelism at the expense of the previously dominant old parties.[52] Challenges from within the NRM caused its leaders to return in 2005 to multi-party competition, not to become more democratic, rather to preserve their dominance. The change was engineered to enhance the NRM's political clientelism. Museveni made this clear: 'Let us rid ourselves of the uncommitted. Then we [the Movement] shall be able to consolidate ourselves.'[53]

After the first multi-party election under the NRM, its leaders mobilized 'nine-person campaign committees ... mirroring the setup' of the tiers of local government and later increased them to thirty members to contend in the 2016 elections.[54] As Museveni noted, 'The NRM ... created a massive structure that could help the leadership more easily explain and implement that vision [of its rebel doctrine].'[55] During election campaigns, this meant a huge expansion in the political clientelist apparatus. '... we created a very powerful structure of village-based committees covering all the 57,792 villages of Uganda. There are 30 NRM leaders in each of those villages.'[56] However, the party practically disappeared between elections which meant the apparatus also shrivelled until needed again.

Paradoxically, after adopting multiparty competition, the government held no local government elections at any level until 2018. Then the secret ballot was replaced with open voting in local elections, which unsurprisingly resulted in the NRM 'winning over 90 per cent of village and parish leadership positions' – further consolidating its political clientelist apparatus.[57] Deploying yet another method for building patronage connections, Museveni appointed an unusually large number of ministers to include prominent regional figures who could connect him with their followers – 'these ... elites are the bridge that links the president to their local communities'.[58] These links multiplied as Museveni expanded the number of districts and accompanying hierarchies of councils and administrations reaching down to the villages.[59]

Funding political clientelism

During his presidency, Museveni accumulated legal and illegal assets for his discretionary use. The national budget includes votes for his official duties which have greatly expanded, often by manipulating the rules. Fraudulent schemes started soon after the take-over and burgeoned in the 1990s and 2000s. The same top government figures have been accused and even prosecuted for their participation, though never punished. Most of them were either Museveni's close relatives, his top officers during the civil war, or both. Co-operating with high political officials who demanded diversion of monies from their budgets meant that bureaucrats violated regulations and often insisted on payment. Museveni often violated existing rules by personally making decisions involving both foreign and domestic business interests. Few of his allies were ever convicted – only those who became opponents of the president. These activities are important for funding political clientelism.

Building political clientelism meant overcoming opposition. Members of the first parliament following the adoption of the 1995 constitution vociferously investigated and publicly denounced many instances of corrupt government behaviour. In response, the president sharply reduced, though without eliminating, the independence of succeeding parliaments by successfully campaigning against MPs who had opposed him and through constitutional amendments that weakened the legislative branch.[60]

Sub-patrons occasionally revealed illegal transactions organized by top officials. Defending himself against a parliamentary censure for his award of a lucrative contract without following established rules, Mayanja Nkangi, then Finance Minister, 'pleaded with MPs not "to kill him" as he had received "orders from above".[61] Elly Kayanja, then the director of the Internal Security Organization (ISO), warned that '"powerful" ministers ... routinely block the Director of Public Prosecutions from prosecuting suspects even after ISO and the Police complete investigations and hand over the files'.[62] Gilbert Bukenya, despite being the vice-president, complained in 2005 of '"an inner circle that is untouchable"' and had to retract his words a few days later.[63] When Jim Muhwezi, then the Minister of Health and formerly a rebel commander during the war, was questioned over misappropriation of foreign grants, 'he declared publicly that he acted on instructions from President Museveni on how to use the funds. A presidential aide ... confirmed this'.[64]

Support for political clientelism occurred partly through legal channels. Some sources of Museveni's funding started legitimately, though as his political domination deepened, he often manipulated the rules. At first, Parliament budgeted funds for the Office of the President (Museveni's official office). Later, it added State House (his private office) as a separate budget item. Expenditures for State House have far outstripped those for the Office of the President.[65] Together the two have grown more rapidly than any other department. 'Politically, this reflects the increasing "informalization" of power in the country, and the fusion of the office of the president with the person of the president'.[66] By 2000, a 'Poverty Alleviation Department was set up in State House to act "as a clearing house for pledges made by President Museveni"'.[67] Museveni often requested large supplementary expenditures. In 2020 the President asked for almost as much in supplementary funding halfway through the year as his original budget.[68]

Reports of NRM corruption began around 1987 and proliferated afterwards. Some of these scandals illustrate the sources of funds accumulated by regime leaders.[69] Perpetrators of these fraudulent schemes usually profited personally. In some cases, low-level bureaucrats had to be included to make a scam work, for example, diverting payments for ghost soldiers. Nevertheless, high-level officials close to the President became rich through these schemes. Museveni tolerated their profits to ensure his allies continued to serve his network. His central purpose was to fund his political operations – 'the two go together'.[70] Preserving these patently illegal arrangements while supporting the full panoply of constitutional and legal regulations is unstable. One consequence is the inflation in rewards demanded which in turn probably led to expansion of corrupt funding.

Military expenditure during the NRM's first two decades in power became an important source of funding for political clientelism. National leaders, who, after all, were soldiers who became rulers, easily diverted military spending without any accounting simply by hiding it through security classification. 'The military is the cash cow in the Ugandan state'.[71] The protection of officers who co-operate in its exercise and punishment of those who challenge its use are prominent features. 'Corruption in the military as well as prosecution of army officers is best understood within a political context, which is shaped by the imperatives of presidential and regime survival'.[72]

Museveni made his brother Caleb Akandwanaho (Salim Saleh) army commander in 1987. 'Corruption went through the roof under Saleh. It is surprising that I have never heard Museveni criticize Saleh for corruption', said Kizza Besigye, a former member of NRM who later became Museveni's main opponent. 'Soldiers were not getting food, salaries, and procurements were all chaotic'.[73] The public outcry forced Museveni to remove Saleh for his first of several dismissals.

In a spectacular incident in 1989, only three years after taking power, army commanders set fire to their headquarters to destroy evidence of 'ghost' soldiers – combatants no longer in the army but still drawing a salary pocketed by various military officers – and of their diversion of funds intended for procurement.[74] The problem worsened in 1990 when more than 4,000 soldiers left to form the Rwandan Patriotic Army but were kept on the Ugandan books for at least the next fifteen years. A Defence ministry committee estimated in 2003 that up to one-third the numbers in the Uganda Peoples Defence Force (UPDF) were missing.[75] Given his close attention to military matters, Museveni surely knew about the corruption over the entire period but did nothing until after the committee filed its report.[76] While several officers were put on forced leave, none were convicted. Museveni's tolerance suggests that he and his allies received income from this long-running scam, though, as in many corruption schemes, part of the funds was probably diverted by those directly involved.

More cases of military corruption appeared in the late 1990s involving overpayments for helicopters incapable of flight, purchases of outdated and overvalued jet fighters, inflated costs to repair a cargo plane, malfunctioning anti-aircraft guns, and obsolete, mostly faulty tanks.[77] In addition, the UPDF commanders were accused of looting gold, diamonds and timber in its invasions in the Democratic Republic of Congo (DRC) in 1996 and 1998.[78] Museveni must have informally known about these activities and probably received some of the profits which would then have been invested to solidify his political position.[79]

The projects involving grand corruption had common elements. All of them were arranged outside the procurement rules and probably involved Museveni directly or his brother Saleh. In the helicopter case, for example, a judicial commission of inquiry not only found that Saleh had received a bribe of $800,000 but received testimony from Museveni acknowledging it.[80] Instead of insisting this illegal money be returned, Museveni told the commission he had instructed Saleh to invest it in the war in the north. Saleh, on the other hand, claimed he used the money for poverty alleviation. The actual destination for these funds could not be traced.[81] At least part of this money as well as overpayments for other military procurements was likely made available for expenditures by Museveni to strengthen his grip on the presidency. Irregularities discovered by parliamentary committees in the defence budget, sometimes the highest in East Africa, indicate that military corruption continued in succeeding years.[82]

Privatization of Ugandan parastatals also generated several cases showing that high government officials, especially those with family ties to Museveni, interfered with government bidding regulations to gain ownership of valuable companies far below market value. They became available for political as well as private investment. Four egregious cases that followed the enactment of the Divestiture Statute in 1993 involved Saleh and Museveni's brother-in-law, Samuel Kutesa.

The most significant was the sale of 49 per cent of the Uganda Commercial Bank to Westmount, a Malaysian company, that lacked any banking experience and whose bid, offered after closure of tendering, amounted to less than one-sixth the value at which government had recapitalized the bank a few years earlier.[83] Even worse, Westmount turned out to be a shell manipulated by a company belonging to Saleh that bureaucratic banking regulators had previously disqualified for lacking financial expertise. Blatantly violating explicit rules, Westmount transferred all its shares to another bank under Salim Saleh's control. Eventually, however, the deal was undone.

The other three cases, involving the government's grain miller, the national airport's ground handling service and the sale of the capital's leading hotel, display equally flagrant violations of Ugandan rules.[84] All three demonstrate the personal capture of large government assets by Museveni's closest allies, none of whom was ever prosecuted despite censure by Parliament.[85] Irregularities in privatization continued for years after these cases in the 1990s, often involving Sam Kutesa.[86] Nine more cases in which corruption accounted for Uganda Shs 5 billion to 230 billion occurred between 2007 and 2012.[87] It is reasonable to infer that the purpose of these manipulations was to transfer control over at least part of these assets to Museveni for funding political clientelism. Rewarding his brother and brother-in-law should be considered a necessary outlay on the expenditure side of Museveni's political budget.

Museveni and top NRM officials' relations with foreign and local businesses exhibited similar conduct.[88] As domestic businesses grow, they must make payments to the regime.[89] Nevertheless, Museveni favoured foreign entrepreneurs over domestic capital in large part to protect his control over funding his centralized political clientelism.[90] Foreign companies paid large bribes to gain government contracts, usually through flagrant violations of bidding or procurement requirements. In the 1990s, Ministry of Finance officials overlooked repeated irregularities in the tender process in contracting with a Swiss firm as the government's procurement agent and with a British firm for pre-shipment inspection.[91] In 2007, Museveni directed the central bank to issue 'the Kenya-based Aga Khan Group an interest-free credit of $70 million – without parliamentary approval'.[92] In 2019, a US federal court sentenced

Patrick Ho for giving a $500,000 bribe each to Kutesa and Museveni in return for arranging 'business advantages' for his company in Uganda.[93]

Given the disproportionate funds intended for development pumped into Uganda from abroad, it is not surprising that 'donor funds became an essential part of the Museveni government's systems of patronage'.[94] Donor resources meant for government humanitarian projects were then embezzled. For example, when the Global Fund to Fight Aids, Tuberculosis and Malaria (GF) discovered its funds had been diverted, it suspended five grants worth $200 million in 2005.[95] Money was also diverted from grants made by the Global Alliance for Vaccine and Immunization (GAVI) at the same time.

Three ministers and a State House employee were suspended and prosecuted for both thefts. Two of the ministers, Jim Muhwezi and Mike Mukula, explained in court that they had sent part of the money to Janet Museveni, the president's wife.[96] The State House employee testified that 'immunization funds were used on Museveni's directive to mobilize political support in the 2004–5 referendum campaigns to return to multiparty politics'.[97] The three ministers were not convicted. Unusually, the State House employee pled guilty and paid a fine to avoid a prison sentence. She was appointed a minister several years later.

Future funding of political clientelism in Uganda will turn significantly on how the government uses its not yet exploited oil and gas wealth. According to one estimate, at a price of $75 per barrel, oil would 'nearly double government revenues'.[98] During the seventeen years since discovering that it would become a significant exporter, manoeuvres to prepare for capturing oil revenues for political clientelism have competed with the formation of a regulatory framework. Two tell-tale signs of the former are the lack of 'transparency and accountability' in the development of the oil sector and the 'overconcentration of powers given to the Minister', as well as the appointment and removal powers of top oil officials given to the president.[99] 'There is evident political interference in the management of Uganda's oil and gas sector. The President has arguably been adamant about maintaining firm control over the oil industry.'[100] One striking example was the 'presidential handshake' scandal in which Museveni arbitrarily rewarded forty-two officials involved in winning tax cases against two oil companies.[101]

Overall, funding clientelism has grown and become institutionalized. It makes routine use of classified and supplementary budgets passed by compliant NRM MPs, and deliberate misapplication of administrative procedures by top bureaucrats.[102] 'The overwhelming majority of NRM ministers, whose appointments primarily serve clientelist relationships at sub-regional levels, are politically weak.'[103] The regime presently benefits financially from gold smuggling, and bribes or electoral contributions from foreign and local businesses dependent on government contracts, grants of public land and tax waivers.[104] The capital accumulated for Museveni's political clientelism continues to enable sufficient expenditure to support this vigorous supplementary form of governance, despite his declining popularity.

Spending political clientelism

Museveni, like other national patrons, solicited political support by distributing resources both legally and illegally. He often deployed legal manoeuvres to cover illegitimate forms of distribution – for example, by creating microfinance programmes for poverty eradication officially and then using their funds to mobilize political supporters. As Andrew Mwenda put it, 'micro finance is actually political finance'.[105] Museveni managed political expenditures differently when targeting an elite as opposed to a mass constituency. Appointments or side-payments to prescribed political officials, legislators or bureaucrats are elite expenditures. Payments to voters in presidential elections or referenda intended to influence their choice are mass expenditures. The clientelist apparatus needed a sophisticated combination of delivery systems to accommodate these different types of disbursements.

The distribution of elite patronage to strengthen the NRM's political position began immediately though innocuously after the NRM take-over and then expanded as Museveni steadily gained influence. As president, many of his appointments were unquestionably legal, some constitutionally mandated. Several expenditures were legitimately expended through his discretionary powers. Others were not, though they were usually given legal cover through misapplication of executive authority or covering legislation. Over time, the number of both sorts of manipulations expanded.

To overcome widespread suspicion of his motives when the NRM took power, Museveni appointed leaders of opposition parties to important positions in his first cabinet a month after becoming president. This decision amounted to a clear departure from the doctrinaire stance the NRM had taken during the rebellion. While the government described it as 'broad-based' and intended it to widen its legitimacy, it amounted to patronage, 'a distribution of offices', that ignored the NRM's rebel doctrines.[106] These selections were Museveni's first patronage appointments. While they were unquestionably legal, his offer of office in return for support was an early indicator that he was willing to build a system of political clientelism.

Throughout his presidency, Museveni frequently used his legal authority to construct political clientelism.[107] In some years, his cabinets were the largest in Africa.[108] He rewarded MPs who helped him protect his network by giving them ministerial appointments or military promotions. For example, in 2009 Museveni elevated to ministerial rank five NRM MPs who broke with the majority in a parliamentary committee's investigation by writing a minority report exonerating three of his close allies from charges of corruption.[109] The majority report had identified the laws they had broken.

Museveni made his brother a minister in 2006 despite the findings of a UN investigation and a Ugandan commission of inquiry that he had stolen assets from the DRC.[110] In 2013, Museveni responded to Amama Mbabazi's presidential challenge by using low-level NRM cadres to nominate him as the sole presidential candidate for the 2016 elections, thus avoiding party elections.[111] Museveni replaced Mbabazi and his supporters in the cabinet and other important posts with these young cadres. More than $1.6 million was given to MPs to 'popularize the sole candidature motion' intended to prevent anyone challenging Museveni for the NRM's presidential nomination in 2016.[112]

Far from all of Museveni's patronage to MPs is legal. He 'relies primarily on financial inducements to win over troublesome MPs'.[113] He also used classified Defence accounts and State House funds to gain MP support.[114] The most significant examples of Museveni's spending for elite political clientelism were his successful manoeuvres rewarding MPs to remove constitutional provisions that would have forced him to leave the presidency. Amending the constitution requires a two-thirds majority. To remove term limits in 2005, he secretly paid 5 million shillings each to selected MPs, about 70 per cent of the members.[115] Later, he was reported to have paid 200 million shillings each (in total more than $17 million!) in three instalments in 2017 and 2019 to the 317 MPs whose votes he needed to remove the age limit in 2017.[116]

The supplementary budgets Parliament granted Museveni covered his promises made during his country tours.[117] In addition, Museveni often pays for 'medical treatment abroad for government officials and purchases of cars for religious and cultural leaders'.[118] The president has authority over a scholarship programme to benefit needy students that began in 1987. He was criticized for awarding these grants to 'children for [*sic*] ministers, NRM cadres, permanent secretaries'.[119] Nevertheless, this patronage was legal. So were Museveni's appointment of over 200 Resident District Commissioners (RDCs), their deputies and 163 Presidential Advisors.[120] Their number grew as he expanded his informal system of governance – as did their patronage cost to taxpayers for their salaries and cars.[121] 'During 2010, the president had approximately US$10.2 million available for ... donations through the State House budget. These funds are handed out at the president's discretion to individuals.'[122] Throughout his regime, Museveni has arbitrarily offered tax incentives and exemptions to close allies.[123]

Another form of political clientelism clothed with legal cover that Museveni exploited to an extraordinary degree was his agreement to re-establish kingdoms and expand local government units.[124] In a controversial reversal of what many thought was NRM rebel doctrine, he initiated the restoration of kingdoms in 1993 and persuaded the National Resistance Council (NRC), then the national legislature, to begin legalizing them as cultural institutions. One of his purposes was to gain support from Baganda, the most intense proponents of the return of kingdoms, in the Constituent Assembly elected the following year. Four of the five kingdoms that had been abolished in 1967 were recognized soon after. Several others followed, often with doubtful claims to a customary monarchy. Each new kingdom presented Museveni with another patronage opportunity for funding kings and their officials.

The remarkable expansion of districts as well as their counties, sub-counties and parishes enormously increased the number of local positions which he could integrate into his network. At its beginning, the NRM regime administered thirty-three districts, each with four subordinate political and administrative levels – the Local Council (LC) system. By 2022 there were 146 districts whose lower tiers also expanded with concomitant positions to fill.[125] 'The new districts thus create opportunities for local elites to access jobs and contracts in the local governments .... [for] winning support of the rural elites for the President and the ruling party.'[126] Officials throughout the hierarchy of district administrations and the kingdoms are paid almost entirely through conditional grants from the central government.[127] By 2010, local government jobs at the district level numbered two and a half times as many as in 1997. They augment the army of low-level sub-patrons expanding Museveni's political clientelism.

Co-ordinating this multitude of new officials required management of the clientelist hierarchy at the centre. The president added a three-person secretariat in State House to coordinate the RDCs and their deputies in each district who reported directly to him.[128] Through them, Museveni established channels of influence over local officials. The boundaries of these new districts, each legally initiated by Parliament, produced new supporters who had previously felt ignored. The creation of kingdoms and new districts invariably occurred just before presidential elections and resulted in increased votes for Museveni.[129]

Mass patronage spent on voters in national electoral campaigns started modestly and then grew remarkably, particularly after the NRM installed village mobilizers in 2009. NRM leaders in the early elections and Museveni alone in later ones directed a complex operation distributing resources, mainly money, to voters. With government resources at his disposal, Museveni outspent his opponents in every election. The campaign for the 1996 election, the first for president under the NRM regime, included 'monetary hand-outs' and *Entandikwa*, a new government poverty alleviation programme conveniently introduced in 1995 and 'administered through the NRM political establishment'.[130]

From that election forward, Museveni used presidential pledges and the LC network the NRM had established as conduits for material benefits to prospective voters. Before each election, start-up capital funds acquired through donor-funded poverty alleviation schemes were dispersed. '... the Parish Development Model (PDM), the much-touted supposedly bottom-up wealth creation [was] born out of the 2021 election. Like its ill-fated predecessors like *Entandikwa*, Operation Wealth Creation, and *Emyooga*, PDM is seen by doubters as just another patronage vehicle to reward NRM constituencies and buy the next election'.[131]

In later elections, the NRM expended more resources to influence voters and did so more openly. NRM expenditures on voters reached a new magnitude in the 2011 presidential election. 'The Museveni campaign's looting of the national budget made the 2011 balloting the most expensive single event in Uganda's post-independence history .... It emerged that $1.3 billion, or more than a third of the entire budget, had been spent in January alone.'[132] While the bulk of these expenditures had to be allocated through Museveni's network of sub-patrons, he personally distributed a surprisingly large proportion. 'Museveni himself was photographed on numerous occasions handing out cash at political rallies around the country. It is very difficult to make a precise estimate of the total amount handed out by the president or by the Office of the President, but the widely quoted figure of $300 million is not unrealistic given the magnitude of the practice.'[133]

The NRM continued to distribute mass patronage to voters through its hierarchy during the 2016 presidential elections. For example, '... a week before the election, each of the more than 60,000 village-level branches was given approximately $75 for mobilization'.[134] One journalist estimated that Museveni's campaign 'spent Shs27 billion ... in two months, 12 times more than his two closest challengers combined'.[135] The NRM apparently invested less in patronage and more in violent disruption of the opposition in the 2021 election campaign. Yet, for Andrew Mwenda, this campaign shows 'the NRM has degenerated into a cash and carry party. Without faith in its mission, it no longer seeks to persuade but to bribe and/ or coerce.'[136]

Protecting political clientelism

To keep his clientelist hierarchy intact, Museveni protected close allies involved in illegally generating and distributing clientelist resources from prosecution, and punished operatives who threatened it or defected. His methods were predictable. To prevent prosecution of high-level NRM operatives caught in corrupt schemes, agents in his informal hierarchy frequently offered bribes to prosecutors to delay or drop cases and threatened them if they refused.[137] Acquittals followed trials after important witnesses declined to appear or changed their testimony after being bribed or threatened. Evidence disappeared.

Museveni seemed closely involved. 'One prosecutor felt his superiors were "on speed dial with the president".[138] Wilful ignorance of corruption was another strategy. Museveni displayed studied obliviousness for more than a decade to his fellow army officers who pocketed salaries of 'ghost' soldiers, enriching themselves and probably helping to fund the clientelist apparatus. In addition, 'by not acting against those involved in the privatization scandals, Museveni was ... lending them his political protection'.[139]

While Museveni responded to public protest over various scandals by making a show of supposed miscreants going on trial, no one essential to raising funds for political clientelism was ever actually punished. Both Saleh and Kutesa, by far his most important fund-raising subordinates, were reprimanded for corruption by political bodies on several occasions and often resigned or were not reappointed, only to reappear at the centre of government. Their resignations were never intended to be permanent, rather a charade for temporary political expediency. Museveni upgraded Kutesa to become Minister of Foreign Affairs where he became implicated in several new corrupt schemes.[140] Saleh has since undertaken several strategic administrative missions.

To protect members of his clientelist hierarchy from prison, Museveni and his NRM allies undercut anti-corruption agencies introduced by the 1995 constitution. The Inspectorate of Government (IG) was formed to investigate, and later to prosecute, abuses in public offices. However, 'by the mid-2000s [it] had hardly investigated any high-ranking political, governmental or military "leaders" or brought any prominent individual to court'.[141] Museveni frequently brought political pressure to prevent indictments of high-ranking officials, and undermined prosecutions by publicly supporting defendants during cases the IG did bring.[142] Museveni often pardoned lower officials convicted of corruption.[143] Protection for funders of political clientelism appears to persist: 'The Inspector General of Government, Justice Irene Mulyagonja, recently observed that 'most corrupt government officials are "hiding behind" the back of President Museveni and use their connection to the Head of State to defeat or escape justice'.[144]

Safeguarding the clientelist hierarchy also requires removal of important members of government who threaten it. Enforcement to manage clientelist operations differs from using coercion and violence against elite and mass opponents. Museveni dismissed three of his closest long-time allies from his cabinet for publicly arguing against removal of term limits.[145] Ministers believed to have considered running against

Museveni found themselves in court.[146] The arrest and court martial of Brigadier Henry Tumukunde after he opposed amending the constitution to let Museveni run again is telling. Tumukunde had been 'one of the president's closest military henchmen, overseeing the use of large amounts of cash (derived from "ghost" soldier wages)'.[147] Given his value to Museveni's network, it is not surprising that after disciplining Tumukunde, Museveni rehabilitated him to work in the 2016 election and afterwards made him a minister.

Managing political clientelism caused Museveni to become more authoritarian

One of Museveni's reasons for strengthening his grip on the Ugandan government was to consolidate his political clientelist hierarchy. The demands of managing this system drove Museveni towards personal domination. It took him time to become its unchallenged head. 'The longer Museveni has ruled, the more authority has shifted to him individually. Today this authority is transmitted from him through a small circle of close family and kin.'[148] As he increased his personal rule, he decreased the resilience of the legal order. His most important unauthorized interventions in all three branches of government were his manoeuvres to build and maintain personal control of political clientelism.

He extended his rule by overcoming the two greatest threats to his personal management of political clientelism. Twice he arranged the amendment of the constitution to remove safeguards intended to prevent indefinite rule by one person. Otherwise, he would have been ineligible to run after he completed his second term in 2006 and after he reached the age of seventy-five in 2019. Without continuing as president, he could not have controlled his clientelist hierarchy.

The removal of term limits was part of an elaborate effort to remove various independent offices that blocked his unrestricted exercise of political clientelism. In 2005, the government attempted to amend or eliminate over 100 constitutional provisions, most seeking 'to reduce the powers of the bodies that check executive power, including the Courts, Parliament and institutions like the Human Rights Commission and the IGG [Inspector-General of Government]'.[149] Parliament still had sufficient autonomy that it used to reject some of these proposals. To ensure passage of the critical amendments, Museveni supplied thinly disguised inducements (supposedly for consulting constituents) but only to MPs expected to give support. The 2018 act to remove age limits was narrower, though he had to supply far larger enticements to selected MPs. Side-payments from public accounts are examples of authoritarianism in the service of political clientelism.

The no-party system was an important early building block that widened the president's authority to act on his own. It contributed to political clientelism by removing constraints on him. No-party rule initially led to constitutional, statutory and policy institutional constraints. But when reforms threatened Museveni's freedom to act, it gave him far greater political resources to fend off challenges and protect his sub-patrons. Ironically, he used his broadened autonomy from the absence of parties to turn the NRM into a partisan organization, one increasingly under his direct control.[150]

Political clientelism further increased Museveni's authoritarianism by weakening the resolve of bureaucrats to oppose his requests by following rules governing their offices. 'He has relied mainly on public positions and resource allocations to keep political leaders and state officials together as well as beholden to him. He has personally made all senior state appointments. He has also personally dispensed state resources, often without following rules and procedures.'[151] As one recent observer of Ugandan governance commented, 'raiding the public budget requires the collusion of bureaucrats, such as permanent secretaries and heads of revenue collecting agencies, statutory authorities and major parastatals – bureaucrats who can manipulate procedures and use public resources for partisan political mobilization'.[152]

To enhance his direct control over funding, Museveni arranged for constant growth in budgets and operations for State House and the President's Office. His relentless demands for finance also weakened the independence of MPs and further reduced the autonomy of bureaucrats. The intimate connection between political clientelism and the official regime required his constant intervention for resources and for his self-protection. Diversion of donor funds to political redistribution diminished the capacity of officials to carry out policy and resist future demands. His actions show that clientelism depends on bureaucracy while simultaneously weakening it.

Museveni's efforts to protect this system also contributed to his authoritarianism. Failing to punish the army officers who set the fire to destroy military records is a spectacular example of undermining the institutionalization of that bureaucracy. Ignoring violations of regulations on privatization and procurement contracts in return for side payments weakened administrative professionalism. Furthermore, engaging in illegal activities on behalf of clients exposed Museveni to potential prosecution. 'Sinning in public has left him extremely vulnerable. The push to remove age limits has exposed him more than the removal of term limits did.'[153] Despite appearing politically invulnerable, he needed more authoritarian practices for self-protection.

The logic of political clientelism led to his falling popularity and consequent insecurity. Its nature is exclusive – favours for supporters only. As Museveni acted more blatantly, especially in personally handing out rewards, he became more disliked by those who received nothing. Money spent on political clients cannot be spent on development projects, further increasing Ugandans' resentment. His popularity also declined in response to his policies to entrench his control over political clientelism. Opinion surveys showed that removing both term and age limits was widely unpopular.[154] Seventy-five per cent of Ugandans, including two-thirds of NRM supporters, did not want the age limit removed. And now want it restored.[155] Over half of the MPs who voted to remove age limits lost their seats in the 2021 election.[156]

Growing unpopularity led Museveni to rely increasingly on authoritarian measures to support his network. Fearing popular protest would become uncontrollable, he intensified repression to break up protests and opposition political rallies. There seems no way out. Museveni has no option but to continue supporting his system and protecting his sub-patrons to avoid jeopardizing himself. While dominant, he has become hostage to the system he created.

Conclusion

To effectively manage the system of centralized political clientelism he constructed, Museveni became an increasingly authoritarian ruler. He used this system to increase his personal control over the Ugandan government and only secondarily to increase the wealth of his allies and relatives. This system supplemented the legal order, in which he constantly intervened. Two NRM doctrines – the four-tiered structure of local councils and the no-party system – facilitated the initial introduction of this form of clientelism.

Museveni paid close attention to its management. He had to develop a political budget to ensure he had enough income to match the patronage expenditures that helped keep him in office. He raised some funds legitimately, others under thin legal cover and more through corrupt schemes carried out by sub-patrons, often members of his extended family.

His resources came from privatization, military and civilian government budgets and donor funds. He spent them on MPs when he needed to change laws, especially to continue as president, and on campaigns when he needed to win elections. He greatly expanded the financing of State House and the President's Office to expend patronage on his network of clients. He was careful to protect both himself and the sub-patrons who carried out corrupt schemes for him. He thwarted or intervened in court proceedings to prevent their prosecution. He crushed anyone who threatened to unmask or replace him.

Through persistent engagement, he developed a certain finesse in the practice of centralized political clientelism. He constantly held meetings with sub-patrons at all levels. To prevent challenges, he appointed 'people who do not have a pre-existing constituency' to high political positions.[157] Because his clientelism is based on years of personal cultivation of multiple informal and direct relationships, it cannot be transferred. Any successor, even his son Muhoozi Kainerugaba or his brother Salim Saleh, would have to build one anew. Many believe he never intends to relinquish rule – 'Museveni's death while in office is more likely'.[158]

Yet, centralized clientelism is not a stable form of governance. Museveni to an ever-greater degree is vulnerable to demands for larger rewards from clients who do his bidding. He must spend political capital defending them from criminal prosecution. He must cope with a vicious circle inherent in political clientelism. His popularity declines as he favours clients at the expense of others and starves social services of funds. He must constantly raise payoffs and add clients, which intensifies his dilemma.

To maintain his clientelist network, Museveni engaged in frequent authoritarian practices by ignoring rules, making side-payments and manipulating officials. The absence of competitive parties during his first two decades of rule removed checks and balances facilitating his development of clientelism. He personally controlled appointment to all high-ranking positions. Most decisively, he initiated amendments to the constitution essential to his continuation in office and intervened to ensure they passed. As he lost popularity, his dependence on centralized political clientelism became ever-more critical to remaining president.

To account for the role political clientelism plays in Museveni's authoritarianism, it is necessary to explore the mechanics of creating and managing this system. Since political leaders will always want to hide their uses of patronage and especially their resort to illegal funding and spending, the voluminous literature on political corruption is not of much help in explaining how it is managed. To the best of my knowledge, this is the first inquiry to try to unravel its 'black box'. I identify the logic of what must happen to make the system work and support it with Ugandan data. Future labourers in this vineyard will provide better evidence for the management techniques patrons use to supplement the legal order and secure their position by developing their own networks of political clientelism. They are likely to discover that rulers who choose to rely on political clientelism become more despotic.

Notes

1   I am grateful for Joe Oloka-Onyango's helpful suggestions.
2   The best of these accounts is Roger Tangri and Andrew M. Mwenda, *The Politics of Elite Corruption in Africa: Uganda in Comparative African Perspective* (London: Routledge, 2013). Excellent cases also connecting political corruption to Museveni's regime preservation include Moses Khisa, 'Inclusive Co-optation and Political Corruption in Museveni's Uganda', in *Political Corruption in African: Extraction and Power Preservation*, ed. Inge Amundsen (Cheltenham, UK: Edward Elgar, 2019), 95–115; Godfrey B. Asiimwe, 'Of Extensive and Elusive Corruption in Uganda: Neo-Patronage, Power, and Narrow Interests', *African Studies Review* 56, no. 2 (2013): 129–44. DOI:10.1017/asr.2013.45; and Joel D. Barkan, Saillie Kayunga, Njuguna Ng'ethe and Jack Titsworth, 'The Political Economy of Uganda: The Art of Managing a Donor-Financed Neo- Patrimonial State', Background Paper Commissioned by the World Bank (2005).
3   This concept of political clientelism expands Inge Amundsen's distinction between corruption for political power and for personal profit. Inge Amundsen, 'Extractive and Power-Preserving Political Corruption', in Amundsen, *Political Corruption*, 4. For the same reason, it excludes grand and petit corruption that concern only wealth.
4   James Q. Wilson, 'The Economy of Patronage', *Journal of Political Economy* 69, no. 4 (1961): 371.
5   Differences among national political and social contexts also cause variation in political clientelist systems.
6   Centralized political clientelism may support developmental goals, but more often it does not. See Tim Kelsall, 'Rethinking the Relationship between Neo-patrimonialism and Economic Development in Africa', *IDS Bulletin* 42, no. 2 (March 2011): 76–87.
7   Richard Joseph, *Democracy and Prebendal Politics in Nigeria: The Rise and Fall of the Second Republic* (Cambridge: Cambridge University Press, 1987), 55–68. Joseph also discusses clientelism but treats it only as a distributive mechanism.
8   For the most trenchant critique of neopatrimonialism, see Thandika Mkandawire, 'Neopatrimonialism and the Political Economy of Economic Performance in Africa: Critical Reflections', *World Politics* 67, no. 3 (July 2015): 563–612. Other extensive critiques that see some value in neopatrimonialism include Ole Therkildsen, 'Working in Neopatrimonial Settings: Public Sector Staff Perceptions in Tanzania and Uganda', in *States at Work: Dynamics of African Bureaucracies,* ed. Thomas Bierschenk and Jean-Pierre Olivier de Sardan (Leiden: Brill, 2014), 113–44; Gero Erdmann and Ulf Engel, 'Neopatrimonialism Reconsidered: Critical Review and

Elaboration of an Elusive Concept', *Commonwealth & Comparative Politics* 45, no. 1 (February 2007): 95–119.

9   Herbert Kitschelt and Steven I. Wilkerson carefully discuss several factors of supply and demand, though without considering how a funding apparatus is organized. Herbert Kitschelt and Steven I. Wilkerson, 'Citizen- Politician Linkages: An Introduction', in *Patrons, Clients, and Policies: Patterns of Democratic Accountability and Political Competition*, ed. Herbert Kitschelt and Steven I. Wilkerson (Cambridge: Cambridge University Press, 2007), 24–8.

10   Alex de Waal, *The Real Politics of the Horn of Africa*: *Money, War and the Business of Power* (Cambridge, UK: Polity Press, 2015), 3.

11   Jean-François Médard, 'Corruption in the Neo-Patrimonial States of Sub-Saharan Africa', in *Political Corruption: Concepts and Contexts*, ed. Arnold Heidenheimer and Michael Johnston (New Brunswick, NJ: Transaction Publishers, 2002), 383.

12   Allen Hicken, 'Clientelism', *Annual Review of Political Science* 14 (2011): 291.

13   See Susan C. Stokes, 'Political Clientelism', in *The Oxford Handbook of Comparative Politics*, ed. Carlos Boix and Susan C. Stokes (Oxford: Oxford University Press, 2009), 648–72.

14   Kitschelt and Wilkerson, 'Citizen-Politician Linkages', 8.

15   Hicken, 'Clientelism', 293.

16   de Waal., *Real Politics*, 213.

17   Erdmann and Engel, 'Neopatrimonialism Reconsidered', 105, 111; Therkildsen, 'Working in Neopatrimonial Settings', 124.

18   Daniel Bach, 'Patrimonialism and Neopatrimonialism: Comparative Receptions and Transcriptions', in *Neopatrimonialism in Africa and Beyond*, ed., Bach and Mamoudou Gazibo (London: Routledge, 2012), 29.

19   Erdmann and Engel, 'Neopatrimonialism Reconsidered', 108.

20   Daniel Compagnon, 'The Model of the Political Entrepreneur', in *Neopatrimonialism in Africa*, 54.

21   Ibid., 53.

22   Marlies Glasius, 'What Authoritarianism Is … and Is Not: A Practice Perspective', *International Affairs* 94, no. 3 (2018): 518–19.

23   Erica Frantz, *Authoritarianism: What Everyone Needs to Know* (New York: Oxford University Press, 2018), 6.

24   Lührmann and Lindberg suggest that 'it is preferable to conceptualize autocratization – the antipode of democratization'. Anna Lührmann and Staffan I. Lindberg, 'A Third Wave of Autocratization Is Here: What Is New about It?' *Democratization* 26, no. 7 (2019): 1098.

25   Glasius, 'What Authoritarianism Is', 519.

26   'To have a healthy situation, the people – working through their democratic institutions – must be the basic determinant in the economy, politics, culture, or even diplomacy.' And '… corruption must be eliminated once and for all'. Yoweri Museveni, 'The Ten-Point Programme', in Museveni, *Selected Articles on the Uganda Resistance War* (Kampala: NRM Publications, 1985), 52, 64.

27   'NRM is committed to the Rule of Law.' *Towards a Free and Democratic Uganda: The Basic Principles and Policies of the National Resistance Movement (NRM)* (Kampala: no pub., n.d. [early 1982]), 7.

28   Nelson Kasfir, 'Guerrillas and Civilian Participation: The National Resistance Army in Uganda, 1981–86', *Journal of Modern African Studies* 43, no. 2 (2005): 285–8.

29   George W. Kanyeihamba, *Kanyeihamba's Commentaries on Law, Politics and Governance* (Kampala: LawAfrica, 2006), 21.

30   Nelson Kasfir and Stephen Hippo Twebaze, 'The Rise and Ebb of Uganda's No-Party Parliament', in *Legislative Power in Emerging African Democracies*, ed. Joel D. Barkan (Boulder, CO: Lynne Rienner, 2009), 78–81.

31   For example, Patrick Chabal and Jean-Pascal Daloz, *Africa Works: Disorder as Political Instrument* (Oxford: James Currey, 1999), 99–101.

32   Janet I. Lewis, *How Insurgency Begins: Rebel Group Formation in Uganda and Beyond* (New York: Cambridge University Press, 2020), 71, 189.

33   'Uganda: The Human Rights Record, 1986–1989', *Amnesty International* (London, 1989), 18.

34   A. B. K. Kasozi, *The Social Origins of Violence in Uganda, 1964–1985* (Kampala: Fountain Publishers, 1994), 200–1.

35   Nelson Kasfir, 'State, *Magendo*, and Class Formation in Uganda', in *State and Class in Africa*, ed. Nelson Kasfir (London: Frank Cass, 1984), 98–9.

36   Yoweri K. Museveni, 'Corruption Is a Cancer', in Yoweri Museveni, *What Is Africa's Problem?* (Kampala: NRM Publications, 1992), 92.

37   'Net Official Development Assistance (ODA) Received (constant 2018 US$)', https:// data.worldbank.org/indicator/DT.ODA.ODAT.XP.ZS?end=2019&locations=UG &start=1971 (accessed 8 May 2022). See also, Tangri and Mwenda, *Politics of Elite Corruption*, 40.

38   'Net ODA received (% of GNI)', https://www.indexmundi.com/facts/indicators/ DT.ODA.ODAT.GN.ZS/compare?country=ug (accessed 8 May 2022).

39   'Net ODA Received (% of central government expenses) – Uganda', Data, The World Bank. https://data.worldbank.org/indicator/DT.ODA.ODAT.XP.ZS?end=2019&locati ons=UG&start=1971 (accessed 8 May 2022).

40   Kristof Titeca and Anna Reuss, 'Museveni and the West: Relationship Status: It's Complicated', *African Arguments* (7 January 2021). https://africanarguments. org/2021/01/museveni-and-the-west-relationship-status-its-complicated/ (accessed 8 January 2021); Jonathan Fisher, 'The Limits – and Limiters – of External Influence: Donors, the Ugandan Electoral Commission and the 2011 Elections', *Journal of Eastern African Studies* 7, no. 3 (2013): 481–4.

41   Tangri and Mwenda, *Politics of Elite Corruption*, 132–6.

42   Barkan et al., 'Political Economy of Uganda, 12–13.

43   Sam Hickey, Badru Bukenya and Haggai Matsiko, 'Pockets of Effectiveness, Political Settlements and Technopols in Uganda: From State-building to Regime Survival?' *Effective States and Inclusive Development*, ESID Working Paper No. 172 (2021), 5.

44   Asiimwe, 'Extensive and Elusive Corruption', 131; Lisa Rolls (pseud.), 'The Shadow State in Uganda', in *The Shadow State in Africa*, Democracy in Africa (7 September 2021), 89, http://democracyinafrica.org/wp-content/uploads/2021/09/The-Shadow-State-in-Africa-Report_FOR-INSTANT-UPLOAD_COMPRESSED_THIS-ONE.pdf (accessed 19 September 2021).

45   Stefan Lindemann, 'Just Another Change of Guard? Broad-Based Politics and Civil War in Museveni's Uganda', *African Affairs* 110, no. 440 (2011): 396.

46   Anna Reuss and Kristof Titeca, 'When Revolutionaries Grow Old: The Museveni Babies and the Slow Death of the Liberation', *Third World Quarterly* 38, no. 10 (2017): 2355–6.

47   Giovanni Carbone, *No-Party Democracy? Ugandan Politics in Comparative Perspective* (Boulder, CO: Lynne Rienner), 85; Luke Patey, 'Oil in Uganda: Hard

Bargaining and Complex Politics in East Africa', WPM 60, Oxford Institute for Energy Studies (2015), 24.

48 Frederick Golooba-Mutebi and Sam Hickey, 'The Master of Institutional Duplicity? The Shifting Politics of Regime Survival, State-Building and Democratization in Museveni's Uganda', *Journal of Eastern African Studies* 10, no. 4 (2016): 606–7, 611–13.

49 For example, Amundsen, 'Extractive and Power-Preserving', 21; J. P. Olivier de Sardan, 'A Moral Economy of Corruption in Africa?' *The Journal of Modern African Studies* 37, no. 1 (1999): 28–9.

50 Aili Mari Tripp, *Museveni's Uganda: Paradoxes of Power in a Hybrid Regime* (Boulder, CO: Lynne Rienner, 2010), 117, see 117–20.

51 Svein-Erik Helle and Lise Rakner, 'The Impact of Elections: The Case of Uganda', in *Crisis in Autocratic Regimes*, ed. Johannes Gerchewski and Christoph H. Stefes (Boulder, CO: Lynne Rienner, 2018), 126.

52 Ibid., 117.

53 'Nation Decides on Political Parties', *The New Humanitarian* (27 July 2005). https://www.thenewhumanitarian.org/report/55602/uganda-nation-decides-political-parties (accessed 11 January 2021).

54 Helle and Rakner, 'Impact of Elections', 122.

55 'Speech to the NRM National Delegates Conference 2014'. Speeches, State House, 15 December 2014. https://statehouse.go.ug/media/speeches/2014/12/15/speech-nrm-national-delegates-conference-2014 (accessed 17 March 2021).

56 Ibid.

57 Bono O. Edward, 'Local Council Elections in Uganda Had Votes Cast but No Democracy' (21 October 2019). https://blogs.lse.ac.uk/africaatlse/2019/10/21/local-council-elections-uganda-votes-democracy-nrm/ (accessed 9 July 2022).

58 Andrew M. Mwenda, 'Uganda Has 3rd Largest Cabinet in the World', *The Independent* (19 January 2011). https://www.independent.co.ug/uganda-3rd-largest-cabinet-world/ (accessed 8 June 2022).

59 Elliott Green, 'Patronage, District Creation, and Reform in Uganda', *Studies in Comparative International Development* 45 (2010): 92–3. DOI 10.1007/s12116-009-9058-8.

60 Michaela Collord, 'From the Electoral Battleground to the Parliamentary Arena: Understanding Intra-Elite Bargaining in Uganda's National Resistance Movement', *Journal of Eastern African Studies* 10, no. 4 (2016): 654–5; Kasfir and Twebaze, 'The Rise and Ebb', 74–5, 105–7.

61 Tangri and Mwenda, *Politics of Elite Corruption*, 93.

62 Ogen Kevin Aliro, 'Corruption: Colonel Kayanja in Danger', *Weekly Observer*, Kampala (8 July 2004). https://www.mail-archive.com/ugandanet@kym.net/msg14765.html (accessed 16 May 2022). Kayanja is also quoted as saying: 'They want to shoot me dead because I am investigating corruption'.

63 Tangri and Mwenda, *Politics of Elite Corruption*, 170; Isaac Mufumba, 'The Fall and Fall of Prof. Gilbert Bukenya', *Monitor*, Kampala (13 September 2020). https://www.monitor.co.ug/uganda/magazines/people-power/the-fall-and-fall-of-prof-gilbert-bukenya-1829858 (accessed 17 May 2022).

64 Tangri and Mwenda, *Politics of Elite Corruption*, 117.

65 Isaac Mufumba, 'Money, Power Tied to Our Presidency', *Monitor* (16 September 2020). https://www.monitor.co.ug/uganda/news/national/money-power-tied-to-our-presidency-1838364 (accessed 21 May 2022).

66 Andrew Mwenda, 'Redefining Uganda's Budget Priorities: A Critique of the 2006/07 Budget', ACODE Policy Briefing Paper, No. 17, 2006, 26. https://www.acode-u.org/uploadedFiles/PBP17.pdf (accessed 14 May 2022).

67 Mufumba, 'Money, Power Tied'.

68 *Business Focus*, 'Worry as State House Spends Shs. 951bn in 4 Months' (20 October 2020). https://businessfocus.co.ug/worry-as-state-house-spends-shs951bn-in-4-months/ (accessed 20 May 2022). Originally, the Budget Act, 2001 limited supplementary expenditures to 3 per cent of the original vote.

69 An excellent early review of corrupt schemes some of which funded Museveni's political clientelist network can be found in Barkan et al., 'Political Economy of Uganda', 47–59.

70 Khisa, 'Inclusive Co-optation', 97.

71 Tangri and Mwenda, *Politics of Elite Corruption*, 109.

72 Ibid., 69.

73 Daniel K. Kalinaki, *Kizza Besigye: And Uganda's Unfinished Revolution* (Kampala: DominantSeven Publishers, 2014), 106.

74 Tangri and Mwenda, *Politics of Elite Corruption*, 85.

75 *The Independent*, 'UPDF Commanders Confess to Existence of Ghost Soldiers', [Report of the Commission of Inquiry], Kampala (20 October 2009), 40–2. Significantly, the three members of the committee were, at the time, close allies of Museveni.

76 Tangri and Mwenda, *Politics of Elite Corruption*, 87, also 86.

77 Ibid., 69–73.

78 *Final Report of the Judicial Commission of Inquiry into Allegations into Illegal Exploitation of Natural Resources and Other Forms of Wealth in the Democratic Republic of Congo 2001* (May 2001–November 2002) [the Porter Report], Kampala (2002).

79 Koen Vlassenroot, Sandrine Perrot and Jeroen Cuvelier, 'Doing Business out of War: An Analysis of the UPDF's Presence in the Democratic Republic of Congo', *Journal of Eastern African Studies* 6, no. 1 (2012): 12.

80 Andrew M. Mwenda, 'Sebutinde Pins Katto, Saleh over Choppers', *The Monitor*, Kampala (12 December 2002).

81 Emmy Allio, 'Chopper Panel Cleared Mbonye but Not Saleh', *New Vision*, Kampala (13 December 2002). https://www.newvision.co.ug/news/1043097/chopper-panel-cleared-mbonye-saleh (accessed 22 October 2021).

82 Gerald Bareebe, 'Predators or Protectors? Military Corruption as a Pillar of Regime Survival in Uganda', *Civil Wars* 22, no. 2–3 (2020): 325.

83 Tangri and Mwenda, *Politics of Elite Corruption*, 58–9.

84 Ibid., 56–60.

85 Ibid., 61–2.

86 Ibid., 64–6.

87 *New Vision*, 'Nine Corruption Scandals to Look back at', Kampala (11 November 2012). https://www.newvision.co.ug/news/1309873/corruption-scandals-look (accessed 21 July 2022).

88 See Tangri and Mwenda's chapter in this volume.

89 Rolls, 'Shadow State', 81.

90 Roger Tangri and Andrew M. Mwenda, 'Change and Continuity in the Politics of Government-Business Relations in Museveni's Uganda', *Journal of Eastern African Studies*, 13, no. 4 (2019): 681.

91 Tangri and Mwenda, *Politics of Elite Corruption*, 92–7.
92 Tangri and Mwenda, 'Change and Continuity', 685.
93 'Patrick Ho, Former Head of Organization Backed by Chinese Energy Conglomerate, Sentenced to 3 Years in Prison for International Bribery and Money Laundering Offenses', Press Release, United States Attorney's Office, Southern District of New York, Department of Justice (25 March 2019). https://www.justice.gov/usao-sdny/pr/patrick-ho-former-head-organization-backed-chinese-energy-conglomerate-sentenced-3 (accessed 28 November 2020).
94 Titeca and Reuss, 'Museveni and the West'.
95 'Uganda: Misuse of Funds Revealed as Global Fund Inquiry Quizzes Ministers', *The New Humanitarian*, News Release (24 March 2006). https://reliefweb.int/organization/tnh (accessed 18 May 2022); Tangri and Mwenda, *Politics of Elite Corruption*, 115–16.
96 Siraje Lubwama, 'Gavi: Muhwezi Hits Back at Judge', *The Observer*, Kampala (14 March 2013). https://observer.ug/component/content/article?id=23224:mukula-guilty-of-embezzling-gavi-funds (accessed 11 June 2022); 'Mukula Claims Giving Gavi Fund Money to Janet Museveni', *Daily Monitor*, Kampala (13 November 2012). https://www.monitor.co.ug/uganda/news/national/mukula-claims-giving-gavi-fund-money-to-janet-museveni-1530120 (accessed 19 May 2022).
97 Tangri and Mwenda, *Politics of Elite Corruption*, 117.
98 Patey, 'Oil in Uganda', 12.
99 Kathleen Brophy and Peter Wandera, 'Keeping Corruption in Check in Uganda's Oil Sector? Uganda's Challenge to Let Everybody Eat, and Not Just the Lucky Few', in *Oil Wealth & Development in Uganda and Beyond: Prospects, Opportunities and Challenges*, ed. Arnim Langer, Ukoha Ukiwo and Pamela Mbabazi (Leuven: Leuven University Press, 2020), 78, 94.
100 Pamela Mbabazi and Martin Muhangi, 'Uganda's Oil Governance Institutions: Fit for Purpose?' in Langer et al., *Oil Wealth*, 42.
101 Brophy and Wandera, 'Keeping Corruption', 78.
102 Rolls, 'Shadow State', 80–1.
103 Ibid., 86.
104 Ibid., 81–5.
105 Mwenda, 'Redefining Uganda's Budget', 17.
106 Mahmood Mamdani, 'Uganda in Transition: Two Years of the NRA/NRM', *Third World Quarterly* 10, no. 3 (1988): 1168–9.
107 In Khisa's apt phrase, 'rule by law'. Khisa, 'Inclusive Co-optation', 105.
108 Mwenda, 'Uganda Has 3rd Largest Cabinet'.
109 Asiimwe, 'Extensive and Elusive Corruption', 134.
110 Ibid., 135.
111 Helle and Rakner, 'Impact', 123.
112 Reuss and Titeca, 'When Revolutionaries', 2358.
113 Michaela Collord, 'From the Electoral Battleground to the Parliamentary Arena: Understanding Intra-Elite Bargaining in Uganda's National Resistance Movement', *Journal of Eastern African Studies* 10, no. 4 (2016): 652.
114 Ibid., 653.
115 Khisa, 'Inclusive Co-optation', 105–6.
116 Sadab Kitatta Kaaya, 'NRM MPs Get Age Limit Cash', *The Observer*, Kampala (16 January 2019). https://observer.ug/news/headlines/59668-nrm-mps-get-age-limit-cash (accessed 14 July 2022). An opposition MP claimed even more was spent.

Ssemujju Ibrahim Nganda, 'Paying the Price for the Life Presidency', *The Observer*, Kampala (20 December 2017). https://observer.ug/viewpoint/56434-paying-the-price-for-the-life-presidency.html (accessed 17 June 2022).

117 Moses Khisa, 'Political Uncertainty and Its Impact on Social Service Delivery in Uganda', *Africa Development*, 11, no. 4 (2015): 182–3.

118 Mufumba, 'Money, Power Tied'.

119 Mercy Nalugo, 'State House Sponsorship Scheme "Not Changing"', *Daily Monitor*, Kampala (6 May 2013).

120 Mufumba, 'Money, Power Tied'.

121 Mufumba estimates the combined annual cost for RDCs' wages, allowances and vehicles in 2020 to be at least UShs. 15.8 billion. Ibid.

122 Svein-Erik Helle and Lise Rakner, 'Grabbing an Election: Abuse of State Resources in the 2011 Elections in Uganda', in *Corruption, Grabbing, and Development: Real World Challenges*, ed. Tina Søreide and Aled Williams (Cheltenham, UK: Edward Elgar, 2014), 164.

123 In fiscal year 2017–18, these waivers and exemptions were estimated to reduce tax receipts by almost $400 million. Rolls, 'Shadow State', 89.

124 Elliott Green, 'Patronage as Institutional Choice: Evidence from Rwanda and Uganda', *Comparative Politics* 43, no. 4 (2011): 431–2. In theory, the kingdoms are cultural units whose principals and administrators are not permitted to engage in politics. The important point here is that the government pays for most new jobs in kingdoms and districts as well as their subunits.

125 'Summary of Administrative Units', Electoral Commission (June, 2022). https://www.ec.or.ug/electoralcommission-statistics (accessed 24 April 2023). The literature on this topic has significantly understated the expansion of patronage involved by ignoring the increase in administrative units *below* the district level, as indicated by comparing 'Summary of Administrative Units in Uganda', Ministry of Local Government, Kampala for different years. I thank my colleague Hippo Twebaze for collecting this data.

126 Mwenda, 'Redefining Uganda's Budget, 19; Asiimwe, 'Extensive and Elusive Corruption', 137.

127 Nicholas Awortwi and A. H. J. (Bert) Helmsing, 'In the Name of Bringing Services Closer to the People? Explaining the Creation of New Local Government Districts in Uganda', *International Review of Administrative Sciences* 80, no. 4 (2014): 777, 776. https://journals-sagepub-com.dartmouth.idm.oclc.org/doi/full/10.1177/0020852314533455 (accessed 12 July 2022).

128 Mufumba, 'Money and Power'. Green's argument in 'Patronage as Institutional Choice' that Rwanda centralized patronage while Uganda decentralized it by creating new districts fails to consider that Museveni also centralized patronage through the RDCs who reported directly to him as well as his informal disbursements to central government bureaucrats and legislators.

129 Awortwi and Helmsing, 'In the Name', 778. By 2010, the Northern and Eastern regions where Museveni had done poorly in previous elections received far more districts relative to the Western and Central regions than in previous rounds of district creation. Ibid., 780. Museveni won in both regions in the 2011 elections and in the two that followed.

130 William Muhumuza, 'Money and Power in Uganda's 1996 Elections', *African Journal of Political Science* 2, no. 1 (1997): 173–4.

131 Charles Onyango-Obbo, 'Museveni 2026 – and 2031? The Hand of an Evil Genius', *Daily Monitor*, Kampala (22 June 2022). https://www.monitor.co.ug/uganda/oped/columnists/charles-onyango-obbo/museveni-2026-and-2031-the-hand-of-an-evil-genius-3855768 (accessed 23 June 2022).

132 Angelo Izama and Michael Wilkerson, 'Uganda: Museveni's Triumph and Weakness', *Journal of Democracy* 22, no. 3 (2011): 68.

133 Joel D. Barkan, 'Uganda: Assessing Risks to Stability', *Report of the CSIS Africa Program*, Washington, D.C.: Centre for Strategic and International Studies (2011), 11.

134 Helle and Rakner, 'Impact', 130.

135 Stephen Kafeero, 'Museveni Spends Shs27b on Campaigns in 2 Months', *Daily Monitor*, Kampala (21 January 2016). http://www.monitor.co.ug/specialreports/elections/museveni-spends-shs27b-on-campaigns-in-2-months/-/859108/3043578/-/ecxk7o/-/index.html (accessed 22 January 2016).

136 'Museveni, Security Clueless on Handling Bobi Wine', *PML*, Kampala (5 December 2020). https://www.pmldaily.com/oped/2020/12/andrew-mwenda-museveni-security-clueless-on-handling-bobi-wine.html (accessed 7 December 2020).

137 '"Letting the Big Fish Swim": Failures to Prosecute High-Level Corruption in Uganda', *Human Rights Watch* (2013): 38–41. https://www.hrw.org/report/2013/10/21/letting-big-fish-swim/failures-prosecute-high-level-corruption-uganda (accessed 20 June 2014).

138 Ibid., 40.

139 Tangri and Mwenda, *Politics of Elite Corruption*, 62.

140 Asiimwe, 'Extensive and Elusive Corruption', 137.

141 Ibid., 132 and see 133–6.

142 Three such cases are reported in *Human Rights Watch*, 'Letting the Big Fish', 16–17.

143 See the cases described in Miria R.K. Matembe, *The Struggle for Freedom and Democracy Betrayed* (privately published: Kampala, 2019), 201–4.

144 'Thieves Hide behind Museveni's Back – IGG', *Daily Monitor*, Kampala (7 June 2018, updated 12 January 2021). https://www.monitor.co.ug/uganda/news/national/thieves-hide-behind-museveni-s-back-igg–1760774 (accessed 18 July 2022).

145 Reuss and Titeca, 'When Revolutionaries Grow', 2352.

146 *Human Rights Watch*, 'Letting the Big Fish', 40.

147 Tangri and Mwenda, *Politics of Elite Corruption*, 88.

148 Mwenda, 'Museveni, Security Clueless'.

149 Oloka Onyango, 'Constitution Bill Is Disaster in Substance', *New Vision*, Kampala (10 March 2005). https://www.newvision.co.ug/new_vision/news/1129431/constitution-disaster-substance (accessed 22 September 2021).

150 Carbone, *No-Party Democracy*, 89–94.

151 Tangri and Mwenda, *Politics of Elite Corruption*, 164.

152 Rolls, 'Shadow State', 80.

153 Ssemujju, 'Paying the Price'.

154 Bernard Tabaire, 'Poll Says 66% Want Museveni to Retire', *Daily Monitor*, Kampala (19 August 2004); *Afrobarometer*, 'Ugandans Overwhelmingly Favour Age Limit for President, Afrobarometer Survey Shows', Kampala (23 September 2017), 1, 3. https://www.afrobarometer.org/wp-content/uploads/2022/02/uga_r7_pr1_presidential_age_limit_23092017.pdf (accessed 15 October 2018).

155 Afrobarometer, 'Most Ugandans Favour Presidential Age Limits, Afro Barometer Survey Shows', Kampala (3 March 2021), 1–3. https://www.afrobarometer.org/wp-

content/uploads/2022/02/news_release-ugandans_favour_age_limits_for_president-afrobarometer-3mar21.pdf (accessed 22 August 2022).

156 Monitor Team, 'Half of MPs Who Backed Age Limit Bill Lose Seats', *Daily Monitor*, Kampala (25 January 2021). www.monitor.co.ug/uganda/news/national/half-of-mps-who-backed-age-limit-bill-lose-seats-3268652 (accessed 19 April 2021).

157 Reuss and Titeca, 'When Revolutionaries Grow', 2357.

158 Maria E. Burnett and Michael Mutyaba, 'Stability, Security, and Uganda's Ever-Elusive Leadership Transition', Centre for Strategic & International Studies (12 August 2022). https://www.csis.org/analysis/stability-security-and-ugandas-ever-elusive-leadership-transition?utm_source=substack&utm_medium=email (accessed 19 August 2022).

2

Heritage, memory and the personalization of NRM rule[1]

Jonathan Fisher and Stephanie Cawood

The collection of chapters in this book charts how the Ugandan government of Yoweri Museveni and the National Resistance Movement (NRM) has evolved, over time, into a highly personalized and autocratic regime. Now well into his fourth decade in office, Museveni is one of the longest-serving heads of state in the world and has overseen the construction of a political settlement whereby success in politics (and often, by association, in the private sector) is tied to personal loyalty to him and to entering the NRM's 'big tent'. This personalization of power has become so acute that Museveni's son and until recently Commander of the Ugandan army's land forces, Muhoozi Kainerugaba, has, since March 2022, taken to Twitter to openly muse about succeeding his father, declaring in March 2023 that 'I will stand for the Presidency in 2026!'[2]

This was not, however, the originally stated NRM plan. The movement – formed in 1981 under Museveni's leadership – committed itself to a political programme which placed the 'restoration of democracy' at its heart.[3] Though it won power through military might, its struggle was premised not simply on seizing the reins of government but on removing a dictator – Milton Obote[4] – and replacing him and his regime with a progressive, inclusive and democratic successor. Famously, Museveni declared on coming to power that the NRM's ascendancy would herald a 'fundamental change to the politics of our country',[5] arguing that 'the problem of … Uganda in particular, is not the people but leaders who want to overstay in power'.[6] Seven years later, almost to the day, the Ugandan president warned those celebrating the NRM's longevity about the rise of 'professional politicians', noting that 'we should not have [them], people should pursue their own professions and then [enter politics] to help the people'.[7]

Much important work has been published – including within this book itself – on the factors and circumstances that have led to Museveni and the NRM ultimately constructing a personalist autocracy rather than an inclusive democracy. This chapter's concern is less focused on explaining this trajectory, however, and more on exploring how it has been justified and articulated in the context of memorializing the liberation struggle which brought the NRM, and Museveni, to power. For while Uganda's autocratic turn under Museveni has been opposed, to varying degrees, by opposition figures, disaffected citizens and (on occasion) Western development 'partners', the greatest moments of peril for the Ugandan leadership have often come from within the NRM elite itself, with struggle-era cadres openly mobilizing against Museveni in the name of reasserting liberation struggle principles.

This chapter therefore explores how the Ugandan liberation struggle – sometimes referred to as the 'Bush War' – has been memorialized since its conclusion in January 1986. What, we ask, can developments in this space tell us about the evolution of thinking within the NRM itself around the political direction of travel under Museveni? To what extent has the progression of struggle memorialization reflected – or sought to neutralize – contemporary elite political debates around personalization of power and 'betrayal' of the struggle agenda, and with what implications?

In taking this approach, we follow a range of scholars who view the liberation struggle as a critical, but ambiguous, political resource in contemporary Uganda. Driving out a violent and abusive dictatorship gave the NRM, and Museveni, almost unparalleled legitimacy on coming to power – not least given the punishing and prolonged character of the military campaign and the near absence of international support provided to the movement. Museveni himself has often referred to his role, and that of the NRM, in the struggle as the moral and political foundation of his right to rule, though other senior NRM struggle veterans – some of whom have since come to found or join opposition parties – have also taken on the same mantle to condemn what they have perceived as corruption and authoritarian creep under his presidency.

Though the struggle itself is increasingly becoming a distant memory for even those Ugandans who lived through it – the average Ugandan was born in 2006 – struggle memorialization and political pageantry have become more, not less, pronounced in recent years. We believe, then, that examining how the struggle has been presented and memorialized by the NRM political establishment reveals an important, and evolving, commentary on the regime's perceived authority, and a 'real time' edification of current thinking on how present-day political developments are justified through the lens of the past.

We do not suggest, in this regard, that state and NRM approaches to struggle memorialization have followed a strategic 'masterplan' since 1986. Nor do we propose that those who have overseen this work have (necessarily) done so with an explicit *intention* to promote or contradict a particular narrative. As the chapter details, these approaches have evolved over time and have involved multiple institutions and actors – although the military leadership and Office of the President have generally been pre-eminent. Instead, we argue that the memorialization sites, debates and processes analysed reflect how ruling elites have, over time, come to justify and represent the Ugandan government's authoritarian trajectory.

In developing this argument, the chapter is organized into four parts. Section 2, immediately below, places the analysis within the wider context of scholarship on 'post-liberation' governance in Africa, and the centrality of struggle discourse and memorialization to elite justifications of establishing personalized, autocratic (or, in the cases of South Africa and Namibia, hegemonic single party-based) systems of government. Section 3 outlines the data on which this study draws – principally elite interviews and archival research undertaken in Uganda during four periods of fieldwork between January 2018 and October 2019. Section 4 provides an overview of struggle memorialization under the NRM, explaining how an initially localized approach has increasingly come under the direction of the military and presidency, and how an early focus on local burial sites has evolved into a series of much grander projects centred on the military and Museveni himself.

Section 5 presents the main analysis of the chapter, highlighting two key ways in which struggle memorialization has developed to reflect emerging elite rationalization of Uganda's autocratic turn – focusing-in on a number of key memorialization sites, occasions and processes. The first of these two themes is the growing 'Movementization' of struggle memorialization. Initially, the NRM sought to incorporate recognition of a wide range of actors and organizations into struggle memorialization, including those not directly associated with the NRM's insurgency. Over time, however, these perspectives have been crowded out in favour of a narrative which presents the NRM as the sole deliverer of Uganda's liberation from tyranny. The second trend we analyse is the growing placement of Museveni at the heart of struggle memorialization spaces, projects and ceremonies and a move from celebrating the NRM – or Movement – as a liberating force to hailing Museveni alone as the country's saviour and sole author of the struggle's success.

The liberation struggle and post-liberation politics in Uganda

Before we outline the scope of this study, and the data upon which our analysis draws, it is first necessary to explain our rationale for focusing on the liberation struggle – and its memorialization – as a lens into elite justifications for Uganda's authoritarian trajectory under the NRM. This requires us to place the Museveni polity in the broader context of African 'post-liberation regimes' and scholarly debates on the longevity and resilience of these political settlements.

The NRM – sometimes referred to in the pre-1986 era by the name of its military wing, the National Resistance Army (NRA)[8] – became, in 1986, the first movement in East Africa to gain power through insurgency, as opposed to military coup or civilian oppositional politics. Perhaps even more significantly, though, it was also one of the first such movements on the continent to seize power in this manner from a black, African, postcolonial government and to do so as a self-styled national liberation movement. Indeed, it is this combination of characteristics – a liberation movement which gained power through violent struggle against a dictatorial African predecessor – which has arguably imprinted itself most profoundly on the political identity of Museveni and many struggle veterans, sometimes called 'Historicals'.

Seven of the fourteen chapters in Museveni's 1997 autobiography are entitled either 'Fighting Amin' or 'Fighting Obote' while the founding document of the NRM – the Ten Point Programme – outlines an explicitly political programme of national independence and liberation.[9] Many of the most damaging internal NRM debates during the 1980s, 1990s and 2000s focused, as mentioned above, not only on questions of governance and creeping authoritarianism but also on whether these developments constituted a betrayal of the NRM's founding political and ideological covenant, with its members and with the Ugandan people.[10]

This political context, together with the movement's 'organizational personality', has led a range of scholars to classify the NRM government as a 'post-liberation regime' – a government which emerged out of an insurgency that fought not only, in the words of Sara Dorman, 'just to seize power, but also to re-shape the state'.[11] For Dorman and others, this places the contemporary Ugandan polity in the same category as a range of others in the region – notably Eritrea since 1991, Rwanda since 1994, and Ethiopia between 1991 and 2019.[12] Other African states in this group, it has been suggested, would be Mozambique and Angola since 1975, Zimbabwe since 1980, Namibia since 1990 and South Africa since 1994. As we and others have noted elsewhere, though, the fact that the East African movements came to power through military means alone (rather than, ultimately, via negotiation) gives them a somewhat distinctive character and, indeed, has rendered the struggle even more central to their governing narratives.

Indeed, the struggle, it is suggested, has not only been critical in providing a founding justification for post-liberation rule, it has more broadly undergirded how many post-liberation elites understand their government's legitimacy and purpose writ-large.[13] The sacrifice and trauma that the struggle entailed have led these ruling elites to feel 'entitled' to power, and hostile to forces, including opposition parties, who seek to end their hegemony. This has been the case not only in increasingly authoritarian post-liberation states like Uganda but also in democratic polities such as Namibia and South Africa. In the latter case, then President Jacob Zuma declared in July 2016 that the ruling African National Congress would rule 'until Jesus comes'.[14]

This combination of ideological cohesion and shared elite history of hardship, struggle and sacrifice, Levitsky and Way argue, renders post-liberation governments – or 'revolutionary regimes', to use their terminology – particularly durable as regime types compared to those which rely principally on patronage and other non-ideational resources to retain power and to weather challenges to their authority.[15]

The struggle – and its discursive marshalling – is therefore of central importance to how, in this case, ruling Ugandan elites have both understood and articulated their authority and legitimacy as political leaders. Debate around who is acting as the true custodian of the struggle legacy has historically been a key dynamic in internal NRM debates and splits concerning governance and Museveni's leadership. It has also been a central motif in many of Museveni's speeches and statements; on National Liberation Day 2017, the Ugandan leader of thirty-one years explained to the citizenry that:

> I am a freedom fighter, that is what I do. I don't do it because I am your servant, I'm not your servant. I am just a freedom fighter, I am fighting for myself and my beliefs. That's how I come in, I'm not an employee … if anybody thinks he gave me a job, he is deceiving himself. I am just a freedom fighter who thought could help you also.[16]

Perhaps more surprisingly, though, this has also been a feature of opposition narratives in recent years. In 2011, long-time presidential candidate Kizza Besigye criticized then prime minister Amama Mbabazi for 'enjoying good meals in [the NRM's external wing in] Nairobi' [during the 1980s] while others (including himself) 'went to the bush', even accusing him of undermining the struggle itself.[17] Besigye was, of course, an early NRM insider – and Museveni's former physician. It is notable, though, that years after leaving the NRM, he became the flagbearer of the main opposition party, and in the lead-up to his third challenge to Museveni, Besigye still framed his critique through the lens of the struggle, indicating, arguably, how embedded this narrative has become in elite Ugandan discourses on legitimate political authority. Nearly a decade later, and months before his fourth tilt at the presidency, Besigye continued in this vein, telling an audience of supporters that he was not quitting 'the struggle to liberate Uganda' and that he would do so 'only when the job that brought [him] into the struggle is accomplished'.[18]

There is, however, a distinction to be drawn between discursive appeals to struggle credentials and custodianship in the heat of political debate or electoral competition, and the spatial inscribing of struggle memorialization upon the landscape. There is, of course, a relationship between the two – and one this chapter will explore in some instances – but the semi-permanence of statues, monuments, memorials and museums ensures a more uncontested version of the past, and its contemporary relevance, is made material.

Spatial memorialization efforts also require sometimes lengthy periods of planning and a degree of consultation, even if – as outlined below – this is principally with a small number of elite actors and bureaucratic functionaries. Hence, a degree of extended reflection and intention around how the struggle (or an aspect of it) should be represented in these spaces is incorporated into these processes in a manner unlikely to be as comprehensive and extended as with the drafting of a speech or preparation for a media interview. An analytical focus on struggle memorialization – including the planning behind it and the ceremonies surrounding it – therefore allows us unique insight into evolving elite reflections on how the 'event' of the struggle links to contemporary claims to political authority.

Researching struggle memorialization in Uganda: Scope and data

This study focuses on physical entities and spaces commissioned, constructed or adapted by the NRM or Ugandan state in commemoration of the liberation struggle, as well as on the ceremonies organized by state actors at these sites, and/or held to mark Uganda's annual National Liberation Day (26 January) and National Heroes Day (9 June). It also examines the inter-elite debates which have taken place in public – notably the Parliament of Uganda – surrounding struggle commemoration. We do not, therefore, examine sites and initiatives developed or launched by non-state/ NRM actors since these do not necessarily reflect elite thinking on how contemporary political authority links to the struggle. We recognize, though, that these alternative memorialization spaces are increasingly widespread and significant, particularly in northern Uganda.[19]

Moreover, we do not draw a clear line between initiatives of the Ugandan state and the NRM. This is because the distinction itself, as other authors in this collection have established, has been deeply ambiguous since 1986. The 'no-party' 'Movement' system of government in place in Uganda between 1986 and 2005 held that all citizens were members of the Movement and that those standing for office did so on 'individual merit' rather than as representatives of a political party. In reality, however, the NRM continued to exist as a *de facto* party when it wished to – establishing a 'Movement caucus' in the 1994–5 Constituent Assembly, for example – while also using the ban on political party activity to side-line politicians at all levels considered to be hostile to the NRM project.[20] Moreover, on coming to power many of the key NRM organs and institutions became the core of reformed state institutions – including the national legislature and military.[21]

By the time that political parties were (re-)legalized in 2005, therefore, the Ugandan state and the NRM had been intertwined to such a degree that drawing a distinction would not only be challenging but also conceptually unhelpful. This ambiguity has arguably continued within Uganda's state institutions and local governance structures while even at the national level, opposition parties have struggled to meaningfully compete as a result of state attempts to disrupt or restrict mobilization and campaigning efforts. The Museveni government has also been extremely skilled at incorporating opposition figures into the ruling party – indeed, this has historically been the Ugandan leader's preferred approach to dealing with civilian political opponents.[22]

The data we draw on comes mainly from work undertaken on four fieldtrips to Uganda in 2018 (January, March, August) and 2019 (October); the first of these coinciding with the 32nd National Liberation Day celebrations, which the authors observed. During these trips, we carried out semi-structured interviews with thirty-five actors who have been involved in commissioning struggle-related memorial sites or organizing struggle-related ceremonies. In most cases, these were current or former NRM, military or public service officials based in the Office of the President, the NRM Secretariat, the National Enterprises Corporation (the army's commercial arm) and the Ministry of Tourism. We also spoke with several NRM and local government (Local Council) officials stationed near to memorial sites (Luweero) or involved with organizing Liberation Day festivities on the ground (Arua), as well as with the Makerere University-based artist commissioned in 2005 to produce a monument commemorating the launching of the NRM struggle. The majority of these actors spoke on condition of anonymity, though in most cases were willing to be cited as an official of the office or unit they are or were based.

This interview material is complemented by two other sources of data. The first is archival. We reviewed newspaper and online media reports relating to struggle memorialization and national ceremonies dating back to c.1993, with those from the 1990s consulted at the Centre for Basic Research's newspaper archive in Kampala. We also undertook field visits to nine memorialization sites in Luweero,

Nakaseke, Wakiso, Mbarara, Mubende and Arua districts. This allowed us to not only observe how these different spaces are (or are not) used and engaged with by local actors but also to speak with local communities about the history of the sites, including – in some cases – their recollection of their commissioning and inauguration.

The sites and spaces we examine in this study vary considerably in size, character, focus and accessibility. Particularly prominent are the *c.*35 'Heroes Graves' constructed between *c.*1991 and 1995 in the Luweero Triangle region north of Kampala, where much of the fighting between the then Ugandan government and its opponents (including the NRM) took place. The constructions themselves are unassuming and functional, consisting of small stone roofed structures erected over mass graves with a short generic inscription dedicated to the 'freedom fighters' who died for the liberation struggle without any personal information of the dead included. In appearance, they seem to echo the functional aesthetic style of nearby local authority buildings. A similar memorial was erected in Rwampara County, Mbarara, in 2012 dedicated to the 'heroes who were killed between 1972 and 1979' in the area 'during the struggle to liberate Uganda from the dictatorial regimes'. This site includes a list of twenty-four named 'Ugandan Heroes', among whom are four people under the age of ten.

Though these graves have a common design and series of dedications, they vary considerably in location, condition and accessibility. In some cases, they are located in prominent spaces and open to all. In others, they are buried in undergrowth, bolted closed or guarded by soldiers or local government officers. In some cases, local state officials enthusiastically provided an overview of the site and its meaning, in others access required the purchase of a ticket from the Gombola Internal Security Officer (local state intelligence representative) or was simply not possible because of the state or location of the space. In one instance, local officials suggested that access was only possible with express permission from the local government and that the sites were 'government property' and not open to the public.[23]

Other relevant sites include the Kabamba barracks monument mentioned above and unveiled by Museveni in 2006. This monument – visible from the highway but located within the grounds of a military academy – is dedicated to the twenty-seven NRM cadres who 'attacked Kabamba on 6/2/1981 marking the beginning of the people's protracted war' and is focused around a 20-metre high statue of a youthful Museveni leading the attack.

The chapter also reflects on a range of memorialization projects which were mooted but ultimately not undertaken, or which are now on-going. Among the latter is a National Military Museum first suggested in the mid-2000s[24] but, at the time of writing, still in the planning phase, with the foundation stone being laid by Museveni himself in December 2020.[25] Through our interviews and archival research we are therefore able to examine not only those sites, spaces and ceremonies which have been established or carried out but also those proposed, debated and planned. Both, we suggest, are revealing of how NRM elites have come to justify the Ugandan government's authoritarian and personalist evolution.

Commemorating struggle under the NRM: An overview

Unsurprisingly, the NRM gave little thought to struggle memorialization during its early years in power, with the exception of establishing two public holidays – the aforementioned Liberation Day and Heroes Day – to mark the anniversary of the movement's seizure of power and to commemorate those killed during the struggle respectively. A third national day – Army Day, or *Tarehe Sita*[26] – was also established, although not as an official holiday. The commemoration and memorialization of struggle 'heroes' begun during the NRM insurgency itself following the summary execution in June 1981 of fifteen NRA fighters, including Edidian 'Lutta' Luttamaguzi by Obote's Uganda National Liberation Army. Luttamaguzi, Museveni writes in the first edition of his autobiography, was declared a hero and gave his name to one of the NRA's six units, taking his place alongside other venerated African liberation and anti-colonial figures, including Kwame Nkrumah, Eduardo Mondlane and Abdel Gamal Nasser.[27] Though the day of Lutta's killing – 9 June – was chosen as the annual date for observing Heroes Day, establishing a physical memorial or monument was not a priority.

In part, this is because the NRM in 1986 was tasked with the rebuilding of a country and society which had been devastated by years of conflict and violent, abusive misrule. As well as reconstituting Uganda's shattered polity and economy, the new government was also necessarily preoccupied with establishing control in areas where it had little presence or where its authority was being openly resisted by insurgencies and remnants of the deposed regime. In addition, it needed to seek accommodation with surviving members of the political establishment who had not aligned themselves with Obote or the rump military regime which briefly succeeded him, and, indeed, to establish constructive relations with international aid donors, many of which approached the leftist NRM with deep suspicion.[28]

It is also suggested, albeit by those sympathetic to the Ugandan leader, that Museveni himself was – at least initially – reluctant to be seen to be glorifying the movement or its leaders for fear of association with tyrannical regimes across the continent. 'The President's own thinking', noted one NRM Secretariat official we interviewed, 'has been to give very little attention to monuments and preserving artefacts of the revolution … I think his fear is that monuments in Africa are associated with oppression.'[29] Another respondent, a former senior NEC official and NRM bush war cadre, agreed that 'the President is shy about this. He is worried about being misunderstood … if you start glorifying your success, the people, they may think other things about you in that area.'[30] Certainly, in its first decade in power, the NRM government placed significant emphasis on being a departure from Uganda's past dictatorships and from personalist regimes elsewhere on the continent. In his inauguration speech in January 1986, for example, Museveni explained that he did 'not like being called 'Excellency' and condemned 'the honourable excellency who is going to the United Nations in executive jets, but has a population at home of 90 per cent walking barefoot' as a 'pathetic spectacle'.[31]

Consequently, the NRM's initial engagement in memorialization work was largely responsive and reactive, centring on the large numbers of unidentified and unburied bones and skulls strewn across the Luweero landscape in the aftermath of the conflict.

A consequence, in large part, of the merciless counter-insurgency campaign launched in the Luweero triangle region by Obote's forces, the NRM ordered the public display of these skeletal remains on makeshift platforms from 1985 onwards as a means to evidence the (from 1986, former) regime's brutality to local and, in particular, international audiences.[32] This served an important propaganda role in both demonizing the regime it ultimately overthrew and legitimizing the NRM's struggle against it – a motif that, as Pauline Bernard has argued, returned in Museveni's 1996 presidential election campaign where pictures of the Luweero skulls were displayed nationwide as a warning of what might return should citizens vote against the president.[33]

As part of this effort, as one local official of Nakaseke District who remembers this period recalls, local NRM officials and soldiers played an active role in collecting skulls and bones, with some displayed openly and others stored, awkwardly, in local government offices.[34] The treatment of these remains – many of which were of civilians – attracted growing outrage from local communities, who wished to see them buried with ceremony and dignity.[35]

From 1991, therefore, the Office of the President took over the situation and, in the words of one senior Tourism Ministry official, begun 'the construction of heroes' graves and monument construction' across Luweero.[36] Between 1991 and c.1995, around thirty-five[37] burial monuments were constructed in the region, each designed in a similar way as discussed in Section 3. In many cases, the dedication of these sites – which included the laying of a plaque commemorating the occasion – was undertaken by Museveni himself and often coinciding with National Liberation Day or Heroes Day. As well as becoming key spaces for commemorating the struggle by national leaders – at least on the day of dedication itself – these sites also served as temporary spaces for general reflection on the NRM's progress as a government (including one 'intellectual discussion on the NRM's seven years in government' held on Liberation Day in 1993) and as opportunities for Luweero residents to lobby for more support from the government.[38]

This memorialization work in Luweero – increasingly directed from Museveni's office – prompted a growing institutionalization and expansion of struggle memorialization efforts from the mid-1990s onwards. This included the transformation of part of the Kololo Airstrip – Kampala's former airport which now serves as an Independence Park and setting for high-profile national ceremonies – into a burial ground for national heroes, and the establishment of a series of national awards and medals linked, in part, to service during the struggle.[39] An act to establish the latter was passed in 1994 – the National Honours and Awards Bill – and amended in 2001.

Though formally under the aegis of the Office of the President, struggle memorialization planning and implementation de facto fell under the control of the army leadership by the early 2000s. Bush war veteran and former army commander Elly Tumwine in particular took on an informal leadership role in this regard (one he held until his death in 2022), acting both as a gatekeeper for memorialization-related planning and resources and as a form of 'official historian' of the struggle in this context. The National Enterprise Corporation (NEC) – led between 1994 and 2010 by struggle veteran and Tumwine ally Fred Mwesigye (at the time of writing, Kampala's High Commissioner to Tanzania) – came to serve as the institutional home for much of this discussion and work during the 2000s and subsequently, though more as the result of the personal relationships and interests of those involved than through official fiat. That is to say, while struggle memorialization work ramped up considerably during the 2000s, this was principally a result of entrepreneurial activity by key military and political leaders; as a former senior NEC official recalls, "I don't think that we have ever sat and held meetings on how our liberation should be remembered."[40]

By the early 2000s, with the NRM well into its second decade in power a range of senior figures appear to have nonetheless begun to reflect critically on this question. In particular, there appears to have been a feeling among some that the NRM and the government had a responsibility to 'tell the story' of the liberation struggle and that what had been undertaken thus far in terms of memorialization and heritage was unduly cautious and minimal.[41] One NRM respondent we spoke with notes that discussions in this regard centred on sentiments such as: 'why are we not preserving this history? These are people who have paid for this sacrifice.'[42] It is within this context – and that of growing division among NRM 'historicals' around Museveni's pursuit of a third term in office – that a range of grander, more triumphalist memorialization initiatives were suggested and commissioned.

The Kabamba barracks monument mentioned in the previous section is a key example of this. Originally proposed as a museum complex ('to make the rest of Uganda feel close to the army'[43]) the monument was carefully designed with input from Tumwine and other bush war veterans,[44] and was unveiled soon after Uganda's 2006 elections, where Museveni faced the most significant electoral challenge to his tenure since coming to power. A second Museveni statue was unveiled at the Special Forces Command (SFC) headquarters in Kampala by the president's son – at the time, SFC commander – shortly after the country's 2021 elections, and coinciding with Army Day.[45] The SFC building itself had been opened three months earlier under the name 'Gen Y K Museveni House'.[46]

Work on a military museum, near Katonga as noted, is also underway – a project overseen by 'bush war' veteran and former army military doctrine chief Pecos Kutesa, until his death in August 2021. In parallel to these developments, the President's Office launched the 'NRA Archives' initiative in 2018. This project focuses on recording and memorializing the liberation struggle through interviewing remaining NRA veterans as well as 'reconstructing [the Heroes] Graves, marking battle grounds, and building two new museums in Mbale and Luweero'.[47] According to the initiative's Twitter account (@NRAArchives), the project 'chronicles the battles of the Uganda Resistance to liberate a damaged Uganda to the peaceful Uganda we have today'.[48]

There has, therefore, been a steady but decisive shift in recent decades towards a military- and military leadership-led approach to managing struggle memorialization efforts in Uganda, although the NRM Secretariat continues to play an important role in organizing and implementing National Liberation Day celebrations.[49] Other state institutions involved in memorialization work appear to do so more as implementers than initiators. The Ministry of Tourism, for example, has been directed by the cabinet since 2016 to conserve and maintain heroes grave sites in Luweero, though according to one official with minimal funding to do so.[50] The Office of the President leads on organizing the National Liberation Day and Heroes Day festivities, though appears to take its direction in this regard from the NRM Secretariat and from Museveni himself.[51]

Struggle memorialization: The flattening of history

The remainder of this chapter examines two central ways in which struggle memorialization by state and NRM actors has evolved since the 1980s. In both cases, the trajectory taken has aligned with the general transformation of the Ugandan polity into an authoritarian and personalized system of government. We first explore how struggle memorialization narratives have flattened Uganda's political history to present the NRM as the sole opponent of past dictatorial regimes, in line with the steady establishment of Uganda as a de facto one-party state. We then chart how struggle memorialization projects have progressively placed focus on the person of Museveni, framing the liberation struggle as a personal crusade and the Ugandan leader as the indispensable liberator of the country. This has been particularly evident since the mid-2000s, at which point the constitutional hurdles to an effective Museveni life presidency were ultimately removed.

The movementization of Ugandan struggle history

While the NRM was undoubtedly the most prominent political and military opponent of the Ugandan government between 1981 and 1986, it was not alone in prosecuting an anti-regime insurgency. The Uganda Freedom Movement (UFM), for example, operated with some success between 1981 and 1982 in the same – central – region of Uganda where the NRM itself focused its campaign. Indeed, NRM veterans – including Museveni and Pecos Kutesa – record how they feared that the UFM would undermine their (potential) support among Baganda leaders and communities in the prosperous and politically important Buganda region.[52] This reportedly prompted Museveni to appeal directly to these communities in a 1982 Kanyanda gathering to switch their support from the UFM because they were 'trying to divide the fighting forces, and in doing so were weakening the struggle against Obote'.[53]

A range of other anti-Obote rebels – notably the Uganda National Rescue Front – also operated in the West Nile (northwest) region of Uganda in the early years of the bush war, eventually being neutralized by a vicious counter-insurgency campaign which reached its peak at the end of 1982.[54] In addition, a low-intensity secessionist movement in Rwenzururu fought the Obote regime to the point where it agreed a political settlement in 1982, including a degree of local autonomy.[55] In other words, while the NRM had emerged as the principal and most effective insurgent movement in Uganda by 1982/3, it was not the sole rebel actor and, indeed, faced 'competition' in this regard even in its main centre of operations for some time.

Moreover, the NRM itself was the product of a merger between Museveni's People's Resistance Army – a movement formed largely of Ugandans from the western Banyankole region and Rwandan Tutsi refugees – and a range of other anti-Obote organizations. Most prominent among these was the Uganda Freedom Fighters (UFF), led by Yusuf Lule, who had briefly held the Ugandan presidency in 1979 and who became the NRM's inaugural Chairman. This was a critical development in the struggle because of the significant support Lule enjoyed among Baganda[56] and, indeed, following Lule's January 1985 death, the NRM leadership pledged that 'the struggle for which Professor Lule stood will continue'.[57]

This complex network of struggle actors has not, however, been reflected in struggle memorialization efforts over time. The plaques unveiled in the Luweero Heroes Graves between 1991 and1995, for example, reveal a series of ambiguities around the centrality of the NRM itself to the struggle. Those unveiled earlier in the period (*c*.1991/2) tend to refer to the struggle in general terms – as the 'People's Protracted War Between 1981–1986' – and to Museveni as 'Leader of the N.R.M./N.R.A. Freedom Fighters 1981–1986', whereas by 1995, a clear language of the 'People's Protracted War *of NRM/ NRA 1981–1986*' (emphasis our own) had been adopted.

This 'movementization' of struggle memorialization became a point of contention by the end of the 1990s during discussion around the National Honours and Awards Bill (1999). In a 2001 parliamentary debate surrounding amending the Bill, opposition MP Stephen Malinga bemoaned how the existing system focused on recognizing only 'those who were in the bush, which makes it very limited in its recognition'. Condemning 'bush syndrome', he proceeded to ask whether a range of other contributors to Uganda's political transformation – including Lule – should be recognized.[58] As the debate progressed the following day into the names of specific medals, this and other similar points were contested by Tumwine, sitting as one of the ten army representatives in parliament, who argued that 'the honours and titles are referring to the geographical and freedom fighter land marks of the history of Uganda and has no character or bias towards NRM alone'.[59]

The National Honours and Awards Act 2001, the outcome of this series of debates, did, in fact, widen the criteria for inclusion and in more recent National Liberation Day festivities, awards and recognition have been afforded to Ugandans from all walks of life. As a senior figure in the Office of the President told us, '[the scope] was expanded after 1999 ... [to] not just look at those who died in the struggle, but ... [from] other areas of excellence'.[60] It is notable, though, that this has been in a context where 'National Liberation Day' has increasingly been described in political speeches and public discourse as 'NRM Liberation Day' or even simply 'NRM Day'.[61]

This apparent contradiction – an opening-up of recognition while also narrowing the overall framing around the NRM and the 'NRM War' – is indicative of a general consolidation that occurred in Ugandan politics during the 1990s whereby the NRM emerged as the de facto sole political party in the country. In its first few years in office, the Museveni government ruled notionally as part of a four-year, bounded interim dispensation, due to end in January 1990. Having formed a 'broad-based government', the new administration consciously incorporated political leaders and (former) opponents from Uganda's (now banned) political parties, extending the interim period in 1989 by five years in order to 'complete the work we have started', in particular in relation to (in)security and economic recovery.[62]

Over the next six years, however, the NRM evolved, effectively becoming the only legal political organization after the constitutionalization of the Movement system was debated and eventually delivered between 1992 and 1995. This period also saw the collapse of the 'broad-based government' and a consolidation of power around Museveni and senior NRM cadres. The prolonging and, ultimately, constitutional embedding of NRM power did not take place without acrimony among struggle veterans; the 1989 extension and, in particular, 1994 constitutional settlement was openly criticized by some senior figures. This included presidential security advisor and former defence state minister David Tinyefuza (latterly Sejusa), who argued during the Constitutional Assembly debates in question that it was 'almost immoral' to further extend the NRM's period in office.[63] The evolving language on the Luweero Heroes Graves is therefore, in part, a reflection of changing elite narratives within the NRM itself on its place and authority in Ugandan politics – from a major player in the struggle against Obote to the 'owner' of the struggle itself.

This context also helps explain the simultaneous opening and narrowing of focus on national days commemorating, in different ways, the struggle. For by the late 1990s/ early 2000s, the NRM's position in the Ugandan polity was largely unassailable and, hence, inclusion no longer threatened to dilute or cut across NRM authority. From this era onwards, Museveni's principal and preferred means to deal with political opponents (with some exceptions) has been to try and incorporate them into (or back into) the NRM; alternative outfits (outside of the military and security forces) have come to present simply an irritation rather than a substantive hazard. As Museveni reportedly explained to one adviser in the mid-2000s, after surviving an internal NRM challenge to his pursuit of a third term in office, the NRM is 'like a railway station – there are arrivals and departures, but the railway station remains'.[64]

This particular comment was reportedly in reference to the 2006 return of long-time NRM cadre and struggle veteran Eriya Kategaya into the NRM fold; Kategaya had effectively quit the NRM and helped to form the opposition Forum for Democratic Change (FDC) in 2004. There are, however, many such examples of this political practice in contemporary Uganda,[65] with another example being the opposition MP Stephen Malinga mentioned above. Malinga, who condemned 'bush syndrome' in 2001, crossed to the NRM in 2005 and was appointed minister of health in 2006.

From movement to man: Uganda's one and only revolutionary president

The mid-2000s was also a period when struggle memorialization increasingly moved from commemorating and lauding the NRM as a collective to acclaiming Museveni as an individual. A comparison of the language used at National Liberation Day celebrations in the 1990s with those of the 2010s exposes a particularly stark change in this regard. Media accounts of the former reveal how central the language of 'the NRM government' was to speeches and discussion during those festivities.[66] During the 1993 celebrations in Bugolobi, for example, local government officials issued a press release which explained, *inter alia*, how the day was to be focused on how 'the NRM – having ensured the security of the people – [has] endeavoured to create political awareness among the people right from the grass-root level to ensure their participation in the administration of the country'.[67]

By the 2010s, however, the focus had shifted decisively to praising Museveni as the architect of the struggle and Uganda's liberation. At the 2018 National Liberation Day celebrations in Arua, for example, the emcee (Alice Muwanguzi, an NRM Secretariat communications official) opened the event with a speech firmly centred on the president, his achievements and his personal qualities. This included a religiously inspired hagiography of Museveni's wisdom ('testimonies …what you have told us, what you have written in your books') and leadership ('an anointing from God'), which concluded with a plea that 'nothing should come as an obstacle in your path until you fulfil that which the Lord appointed you to do'.[68] Later in the ceremony, a group of local primary school children performed a poem dedicated to Museveni – entitled 'Revolutionary Presidents' – which described Museveni as 'the only revolutionary president' and the person responsible for rebuilding Uganda's state and economy following decades of 'untested leaders'. The poem concluded with its reciters kneeling and addressing Museveni, explaining that 'old age is never inability'.[69]

It is also noteworthy, in this regard, that a Heroes Grave-style memorial was unveiled in 2012 by Museveni on National Heroes Day that year. Unlike those in Luweero, however, this monument – erected in Rwampara, in Western Uganda – commemorated not the NRM struggle per se but those killed between 1972 and 1979 'during the struggle to liberate Uganda from the dictatorial regimes'. The NRM did not exist during this period, although Museveni was at the time leading the Front for National Salvation (FRONASA), a rebel movement formed in opposition to Idi Amin's dictatorship. Museveni's name – 'His Excellency General Yoweri Kaguta Museveni' – appears in the largest letters on the monument and two of our interviewees – a local educator and a religious leader – recall the planning and establishment of the memorial as having a heavy focus on the president:

> In 2012 there was a directive from our president, because we can still remember what happened in this area [during the 1970s]. We invited the president to the church [now adjacent to the monument] and he said 'this is my church' and promised that he would help build it, so we called it 'Museveni's church'.[70]

This increasing emphasis on Museveni and under-playing of the NRM also came across in some of our interviews with NRM officials involved in struggle memorialization and ceremonial planning work. One NRM Secretariat official, for example, described the NRM as a 'rider' on Museveni's 'very strong vision', opining that 'his vision [for] the country is stronger than [that of] the organisation'.[71] Together with some others, though, he also acknowledged that the steady emphasis on Museveni in memorialization and commemoration events did not necessarily resonate with many Ugandans, suggesting that 'for young people there is a need for a different message ….the [memorialisation] unveilings are not well-attended, I would actually say they are badly-attended'.[72]

This refocusing of discourse in and around national struggle memorialization ceremonies is reflective of a broader shift in Ugandan politics and inter-NRM political narratives in recent decades where the leadership and centrality of 'the Movement' have been superseded by that of Museveni. As noted above, the likelihood that the NRM would continue to dominate Ugandan politics far into the future was unclear for many NRM cadres during the first few years of NRM rule, though this question had been largely settled by the mid-1990s. Relatedly, Museveni's continued tenure remained a matter of considerable debate within the NRM during its second decade in power.

In the aftermath of the divisive Constituent Assembly debates where some NRM veterans had opposed a continuation of the no-party, Movement system, senior

NRM cadre David Tinyefuza reportedly sought to persuade Museveni not to stand in the 1996 election which he eventually won decisively.[73] In 2000, Kizza Besigye announced that he would challenge Museveni for the presidency in the upcoming 2001 elections, arguing that the NRM leadership had become mired in corruption and an 'arrogant' disregard for democracy.[74] The vast majority of NRM figures, though, supported Museveni's leadership and presidential candidacy in both 1996 and 2001, albeit with a number assuming that the Ugandan leader would honour the presidential term limits clause in the Ugandan constitution and step down as president in 2006.

This was, of course, not to be, though, as noted, the removal of term limits led to unprecedented public and private division within the NRM leadership. The period between March 2002 – when the NRM's National Executive Committee proposed a motion to delete the presidential term limit clause from the Ugandan constitution – and June 2005 – when MPs voted to do so – was not simply a time of fractious debate; however, c.2002–05 was also the period when it became clear to many in the ruling party that Museveni would not soon depart the political stage and would potentially remain in office for many years to come.

The shift in focus in the memorialization of the struggle therefore reflects a series of emerging realities of the 2000s for many NRM officials. First, a growing acceptance – and, for some, a welcome one – that political power in Uganda would increasingly be synonymous with Museveni rather than the NRM as a collective. As noted elsewhere in this book, this personalization and centralization of power intensified considerably during the 2000s and 2010s. Second, it significantly altered and, in some respects, weakened the independence of the NRM. As Sabiti Makara et al. and others have noted, the presidential term limits debate took place in parallel to debates on ending the no-party political system and re-introducing multi-partyism to Uganda – which occurred in 2005.[75] In some respects the latter helped to strengthen the NRM, in terms of enabling it both to adopt formal party structures and processes and to 'flush out' internal opponents who had previously been notionally all members of 'the Movement'.[76]

These processes also, however, lead to a closure of space for debate within the party and a growing emphasis on loyalty to the president and his circle. As Makara et al. explain, 'the Movement grew intolerant of divergent views [internally] and increasing power became centralised around the president, his family and loyalists from his home area'.[77] An NRM official involved in the planning of the 2018 National Liberation Day celebrations in Arua we spoke with described a similar dynamic, noting that 'you hear so much about the president but not about the NRM. That is one of the weaknesses of the NRM as a party. You know, I am here with the Movement and I am supporting Museveni because it is how you get on in politics here in Uganda today. You want politics? You go with Museveni'.[78]

The commissioning and unveiling of the Kabamba barracks monument and Museveni statue in 2005–6 was a central turning point in this regard and symbolic of this shift in Ugandan politics and elite thinking from Movement to man, from NRM to Museveni. The monument commemorates the launch of the NRM insurgency but centres around a statue of Museveni; the first to be erected in Uganda. As the artist in charge of the team who produced the statue recalls, the timing of the commissioning was clearly linked to contemporary political events: 'This was 2005', he noted in a

2018 interview, 'here in Uganda, another election was in the offing and voices were already out there about the controversial lifting of the presidential term limits to allow president Museveni to contest in the 2006 polls'.[79] Moreover, the statue was not the initiative of the NRM *per se* but of struggle veterans in the military leadership – this case some of Museveni's closest allies. The idea for the statue – which was originally also to be accompanied by a military museum – came from the NEC, with the strong support of senior generals including Tumwine who closely supervised the project.[80]

Conclusion

This chapter has plotted the authoritarian trajectory of the Museveni-led government against trends in state/NRM memorialization of the liberation struggle which brought it to power. The latter, we argue, not only provides a – sometimes physical – 'commentary' on political developments but also speaks to how ruling elites (principally members of the NRM) have understood the authority and legitimacy of their government over time. Focusing on a number of spaces, ceremonies and political debates within the NRM itself and the Ugandan Parliament, we show how struggle memorialization in Uganda has gradually come to promote two central and linked narratives on political authority in contemporary Uganda: the right of the NRM and, above it, Museveni alone to stay in power.

Many of the struggle memorialization phenomena we analyse in this chapter are not unique to Uganda. A growing emphasis on and lionization of struggle leaders is evident in post-liberation polities as different as Rwanda and South Africa.[81] A 'flattening' of struggle history which underplays the role of actors other than the – now – ruling movement has also been a criticism levelled by many scholars at the ANC of South Africa[82] – though few would suggest that the ANC and NRM governments' trajectories share many characteristics. Most post-liberation polities do, however, experience the common challenge of making the founding events of their political legitimacy – the liberation struggle – pertinent to successive generations of citizens who did not live through this period of history. This is particularly so if, as has often been the case, post-liberation governments have failed to deliver on the promises of democracy, development and peace which underlay their struggle.

In the case of Uganda, struggle memorialization has increasingly come to take on a somewhat dual character. On the one hand, a 'frozen' version of the struggle, where Museveni enjoys centre stage, has come to be presented. One example of this from recent years was a January 2020 jungle trek by the Ugandan leader following, as his press secretary noted, 'a route the liberators led by Museveni took to liberate the country' during the bush war.[83] Eighteen months earlier, Museveni's daughter released a film she had directed – *27 Guns* – which focused on 'a young man [Museveni] and his unlikely group of young idealists who leave all to fight for salvation of a nation'.[84]

On the other hand, and as evidenced in the 2018 National Liberation Day celebrations described above, memorialization has increasingly come to be intermingled with claims surrounding the achievements of the Museveni/NRM government since 1986, particularly in relation to security. As one of our NRM interlocutors noted, though, 'the threats we face now are totally different to at the time of the struggle … the past is gone, the youth don't see that threat of peace and security as imminent now … social justice is the war being fought now and that we are struggling to address'.[85]

Notes

1   Earlier versions of this study were presented at an expert workshop held in Kampala on 29 August 2018, at the UK African Studies Association in Birmingham in September 2018, at the Stellenbosch Institute for Advanced Study (STIAS) and at the International Development Department at the University of Birmingham in February 2021. We are grateful to participants and discussants in these events for valuable feedback. We would also like to thank Hippo Twebaze for feedback on the research project underlying this work and to acknowledge generous support provided by the Newton Fund (AF160100) which made the research possible. Finally, Jonathan Fisher would like to thank STIAS for hosting him as a Visiting Fellow during this research project in 2019.

2   As has been commonplace with the First Son's more sensitive political and diplomatic online declarations, this particular tweet has since been deleted. Moses Baguma, 'What's beneath Muhoozi's Ridiculous and Outrageous Tweets'? *The Observer* (1 March 2022). https://observer.ug/viewpoint/72907-what-s-beneath-muhoozi-s-ridiculous-and-outrageous-tweets (accessed 12 August 2022); Job Bwire, 'I'm Tired of Waiting, I'll Stand for Presidency in 2026 – Muhoozi', *Daily Monitor* (17 March 2023). https://www.monitor.co.ug/uganda/news/national/i-m-tired-of-waiting-i-ll-stand-for-presidency-in-2026-muhoozi-4160712 (accessed 20 March 2023); Kristof Titeca, 'The "Muhoozi Project" in Uganda: Testing the Water or Preparing the Ground'? *Democracy in Africa* (27 May 2022). http://democracyinafrica.org/the-muhoozi-project-in-uganda-testing-the-water-or-preparing-the-ground/ (accessed 12 August 2022); Sam Wilkins and Richard Vokes, 'Museveni's First Son Muhoozi: Clear Signals of a Succession Plan in Uganda', *The Conversation* (22 May 2022). https://theconversation.com/musevenis-first-son-muhoozi-clear-signals-of-a-succession-plan-in-uganda-181863 (accessed 12 August 2022).

3   Yoweri K Museveni, *What Is Africa's Problem?* (Kampala: NRM Publications, 1992), 279.

4   During the final six months of the NRM insurgency, Obote was overthrown by senior military commander Bazilio Olara-Okello, as Chairman of the (ruling) Military Council. Olara-Okello was himself replaced shortly after in this role by Tito Okello, who ruled Uganda as president for six months until the NRM took Kampala in January 1986.

5   Museveni, *What Is Africa's Problem*, 21.

6   'How Events Unfolded at the 1986 Swearing In', *Daily Monitor* (25 January 2016). https://www.monitor.co.ug/uganda/news/national/how-events-unfolded-at-the-1986-swearing-in-1638260 (accessed 12 August 2022).

7   Lillian Nsubuga, 'Museveni Fans Walk 123 Miles', *The Monitor* (29 January 1993).

8   Between January 1986 and October 1995, the NRA became the name of the Ugandan military itself. Following the promulgation of the 1995 Constitution of Uganda, the NRA UPDF.

9   Yoweri Kaguta Museveni, *Sowing the Mustard Seed*, First Edition (New York, NY: St Martin's Press, 1997); Museveni, *What Is Africa's Problem*, 279–82.

10   The contours of these debates are analysed in, *Inter Alia*, Ondoga Ori Amaza, *Museveni's Long March from Guerrilla to Statesman* (Kampala: Fountain Publishers, 1998), 203; Jonathan Fisher, *East Africa after Liberation: Conflict, Security, and the State since the 1980s* (Cambridge: Cambridge University Press, 2020), 236–42; Moses Khisa, 'Shrinking Democratic Space? Crisis of Consensus and Contentious Politics in Uganda', *Commonwealth and Comparative Politics* 57, no. 3 (2019): 351–3; Sabiti Makara, Lise Rakner and Lars Svåsand, 'Turnaround: The National Resistance Movement and the Reintroduction of a Multiparty System in Uganda', *International Political Science Review* 30, no. 2 (2009): 185–204; Roger Tangri, 'Politics and Presidential Term Limits in Uganda', in *Legacies of Power: Leadership Change and Former Presidents in African Politics*, ed. Roger Southall and Henning Melber (Pretoria: HSRC Press, 2004).

11   Sara Rich Dorman, 'Post-Liberation Politics in Africa: Examining the Political Legacy of Struggle', *Third World Quarterly* 27, no. 6 (2006): 1097. See also Redie Bereketaeb, ed., *National Liberation Movements as Governments in Africa* (Abingdon: Routledge, 2018); Christopher Clapham, *From Liberation Movement to Government: Past Legacies and the Challenge of Transition in Africa* (Johannesburg: Brenthurst Foundation, 2012); Fisher, *East Africa after Liberation*, 20–4; Terrence Lyons, 'The Importance of Winning: Victorious Insurgent Groups and Authoritarian Politics', *Comparative Politics* 48, no. 2 (2016): 167–84; Philip Roessler and Harry Verhoeven, *When Comrades Go to War: Liberation Politics and the Outbreak of Africa's Deadliest Conflict* (London: Hurst, 2016), 30–43; Mohamed Salih, 'African Liberation Movement Governments and Democracy', *Democratization* 14, no. 4 (2007): 669–85.

12   The Ethiopian People's Revolutionary Democratic Front (EPRDF) which seized power in Addis Ababa in 1991 was formally dissolved in December 2019.

13   Clapham, *From Liberation Movement;* Dorman, 'Post-Liberation Politics'; Salih, 'African Liberation Movement'.

14   Karabo Ngoepe, 'ANC Will Rule Until Jesus Comes, Zuma Says Again,' *News24* (5 July 2016). https://www.news24.com/elections/news/anc-will-rule-until-jesus-comes-zuma-says-again-20160705 (accessed 12 August 2022).

15   Stephen Levitsky and Lucan Way, 'Beyond Patronage: Violent Struggle, Ruling Party Cohesion, and Authoritarian Durability', *Perspectives on Politics* 10, no. 4 (2012): 869–89.

16   Abdur Rahman Alfa Shaban, 'I'm Not Anybody's Servant, I'm Just a Freedom Fighter" – Ugandan President', *Africanews* (27 January 2017). https://www.africanews.com/2017/01/27/i-m-not-anybody-s-servant-i-m-just-a-freedom-fighter-ugandan-president (accessed 12 August 2022).

17   Gerald Bareebe, 'Security Minister Sabotaged Bush War', *Daily Monitor* (14 February 2011).

18   Damali Mukhaye, 'I am Not Quitting the Struggle, Says Dr Besigye', *Daily Monitor* (29 July 2020).

19   See, for example, David Mwambari, 'Transcultural Memory in Post-Conflict Northern Uganda War Commemorations', *Africa Development* 46, no. 4 (2012): 71–96 and the National Memory and Peace Documentation Centre in Kitgum.

20   Nelson Kasfir, 'African Ambiguities: "No-Party Democracy" in Uganda', *Journal of Democracy* 9, no. 2 (1998): 49–61; Justus Mugaju and Joe Oloka-Onyango,

eds., *No-Party Democracy in Uganda: Myths and Realities* (Kampala: Fountain Publishers, 2000).

21   Fisher, *East Africa after Liberation*, 103–5.

22   Frederick Golooba-Mutebi and Samuel Hickey, 'The Master of Institutional Multiplicity? The Shifting Politics of Regime Survival, State-Building and Democratisation in Museveni's Uganda', *Journal of Eastern African Studies* 10, no. 4 (2016): 601–18; Moses Khisa, 'Inclusive Co-optation and Political Corruption in Museveni's Uganda', in *Political Corruption in Africa*, ed. Inge Amundsen (Cheltenham: Edward Elgar Publishing, 2019).

23   Discussion with local government officials, Kikamulo Sub-County Headquarters, Nakaseke District, 23 August 2018.

24   Interview with former senior NEC official, Kampala, 21 August 2018.

25   Wilson Kutamba and Al-Mahdi Ssenkabirwa, 'Military Museum Works Stall', *Daily Monitor* (23 February 2022). https://www.monitor.co.ug/uganda/news/national/military-museum-works-stall-3725906 (accessed 12 August 2022).

26   Meaning "sixth day" in Kiswahili, the name refers to the date – February 6 – on which the NRM insurgency formally commenced in 1981 with an attack on the Kabamba barracks in Mubende, central Uganda.

27   Pecos Kutesa, *Uganda's Revolution, 1979–1986: How I Saw It* (Kampala: Fountain Publishers, 2006), 83; Yoweri Kaguta Museveni, *Sowing the Mustard Seed: The Struggle for Freedom and Democracy in Uganda*, Second Edition (Nairobi: Moran Publishers, 2016), 131–2.

28   Holger Bernt Hansen and Michael Twaddle, eds., *Changing Uganda: The Dilemmas of Structural Adjustment and Revolutionary Change* (Athens: Ohio University Press, 1991); Florence Kuteesa, Emmanuel Tumusiime-Mutebile, Alan Whitworth and Tim Williamson, eds., *Uganda's Economic Reforms: Inside Accounts* (Oxford: Oxford University Press, 2010).

29   Interview with NRM Secretariat official, Kampala, 29 January 2018.

30   Interview with former senior NEC official, Kampala, 21 January 2018.

31   Museveni, *What Is Africa's Problem*, 24 and 26.

32   Pauline Bernard, 'The Politics of the Luwero Skulls: The Making of Memorial Heritage and Post- Revolutionary State Legitimacy over the Luwero Mass Graves in Uganda', *Journal of Eastern African Studies* 11, no. 1 (2017): 193–6.

33   Ibid., 188 and 199–201.

34   Interview with local government official, Nakaseke District, 23 March 2018.

35   Interview with local government official, Nakaseke District, 23 March 2018; 'Bernard, The Politics of the Luwero Skulls', 196–7.

36   Interview with senior Tourism Ministry official, Kampala, 22 January 2018.

37   Uganda's Ministry of Tourism holds an 'official list' of 33 Heroes Graves, though during our research we encountered mentions of at least two others in newspapers from the time (*New Vision*, 11/06/1994 and 12/06/1994).

38   Frederick Kiwanuka, 'Luwero: "We Won the War to No Avail"', *Sunday Vision* (16 January 1994); Timothy Kalyegira, 'NRM: A Step beyond Anarchy', *New Vision* (26 January 1994); *New Vision*, 'Cause for Jubilation' (27 January 1994); *The Star*, 'NRM Championed End to State Genocide' (27 January 1993).

39   Martin Lutalo Mpungu, 'Top Ugandans to Get New Honours', *The Monitor* (12 December 1994); *New Vision*, 'Jet for Hero's Burial' (6 October 1998).

40   Interview with former senior NEC official, Kampala, 21 January 2018.

41   Stephanie Cawood and Jonathan Fisher, "'It should be a constant reminder": Space, Meaning, and Power in Post-Liberation Africa', *Political Geography* 99 (2022), Online First.

42   Interview with NRM Secretariat official, Kampala, 29 January 2018.

43   Interview with former senior NEC official, Kampala, 21 January 2018.

44   Interview with George Kyeyune, Associate Professor (Makerere University) and artist, Kampala, 21 January 2018.

45   'SFC Unveils Museveni Statue Ahead of 40th Tarehe Sita Celebrations', *Kampala Post* (5 February 2021). https://kampalapost.com/content/sfc-unveils-museveni-statue-ahead-40th-tarehe-sita-celebrations (accessed 12 August 2022).

46   Javira Ssebwami, 'SFC Headquarters Named After Museveni', *PML Daily* (6 November 2020). https://www.pmldaily.com/news/2020/11/sfc-headquarters-named-after-museveni.html (accessed 12 August 2022).

47   Email communication with Mr Stephen 'Hippo' Twebaze, Presidential Advisor (NRA Archives), 13 September 2022.

48   Twitter page available at https://twitter.com/NRAArchives; (accessed 25 March 2023).

49   Interview with NRM Secretariat official, Kampala, 29 January 2018.

50   Interview with senior Tourism Ministry official, Kampala, 22 January 2018.

51   Interview with Office of the President official, Kampala, 29 January 2018.

52   Kutesa, *Uganda's Revolution*, 146–7; Museveni, 1997, 149–51.

53   Museveni, *Sowing the Mustard Seed*, First Edition,150–1.

54   Chris Day, 'The Fates of Rebels: Insurgencies in Uganda', *Comparative Politics* 43, no. 4 (2011): 451–2.

55   Anna Reuss and Kristof Titeca, 'Beyond Ethnicity: The Violence in Western Uganda and Rwenzori's 99 Problems', *Journal of Eastern African Studies* 44, no. 151 (2017): 132.

56   Museveni, *Sowing the Mustard Seed*, First Edition, 149.

57   'Yusuf Lule Dies; Ex-Uganda Leader', *New York Times* (23 January 1985).

58   Uganda Hansard 30 January 2001, Second Reading of National Honours and Awards Bill, 1999.

59   Uganda Hansard 31 January 2001, Second Reading of National Honours and Awards Bill, 1999.

60   Interview with Office of the President official, Kampala, 29 January 2018.

61   Field notes, Kampala and Arua during and in the aftermath of National Liberation Day celebrations, January and March 2018.

62   Museveni, *What Is Africa's Problem?* 61.

63   Fisher, *East Africa after Liberation*, 237.

64   Tamale Mirundi, 'Kategaya's Return Is Proof of How the Movement Works', *New Vision* (31 May 2006).

65   Golooba-Mutebi and Hickey, 'The Master of Institutional'; Khisa, 'Inclusive Co-optation'.

66   The Star, 'NRM Championed End'; Kalyegira, 'NRM'; Alfred Wasike, 'Nakawa Jubilates', *New Vision* (27 January 1994).

67   *The Star*, 'NRM Championed End'.

68   Field notes, National Liberation Day ceremony, 26 January 2018.

69   Ibid.

70   Interview with local educator and local religious leader, Rwampara County, 27 January 2018.

71   Interview with NRM Secretariat official, Kampala, 29 January 2018.

72 Interview with NRM Secretariat official, Kampala, 29 January 2018.

73 Benson Herbert Oluka and Siraje Lubwana, 'I helped Museveni's Opponents – Sejusa', *The Observer* (5 November 2014).

74 Fisher, *East Africa after Liberation*, 238–9.

75 Makara et al., 'Turnaround', 190.

76 Ibid.

77 Ibid., 190.

78 Interview with local NRM official and councillor, Arua, 23 March 2018.

79 Stephen Ssenkaaba, 'Kabamba Monument: Art's Towering Tribute to Uganda's Liberation', *New Vision* (9 March 2018); Interview with George Kyeyune, Associate Professor (Makerere University) and artist, Kampala, 21 January 2018.

80 Interview with former senior NEC official, Kampala, 21 January 2018; Ssenkaaba, 'Kabamba Monument'.

81 Cawood and Fisher, 'It should be'.

82 David Mwambari and Iris Nxumalo, 'Harnessing Memory Institutions for Peace and Justice: The Case of South Africa', in *Postconflict Institutional Design: Peacebuilding and Democracy in Africa,* ed. Abu Bah (London: Zed Books, 2020).

83 'Ugandan Leader Yoweri Museveni Begins Six-day Trek through Jungle', *Guardian* (4 January 2020). https://www.theguardian.com/world/2020/jan/04/yoweri-museveni-begins-six-day-trek-through-uganda-jungle (accessed 12 August 2022).

84 https://filmfreeway.com/27Guns (accessed 12 August 2022).

85 Interview with NRM Secretariat official, Kampala, 29 January 2018.

3

Museveni and government-foreign business relations in the electricity sector[1]

Roger Tangri and Andrew M. Mwenda

In the 1990s, Uganda had a moribund, state-run power sector.[2] As part of its reform agenda oriented towards creating a market economy based on private ownership, the World Bank began advocating for privately owned companies to revive the country's ailing electricity system. Under its 1999 Electricity Act, the NRM government agreed to liberalize the electricity market and turn to large-scale private firms to alleviate serious power supply problems. In 2002, the government released its power strategy which prioritized greater foreign private company participation in the construction of hydroelectric dams as well as investment in power distribution.[3] In fact, in 2001, the government had on the advice of the World Bank awarded a contract to a United States energy giant, AES (Applied Energy Services), to build a new dam on the River Nile. After this scheme – referred to here as Bujagali 1 – collapsed in 2002–03, the government, again in consultation with the Bank, awarded another contract to an international consortium, Bujagali Electricity Limited (BEL), to build and operate a hydropower dam – Bujagali 2 – on the Nile.[4] In 2005, and on the Bank's advice, a major concession was awarded to another foreign consortium, to be known by its acronym UMEME (the KiSwahili word for electrical power) to invest and manage electricity distribution.

During the 1990s and 2000s, both the NRM government and these foreign companies cooperated closely especially as their mutual interests dovetailed. But they diverged in the 2010s when private profit exceeded public benefits and as major financial liabilities were created for the government. In the past decade, President Yoweri Museveni has looked to Chinese state companies to build new hydropower plants instead of relying on much-criticized World Bank-supported private Western consortia. But profit-making Chinese dam construction firms are producing additional budgetary burdens on government while access and affordability outcomes remain limited.

This chapter provides a political account of the relations between the NRM government and Western and Chinese firms investing in the construction of hydropower dams (generating nearly 90 per cent of Uganda's electricity) as well as in distribution networks. It focuses especially on the relations between President

Museveni and these international companies and how their respective interests and interactions have shaped electricity outcomes. The next section outlines our main argument, namely, that cooperation between the Museveni government and the World Bank and later China's Eximbank regarding electricity provision has benefitted foreign firms at the expense of domestic consumers and public finances. Although in Uganda's semi-authoritarian political system, Museveni has had the final say in the making of electricity deals, the greater bargaining strength of World Bank and Chinese-supported foreign companies *vis-à-vis* the president and his advisors has influenced power sector contract negotiations. We also argue that Museveni's strong personal involvement in electricity governance involving limited parliamentary and public consultation has tarnished his reputation as a reforming leader protecting and promoting the national interest.

Outline of the Argument

There are two key interconnected themes in the governance of energy in Uganda. The first concerns the specific terms of power sector contracts negotiated by foreign firms with the NRM government. These contracts, we contend, have been structured more in the interests of foreign companies than to the electric power needs of Ugandan citizens.

The World Bank was at the forefront in urging the government and most prominently the president to adopt a market and private sector approach to electricity provision. But in the 1990s and 2000s, foreign capital was reluctant to invest in Uganda's dilapidated power sector unless it was assured of guarantees covering various commercial, financial and hydraulic risks. The Bank advised the government on the required risk-mitigation measures which were incorporated into power purchase and concession agreements signed with foreign investors.[5]

For instance, foreign firms required guarantees of a fixed and high rate of return on investment. They required an assurance as well from government to bulk-purchase all the electricity they generated and bulk-supply all the power they needed for distribution. And they sought buy-out clauses, which would make it costly for the government to terminate contracts. In addition, the Bank was closely involved with the government in implementing pricing reforms to improve cost recovery and operational efficiency. Cost-reflective tariffs would cover the full cost of supplying electricity and generate the desired returns on investment for foreign profit-seeking companies.

With the backing of the World Bank as well as several Western embassies, especially from the UK and the United States, companies from these countries held the upper hand in their negotiations with the government. International firms were able to win important contractual terms and conditions which minimized their investment risks as well as enabling them to achieve high profit levels. The Bank had also for several years been cultivating the president and senior finance and energy ministry officials to its pro-market ideas, making the latter ideologically disposed to accepting the specific power sector contract terms which foreign companies required as a condition of local investment. As we will see in the case studies, because so few foreign companies were interested in investing in Uganda's decrepit power sector, the successful bidders were able to virtually dictate the terms of the power purchase and concession agreements they desired. Noteworthy, too, was that non-transparent contracts were kept secret and therefore unavailable for public scrutiny.

Explicit emphasis was placed in the contracts and concessions awarded to BEL and UMEME to expand electricity generation capacity, rehabilitate and strengthen distribution infrastructure as well as implement cost-covering tariffs. Only with the commissioning of Bujagali 2 in 2012 did government's key policy goals of ensuring affordable consumer tariffs and expanding access to electricity assume prominence on the reform agenda. However, various contractual guarantees, anti-risk measures and cost-reflective tariffs have negatively impacted the achievement of access and affordability objectives.

For instance, the high rate of return on investments, which was factored into the tariff, contributed to persistently elevated consumer power prices and, in consequence, low access to electricity. Contracts also allowed 'for the pass-through of all costs to the tariff'.[6] Foreign companies were able to recoup their investments as well as the cost of their loans directly from the tariff. Transferring all these and other costs to the retail tariff led to rising prices stifling business as well as making electricity expensive for domestic households. On the other hand, international firms derived high profits from their investments at the expense of local consumers. As Bosshard noted in his critique of Power Purchase Agreements (PPAs) in developing countries, they provided 'sweetheart deals for private investors, guaranteeing them high profits at low risk, while entailing major costs for the public'.[7]

The Electricity Regulatory Authority (ERA), established in 2000, was given the mandate to oversee foreign companies to ensure they complied with their licences. The ERA was responsible for setting the end-user power tariffs after computing the generation, transmission and distribution companies' reasonable costs. The retail price of electricity had to cover the full cost of provision under the system of cost-recovery which was essential to the profitability of foreign capital. Up to 2012, an inexperienced ERA was hardly able to constrain the operations of foreign business in the power sector. In recent years, however, ERA officials have expressed concern that the cost-reflective tariff placed a heavy burden on consumers and industries. The regulator now includes among its core focus areas affordable tariffs and accelerating access, which it seeks to achieve mainly through cutting generation and distribution costs.[8] But protecting electricity consumers from 'unrealistic' costs has led to considerable friction between the regulator and especially UMEME, the monopoly power distributing company.[9] On the other hand, finance ministry officials as well as the ERA have sought to constrain BEL's huge generation costs on the tariff by re-negotiating agreements, especially with the foreign consortium's financiers.

Our second main theme relates to President Museveni's prominent involvement, initially with the World Bank and later with China, in key aspects of the governance of electricity. Uganda is a semi-authoritarian state where since 1986 political power has been concentrated and centralized in the hands of a powerful president. From the early

1990s, President Museveni became committed to developing Uganda's electrification by partnering with Western firms, in the belief that this would help promote industry, citizen well-being and legitimize his leadership. By developing close working relations with him, the World Bank enhanced the centrality of the president in electricity decision-making. Because of his prominent position, foreign company representatives often directly approached the president, with numerous meetings involving foreign firms, Museveni and his small circle of advisors taking place at State House. Museveni has been ultimately responsible for approving which companies obtain power sector contracts and concessions. As we will see, this was most evident regarding Chinese dam construction companies, where Museveni personally selected which companies should be awarded contracts, a decision also informed by political considerations. For instance, and as detailed below, he was able to choose Chinese firms which were being fronted by close political allies and family members. Alternatively, he turned against Chinese companies being supported by political rivals.

However, and as noted above, the much stronger bargaining strength of international economic actors has meant that they have been able to determine the specific terms and conditions of contracts favourable to the interests of foreign companies. Museveni has also generally allowed international firms operational independence and hardly intervened in their operations. Moreover, he has avoided breaching contracts regarding foreign firms he was critical of. Such interventions would have undermined Uganda's credibility among foreign investors as well as damaged the country's cordial relations with the West and China, whose diplomatic and political benefits have been important for Museveni's preservation of power.

During the 1990s and 2000s, the president's relationship with BEL and UMEME was a cooperative one on account of mutually shared interests. Museveni directly engaged the firms in private talks and personally approved specific terms and conditions of their contracts and concessions. Especially between 2002 and 2007, when the need to expand power supply was urgent, Museveni accepted the demands of these companies for contractual guarantees, which forced the government to bear most of the costs and risks. Many of the senior technocrats in the finance and energy ministries also accepted that specific guarantees were a necessity in order to lower investment risks in the generation and distribution sectors. Otherwise, according to a former energy minister, no agreement would be concluded, and Uganda's power problems would be compounded.[10]

From the 2010s on, and as we will consider below, the president has faced a drumbeat of criticism from civil society and parliament regarding the power contracts focusing more on the interests of Western private firms than on the benefits to Uganda's wider society. As Museveni himself has grown displeased with the excessive terms of the agreements – and sought to renegotiate parts of them – his relationship with BEL and UMEME has become more conflictual. Museveni, the finance ministry and the ERA have sought cuts in guaranteed returns on investments as well as a decrease in the price of generated power and distribution, both to lower end-user tariffs and to ease the financial burdens on government.

Since 2012, Museveni has become outspoken in his criticism of profit-seeking private Western investors. Thus, the president has sought to reclaim control of generation and distribution projects by reverting towards government ownership and management. Because of budgetary constraints, however, Museveni has instead turned to Chinese-funded investment to finance Uganda's power needs. He has personally awarded contracts to Chinese state companies to construct hydropower plants, which would be owned and operated by government and meet goals of public access and affordability. But Uganda's power tariffs have remained high in comparison to other East African countries, and new problems of excess capacity and accompanying budgetary liabilities have emerged. As we seek to show in the following case studies, the Ugandan experience of pursuing national electricity provision *via* profit-seeking international firms has proven to be highly contentious, as well as damaging to Museveni's political reputation to achieve publicly stated government goals in the national interest.

Bujagali 1

Up to the 1990s, Uganda's sole energy source was the Owen Falls (now Nalubaale) hydroelectric dam built in 1954. It was refurbished in 1991 but still only generated 180-megawatt (MW), at least 100MW less than required. Construction of a second power plant, Kiira, began in 1993 but took ten years to complete. To relieve Uganda's power supply deficit, the World Bank advised President Museveni to approve construction of a new, large-scale electricity generation plant. In 1994, however, only one foreign company responded to Uganda's invitation to overseas energy firms to construct a hydroelectric dam. The same year, President Museveni signed a Memorandum of Understanding with AES Nile Power Limited (AESNP), an affiliate of the big US-based energy corporation, AES, which gave the company the first right of refusal to build a new dam at Bujagali Falls on the Nile.[11]

In 1997 the Bank offered financial support for a new hydropower project in Uganda. The following year, the government invited AESNP to enter a contract to build and operate a power dam at Bujagali. President Museveni spoke publicly in favour of the company, which also had a close working relationship with the World Bank, being one of the biggest recipients of funding in recent years from the Bank's private finance arm, the International Finance Corporation.[12] Interviews with finance ministry officials in 1998 and 1999 also indicated that Museveni was under pressure from the US ambassador to give the contract to an American company and thereby cement his emerging cordial relationship with the Clinton administration. Later in 1998, a draft PPA was negotiated between the Ministry of Energy and Mineral Development (MEMD) and AESNP.

In January 1999, the Minister of Energy Richard Kaijuka took the PPA to Parliament for approval of the contract for the $523 million 250MW power generation facility. The parliamentary Committee on the National Economy, however, objected to various provisions, including the hydraulic guarantee as well as the 'take-or-pay' clauses, which respectively required the government to pay for a predetermined volume of electricity even if the plant was unable to generate this amount because of low water flows, or even if there was insufficient demand for the power from consumers. The legislators also criticized a provision which compelled the government to buy all the power produced at a cost of $0.06 per kilowatt-hour, amounting to a cost of $100 million a year for thirty years. Isaac Musumba, the committee chair, calculated that within eight years, AESNP would recoup enough to cover initial investment and interest, constituting an excessive rate of profitability. He questioned that the tariff charge was too high. A comparative price in Kenya at the time was about $0.036.[13]

The Committee also had another major concern, namely, that a Norwegian consortium, NORPAK Power Limited, lobbying for a concession to build a power dam at Karuma Falls on the Nile appeared to be offering a much better deal, which undercut AESNP's proposal in several ways. Committee members contended that the AESNP scheme would not only take longer to produce power but would also do so at much higher expense and would result in a higher tariff for the consumer. NORPAK was offering to build a 200MW underground facility for $300 million, which showed that Bujagali was more expensive.[14]

NORPAK and AESNP became engaged in an intense contest to win the contract for building a new power plant in Uganda and be supported by World Bank funding. The energy minister was alleged to have been given incentives by AESNP to advocate its case within the energy ministry as well as to block NORPAK's proposal in government circles.[15] After MPs rejected three attempts by Kaijuka to have them approve the PPA, the government began renegotiating with AESNP. The revised PPA reduced the price of power, removed the hydraulic guarantee and AESNP also agreed to put up a performance bond of $12 million.

In March 2000, an amended agreement was presented by Kaijuka's successor and approved by Parliament. Allegations surfaced that many committee members received financial inducements to approve the revised PPA, and some MPs complained 'they were bullied into it by President Museveni amid threats that the U.S. aid budget depended on accepting the AES bid'.[16] Critics of the PPA were regularly dismissed by the president as 'ignorant' and 'economic saboteurs', especially when, like Isaac Musumba, they argued that the annual capacity payment would cause 'the financial ruin of Uganda' as well as high tariff levels.[17] In his determined support of the dam project, Museveni ignored the financial obligations inherent in successive versions of the PPA. For his part, Musumba would be vindicated in calling for the overpriced dam project to be reviewed.

The Ugandan government and the World Bank decided not to make the PPA public. When the High Court obliged the government to release the PPA as a public document in November 2002, an independent team of energy experts from India, the Prayas Energy Group, determined the dam project capital cost to be 'excessively high' and likely to produce electricity that would be unaffordable to most consumers. The review claimed the World Bank had misled the government and the public about how grossly overpriced the Bujagali project was, especially compared to NORPAK's Karuma dam on which the Bank had been silent. According to Prayas, the PPA obligated the government to make yearly payments of $132 million amounting to around $4 billion over the thirty-year lifetime of the contract.

In sum, the PPA was deemed to be 'substantially unfavourable' to the Ugandan government and people.[18] However, in 2001 the World Bank had approved a

$225 million package of loans and guarantees for the project. And financial closure was reached the same year between AES Corporation and the government. Bujagali 1 was to commence construction in early 2002 and be commissioned by the end of 2005. But in 2002, AES Corporation suddenly pulled out of the project, writing off $75 million it had invested. The Bank terminated the project in September 2003.

Bujagali 2

Despite these setbacks, President Museveni and the World Bank remained strongly committed to the Bujagali dam project. In early 2004 the NRM government with the support of the Bank initiated a process soliciting the interest of prospective private investors to develop the hydropower plant. Three companies reached the final assessment stage and following a transparent selection process, BEL was invited to negotiate a contract.

Subsequently, in December 2005, a PPA was signed between BEL and the government to construct and operate the now $565 million 250MW dam. BEL was a consortium owned by Industrial Promotion Services (IPS), a holding company of the Kenya-based Aga Khan Fund for Economic Development, and SG Bujagali Holdings, an affiliate of Sithe Global Power, part of Blackstone, a large US-based private equity fund. In April 2007, the World Bank approved $374.8 million in loans and guarantees for the new project. Financial closure was reached between the Bank, BEL and financiers, with BEL being awarded a thirty-year concession over the now $682 million dam.[19] Construction began in September 2007.

President Museveni was anxious to conclude a contract with BEL, especially after the debacle of the Bujagali 1 project. From 2004, Uganda also began facing an increasing electricity deficit, partly because of limited power production from the Kiira and Nalubaale dams. And when a severe drought struck in 2005 and reduced the amount of water, the two dams began producing at only one-third of their capacity. It was in this context of a severe power shortfall that the government rushed into accepting what the president later often referred to as a highly 'unfavourable' contract with BEL.

Although there was a competitive bidding process, overseen by the World Bank, much of the contracting, according to interviewees, was conducted privately between President Museveni and the Aga Khan, accompanied by their officials. Museveni was determined to see the project start producing energy as quickly as possible and end acute power shortages. The president was willing to agree to extremely attractive terms in the thirty-year PPA being offered to the consortium. For instance, the rate of return specified in the agreement was 19 per cent a year on the equity invested in the project. The PPA contained a 'take-or-pay' clause which obliged the government to pay for a set quantity of electricity – 250MW – even if demand for this amount could not absorb it. The government also assumed the hydrological risk of the dam, agreeing to pay for the full amount of power when low water levels generated less than the projected supply.

In addition, Museveni personally approved without consulting the finance ministry a corporation tax holiday for the first ten years – 2007–17 – of operations.[20] Noteworthy was that in its press release, Blackstone reported the project would produce 'power at a levelised cost of approximately $0.065' per kilowatt-hour. The PPA was not publicly released because it would have caused controversy, not least for the president. Nor was it approved by parliament, as was also the case with loans for the project.[21]

In late 2007, when the Aga Khan was unable to give the main contractor a letter of credit for $97 million, Museveni agreed to advance BEL the money to kick-start the project to avoid any further delays. By then, the estimated cost of the dam had increased to $798 million, with the approval of the government. Why the cost of the dam had risen so appreciably since the signing of the PPA in 2005 remained unclear. Part of the reason was, as reported many years later in a World Bank publication, that 'in a situation of limited competition and a large difference in bidding prices, the price increased by $90 million (19 per cent) during negotiations'.[22] That Bujagali 2 would be a high-priced dam was evident to energy and finance ministry officials during the contract negotiations. Yet they agreed with Museveni that expensive hydropower was better than none.[23]

Of the five years it took to complete Bujagali 2, two were marked by an acute electricity crisis in Uganda. To alleviate the power shortages, the government brought in expensive, new emergency diesel power plants. To keep the price of electricity from these plants down, the government spent a staggering $624 million on electricity subsidies between 2005 and 2011. When the Bujagali 2 power plant was commissioned in October 2012, it boosted Uganda's power capacity, reduced the frequent power cuts and outages and abolished the extremely costly subsidies. At the inauguration of the dam, the chairman of BEL reported that it had cost $902 million to construct the plant.[24] Shortly thereafter, however, MPs on a parliamentary committee on energy claimed that the actual cost was even higher and contended that Bujagali 2 was the most expensive dam in the world for its size. For instance, each megawatt of power cost $3.6 million, more than double the average cost for similar power plants in developing countries.[25]

The significant increase in the cost of Bujagali 2 was also the result of expensive loan financing. The World Bank estimated the total cost of the project at $798 million of which three-quarters was borrowed from a group of international financiers. BEL secured 22 per cent of equity financing but the government borrowed the remaining 78 per cent. The high borrowing costs were to be repaid by local customers from the end-user tariff.[26] Because of expensive generation, BEL was to sell power at $0.10 per kilowatt-hour with the tariff set to rise to $0.13 when the corporate tax holiday Museveni had personally awarded expired in 2017. The excessive cost of Bujagali power continued to put electricity beyond the reach of most Ugandans. The subsequent response of BEL to multiple criticisms regarding project costs and expensive power was that 'the Government approved the entire project, including project cost and terms of financing'.[27]

On the other hand, the contract deal ensured huge corporate profits for BEL investors. This began when BEL as per the PPA started earning its 19 per cent rate of return immediately dam construction started. During the first four years of construction, BEL did not earn a return because no revenue was being generated. Instead, the rate of return was compounded to the equity, as follows:

Year	Equity	Return
2008	$179 million	$34 million
2009	$213 million	$40 million
2010	$253 million	$49 million
2011	$302 million	$57 million

In 2012, BEL received revenue and a rate of return on $360 million. It earned legally $200 million while constructing the dam, much to the dismay of Museveni and finance ministry officials who, according to interviews, were unaware of the contractual conditions.[28]

BEL has posted regular after-tax profits since 2011–12, when it made $20 million. In 2012, the plant was reported to have made $32 million; in 2013, $66 million; and in 2014, $42 million.[29] 'A cash flow projection', showed that BEL would 'earn enormous profits' in subsequent years. In the first thirteen years, when BEL was paying back its huge loans, it was expected to earn between $906 million and $1.4 billion, depending on the tariff for Bujagali power.[30] The profitability of BEL was also evident in figures from the sale of Sithe Global. Sithe had served as the lead investor and invested $116 million of equity in BEL (compared to $63 million from IPS). In July 2018, a Norwegian company announced it had acquired Sithe's two-thirds stake in BEL for $278 million.[31] Ugandan tax authorities were thwarted in collecting capital gains tax amounting to $83 million from the transaction for various reasons; perhaps because the deal was done in off-shore, low-tax jurisdictions as well as because Museveni did not want to upset relations with prospective US investors.

President Museveni publicly decried the high cost of Bujagali power. Because Bujagali 2 was unable to deliver electricity at cheaper rates, the president's claims that the project was a vital instrument of economic transformation were proving a pipe dream. In his 2014 'State of the Nation' address, Museveni declared he was 'going to engage the developers to find ways of refinancing this project' so that the end-user tariff would be $0.05 per kilowatt-hour and make local industries competitive. During his 2015 'State of the Nation' address, he proposed a buyout to take over the dam. He wished he had asked BEL only to build the dam and not also operate it. However, he soon dropped the proposal when made aware of the stiff penalties involved in terminating the contract. It is also doubtful he would have bought Bujagali 2 outright as that would have alienated him from foreign investors, the World Bank as well as the US Commerce department.

Museveni's bargaining power was clearly limited on this matter. Instead, finance ministry officials began working with BEL and the lenders to restructure and refinance loans that would lower Bujagali's power tariffs. BEL's representatives were unreceptive to the idea put forward by finance officials of reducing the fixed rate of return to bring down the cost of power. Such an arrangement would also complicate Sithe's proposed Norwegian deal which was based on maintaining the existing high level of profitability.

In July 2018, Museveni directed finance officials to break a deadlock in negotiations by accepting all the demands of the financiers, which included extending loan maturities to 2032 rather than the original 2023; providing a corporation tax waiver of about $28 million per annum until 2027 instead of 2017; and not compromising the proprietor's guaranteed rate of return of 19 per cent (instead of reducing BEL's return on equity from 19 to 15 per cent as the Ugandan officials wanted).[32] Finance ministry officials suggested to us that Museveni was willing to commit the government to huge annual payments just to be able to claim that he had reduced the end-user tariff, although still not to $0.05 per kilowatt-hour.

The re-financing agreement led to generation costs dropping from $0.13 to $0.08 especially for industry. This was publicly welcomed by the president, even though it was a short-term reduction for six years, whereas BEL continued to receive annual income tax waivers of $28 million for a further ten years. The government was also still left with huge financial liabilities stemming from expensive dam construction loan terms and which are passed through directly to the tariff. For instance, the average annual capacity payment to repay BEL's loans as well as the guaranteed rate of return from the tariff amounted to $120 million in 2021.[33] Moreover, because of low water levels, Bujagali 2 has been unable to generate at full throttle – on average it has operated at 67 per cent capacity. But the government is contractually obliged to pay for the full volume of power through the tariff.

Much anger was expressed by government officials about high returns and profits for BEL derived at the expense of the energy needs of local people. In 2020 BEL's profit for the year was $56.8 million while in 2021 it had risen to $79.8 million.[34] Legislators and environmental organizations also did not spare Museveni from criticism. They scoffed at his excuses for explaining the high cost of Bujagali power. As the head of the National Association of Professional Environmentalists put it, 'We are telling the government that to benefit from these mega projects …, it needs to consult widely and listen instead of rushing into agreements that turn out to be too costly for us.'[35] Confronted by a cascade of criticism, Museveni initially denied the crisis was of his making, and that he had accepted unrealistic claims from the World Bank. Speaking at the NRM's National Conference in 2020, however, Museveni described his decision to sanction the Bujagali financial arrangements as a grave error of judgement on his part: 'I made a mistake of accepting expensive money without adequate consultations,' he said.[36]

UMEME

From 2002, the government began engaging with foreign companies to find a private sector operator for the electricity distribution system. Several companies conducted their due diligence on the sector. All but one left the country without submitting a bid. In 2004, however, following a protracted two-year negotiation process, a joint venture between the UK government's Commonwealth Development Corporation and specifically its subsidiary Globeleq Holdings Limited (with a 56 per cent shareholding) and the South African parastatal, ESKOM Enterprises (with 44 per cent) was offered the concession for managing power distribution. In March 2005, the consortium concluded a twenty-year concession agreement with the government. It also entered a power sales agreement with Uganda Electricity Transmission Company Limited (UETCL) to avail it of power to distribute and negotiated a lease agreement to use the distribution assets of Uganda Electricity Distribution Company Limited (UEDCL). The private concessionaire came under the regulation of the ERA.

The consortium, later renamed UMEME Limited, was virtually the only viable foreign firm considered for the distribution concession. As such, it was able to secure highly favourable contract terms and guarantees. The contract itself has remained a closely guarded document. Under the agreement, UMEME became Uganda's predominant power distributor as well as a profitable private monopoly. The contract assured UMEME a return on investment of 20 per cent per annum. World Bank guarantees also underwrote the agreement, protecting the investor from financial, regulatory and political risks. For instance, severe penalties would be payable by government in case of a breach or termination of contract.

The agreement tasked UMEME between 2005 and 2012 to invest a minimum of $65 million to improve the distribution network, reduce power losses, expand the collection rate and increase the number of connections to end-users.[37] With the exit of ESKOM in 2006, Globeleq, now the sole owner of UMEME, was confronted by a serious drought resulting in huge power shortages. Supported by the International Finance Corporation of the World Bank, Globeleq renegotiated parts of the concession agreement with the government. The ERA accepted that UMEME not be bound by the original performance targets, particularly the loss-reduction targets, at least until Bujagali 2 came on stream.

Following incessant criticism of the power distributor for multiple tariff hikes amid frequent blackouts and load-shedding, UMEME became the subject of two official inquiries. In 2009, the Ministry of Energy constituted a 'Committee for Interim Review of Electricity Tariff' chaired by the President's brother, General Salim Saleh, a presidential advisor.[38] Its recommendations, all damning of UMEME, called for the termination of the company's distribution concession, primarily because it was not in the national interest.[39] The second public inquiry undertaken in 2011–12 by an *ad hoc* parliamentary committee investigated what it termed 'the electricity crisis in the country'.[40]

In a provocative November 2013 report, it argued that UMEME had failed to reduce 'high energy losses', lower 'high power tariffs' and had exaggerated its investments in allegedly seeking to rehabilitate the 'still dilapidated infrastructure'. The committee also objected to UMEME's concession contract which was 'crafted to strongly favour the private concessionaire at the expense of Uganda in terms of return on investment, arbitration, buy-out conditions on termination of the contract and risk allocation'. The report referred as well to 'the soft targets set for UMEME' and claimed that for each '1 per cent loss UMEME was compensated the equivalent of $4 million through the tariff'.[41] It followed the Saleh report in proposing that UMEME's power distribution concession be cancelled, a recommendation endorsed in April 2014 by the full Parliament. Both inquiries also commented that while Ugandans were suffering severe power shortages and rising power tariffs, UMEME was making 'supernormal' profits. In 2010, the company was reported as having made a gross profit of $24 million compared to its share capital of just $9.8 million.[42]

UMEME responded by declaring the parliamentary report erroneous and misinformed.[43] It claimed, for instance, that its distribution costs contributed only 25 per cent to the power tariff, the remaining 75 per cent being the result of high generation and transmission costs. However, critics have always disputed these figures, with President Museveni and others stating, as noted below, that UMEME's costs contributed around 35 per cent of the final consumer price. Secondly, UMEME reported that the ERA had re-established collection and loss reduction targets in 2010 as electricity supply constraints gradually eased. From that time, the company had reduced energy losses from 38 per cent to 26 per cent, increased collection of revenue from 75 per cent to 98 percent, made 220,000 instead of 60,000 connections, and markedly improved the distribution network because of its investments totalling $130 million – all in the first seven years of the contract. Indeed, UMEME claimed it had surpassed all the performance targets set for it under the concession and was well on its way to achieving the new targets it had negotiated with the regulator for the next period.[44]

President Museveni as well as the cabinet dismissed the reports' recommendations for cancelling the contract with UMEME. The energy minister supported the power distributor's claims by saying 'it is a fact that UMEME fulfilled the targets set in the concession agreement'.[45] She shunned the criticisms of legislators, warning that terminating UMEME's concession would oblige the government to pay huge sums in severance costs. She also argued that cancelling the contract would alienate the World Bank as well as seriously deter potential foreign investment in Uganda's energy sector.[46]

Noteworthy, too, was that in May 2012, UMEME had sold 38 per cent of its stock to the public and was listed on the Uganda Securities Exchange (USE). An estimated 4,300–6,000 Ugandans bought shares and would have to be compensated if government ended the concession. By listing on the USE, UMEME cushioned itself against hostile actions such as those called for by Uganda's Parliament. As a publicly listed company, UMEME has also sought to counter widespread concerns of it being a foreign company, indeed a private monopoly, controlling distribution in a national strategic economic sector. Since November 2016, Uganda's state pension fund, the National Social Security Fund (NSSF), has become the largest shareholder in UMEME with a stake of 23 per cent. Ugandan investors hold a further 13 per cent and combined with NSSF own a significant stake in UMEME.[47] Yet, public and parliamentary perceptions of the private operator have remained quite negative, not least because of clear evidence that a foreign company is profiting at the expense of Ugandans.

ERA vs UMEME

In 2012, the ERA set performance targets for UMEME's next seven-year contract period, 2012–19. Under the new plan, the concessionaire agreed to reduce energy losses which legislators deemed as unacceptably high at 26 per cent in 2012. In 2018, UMEME declared it had reduced losses to 16.9 per cent although this was still well below the target set by ERA of 14.7 per cent. Critics continued to point to losses declining too slowly, despite claims by the chairman of UMEME that the company had invested $627 million in the distribution network by the end of 2018.[48] Indeed, the Saleh report accused UMEME of defrauding government to the tune of UGS34.4 billion between 2005 and 2009 by over-declaring losses. UMEME received $61.5 million in 2014 in compensation for losses and it was projected to receive $55.5 million in 2015, $51.3 million in 2016, $47.7 million in 2017 and $44.7 million in 2018, all through the tariff.[49]

In 2018, UMEME and the industry regulator began negotiating new performance targets for the period 2019 to 2025. ERA officials generally accepted that improvements in operational efficiency and financial performance had occurred over the previous seven years. However, they wanted the power distributor not only to continue improving in many areas but specifically bring down energy losses as well as various costs which could be recovered from consumers through the power tariffs. To reduce end-user electricity tariffs, which, according to phone interviews with ERA officials in 2020, were nearly double the price at which UMEME purchased power from UETCL, the regulator proposed that UMEME reduce the investments it makes as well as only earn a 20 per cent return on investments with ERA's approval. ERA capped UMEME's operation, distribution and maintenance costs to about one-half of what UMEME proposed for the period. With its improved planning capacity, ERA sought to guide UMEME to invest in critical areas and disallow the company from dictating where and how to invest as well as what would be absorbed in the tariff.

UMEME appealed the new targets, arguing it needed to invest more money if more Ugandans were to be connected to the grid. It would then recoup this investment through the power tariff. But the ERA 'faced with some public unrest over the power tariff that many feel is too high' countered, by claiming the power distributor could achieve the customer connections with less money.[50] Finally, to achieve affordable tariffs, ERA also required UMEME in the new performance period to reduce energy losses to 11.13 per cent by 2025. UMEME responded by warning the regulator that the proposed spending cuts would also limit its ability to meet the loss reduction target. Indeed, in 2018–19, UMEME's distribution losses had grown to 17.2 per cent.

UMEME concession extension

In 2017, there was an urgent need to extend the transmission and distribution infrastructure to evacuate new generated power from the upcoming Karuma and Isimba dams (see below). The finance ministry estimated that a total of $3 billion would be needed of which 30 per cent would be for transmission and 70 per cent for distribution. Various companies expressed interest and lobbied to get the potentially lucrative distribution contract. The overseers of the UMEME concession, the UEDCL proposed reducing gradually the investments UMEME was making and calling on government to invest more of its own money in the network. In 2025, UMEME's concession would expire, and government would be the primary investor in modernizing the power distribution system.

UMEME, too, began expressing a strong interest in having its concession extended beyond 2025. UMEME had been making an after-tax profit every year since 2011.

The company's guaranteed 20 per cent return on investment as well as monopolistic position ensured its profitability: in 2011 – $9.22 million; 2012 – $21.26 million; 2014 – $24 million; 2016 – approximately $38 million; dropping in 2017 to $9.8 million, rising to $33.7 million in 2018 and $35.3 million in 2019. In 2018 it started lobbying for an extension, both touting its achievements over the years as well as arguing that given its experience it was better placed than any other company to distribute power in Uganda. To achieve its new performance targets, it announced plans for further financial investment. It also proposed investing $120 million ahead of the proposed commissioning of the Karuma dam in 2020. UMEME estimated Uganda would need to invest $1.2 to $1.5 billion over the next seven years to expand the distribution network and absorb the electricity capacity. But to mobilize long-term capital for such massive investment UMEME required a long-term contract, it argued.

However, in a March 2018 letter to the Minister of Energy, President Museveni advised that UMEME's concession not be renewed because of the persistently high costs of distributing electricity and continuing high energy losses. Referring to the *ad hoc* parliamentary committee report of 2013, Museveni reiterated its argument that the concession 'started with fraud of inflating the magnitude of the technical and commercial losses' from 28 per cent to 40 per cent.[51] He also wanted to know 'if they have invested so much money, why do the technical losses not decline'? In the meantime, 'there should be no question of renewing UMEME's concession'.[52] In his January 2019 New Year's message, Museveni alleged that UMEME's distribution costs accounted for 34 per cent of the end-user power tariff and were a key 'distorter' in the energy supply chain, stifling government efforts to bring down the cost of power for consumers, especially industrialists.[53] Talk of a possible termination of the twenty-year concession hit UMEME shares on the Uganda Securities Exchange.

Museveni's highly unusual letter provided little factual basis for its many assertions. Government officials suggest it may have been part of a plan to influence subsequent negotiations with the power distributor. Museveni may have been posturing as within a month he was in private talks with UMEME representatives. In November 2018, following a series of meetings which included finance ministry officials, Museveni suddenly directed the Minister of Energy and the Attorney General to finalize negotiations for the extension of UMEME's concession beyond 2025 to enable the concessionaire to undertake the urgent investments needed to distribute the new generated power. In Museveni's words, drawn from media reports, the negotiations should seek to 'provide better terms that lower tariff'.[54]

For the government there were many contentious provisions in the concession contract. The fixed rate of return stipulated in the contract rankled the president and finance ministry officials, especially as they believed it had a significant impact on the final consumer tariff. They wanted UMEME to accept a cut in the fixed rate of return from 20 to 12 per cent while the company was insisting on at least 15 per cent.[55] There were also serious concerns about UMEME's compensation from distribution losses being factored into the end-user tariff, and which contributed to the high electricity rates. In addition, UMEME's purported levels of investment had for over a decade been viewed by government as highly exaggerated. Government officials insisted that only those investment costs verified by ERA should be recouped from power tariffs, a view that had engendered much heat between the two parties, although it was incorporated in the new performance targets set for UMEME.

In 2020 it was rumoured that Museveni had agreed to extend UMEME's contract for twenty years while UMEME had accepted a reduction in its rate of return to 13 per cent. Agreement was also reported to have been reached on the distributor's $450 million 2019–25 investment agenda. The ERA approved UMEME's plan to invest $83 million to connect 300,000 customers in 2020. But in a dramatic turnaround, President Museveni appeared to reverse himself on the terms of the proposed concession renewal. Speaking at Independence Day celebrations in October 2020, he declared that 'UMEME's drive to generate profits for its shareholders has been the reason for the high-power costs in Uganda'. He contended that a private company could not sell power cheaply on account of its profit-making 'mentality'.[56] Six months later, Museveni was directing that power 'go straight from generation to the industrial parks, not through UMEME' as a way of cutting costs, a move that UMEME saw as terminating its concession.

Worthy of note in this acrimonious tussle is that UMEME does not have a major international godfather, such as the United States in the case of BEL. The president does not need to appease important international partners when making electricity distribution decisions. In addition, NSSF shareholders do not carry much political weight. Thus, unlike the situation in the 2000s when one-sided deals favourable to the interests of foreign companies were negotiated, the bargaining power of President Museveni is presently greater than that of UMEME on contract renewal.

Chinese hydropower dams

'Privately funded electricity was unaffordable for Uganda', declared President Museveni in 2014. 'We're not going back to private investors', he said.[57] Museveni preferred that government build its own power plants. 'Government-funded hydroelectric dams were cheaper' and would result in lower generation and end-user tariffs. Although publicly owned power plants would recoup their investment through the tariff like private power ones, there would be no return on equity and specific financial liabilities would be met by the national treasury. The tariff would therefore reflect debt servicing and operational costs and be able to produce more affordable power to households and businesses.

Under Uganda's Second National Development Plan (2015/16–2020/21), the government prioritized two big power projects, Karuma and Isimba to boost generation capacity. After ten years of Western private undertakings running the power sector, President Museveni turned to China to build and finance these dams while the government would, through UEGCL, own, manage and operate them. But as the following cases on Karuma and Isimba show, the agreements concluded between the Museveni government and Chinese firms have only partly produced the desired electricity development outcomes.

Karuma dam

In 2010, the Ministry of Energy invited bids for the construction of the 600MW hydropower plant in north-western Uganda. Three firms, two of which were Chinese, reached the pre-qualification round out of a total of six companies that bid. This was, however, the beginning of a protracted bidding process, mired in allegations of impropriety prompting lawsuits and investigations. A Chinese firm – China International Water and Electric Corporation (CWE) – was ranked first in the evaluation. CWE is the international arm of China Three Gorges Corporation (CTGC), a Chinese state corporation. CTGC was reported by Ministry of Energy officials after visiting China as having a good track record in building dams in China, Ethiopia and Ghana. SinoHydro Corporation was the other Chinese company. Allegations of bribery and police investigations as well as queries regarding CWE's technical and financial capacity to execute the project delayed the procurement process.[58]

In August 2012, however, the Attorney General and energy minister presented CWE corporate executives to President Museveni as representing the company that had won the deal. Reports appeared subsequently that the president had agreed to a secret deal for CWE to build the Karuma dam, while CTGC had agreed to guarantee the performance of CWE. A secret offer was made to CWE but was almost immediately withdrawn following presidential reservations.[59]

In January 2013, CWE was evaluated again as the best bidder. But the Inspector General of Government (IGG) – the Ombudsman – halted the bidding process on grounds of multiple irregularities.[60] In March, with the project over two years behind schedule, Museveni personally took charge to expedite the procurement. The president chose to work within a bilateral agreement with China rather than go through another lengthy evaluation process. He met with the new Chinese President, Xi Jinping, in South Africa and shortly afterwards China and Uganda sealed an agreement whereby China would fund the project and Uganda would choose either of the two qualified Chinese companies.[61]

Museveni sent a State House technical team to China to evaluate the technical competences of CWE/CTGC and SinoHydro. It discovered that CWE had not built any dams, although its parent firm, CTGC, was the largest producer/owner of hydropower dams in the world. The team also found that SinoHydro had built many dams, including dams for CTGC.[62] In June, following discussions with the Chinese embassy, a Memorandum of Understanding was signed between the Ministry of Energy and SinoHydro.

The direct award of the contract by Museveni was subsequently criticized by the Auditor General as contravening Uganda law. Hardly any engineering and financial audit was carried out of SinoHydro.[63] Museveni, however, according to several people with knowledge of the matter, gave the deal to SinoHydro on learning that CWE was being fronted by one of his leading NRM rivals. Moreover, a former US Trade Secretary and public relations consultant/advisor of the president was lobbying strongly for SinoHydro. By selecting SinoHydro for the Karuma contract, Museveni won support in both US and Chinese circles.

Museveni broke the ground for the start of construction in August 2013 well before the contract – which was not disclosed to the public – was signed and funding arrangements agreed. Only in mid-2015, did the state-backed China Eximbank agree to fund 85 per cent of the total project costs of $1.65 billion.[64] The power station was estimated to cost $1.38 billion and $287 million was for the associated transmission lines. Critics claimed that the project had in 2011 been costed by the Ministry of Energy at $900 million but the government argued the final figures corresponded to those quoted by CWE in its Karuma bid.[65] The government borrowed $1.435 billion from Eximbank of which $789 million was loaned at 2 per cent per annum repayable over twenty years, while $645 million would attract 4 per cent interest payable over fifteen years. Karuma would deliver electricity at $0.05 per kilowatt-hour, far more cheaply than the privately financed Bujagali 2 dam, declared a jubilant President Museveni.

Karuma's commissioning, however, has been delayed several times and pushed now to the middle of 2023. Part of the reason for the postponement was because the transmission lines would not be ready to evacuate power from the dam. SinoHydro demanded $166 million as compensation, arguing that delays were caused by the Ministry of Energy failing to acquire land for transmission lines. Relations between UEGCL and SinoHydro were often strained over various issues during construction. But unlike Bujagali 2 where UEGCL, the generation authority, was obliged to cover BEL's spiralling financing costs, in the words of SinoHydro's East Africa representative, the company 'will probably make some money' on the project but it 'cannot raise the [contract] price and has to bear the risk'.[66]

Chinese state companies are, however, largely profit-oriented while Eximbank allegedly inflated Karuma's costs to cover any contingencies as well as ensure a good return on the project. Worth noting is that in August 2020, the government requested a delay on the repayment of its loans for Karuma because the construction of the dam was taking much longer than planned. Eximbank, however, exists to make profits. It rejected the request and declared the government was obligated to repay its debts when the repayment period commenced on 25 December 2020. Uganda started paying interest on loans in 2021 while payment of the principal began in 2022. Also, according to information provided by finance ministry officials in 2022, the government is paying $500,000 per day for energy that Karuma is still not producing: the Ministry of Energy is contractually obliged to pay for this non-existent power.

Isimba dam

Although the IGG had in March 2013 described CWE's Karuma bid as riddled with 'irregularities and falsehoods', in July the government signed a Memorandum of Understanding with the Chinese company to construct a 183MW hydropower dam at Isimba Falls, also under a bilateral arrangement between Uganda and China. According to interviews with close advisors, Museveni chose CWE principally because he did not want to antagonize CTGC's politically well-connected top officials who could influence Chinese Communist Party leaders to continue supporting the NRM. But as the Auditor General remarked, 'there was no tendering undertaken and therefore no bidding done'. He also stated that 'there is no evidence that this firm had the technical capacity to construct the dam'.[67] Isimba would cost $589 million including $27.7 million for the transmission lines. The government borrowed $482.5 million from Eximbank at 2 per cent annual interest payable over twenty years. However, 'since there was no bidding, the contract price ... had no basis ... and could be exaggerated', commented the Auditor General. Indeed, it was $186 million above the initial cost estimates, which covered a slightly different project design.[68]

Museveni flagged off the project in October 2013, although construction only commenced in April 2015 because of delays in concluding financing arrangements with Eximbank. Isimba's completion was delayed by design, engineering problems as well as allegations of shoddy work. At the commissioning in March 2019, Museveni declared that at $0.04 per kilowatt-hour, Isimba power would be much cheaper than that generated at the Bujagali station.

General analysis and discussion

In all, the Ugandan government has signed expensive 'take-or-pay' agreements denominated in hard currency with foreign companies generating electricity. These deals stipulate that the companies are paid for the full generation capacity of the dams even if they produce or sell less to UETCL, the transmission authority. In the case of BEL, power which is not sold to UETCL – known as 'deemed energy' – is paid for through the tariff. In the case of Karuma and Isimba, however, the government has agreed to compensate UETCL for unused power and thereby meet the loan service obligation without raising the tariff of the power plants.[69]

In 2019/20, UGS 126 billion ($36 million) of Isimba power was sold to UETCL but this was far below the UGS 223 billion ($63 million) the transmission company was to pay annually to fulfil Isimba's debt servicing. The government covered the $27 million shortfall in Isimba's loan repayment. The Secretary to the Treasury was quoted as saying that because of Uganda's hydropower dams producing much more power than could be consumed – in 2019, 1167MW compared to peak demand of 724MW – compensation for 'deemed energy' from the two Chinese dams would constitute a 'huge dent in the budget' for the next five years.[70] Power generation is estimated to reach more than 1850MW with the addition of the Karuma plant, thereby exacerbating the problem of electricity surplus.[71] Important to note is that if the capacity utilization of Karuma and Isimba dams is affected by low electricity demand, then the effective tariff will be much higher than the current projected $0.04–0.05 per kilowatt-hour, especially if the government is unable to pay the full compensation amount for 'deemed energy'.

In the 2000s, Museveni lauded Bujagali 2 as a vital instrument of economic transformation. Following the commissioning of the dam in 2012, however, the president grew disillusioned with BEL for producing expensive power which contributed to high generation tariffs while earning excessive profits, all this while receiving presidential tax benefits. Museveni also took umbrage with BEL for consistently refusing to renegotiate its contractual terms, especially its costly 'take-or-pay' and 'hydraulic' agreements, which involved repayment through the tariff, and were to the detriment of cheap power for local industry and domestic households. Yet notwithstanding Museveni's remonstrations, he has done little to contest these agreements by, for instance, seeking to de-risk the dam project, given Uganda's present much more favourable risk-profile. Nor has he seriously considered terminating BEL's thirty-year contract, which, as of this writing, still has many highly lucrative years to run for the financial benefit of foreign capital. Museveni's reluctance to take stronger action against BEL is partly because government would be liable to massive penalties for any breach of contract; and partly because Museveni does not want to upend his long-standing relations with the Aga Khan, the World Bank and the United States.

The president has also regularly complained of UMEME's inflated costs of distributing electricity. He criticized UMEME's bid to renew its concession unless it agreed inter alia to cut its fixed 20 per cent rate of return by half to reduce high power prices. Interestingly, Museveni has publicly focused attention on UMEME's high distribution costs while only occasionally commenting on BEL's even higher generation costs.

Much of the public's discontent with the electricity sector has also tended to be heaped on UMEME, simply because it was the part of the sector most people encounter directly. By attributing blame on UMEME for Uganda's electricity travails, Museveni could divert attention from BEL, which was earning exorbitant profits at the expense of Ugandans, derived partly from the favourable contract terms the president had approved for it. Perhaps also because UMEME does not have a major international patron to promote and protect its interests, the president appears bent on not renewing its contract in 2025, even though the power distributor has now met most of Museveni's demands including lowering the fixed rate of return to 10 per cent.[72]

In the 2010s, Museveni turned increasingly to Chinese state-owned enterprises in the belief that they could produce cheap hydroelectric power. And, indeed, low interest Chinese loans have enabled Isimba Dam to produce much cheaper electricity than Bujagali Dam. But for many years electricity demand has not matched expanding generation capacity resulting in power tariffs remaining high as well as in compensation costs for 'deemed energy' from Isimba and loan repayments for Karuma which has yet to be completed and commissioned posing significant budgetary costs for government.

Museveni's embrace of foreign companies – Western and Chinese – and their failures to bring the desired electricity benefits to Uganda's businesses and households has seriously dented his reputation as a public-spirited, reforming leader. For far too long, the president and senior government officials were convinced that liberalizing reforms and market-based approaches were conducive to achieving the government's electricity priorities. On the advice of influential international economic actors, Museveni approved specific contract terms and personally provided tax benefits as well as relief from capital gains taxes, which favoured the interests of foreign investors. All these contracts enabled strong financial returns for foreign firms but failed to secure affordable power for domestic users.

The failure to reduce electricity prices has stirred protest and vandalism. The Uganda Manufacturers Association has regularly pressed President Museveni for a power tariff of $0.05 per kilowatt-hour. 'We can't have a competitive manufacturing sector when electricity is so expensive' has been a consistent refrain of industrialists who currently use 70 per cent of Uganda's electricity and in 2022 paid an average tariff of $0.09 cents per kilowatt-hour. They also point to countries in the region subsidizing their energy sectors. Moreover, among domestic consumers, who pay $0.19 cents per kilowatt-hour, vandalism of electricity infrastructure and theft of electricity have led to UMEME's distribution losses increasing to over 18.4 per cent with negative consequences for tariffs. Also, although 38 per cent of Ugandans were reported in 2020 as being connected to solar energy,[73] mainly for lighting, for cooking they were still predominantly using charcoal and firewood, which contributes to the forest cover depletion. It is evidently clear there is urgent demand for affordable power in Uganda if key national development challenges are to be met.

Conclusion

President Museveni and the NRM government have viewed electricity as a private good to be bought and sold in the marketplace. Thus, the price charged has reflected the cost of capital investment and operating expenses as well as any guaranteed profit returns for foreign investors. However, over the years, many government officials including the president have grown sceptical of the value of such an overtly market-driven approach. But unlike governments in other East African countries, which subsidize electricity and treat it as a public good, Uganda under Museveni is still far from viewing electric power as a strategic good which government should ensure is affordable as well as promote wider economic and social benefits.

More recently, and as noted above, the government has agreed to meet the loan service obligation of the two Chinese-built dams and not have the debts paid through the tariff. Moreover, the recent passing of the Electricity (Amendment) Act, 2022, does contain some indication of the state playing a gradually more interventionist role in the electricity sector such as allowing UEDCL, the distribution authority, to supply electricity to industrial parks 'at a tariff to be determined by government'.[74]

In November 2022, the energy ministry declared that the government had decided against renewal of UMEME's concession when it expires in 2025. Instead, the government proposed creating the Uganda National Electricity Company Limited (UNECL), a state-run company to manage the generation, transmission and distribution segments of the entire electricity sector. According to media reports, state management was expected to 'minimise expensive private capital in the electricity sub-sector' which Ministry of Energy officials declared was what was called for by the president in his repeated claims that private companies were primarily responsible for high power tariffs and failing to bring down energy losses.

The government appears to be signalling greater intervention in a vital economic sector in which it has limited expertise as well as financial resources to build its own dams or invest in power distribution. For the past three decades, the NRM government has been obliged to partner with foreign companies supported by influential international economic actors. President Museveni has been at the centre of dealings with foreign companies. But heavily one-sided agreements have enabled foreign actors to place limits on the government's bargaining power as well as on the actions that even a domestically dominant president can take.

For technical and financial reasons, however, private foreign firms remain important for promoting Uganda's electrification, albeit as minority partners in any joint venture. How the president and government relate to international companies to manage the energy priorities of Ugandans will depend on their ability to influence inter alia power sector contracts which have made electricity expensive and tarnished Museveni's reputation as a modernizing leader promoting the national interest.

This study contributes to research on authoritarian rule in several ways. The existing literature demonstrates that President Museveni has possessed considerable autonomy to play a leading role in decision-making. For instance, he has personally intervened to award public contracts to favoured businessmen. He has also directed that investors be availed of urban land without any public bidding.[75] However, our present research shows that Museveni has faced serious limits when dealing with the World Bank and private Western firms involved in the construction and operation of large dams. Only in the case of Chinese state firms was Museveni able to select which firms should be personally awarded power generation contracts. Otherwise, as in the case of Western companies, the terms and conditions of the contracts and concessions have reflected the greater bargaining strength of Chinese banks and companies.

Museveni's leverage in contract negotiations has been very limited. These contracts have followed market-based principles as well as incorporated various contractual guarantees, anti-risk measures and cost-reflective tariffs favourable to the interests of foreign capital. President Museveni has experienced little agency and much frustration in his relations with foreign companies.

Notes

1   We wish to thank Kate Bayliss (SOAS/Leeds University), Mette Kjaer (Aarhus University), Nelson Kasfir (Dartmouth College) and Joe Oloka-Onyango (Makerere University) for their many helpful comments on earlier versions of this chapter.
2   Christopher D. Gore, *Electricity in Africa. The Politics of Transformation in Uganda* (Woodbridge: James Currey, 2017), 115–18.
3   Ministry of Energy and Mineral Development (MEMD), *The Energy Policy for Uganda* (Kampala: MEMD, 2002).
4   We do not consider the cases of Nalubaale and Kiira dams which were operated from 2002 to 2023 by EUL, a subsidiary of South Africa's state-owned power utility, ESKOM Holdings.
5   Kate Bayliss, 'Private Sector Participation in African Infrastructure', Brasilia, Brazil: International Policy Centre for Inclusive Growth, 2009, 17–19; and Vivien Foster and Anshul Rana, *Rethinking Power Sector Reform in the Developing World* (Washington, DC: The World Bank, 2019).
6   World Bank, *Uganda Economic Update: Infrastructure Finance Deficit* (Washington, DC: The World Bank, 2017), 34.
7   Peter Bosshard, *Private Gain – Public Risk? The International Experience of Power Purchase Agreements of Private Power Projects* (Berkeley, CA: International Rivers Network, 2002).
8   Electricity Regulatory Authority (ERA), *Annual Report 2017–2018* (Kampala: ERA, 2018), 51–5.
9   Catrina Godinho and Anton Eberhard, *Learning from Power Sector Reform. The Case of Uganda* (Washington, DC: The World Bank, Policy Research WP 8820, 2019), 36–42.
10 Daudi Migereko, 'Energy PPAs Were Necessary to Rid Uganda of Power Shortage', *Daily Monitor*, Kampala (23 March 2020). https://www.monitor.co.ug/uganda/

oped/commentary/energy-ppas-were-necessary-to-rid-uganda-of-power-shortage-1882068

11   Gore, *Electricity in Africa*, 121–2.

12   Lori Pottinger, 'Uganda's Bujagali Dam: A Case Study in Corporate Welfare', Berkeley, CA: International Rivers Network (2009), 3.

13   Isaac Musumba, 'Who Is Not Telling the Truth on Bujagali Power'? *The Monitor* (25 February 1999).

14   Roger Tangri and Andrew M. Mwenda, *The Politics of Elite Corruption in Africa. Uganda in Comparative African Perspective* (New York: Routledge, 2013), 98–100; Gore, *Electricity in Africa*, Chap.4.

15   Ibid., 100.

16   Charlotte Denny, 'Nile Power Row Splits Uganda', *The Guardian*, London (15 August 2001).

17   Interviews with Musumba 2000, 2002.

18   Prayas Energy Group, *The Bujagali Power Purchase Agreement – an Independent Review* (Berkeley, CA: International Rivers Network, 2002).

19   Blackstone, 'Sithe Global and IPS Establish a New Hydroelectric Station in Uganda', Press Release (21 December 2007).

20   Museveni's tax intervention was to cost the country over $240 million for the ten-year period.

21   National Association of Professional Environmentalists, 'Key Civil Concerns over the Bujagali Project', Kampala (16 December 2005).

22   World Bank, 'Uganda: Economic Update', 35.

23   Migereko, 'Energy PPAs Were Necessary'.

24   Aga Khan Development Network, 'Ugandan President and Aga Khan Inaugurate Bujagali', press release (8 October 2012).

25   Agather Atuhaire, 'Taxpayers to Fork Extra $438 Million for Bujagali Dam – MPs', *The Observer* (5 September 2012). https://observer.ug/component/content/article?id=20780:taxpayers-to-pay-extra-438m-for-bujagali-dam-mps; Rene Meyer, Anton Eberhard and Katharine Gratwick, 'Uganda's Power Sector Reform: There and Back Again'? *Energy for Sustainable Development* 43, (2018): 85.

26   World Bank, 'Uganda: Economic Update', 35.

27   Haggai Matsiko, 'Inside the Shs. 1.4 Billion Bujagali Deal', *The Independent*, Kampala (9 September 2016). https://www.independent.co.ug/analysis-inside-shs1-4-trillion-bujagali-deal/

28   This paragraph draws on confidential interviews with government and State House officials.

29   Matsiko, 'Inside the Shs. 1.4 Billion'.

30   Agather Atuhaire, 'Why Is Bujagali Power Expensive?' *The Independent*, Kampala (9 March 2012). https://www.independent.co.ug/bujagali-power-expensive/

31   'Norwegians Buy Uganda's Bujagali Hydropower Dam', press release SN Power (30 July 2018).

32   Jeff Mbanga, 'Will Uganda Meet WB, ADB New Conditions on Bujagali'? *The Observer*, Kampala (22 May 2018). https://observer.ug/businessnews/57732-will-uganda-meet-wb-adb-new-conditions-on-bujagali; Nelson Wesonga and Paul Tajuba, 'African Development Bank to Steer Restructuring of Bujagali Loan', *Daily Monitor*, Kampala (14 May 2017). https://allafrica.com/stories/201705160032.html

33   Before re-financing, the annual payment before 2020 amounted to $168 million. See Electricity Regulatory Authority, *Tariff Review Report for 2018* (Kampala: ERA, 2020), 5.

34   Profit figures are from BEL's Annual Report and Financial Statements for the year ended 31 December 2021.

35   Quoted in Henry Lutaaya, 'We Warned You on Bujagali – Environmentalists Tell Museveni' (12 June 2015). Sunrise.ug/news/201506.

36   'Museveni Regrets Bujagali Financing Mechanism', *New Vision*, Kampala (26 January 2020). https://www.newvision.co.ug/news/1514023/museveni-regretsbujagali-financing-mechanism

37   Andrew M. Mwenda, 'Between UMEME and Parliament', *The Independent* (29 November 2013). https://www.independent.co.ug/between-umeme-and-parliament/

38   Andrew M. Mwenda and Molly Lister, 'Inside the UMEME Power Tariff Scandal', *The Independent* (18 June 2009). https://www.independent.co.ug/inside-umeme-power-tariff-scandal/

39   Andrew M. Mwenda, 'Report Shows How Government Lost UGS. 452 Billion in UMEME Deal', *The Independent* (20 October, 2009). https://www.independent.co.ug/report-shows-govt-lost-shs-452-billion-umeme-deal/

40   Parliament of Uganda, Report of the *Ad hoc* Committee on Energy on the Performance of the Electricity Sub- Sector in Uganda, September 2011 – October 2012 (Kampala, 2013).

41   Ibid.

42   Halima Abdallah, 'Uganda Parliament Investigates UMEME's profits', *East African*, Nairobi (4 December 2011). https://allafrica.com/stories/201112051659.html

43   Mwenda, 'Between UMEME and Parliament'.

44   Ibid.

45   Haggai Matsiko, 'Speculators Fighting UMEME', *The Independent* (13 December 2013). https://www.independent.co.ug/speculators-fighting-umeme/

46   Ibid.

47   Godinho and Eberhard, 'Learning from Power Sector', 28–30.

48   Julius Businge, 'UMEME's License Renewal', *The Independent*, Kampala (24 May 2019). https://www.independent.co.ug/umemes-licence-renewal/

49   Nelson Wesonga, 'Should Government Terminate UMEME Contract'? *Daily Monitor*, Kampala (31 March 2014). https://www.monitor.co.ug/uganda/special-reports/why-mps-advised-government-to-end-umeme-contract-1571994

50   Jeff Mbanga, 'UMEME, ERA Seek Middle Ground Over Six-Year Target', *The Observer*, Kampala (27 August 2019). https://observer.ug/businessnews/61781-umeme-era-seek-middle-ground-over-six-year-target

51   Daily Monitor, 'Letter from Yoweri K. Museveni to Minister of Energy and Minerals' (12 March 2018).

52   Ibid.

53   National Resistance Movement (NRM), 'President Museveni's New Year Message 2019' (31 December 2018); and *The Independent*, 'Electricity Supply Cost: Museveni, UMEME Differ', Kampala (7 January 2019). https://www.independent.co.ug/electricity-supply-cost-museveni-umeme-differ/

54   See Nelson Wesonga, 'Negotiate Extension of UMEME Concession, Museveni Directs', *Daily Monitor*, Kampala (19 December 2018). https://www.monitor.co.ug/uganda/business/finance/negotiate-extension-of-umeme-concession-museveni-directs-1796278

55   Haggai Matsiko, 'Should Government Take Over UMEME Job'? *The Independent*, Kampala (26 January 2018). https://www.independent.co.ug/government-takeover-umeme-job/3/

56   53 Business Focus, 'Museveni Attacks UMEME, Reveals Why He Has Refused to Renew Its Contract', Kampala (9 October 2020). https://businessfocus.co.ug/museveni-attacks-umeme-reveals-why-he-has-refused-to-renew-its-contract/

57   Simon Clark, 'Privately Funded Electricity Is Too Expensive for Uganda, President Says', *Wall Street Journal*, New York (20 October2014). https://www.wsj.com/articles/privately-funded-electricity-too-expensive-for-uganda-president-says-1413827013

58   Mubatsi Habati, 'Bribery Hits 600MW Karuma Power Dam', *The Independent*, Kampala (14 May 2012). https://www.independent.co.ug/bribery-hits-600mw-karuma-power-dam/

59   Tabu Butagira, 'Government Abandons Plan to Give Chinese Firm Karuma Hydropower Project', *Daily Monitor* (1 October 2012). https://www.monitor.co.ug/uganda/news/national/government-abandons-plan-to-give-chinese-firm-karuma-hydropower-project-1526866

60   Ibrahim Kasiita, Samuel Sanya and Darious Magara, 'Karuma Dam Bidding Halted', *New Vision*, Kampala (28 January 2013). https://www.newvision.co.ug/news/1313339/karuma-dam-bidding-halted

61   See, 'President Xi Jinping Meets with Ugandan, Mozambican and Ethiopian Leaders', http://nl.china-embassy.gov.cn/eng/zgyw/201303/t20130329_10044007.htm

62   In fact, SinoHydro would be hired by CWE to build the Isimba dam.

63   Office of the Auditor General (OAG), *Annual Report of the Auditor General for the Year Ended 30 June 2015* (Kampala: OAG, 2016).

64   An impeccable source revealed to us that $90 million was shared between Exim Bank and Ugandan government officials and commission agents for negotiating Karuma.

65   Elias Biryabarema, 'Uganda Seeking Ways to Refinance Bujagali Power Dam', *Reuters* (4 June 2015). https://www.reuters.com/article/uganda-electricity/uganda-seeking-ways-to-refinance-bujagali-power-dam-idUSL5N0YQ3I820150604

66   David Blair and Xiao Xiangyi, 'Dams to Power Uganda's Growth', *China Daily Africa*, Beijing (31 August 2018). http://africa.chinadaily.com.cn/weekly/2018-08/31/content_36849089.htm

67   OAG, *Annual Report*, 300.

68   Michael Wakabi, 'New Hydro Projects to Ease Uganda's Power Costs', *The East African* (12 October 2013). https://www.theeastafrican.co.ke/tea/news/east-africa/new-hydro-projects-to-ease-uganda-s-power-costs-1319966

69   Electricity Regulatory Authority (ERA), *Tariff Review t Q3 for 2020*, Kampala (2020), 14.

70   Uganda Radio Network (URN), 'Unconsumed Power Will Hit the Budget Hard – Muhankanizi' (6 December 2019). https://ugandaradionetwork.net/story/unconsumed-power-will-hit-the-budget-hard-muhakanizi

71   In an alternative scenario based less on installed capacity than on available supply, installed capacity in 2022 was 1378MW whereas actual electricity supply was 902MW with peak demand at 870MW. According to the CEO of UMEME (phone conversation 17 May 2022), electricity demand will exceed available supply by 2023 unless Karuma comes on line. He argues that Uganda needs new hydropower dams. We understand that the government has approved contracts for a new Chinese dam at Ayago.

72   Andrew M. Mwenda, 'Museveni's UMEME Mistake', *The Independent*, Kampala (20 May 2022). https://www.independent.co.ug/musevenis-umeme-mistake/

73   Uganda Bureau of Statistics, *National Household Survey 2019/2020* (Kampala: UBOS, 2021) 142–53.

74   Quoted in Parliament of Uganda, Press Release. 'Heavy Penalties for Vandalism of Electricity Infrastructure', Kampala (14 April 2022).

75   See Tangri and Mwenda, *Politics of Elite Corruption*, 45.

Part Two

Co-optation, coercion and social control

4

State co-optation of feminism: Unpacking the paradoxes of political representation

Tabitha Mulyampiti

The foundations of the resilience and longevity of President Museveni's regime have been anchored in part on the trust gained in the area of gender equality and the women's empowerment. Some people have interpreted this boon as a piece of political golden luck for the womenfolk of Uganda. In this respect, the affirmative action quota for women in parliament and their appointment to top decision-making arenas have been used by the National Resistance Movement (NRM) government to increase support in parliament and to capture the female vote. In fact, the women parliamentary bloc has been perhaps the most important pillar of the NRM's parliamentary super-majority without which Museveni and the NRM would not have been able to maintain such a consistent and commanding control of the legislature. The gender-equality debate is therefore controlled and affected by the women's closeness to the current regime. The loyalty expected in return from the political favours conferred via cabinet positions, representation in parliament and a fixed percentage of seats in lower local councils translates into a de facto marriage between the women of Uganda and the NRM government.

Aili Mari Tripp's application of the term 'hybrid regimes' to the NRM political system reflects analytically on the distinctiveness of this type of system and on its implications for civil society, particularly women's organizations.[1] Similarly, Jasmin Lorch and Bettina Bunk connect debates on authoritarian resilience to state feminism arguing that authoritarian regimes employ the areas of women's rights and gender to contribute to regime resilience.[2] But for women there is a downside. As Anne Marie Goetz notes, the political value of specially created new seats has been eroded by their exploitation as currency for the NRM's patronage system. The trade-off has undermined women's effectiveness as representatives of the interests of women once in office.[3] This is because the gate-keepers of access to reserved political space are not the women's movement, or even female voters, but NRM elites.

There have been studies on state feminism in non-democratic regimes, as well as whether and how state feminism translates to women-friendly policies and institutions, for example, enhancing the situation of women and addressing gender imbalances.[4] These studies also reveal factors that can thwart democratic transition by showing regime performance in different policy fields, such as economic development or the provision of social services. In the light of these analyses, the present chapter attempts to link the arguments around state feminism and the struggle for gender balance in political representation and the women's involvement in politics to the broader discussions about African authoritarian regime resilience. The analysis is rooted in feminist political theories of gender, women's representation in politics, feminist co-optation and state survival.

The major aim of the chapter is to analyse the paradox of, on the one hand, women's longstanding efforts to organize and to exercise their political power, and on the other, the loyalty that is expected of women in return for the political favours conferred by the Museveni regime. The chapter identifies and analyses ways that the Museveni regime has used gender to co-opt feminism, attain feminist compliance and acceptance of state feminism culture. The chapter examines three examples of authoritarian state capture of the feminist agenda. These are: (i) securing female representation in the regime's legislative and executive structures, culminating with President Museveni's 'fishermen' cabinet of 2021; (ii) the First Lady 'Maama' Syndrome; and (iii) the collapse of the Women's Movement. Specifically, the chapter asks: how does Museveni's regime use state feminism to preserve its rule? How has state feminism affected the nature of women's leadership, influence on decision-making and the chances that they will promote a gender-equality agenda?

Methodologically, the chapter synthesizes the different literature on autocratic politics, gender and co-optation in various feminist subfields in order to pull together concepts and empirical insights that are central to developing a feminist-based approach to the analysis. The chapter draws mostly from secondary data, supported by key informant interviews consisting of purposively selected political actors and experts in both government and civil society.

State feminism, co-optation and regime resilience: A theoretical framework

Scholarly analysis relating to political co-optation of women's rights discourse is here termed as co-opting feminism.[5] In this sense, the term 'state feminism' is linked to the co-optation of feminist interests and activists by the state. The terms 'gender' and 'feminism' here are merely a guide to the central theory. State feminism seeks to convert the feminist agenda into small changes within a flawed system rather than holding out for revolutionary dreams and outcomes.[6] It relates mostly to changes in power relations by means of the promotion of feminist goals through public policies and measures taken by the state.[7] The debate on state feminism has travelled outside the Western world and been applied to post-socialist political systems and authoritarian states in developing countries.

The question of why some authoritarian regimes have the ability to sustain themselves while others fail to do so has emerged as an important topic for scholarship on gender and politics.[8] Researchers have demonstrated that various 'democratic' institutions such as legislatures, political parties and elections are foundations of authoritarian resilience. Authoritarian regimes often rely on a mix of strategies, including not only repression but also legitimation and co-optation. The co-optation mechanisms, such as patron-client networks and arrangements for selective political inclusion can be used to make non-democratic rule more resilient.[9] It is in this regard that we situate the role of state feminism, the state-centric notion of feminism that is facilitated, created or approved by the government.[10] Some scholars have considered state feminism as a policy approach where the government or the state adopts policies that are beneficial to women's rights and may lead to the improvement in women's lives.

Co-optation on the other hand is defined as a process whereby 'opponents adopt aspects of the content of a movement's discourse, while subverting its intent', and which 'may have diluting, demobilizing, depoliticizing, and disempowering effects on the movement'.[11] A central locus for feminist co-optation is the movements for representation in legislatures and assemblies.[12] In many ways, these have always been movements for presence that challenge political arrangements and seek to insert women's interests into policy-making by ensuring that they are well positioned among the policy-makers. Feminist co-optation breeds a range of constraints which undermine the ability of feminist movements to effectively pursue their agendas through means such as marginalization, role assignment and stigmatization.[13]

Closely related to the argument on state feminism are the concepts of gender and feminism. Ridgeway and Smith-Lovin present the gender system as including processes that both define males and females as different in socially significant ways, and justify inequality on the basis of that difference.[14] The continued, everyday acceptance of the gender system is inculcated in both people's experiences and cultural beliefs in ways that justify men's greater power and privilege. Feminism, on the other hand, provides the lens to analyse gender inequality, and the construction of patriarchy and power in society.

Women's agency is a central tenet within the feminist discourse. Lorber classifies feminism as reformative or gender-resistant.[15] In her typology, gender reform feminisms are rooted in the political philosophy of liberalism with its emphasis on individual rights, whereas gender-resistant feminisms focus on specific behaviour and group dynamics through which women are kept in a subordinate position, even in subcultures which claim to support gender equality.[16] However, the image in Western feminist scholarship of African women as passive victims marginalized without a voice has been challenged in recent work.[17]

The blending of feminist thought into political science literature has given rise to the construction of an unconventional theoretical base towards understanding women's issues in politics. Feminist thinkers have varied conceptualizations of politics and political concepts that are woman-centric,[18] which incorporate a broad scope of approaches, including feminist understanding of the state, feminism and the concept of power, feminist critique of rationality and feminist notion of citizenship.

In the language of gendered politics, the term 'gender' is often used to mean women in need of protection. Through this description, women are mainly portrayed as victims in need of protection in a situation where politics and the state (the supreme symbol of power and hegemony against the women) are constructed with contradictions in terms of uneven allocation of resources, gendered institutions, androcentric leadership and male bias.[19] Gender politics focusses on the social construction of gender, the role of gender in social and political life, and women's political participation in the context of patriarchal political systems is a particular focus.[20]

State feminism and Uganda's political history

Women's involvement in politics under the NRM has its roots in women's political and social activism that began in the 1940s with the birth of national movements for the advancement of women.[21] The women's rights movement was strengthened by the organizational capacity and activities of the Uganda Council of Women (UCW) that was started in 1946, emerging from the Uganda Women's League.[22] Barbara Saben and Alice Boase were the first women representatives to be duly represented in the Legislative Council (Legco) in 1954 out of the total of sixty members in the house. Their entrance onto the political scene was unsurprising given that Saben was one of the founding members of UCW while Boase was its president between 1953 and 1955. Pumla Kisosonkole – mother-in-law to Kabaka Edward Mutesa II and a prominent actor in the movement to independence – was President between 1957 and 1960.[23]

Participation in the legislature further involved women including Florence Lubega, Eseza Makumbi and Sugra Visram (a Ugandan of Indian origin) who were elected to the Lukiiko (the Parliament of the kingdom of Buganda) in February 1962, and were later nominated to the National Assembly as representatives of Buganda. Makumbi served on the East African Legislative Assembly between 1962 and 1977.[24] During the tumultuous regimes of presidents Milton Obote (1966 to 1970, then again from 1980 to 1985) and Idi Amin (1971 to 1979) all power was vested in the presidency.[25] Aili Mari Tripp reports that this took its toll on the political representation of women in Uganda's political structures.[26] Except for the brief appearance of Rhoda Kalema and Geraldine Bitamazire in 1979–80 and Theresa Odongo-Oduka in 1980–5, no other women held seats in parliament from 1962 until 1986. In 1964, then Prime Minister Obote rejected a request by the women's organizations for seats reserved for women in the National Assembly although he enjoyed their support.[27]

Fast forward to 1986, the NRM and President Yoweri Kaguta Museveni introduced a political system where candidates were elected on individual merit. This meant that all candidates (men and women) were allowed to speak freely and run for election on their own merit, without necessarily belonging to any political party. Hence, the NRM system created a broad-based and all-inclusive political system which made it possible for women to enter the political sphere. In addition, in 1989 the Museveni government adopted the system of seats reserved for women at all levels from local councils to the parliament.[28] This ensured that at least one-third of seats were held by women. As a result, female representation in Parliament grew from 51 out of 276 members (19 per cent) in 1996 to 167 out of 529 (32 per cent) in 2021.[29]

The 1995 Constitution has often been referred to as the most gender-sensitive in Uganda's history.[30] It underlined the affirmative action policies that are still in effect today. However, critics have maintained that although the number of women members of parliament increased under the NRM, women were still denied real power.

Although women gained in numerical representation, they struggled to match this with impactful legislative outcomes.[31] What is more, women's affirmative action quota in parliament and appointments to top decision-making arenas have been used by the NRM government to increase and sustain support in parliament and to capture the female vote.

The gender-equality debate is therefore controlled and affected by the women's closeness to the current regime. Loyalty is expected in return for the political favours in terms of cabinet posts, parliamentary representation and presence within the lower local councils could be translated as a de facto marriage between women and the NRM government. As a general rule, women representatives found it difficult to challenge the government over controversial matters. As Kari Hanssen succinctly puts it: 'can you really fail to support the one who feeds you?'[32] Similarly, Jacqueline Asiimwe-Mwesige, a women rights activist, noted that women were unsure of their new roles in the political parties and did not appreciate the difference created by the 2005 transition from the Movement system to multi-party politics.[33] Instead, women were more interested in taking the state to task to account for its soft-peddling on actualizing women's democratic rights as enshrined in the constitution:

As we mobilized for the first time in 20 years under multi-party elections, the women's movement rallied its cry around three main issues: why Museveni and his men were interfering with the land co-ownership women's clause; why parliament was sitting on the domestic relations bill; and why the establishment of the equal opportunities commission was being deferred.[34]

Asiimwe-Mwesige further noted that Ugandan women were aware that the majority of men (the both no-party/movement and multi-party enthusiasts) who were agitating for political power continued to harbour patriarchal views that justified women's subordination and exploitation.[35] Even while their political manifestoes often included proclamations for democracy and even gender equality, their actions as legislators revealed a strong and embedded patriarchal mind-set. For example, many male legislators were hesitant to discuss sex discrimination, domestic violence, sexual violence, gender equity and often dismissed whatever women said while on the parliamentary floor.[36]

Dating back to the colonial period and beyond, *de jure* women had no rights to participate in top decision-making bodies, and de facto they were largely excluded. Their participation at these levels depended on the mercies and mood of the ruling group at the top. When Museveni and the NRM came to power in 1986 there was a dramatic turnaround with the introduction of women quotas. Henceforth, from the no-party transition to the multi-party political system, participants in the Uganda women's movement embraced a strategy of electing women to parliament and raising matters important for the female constituency. However, women found it difficult to challenge the government on controversial matters given that it was this government's support that had allowed them to access the new positions of power. The gender-equality debate and the election or appointment of what can be termed serious female voices may have weakened following the transition to the multiparty system.[37]

The paradox of increased female legislative and executive representation

Three interlinked phenomena illuminate the paradox of increased female legislative and executive representation. These are considered to be the overarching mechanisms through which Museveni's regime has managed to institute state feminism and co-opt the women's movement and political voice. The following phenomena of co-optation are elaborated: descriptive *versus* substantive representation in parliament and cabinet and use of quotas; the First Lady syndrome and its impact on women's presence and impact in contemporary Ugandan politics, and the choice of political women in Museveni's Fishermen' cabinet.

Women's descriptive versus substantive representation and the use of quotas

There has been sustained interest in how political institutions such as electoral systems and candidate recruitment and selection procedures shape the legislative agendas and the representative roles of individual MPs.[38] Hence, a core aspect in promotion of representative democracy has been the introduction of electoral gender quotas.[39] Researchers on women and politics often analyse women's political representation as descriptive (women's presence in numbers) and/or substantive (representation outcomes such as relevant policies).[40]

Usually, the descriptive representation is expected to bring about changes in women's substantive representation. However, for women's descriptive representation to bring about change in a more women/gender friendly direction, female politicians should have distinct views on women's issues to be able to bring a women's perspective into political decision-making, or bring a different style to politics.[41] As such, women are not by their numbers automatically regarded as bringing about change.

Since 1989, Uganda has reserved seats for female legislators. Women are also allowed to compete against men for unreserved seats. This provision is stipulated in articles 31, 32 and 33 of the 1995 Constitution, which outline the rights of women and provide for affirmative action for the purpose of redressing the imbalances created history, tradition or custom. With regards to the nature of reserved seats for women, Article 78(1) of the Constitution states that the Parliament shall consist of one woman representative for every district – the highest unit of decentralized government.

The table below summarizes the proportion of women legislators up to 2016. It shows that the National Resistance Council (NRC) in 1989 consisted of 38[42] Historical Members of the NRM/National Resistance Army and a total membership of 280, which included a total of 50 women (18 per cent). In 1993, the NRC passed the Constituent Assembly Statute, providing for elections to the Constituent Assembly (CA), but the number of women delegates to CA remained almost the same with the NRC (17.4 per cent). Despite the prescription for affirmative action by the CA, the number of women legislators remained below the 30 per cent requirement until 2006 when multi-party elections were held after a twenty-year freeze. By 2011, the number of districts in Uganda had been increased dramatically to 122 and the number of women MPs grew to 35 per cent.

As of 23 July 2021, there were a total of 188 women out of 556 members, or nearly 34 per cent representation. Of these, 15 were elected as Constituency Representatives and 146 were District Women Representatives. The number of districts also increased to include newly created cities. Another twenty-seven women come in as a result of an indirect election of representatives of interest groups and as ex officio members appointed by the President. Currently, with a 33.81 per cent female representation in parliament, Uganda[44] becomes the eleventh African country with the highest number of female legislators.[45]

Considering that the great majority of quota representatives are NRM members, the quota system has helped boost NRM's electoral strength and share of parliamentary seats. Such a boom is possible largely because NRM is the only party able to field candidates in almost all districts. In the 2016 elections, for instance, NRM fielded 110 candidates for 112 districts, and in 2021, won 119 of the 152 women elected in both district and cities parliamentary seats. Thus, all types of candidates (not just women) benefit by becoming NRM flag bearers, since they have access to the support and backing of the NRM and state machinery.

The Women's Parliamentary Caucus, which was initiated as a cross-party lobby group for gender issues, quickly became the NRM Women's Caucus synonymous with the NRM political agenda. Hence, the structure has been eroded of its effectiveness due to its exploitation as currency for the NRM's patronage system.[46] In many instances the caucus failed to stand up for women's rights. For example, during the 1994–95 CA debates, the caucus did not take a stand on the debate on the country's political system, claiming to be non-partisan nor did it work with the multiparty caucus, the National Caucus for Democracy, made up mostly of individuals known to be associated with opposition parties.[47] In the end, the CA adopted a Movement system as an alternative

Table showing trends in the number of women in the national Assembly 1989–2016[43]

Year	No. of districts	Assembly	Affirmative action	Open seat	Others	Total women	Total MPs	% women
1989	39	NRC	39	2	9	50	280	18
1994	39	CA	39	8	3	50	286	17.4
1996	39	Parliament	39	8	4	51	276	19
2001	56	Parliament	56	13	6	75	304	24.4
2006	79	Parliament	79	14	1	100	319	31
2011	112	Parliament	112	11	8	131	375	35
2016	112	Parliament	112	18	9	139	428	33
2021	146	Parliament	146	15	27	188	566	33.81

to multiparty politics, a move that contributed to the entrenchment of Museveni's authoritarianism that persists to the present day.

The problem with women's elections is that women have been generally targeted as a group who can mobilize votes to enable the NRM party to win. That is why civic education as a precursor for smooth and informed election was not given the requisite attention required for the various franchises conducted in the early days of the NRM rise to power. Evaluation of the effectiveness of civic education programmes found no change in women's political participation or in views of gender norms in local politics. The programmes were hampered in part by incomplete implementation and the lack of support from local political party leaders who may have feared an electorally risky association with the sometimes-controversial social messages.[48] Another glaring gap was the failure to address issues of sexual and gender-based violence (SGBV), which seemed to be prevalent during elections.[49] Some sceptics had warned that Museveni was not interested in the women's cause, but only in winning another term in office.[50]

Another action was the election of female Speakers and/or deputy Speakers as a means to control the legislature. Uganda again made history in consecutively electing women to the position of Speaker of Parliament from 2011 to 2026.[51] Lawyer and ardent NRM enthusiast, Rebecca Alitwala Kadaga served as Speaker of the Parliament of Uganda from 19 May 2011 until 21 May 2021. After being controversially shunted out of the position in favour of her then-deputy, Jacob Oulanya, Kadaga was moved to the less powerful position of First Deputy Prime Minister and Minister of East African Community Affairs.

Anita Annet Among who is the incumbent Speaker of the 11th Parliament of Uganda concurrently serves as the elected member of parliament for the Bukedea District, first elected in 2016 to the 10th parliament.[52] Before joining the ruling NRM, Among was in the FDC, later running as an independent before joining NRM and eventually being elected Deputy Speaker in 2021 for the 11th Parliament, then Speaker in 2022 following the death of Speaker Jacob Oulanyah. The election of both Kadaga and Among ignited debates around the effectiveness of female Speakers of Parliament. A number of positive arguments have been put forward to hail this move by the NRM. Many people in different circles view this as trust of women's leadership by the regime, as it broke the stereotypes about women's abilities and competencies in politics. A member of the women's movement in Uganda for examples asserted: 'As an African woman working in development, I am delighted to finally see years of meaningful measures to promote gender equality being reflected in Uganda.'[53]

A number of women activists were excited to have women serving in such positions. Kadaga's speakership ended with a lot of praise and awards for good stewardship from across Africa. But from the literature and interviews conducted for this chapter, there appears to be more mixed feelings than outright approval of female parliamentary leadership in Uganda. The major argument has been that the inability of parliament to move critical women's Bills indicates that descriptive representation of women legislators is not tied to similar improvements in substantive representation.[54]

A number of writers have discussed the relationship between regime type and the adoption of quotas in Africa in general and Uganda in particular. Ragnhild Muriaas and Vibeke Wang note that the NRM has employed the reserved seat policy strategically to maintain its dominant position and that strategies for using the quota system have displayed vested interests in its survival.[55] Amanda Clayton et al. also note that the introduction of electoral gender quotas in Uganda has raised questions of whether female MPs have the incentives and capabilities to vocally represent women's interests in the policy-making process.[56]

Aili Mari Tripp and Alice Kang note that whereas democracies were proportionately most likely to adopt party quotas, the authoritarian regimes were most likely to adopt reserved seats.[57] Since women were not involved in the design of such affirmative action measures, there have been constraints in effectively implementing the reserved seat policy. The Ugandan model has been criticized for creating a gendered perception that constituency seats were for males and reserved seats for females.[58] This perception affects each step of the switch to a non-quota seat, which has stagnated the number of women coming in through the open seat.[59] Moreover, there is a growing trend where women's effectiveness in Parliament would be influenced by their strong connection to the NRM regime.

Freedom House's Freedom in the World (2022) report ranked Uganda as a 'Not Free' country with 34/100 reflecting both the constraints and the possibilities of advancing a women's rights agenda in an authoritarian country. This situation raises a crucial question about women's accessibility to real power and influence, in terms of lobbying or via direct participation in decision-making. A related concern has always focused on the ways in which women were being used to further promote dictatorship and to erode democracy and freedom of citizens.

The First Lady 'Maama' syndrome

The phenomena of 'First Lady' syndrome (used by African writers Amina Mama in 1995 and Amanda Gouws in 2021)[60] refers to the role of high-level women based on their personal ties with men in power rather than personal achievement as leaders in their own right. Historically, First Ladies in Africa have lived in the shadows of their husbands, tending to their families. Increasingly, however, many have come to the fore and some have become influential decision-makers as both state and non-state actors.[61] In many African countries, the First Lady phenomenon has created a dynamic in which political space has been appropriated and used by the wives and friends of men in power for purposes of personal aggrandizement, rather than for furthering the interests of women.[62] Many First Ladies have been at the front such as Maryam Babangida (Nigeria), Grace Mugabe (Zimbabwe), Denise Nkurunziza (Burundi), Elizabeth Diouf (Senegal), Margaret Gakuo Kenyatta (Kenya), Ana Afonso Dias Lourenço (Angola) and Jeannette Nyiramongi Kagame (Rwanda).

The phenomenon was also used to refer to the Nigerian first lady Mrs Mariam Babangida who launched her 'Better Life Programme' and managed to secure access to government funding and garner considerable publicity in the name of promoting women's interests.[63] In the case of Nigeria, the national gender machinery was also taken over by the First Lady.[64] Often these First Ladies and their organizations ended up serving the ruling party mobilizing support from female voters, aside from performing mundane tasks such as entertaining and serving at party rallies.

The Independent news magazine reported a study on the role played by the wives of heads of state in Africa and ranked Uganda's Janet Museveni among the top three most influential first ladies.[65] The others were Grace Mugabe, the wife of then-Zimbabwe's former president Robert Mugabe; and Denise Nkurunziza, wife of Burundi's President Pierre Nkurunziza. Janet Museveni is widely considered to be politically ambitious and to actively support her husband's rule.[66] Maama Janet as she prefers to be called is the first lady with the longest involvement in the cabinet and parliament of Uganda, having been Minister of Education and Sports since 6 June 2016.[67] Earlier, from 27 May 2011 until 6 June 2016, she was Minister for Karamoja Affairs, and was the elected Member of Parliament representing Ruhaama County in Ntungamo District, between 2006 and 2016.

Janet Museveni is also among the first ladies of the ten longest-ever African serving leaders.[68] Well into her thirty-sixth consecutive year in power and supporting her husband, Janet was beside her husband as he was sworn in for his sixth term as president of Uganda in 2021. Because of her proximity to the executive and other decision-makers, she wields considerable political influence and was previously reported to have political ambitions for the highest office.[69] Given her role in the executive branch, she has actively contributed to Uganda political trajectory including the entrenchment of autocratic rule. It is believed that she wields influence in, for example, appointments of government ministers and other top executives in government. She is in fact the de facto leader of the gender agenda in the NRM party.[70]

The Maama Syndrome in Uganda has turned out to be a deeper manifestation of elite patronage politics where individual members of the dominant groups are characterized by their accumulation of power in the sense of having the ability and resources needed to influence and control key decisions of state. The Maama Syndrome poses a huge challenge for other NRM women leaders who should see Janet Museveni as their role model because it has impacted their effectiveness as appointed and elected leaders participating in policy-making processes. The syndrome is an emerging trend in Uganda where to enter and survive in public decision-making spaces – through elections or appointment, Maama herself must have blessed and opened the doors for them: 'In this country the top first lady (Maama) has a peculiar work method. She always protects her loyal confidants while dismissing those with dissenting views.'[71]

Janet Museveni thus benefits from and leverages her personal relations to strengthen her own personal position in the power matrix. After the 2016 election, analyst Angelo Izama, for example, speculated that Janet Museveni was rumoured to be the most likely successor to her husband as Museveni may have been at the stage when he needed to consider who can ensure the survival of his regime.[72] Her direct political roles and positions have augmented her power as the First Lady by creating specific state and non-state structures that provide her with instruments of political power and influence though not for the benefit of women as a social group. This phenomenon has been christened 'femocracy'. According to Amina Mama, femocracy is:

> an anti-democratic female power structure, which claims to exist for the advancement of ordinary women, but is unable to do so because it is dominated by a small clique of women whose authority derives from their being married to powerful men, rather than from any actions or ideas of their own.[73]

Mrs. Museveni's leadership has been criticized as instrumentalizing gender for political gain, rather than seeking to genuinely improve the status and welfare of women and girls. For example, in her work as Minister of Education, she was accused of failing to implement the presidential directive to provide sanitary towels to female pupils.[74] She allegedly told MPs that she doesn't agree that government should be providing sanitary pads to students, and that provision of school lunch and pads should be the responsibility of parents and not government.[75] This was confirmed by a girl-child education activist who was following up on the promise of providing sanitary pads. During the interview she revealed that:

> … But Mrs Museveni told the parliamentary committee on education that funding for the purchase of sanitary towels was not available. A packet of quality sanitary towels go for about four thousand Shillings (equivalent of just over one dollar). This is not going to solve the problem because parents of these girls do not have the money in the first place. It is as if she was mocking poor parents and not even interested in education for the girl-child and yet she is the concerned Minister.[76]

Maama has also been seen to fail in addressing or even focusing on the plight of the girl child in the areas of ending corporal punishment, elimination of harmful cultural practices like female genital mutilation, elimination of child marriage, promotion and protection of their rights and increased support towards their education.[77]

Women in Museveni's 'Fishermen' Cabinet

The appointment of thirty-four women in President Museveni's 82-member cabinet, including Jessica Alupo as Vice-president, and Robinah Nabbanja as Prime Minister followed President Museveni's 2021 re-election. In addition to these posts, two of the three Deputy Prime Ministers are also women, with others were placed in key ministries including education, health, energy and mineral resources, lands, communication, science and technology. The percentage of women in cabinet increased from 27 to 43 per cent and, for the second time, Museveni appointed a woman vice-president.[78] The new cabinet was a complete departure from the usual dominance of men. Even NRM loyalists were puzzled by Museveni's new line-up.

President Yoweri Museveni explained the logic behind his new cabinet by saying he followed Jesus Christ's footsteps and opted for 'fishermen' instead of intellectuals or highly learned people.[79] He was quoted in the media to have said: 'Jesus didn't recruit Pharisees, Sadducees or the Levites but he went for Simon Peter. Of course, he also had some intellectuals such as Luke who was a doctor. So, when you look at my list, know that I am in the path of Jesus Christ.'[80]

The general view is that this cabinet favours loyalty over competence and intellectualism, a view the president himself acknowledges.[81] In many respects this is a contradiction of the way NRM has hitherto presented itself as a grouping of educated, experienced and more technically competent people than their main rivals in 2021, the National Unity Platform (NUP).[82] The NRM supporters sought to contrast candidate Museveni, with his grasp of East African history, economic policy and security strategy, with the inexperienced NUP candidate Robert Kyagulanyi.[83] Yet public sentiments ridiculed Museveni's cabinet, asking if it can or will it deliver in tackling the difficult problems the country faces. One view is that the current cabinet cannot perform and deliver services to the public because it is not a meritorious cabinet. As one analyst noted, 'The challenges facing Uganda over the next five years increasingly require technical and technocratic knowledge. … our lives, businesses and public utilities are being built around electronic communications, money transfers, data storage and the interpretation of digital data.'[84]

Scholars have shown how women in elite political positions face negative gendered portrayals. Furthermore, the trivializing of women leaders in the media undermines their leadership.[85] The media ridiculed Museveni's appointees, particularly to the top positions of vice-president and prime minister, both women, with statements such as: 'we all know that the President doesn't look for the best and brightest. In fact, the best and brightest are shunned to keep patronage afloat on the shark-infested seas of Ugandan politics …. It's well known that President Museveni prefers uncritical cadres to critical Cassandras who would tell him the truth about his government being an express train to nowhere.'[86]

Despite the negative portrayal, the general feeling is that co-option of women in state structures makes them voiceless hence lending credibility to the system, which is responsible for the marginalization and exploitation of women as a social group. As such, women are appointed into leadership positions as tokenism. This scepticism deepens when the women leaders in government fail to present adequate protection and support to other women groups outside government.

The women's movement and its collapse

Over the past two decades the contributions and achievements as well as failures of women's movements and women's activism have been well documented.[87] The word 'movement' means 'to create action', to go from one place to another; sustaining a movement is about sustaining action.[88] Autonomous women's movements play significant roles in influencing progressive policy on violence and have held governments accountable for commitments to transform laws and policies into inclusive development.[89] In Uganda, women's active mobilization and power predate colonialism. Strengthened by the organizational capacity and activities of the UCW, discussed earlier in this chapter, the movement managed to live through the test of time resisting different regimes and worked to improve the lot of women through various initiatives.[90]

Although Uganda's women's movement survived the tumultuous times of Idi Amin,[91] a number of factors threaten its survival today. For example, pervasive militarism importantly reshapes local dynamics in a way that contributes to a patriarchal social order while also reinforcing authoritarianism in Uganda. Rebecca Tapscott discusses these dynamics, and how they can erode many forms of local and political organization – to which I add women's movements.[92] According to Tapscott, the militarized and gendered performances of power enacted by Museveni and the

NRM party are central to these dynamics.[93] National-level authoritarian power is produced and diffused into society through gendered local encounters, which mirror executive power and reproduce it through tensions and ambiguities between restraint and impunity.[94] Hence, the militarized masculinities serve for the autocratic rulers as a key mechanism of social control, including the control of women's rights activities. Confronted by these ambiguities, ordinary citizens learn to 'live with' authoritarian power in their everyday lives.[95]

State coercion also directly inhibits the ability for Ugandans to mobilize politically, again with direct consequences for the women's movement. This remains a pervasive problem despite repeated denunciations by local actors and the international community against the use of excessive force by the police and other security agencies to suppress demonstrations, and intimidation human rights defenders.[96] The security forces use unnecessary lethal force during protests, and have also taken advantage of the NGO Act, 2016 to silence civic activity. On 10 August 2021, the National Bureau for Non-Governmental Organizations indefinitely suspended fifty-four civil society groups, some of them belonging to the women's movement.[97] In the same year, the government indefinitely suspended the Democratic Governance Facility (DGF), a European Union fund for nongovernmental groups, leaving many women organizations stranded without funding.

Other studies have also indicated that the government-led institutionalization of gender has contributed to a deep rift between women in government settings and those in women's movements.[98] In addition, women's organizations often did not trust women in government and were therefore rarely consulted on policy issues by their official counterparts. In fact, it has also been claimed that the Ministry in charge of directing women's organization instead actively worked against them. For Uganda, the biggest blow came with the defeat of the 2009 Marriage and Divorce Bill, one of the most debated laws in the history of Uganda having been debated in parliament for almost five decades as far back as the colonial times. One of the main reasons why the Bill has been shelved every time it comes before Parliament is that it has faced stiff resistance from traditionalists, Muslims and Christians alike. The Bill is intended to reform and consolidate the law relating to marriage, separation and divorce in Uganda and therefore addresses issues like marital property, bride price, sexual abuse among spouses, cohabitation and polygamy.[99]

Conclusion

This chapter has assessed, through various angles, the extent to which Museveni's regime survival techniques use gender to co-opt feminism, and gain feminist compliance and acceptance of state feminism culture. The basic authoritarian practices or means through which Museveni and NRM have controlled the feminist agenda include the nature and type of securing female representation in the regime's legislative processes through quotas and direct appointments, support to gender institutionalization and corresponding gender policies, and the expansion of women in the cabinet. As a result, Uganda holds a distinction of having 43 per cent women in Cabinet, 46 per cent in local government positions and 33.8 per cent in parliament, while still performing poorly on substantive measures of gender equality.

President Museveni's regime appears to lead in the implementation of state feminist policies and nationalizing gender across political structures. In this scenario, Ugandan women are able to join government leadership and have gained access to private opportunities too, forming part of a wider ensemble of the functioning of national authoritarian institutions with the attendant implication of capitulating to mechanisms of authoritarian co-optation. On the other hand, rather than act as a transmission belt for Museveni's autocratic ideologies, in some sense the women's movement appears to have pulled back into oblivion. Many prominent members of the women's movement remain unconvinced by the current government's commitment to women's rights.[100]

The Ugandan example raises broader questions that extend beyond the experience of autocratic NRM governance: can states ever truly be feminist? Is state feminism not a form of co-option? In general, the NRM government appears to have broken political trust between the state and women, and Museveni's regime is recognized as using the institution of gender as a core survival strategy to secure and retain power. Numerous studies have synthesized state feminism and co-optation in various feminist fields. However, more research is needed to achieve deeper empirical insights that could help develop a feminist research agenda to identify theories and strategies to reverse feminist co-optation trends.

Gains by women are often contingent on systems becoming more just. It is antidemocratic to reverse these trends. Also, the women's movement can resist the tendency to deprioritize its own autonomy and ambition and choose not to disempower itself. The efforts to revitalize the women movement in Uganda at a minimum require actively recruiting and retaining women organizers, activists, community leaders and public figures to build a deep coalition of women participants. It also means providing many different points of entry for participating in the movement while recognizing the need to involve women of varied social standing.

Notes

1   Aili Mari Tripp, *Museveni's Uganda: Paradoxes of Power in a Hybrid Regime* (Boulder, CO: Lynne Reiner Publishers, 2010).

2   Jasmin Lorch and Bettina Bunk, 'Gender Politics, Authoritarian Regime Resilience, and the Role of Civil Society in Algeria and Mozambique', GIGA Working Papers, No. 292: 2016. GIGA German Institute of Global and Area Studies. http://hdl.handle.net/10419/147547

3   Anne Marie Goetz, 'Women's Political Effectiveness – A Conceptual Framework', in *No Shortcuts to Power: African Women in Politics and Policy Making*, ed. Anne Marie Goetz, Shireen Hassim and Robin Luckham (London: Zed Books, 2003).

4   Bradley L. DiMariano, *Gender and the Authoritarian Dynamic: An Analysis of Social Identity in the Partisanship of White Americans*, PhD diss. (University of Missouri-Saint Louis, 2021); Gökten Huriye Dogangün, *Gender Politics in Turkey and Russia: From State Feminism to Authoritarian Rule* (London: Bloomsbury Publishing, 2019); Daniela Donno and Anne-Kathrin Kreft, 'Authoritarian Institutions and Women's

Rights', *Comparative Political Studies* 52, no. 5 (2019): 720–53; Lorch and Bunk, 'Gender Politics'; Mary Gallagher and Jonathan K. Hanson, 'Authoritarian Survival, Resilience, and the Selectorate', in *Why Communism Didn't Collapse: Understanding Regime Resilience in Asia and Europe*, ed. Martin Dimitrov (Cambridge: Cambridge University Press, 2013); Anne Marie Goetz, 'No Shortcuts to Power: Constraints on Women's Political Effectiveness in Uganda', *The Journal of Modern African Studies* 40, no. 4 (2002): 549–75; Joe Oloka-Onyango, 'On the Barricades: Civil Society and the Role of Human and Women's Rights Organizations in the Formulation of the Bill of Rights of Uganda's 1995 Constitution', Working Paper No. 60 (Kampala: Centre for Basic Research, 2000).

5   Co-opting feminism is a term adopted by de Jong Sara and Kimm Suzanne, 'The Co-optation of Feminisms: A Research Agenda', *International Feminist Journal of Politics* 19, no. 2 (2017): 185–200.

6   Pauline Stoltz, 'Co-optation and Feminisms in the Nordic Region: "Gender-friendly" Welfare States, "Nordic exceptionalism" and Intersectionality', in *Feminisms in the Nordic Region: Gender and Politics*, ed. Suvi Keskinen, Pauline Stoltz and Diana Mulinari (New York: Palgrave Macmillan, 2021); Jennifer Allsopp, 'State Feminism: Co-opting Women's Voices', *Open Democracy* (2012). https://www.opendemocracy.net/en/5050/state-feminism-co-opting-womens-voices/

7   Lorch and Bunk, 'Gender Politics'.

8   See, for example, Sapkota Mahendra and Dahal Kabita, 'Gender and Politics: A Feminist Critique of the State', *Journal of Political Science* 22 (2022): 75–91; Diana Højlund Madsen, ed., *Gendered Institutions and Women's Political Representation in Africa* (London: Zed books, 2021); Yongshun Cai, 'Power Structure and Regime Resilience: Contentious Politics in China', *British Journal of Political Science* 38, no. 3 (2008): 411–32. Dogangün, *Gender Politics;* Donno and Kreft, 'Authoritarian Institutions'; Gallagher and Hanson, 'Authoritarian Survival, Resilience'; Tripp, *Museveni's Uganda*.

9   Lorch and Bunk, 'Gender Politics'.

10   Mahendra and Dahal Kabita, 'Gender and Politics'; Gary Goertz and Amy G Mazur, *State Feminism* (Cambridge: Cambridge University Press, 2010); Joni Lovenduski, 'State Feminism and Women's Movements', *West European Politics* 31, no. 1–2 (2008): 169–94.

11   Mary C. Burke and Mary Bernstein, 'How the Right Usurped the Queer Agenda: Frame Co-optation in Political Discourse', *Sociological Forum* 29, no. 4 (2014): 831.

12   Madsen, *Gendered Institutions;* Tripp, *Museveni's Uganda;* Lorch and Bunk, 'Gender Politics'.

13   Goertz and Mazur, *State Feminism;* Lovenduski, 'State Feminism'.

14   Cecilia L. Ridgeway and Lynn Smith-Lovin, 'The Gender System and Interaction', *Annual Review of Sociology* 25 (1999): 191–216.

15   Judith Lorber, *Gender Inequalities: Feminist Theories and Politics*, Fifth Edition (Oxford: Oxford University Press, 2012).

16   Ibid.

17   Sylvia Tamale, *Decolonization and Afro-Feminism* (Ottawa: Daraja Press, 2020); Madsen, *Gendered Institutions;* Amina Mama, 'We Will Not Be Pacified: From Freedom Fighters to Feminists', *European Journal of Women's Studies* 27, no. 4 (2020): 362–80.

18   E.g., Tripp, Goetz, Lovesdaski, cited above.

19   Sapkota and Dahal, 'Gender and Politics'.

20   Moa Frödin Gruneau, 'Why History Matters for Gender Balance in Political Representation', *LSE European Politics and Policy (EUROPP) blog* (21 July 2021). https://blogs.lse.ac.uk/europpblog/2021/07/21/why-history-matters-for-gender-balance-in-political-representation/

21   See Aili Mari Tripp, 'Women in Ugandan Politics and History: Collective Biography', in *Oxford Research Encyclopedia of African History* (Oxford: Oxford University Press, 2020). Also Aili Mari Tripp, *Women in Politics in Uganda* (Madison: The University of Wisconsin Press, 2000).

22   Tripp, *Women in Politics*.

23   Ibid., 39.

24   Ibid.

25   See Hanibal Goitom, 'Today in History: Idi Amin Overthrows President Milton Obote in Uganda', *Library of Congress Blogs* (25 January 2018). https://blogs.loc.gov/law/2018/01/today-in-history-idi-amin-overthrows-president-milton-obote-in-uganda/

26   Tripp, *Women in Politics*, 277.

27   Ibid., 278.

28   Vibeke Wang and Mi Yung Yoon, 'Recruitment Mechanisms for Reserved Seats for Women in Parliament and Switches to Non-quota Seats: A Comparative Study of Tanzania and Uganda', *The Journal of Modern African Studies* 56, no. 2 (2018): 299–324.

29   Aili Mari Tripp, 'The Instrumentalization of Women Opposition Leaders for Authoritarian Regime Entrenchment: The Case of Uganda', *Politics and Governance* 11, no. 1 (2023): 156.

30   Dan Ottemoeller, 'The Politics of Gender in Uganda: Symbolism in the Service of Pragmatism', *African Studies Review* 42, no. 2 (1999): 89.

31   Ibid; Hanssen Kari Nordstoga, 'Towards Multiparty System in Uganda: The Effect on Female Representation in Politics', Chr. Michelsen Institute (2006); Goetz, 'No Shortcuts to Power'; Tripp, *Women in Politics*.

32   Nordstoga, 'Towards Multiparty System'.

33   Jacqueline Asiimwe-Mwesige, 'Women's Experiences in the Transition from the Movement System to Multiparty System of Governance.' Briefing Paper, Konrad Adeneur Stiftung (2006). https://library.fes.de/pdf-files/bueros/uganda/05918.pdf

34   Interview, Kampala 16 November 2021.

35   Ibid.

36   Asiimwe-Mwesige, 'Women's Experiences'.

37   Ibid.

38   Ragnhild L. Muriaas and Vibeke Wang, 'Executive Dominance and the Politics of Quota Representation in Uganda', *The Journal of Modern African Studies* 50, no. 2 (2012): 309–38.

39   Amanda Clayton, Cecilia Josefsson and Vibeke Wang, 'Quotas and Women's Substantive Representation: Evidence from a Content Analysis of Ugandan Plenary Debates', *Politics & Gender* 13, no. 2 (2016); Gretchen Bauer, 'Reserved Seats for Women MPs: Affirmative Action for the National Women's Movement or the National Resistance Movement', in *Women and Legislative Representation*, ed. Manon Tremblay (New York: Palgrave Macmillan, 2008); Muriaas and Wang, 'Executive Dominance'; Aili Mari Tripp, 'Women Appointed to Top Positions in Uganda, but Feelings Are Mixed', *The Conversation* (15 June 2021).

40   Amanda Gouws, 'Reducing Women to Bare Life: Sexual Violence in South Africa', *Feminist Encounters: A Journal of Critical Studies in Culture and Politics* 5, no. 1 (2021): 1–12; Goetz, 'No Shortcuts to Power'; Lena Wängnerud, 'Women in

Parliaments: Descriptive and Substantive Representation', *Annual Review of Political Science* 12 (2009): 51–69; Josephine Ahikire, Peace Musiimenta and Amon Mwiine, 'Making a Difference: Embracing the Challenge of Women's Substantive Engagement in Political Leadership in Uganda', *Feminist Africa* 20 (2014): 26–42.

41   Madsen, *Gendered Institutions*; Ahikire et al., 'Making a Difference'.

42   See History of Uganda Parliament found at: https://www.parliament.go.ug/page/history-parliament

43   Source: Solome Nakaweesi-Nakimbugwe, 'Country Analysis: Leadership in Advancing Women's Rights in Public Decision-Making Processes in Uganda', *Robert Bosch Stiftung* (2018). https://www.bosch-stiftung.de/sites/default/files/publications/pdf/2019-08/Uganda%20Country%20Analysis_0.pdf Table is reproduced with permission of the authour.

44   The top 10 are: Rwanda 61.25 per cent, South Africa 46.5 per cent, Namibia 44.23 per cent, Senegal 42.68 per cent, Mozambique 42.4 per cent, Ethiopia 41.49 per cent, Cape Verde 38.89 per cent, Burundi 38.21 per cent, Tanzania 36.86 per cent and Cameroon 33.89 per cent.

45   Rwanda, for example, jumped from 17 per cent of parliamentary seats held by women in 1998 to 56 per cent in 2008 and stabilized at 61.3 per cent since 2018, the first country in the world with a female majority in parliament.

46   Goetz, 'No Shortcuts to Power'.

47   Ibid., 560.

48   United Nations Democracy Fund, *Strengthening CSO Engagement with Defence Institutions to Reduce Corruption and Strengthen Accountability* (New York: UNDEF, 2017).

49   Ibid.

50   Tripp, 'Women Appointed'.

51   Aili Mari Tripp, 'New Trends in Women and Politics in Africa', in *The Palgrave Handbook of African Women's Studies* (New York: Palgrave, 2021), 517–37.

52   Among was one of the few legislators who was elected unopposed to join the 11th parliament though her victory was contentious because the electoral commission blocked some of her competitors from nomination. In the 10th Parliament, she served as Vice Chairperson of the Committee on Commissions, Statutory Authorities and State Enterprises (COSASE). Among was elected the new Speaker of the parliament of Uganda on 25 March 2022 replacing the late Jacob Oulanyah who passed away.

53   Interview with a women's rights activist, Kampala 13 November 2021.

54   Tripp, 'Women Appointed'.

55   Muriaas and Wang, 'Executive Dominance'.

56   Clayton et al., 'Quotas and Women's'.

57   Aili Mari Tripp and Alice Kang, 'The Global Impact of Quotas on the Fast Track to Increased Female Legislative Representation', *Comparative Political Studies* 41, no. 3 (2008): 338–61.

58   Ibid.

59   Wang and Yoon, 'Recruitment Mechanisms'; Clayton et al., 'Quotas and Women's'; Ahikire et al., 'Making a Difference'.

60   Madsen, *Gendered Institutions*.

61   Jo-Ansie van Wyk, Arina Muresan and Chidochashe Nyere, 'African First Ladies, Politics and the State', *Politeia* 37, no. 2 (2018): 1–20.

62   Jo-Ansie Van Wyk, 'The First Ladies of Southern Africa: Trophies or Trailblazers'? *South African Journal of Political Studies* 44, no. 1 (2017): 157–72; van Wyk et al., 'African First Ladies'.

63   van Wyk, 'The First Ladies'.

64   Ibid.

65   The Independent, 'Janet Museveni Power Analysed' (3 June 2019). https://www. independent.co.ug/janet-museveni-power-analysed/

66   Ibid.

67   The term 'Maama' is a Luganda/Swahili word referring to an elder, opinion leader or mother.

68   Shaban Abdur Rahman Alfa, 'The African First Lady: Powerful yet Unelected Politicians', *Africanews* (21 July 2017).

69   See Yusuf Kalyango and Betty H. Winfield, 'Rhetorical Media Framing of Two First Lady Political Candidates across Cultures', *Global Media Journal* 8, no. 15 (2009): 1–34.

70   See *The Independent*, 'Janet Museveni Power'.

71   Interview, Kampala, 2 December 2021.

72   Angelo Izama, 'The Queen of Uganda's Museveni Dynasty', *Foreign Policy* (24 February 2016). https://foreignpolicy.com/2016/02/24/the-queen-of-ugandas-museveni-dynasty/

73   Amina Mama, 'Feminism or Femocracy? State Feminism and Democratisation in Nigeria', *African Development* 20, no. 1 (1995): 37–58.

74   Michael Wambi, 'Janet Museveni Faces Criticism over Sanitary Pads', *URN News* (7 March 2017). https://ugandaradionetwork.net/story/janet-museveni-criticised-over-sanitary-towels-budget; The Observer, 'First Lady Opposes Museveni's Sanitary Towel Pledge' (17 January 2020). https://observer.ug/news/headlines/63231-first-lady-opposes-museveni-s-sanitary-towel-pledge

75   *The Observer*, 'First Lady Opposes'.

76   Interview, Kampala, 30 October 2022.

77   Proscovia Nakibuuka Mbonye, 'On the International Day of the Girl Child, Rural Adolescent Girls Highlight Their Plight', *UNICEF* (11 December 2016). https:// www.unicef.org/uganda/stories/international-day-girl-child-rural-adolescent-girls-highlight-their-plight

78   Dr. Specioza Wandira Kazibwe served as Vice-president from 1994 to 2003.

79   Phillip Matogo, 'Museveni Mistaken on Parable of Fishermen Cabinet', *Sunday Monitor* (25 July 2021). https://www.monitor.co.ug/uganda/oped/commentary/museveni-mistaken-on-parable-of-fishermen-cabinet-3485632

80   See Uganda Update, 'Museveni Explains the Logic behind His New Cabinet Full of "Fishermen"' (11 June 2021). https://ugandaupdatenews.com/museveni-explains-the-logic-behind-his-new-cabinet-full-of-fishermen/

81   Godfrey Olukya, 'Mixed Response to Appointment of Women in Top Positions in Uganda'. Kampala: Anadolu Agency (30 August 2021). https://www.aa.com. tr/en/africa/mixed-response-to-appointment-of-women-in-top-positions-in-uganda/2350290

82   Matogo, 'Museveni Mistaken'.

83   Ibid.

84   Timothy Kalyegira, 'Will Museveni's Cabinet of Fishermen Deliver'? *Sunday Monitor* (13 June 2021). https://www.monitor.co.ug/uganda/magazines/people-power/will-museveni-cabinet-of-fishermen-deliver–3435080

85   Nakaweesi-Kimbugwe, 'Country Analysis'; Kalyango and Winfield, 'Rhetorical Media'.

86   Matogo, 'Museveni Mistaken'.

87   Amanda Gouws and Azille Coetzee, 'Women's Movements and Feminist Activism',
      Agenda 33, no. 2 (2019): 1–8; Mama, 'We Will Not Be Pacified;' Aili Mari Tripp,
      Isabel Casimiro, Joy Kwesiga and Alica Mungwa, *African Women's Movements:
      Changing Political Landscapes* (Cambridge: Cambridge University Press, 2009).

88   Hildy Gottlieb, 'Building Movements, Not Organizations', *Stanford Social Innovation
      Review* (28 July 2015). https://doi.org/10.48558/RKWS-DG43

89   Tabitha Mulyampiti, 'Women Organizations and the Development AID Discourse:
      Framing Feminist Agency and Capabilities' (Unpublished, 2023).

90   Richard Ssewakiryanga, 'Tangible or Superficial Power: The Role of Civil Society in
      Advancing the Women's Agenda' (unpublished, undated).

91   The regime banned women from wearing miniskirts, and any woman found
      in a miniskirt would be molested and sometimes even raped. There were other
      outrageous pronouncements like stopping women from wearing perfumes and
      make-up of any nature as conditions that the state imposed on women. 'Unmarried
      women' were banned from the streets of Kampala.

92   Rebecca Tapscott, 'Militarized Masculinity and the Paradox of Restraint: Mechanisms
      of Social Control under Modern Authoritarianism', *International Affairs* 96, no. 6
      (2020): 1565–84.

93   See also Tapscott's chapter in this volume.

94   Tapscott, 'Militarized Masculinity'.

95   Ibid., 2.

96   Women Initiative for Gender Justice, 'Ugandan Women Civil Society Organisations
      Protest Use of Excessive Force' (1 June 2011). https://4genderjustice.org/
      uncategorized/ugandan-women-civil-society-organisations-protest-use-of-excessive-
      force/

97   Oryem Nyeko, 'Court Ends Suspension of NGO in Uganda', *Human Rights Watch*
      (24 May 2022). https://www.hrw.org/news/2022/05/24/court-ends-suspension-
      ngo-uganda#:~:text=The%20Ugandan%20High%20Court's%20decision,civil%20
      society%20groups%20in%20Uganda.

98   Ahikire, Josephine, 'African Feminism in Context: Reflections on the Legitimation
      Battles, Victories and Reversals', *Feminist Africa* 19 (2014): 7–23; Tripp, *Women in
      Politics*; Sylvia Tamale, *When Hens Begin to Crow: Gender and Parliamentary Politics
      in Uganda* (Boulder, CO: Westview Press, 1999). Diana Højlund Madsen, Amanda
      Gouws and Asiyati Lorraine Chiweza, 'Gender Mainstreaming in Africa: Local
      Translations and Institutional Challenges in Ghana, Malawi and South Africa', in
      Routledge Handbook of Public Policy in Africa, ed. Gedion Onyango (London and
      New York: Routledge, 2021), 524–35.

99   Godiva Akullo Monica, 'How Long Shall We Wait? An Analysis of the
      Marriage and Divorce Bill 2009' (2018). https://cepa.or.ug/wp-content/
      uploads/2018/06/270900389-HOW-LONG-SHALL-WE-WAIT-AN-ANALYSIS-OF-
      THE-MARRIAGE-AND-DIVORCE-BILL-2009.pdf

100   One of the most important voices in recent years is former minister Maria Matembe
      who was sacked from cabinet and became an outspoken critic of Museveni and his
      government. See her memoirs, Miria R. K. Matembe, *The Struggle for Freedom and
      Democracy Betrayed* (Kampala: Self-Published, 2019).

5

Obstructing civil society: State backlash, co-optation and coping mechanisms

Mesharch W. Katusiimeh

The concept of civil society has closely been associated with democracy and democratization. There was a significant upsurge of civil society organizations (CSOs) in countries of the developing world in the 1980s and 1990s, especially with donors pushing for the adoption of policies on 'good governance' and liberal democracy.[1] Since that time, CSOs have been very active in the areas of governance, protection of human rights and the promotion of political freedoms. Among the many forces that contributed to the political liberalization of many African nations, civil society actors played a big role in opening public space for wider political representation.[2]

Following these developments, several African countries adopted frameworks for civil society engagement including standards to respect, empower and protect civil society.[3] In contrast, many regimes have increased the regulation of civil society actors and also adopted repressive tactics to maintain power. The existence of these contradictions invites a re-examination of the current state of civil society. Despite the wide literature on civil society and the increased attention CSOs have received, their role in relation to the deepening of autocratic regimes is at best unclear. In the light of the above, this chapter addresses the dilemmas facing civil society in Uganda, where the processes of democratization and autocratization have gone hand-in-hand. How have civil society actors dealt with the challenges presented by the clamp-down on civil liberties and how have they coped with government repression but also contributed, inadvertently, to the extant system?

Civil society means different things to different people, and indeed, the meaning of the term has changed on a number of occasions. According to the report by the Uganda NGO Forum, the relationship between civil society and the state is viewed from two lenses: civil society that provides public services is perceived as 'pro-government' and that which champions human rights and accountability is perceived as 'agents of foreign interests'.[4] Thus, of late there has emerged the recognition of informal associations and movements that are distinct from the traditional CSOs.[5] They also set themselves apart from traditional groups such as trade unions, cooperatives and student or women's movements, whose very existence tends to depend on favours from the state or on different forms of patronage.[6] However, in this chapter, the concept of civil society is defined to include free associations such as NGOs, media, religious organizations and other self-organizing organizations not controlled by the state.[7]

The chapter is based on three sources of information: primary sources including in-depth interviews with key informants, secondary sources (published and unpublished, academic and non-academic, including newspapers) and conversations and interviews with civil society activists of different kinds at all levels. The chapter therefore combines literature review and empirical investigation. The second section of the chapter provides an overview of the historical context of civil society and democratization in Uganda, while the third is an empirical examination of the types of CSOs, their experiences and challenges they face including how they relate with the NRM government. The final section outlines the main conclusions and implications of the study.

Evolution of civil society in Uganda

Civil society as it existed in pre-colonial Uganda was composed of community institutions including self-help and solidarity groups whose objective was to cultivate solidarity among members. During colonial rule, Ugandans mobilized themselves to oppose colonial policies through associations such as Uganda African Drivers Association formed in 1939 and Uganda African Farmers Union formed in 1949.[8] Communities in Uganda mobilized themselves for collective benefit for instance associations like 'Munno Mukabi' and 'Bataka Twezikye', among others.[9] Other non-state groups included age grade, secret societies and religious groups which employed diverse means in collaboration with traditional governing authorities to promote various socio-cultural interests in quest of a collective mission. The arrival of missionaries led to the growth of religious/faith based groups, which established churches, schools and hospitals. According to Doyle, by 1932 the Christian Missionaries had already established twenty-three clinics especially dealing with maternity and child welfare issues.[10] Missionaries were closely followed by the colonizers.

The colonial government in Uganda regarded civil society groups with great suspicion fearing that they could be instrumental in mobilizing against them, hence it set out to actively define and control associational life. Despite the colonial efforts to prevent most attempts at mobilization, Ugandans still found ways to create and join informal associations. For example, as early as 1922, the Uganda African Civil Servants Association was established to contest African exclusion from the extension of government bonuses to Europeans and Asians.[11] Cooperative organizations which were mainly grounded in rural communities were largely concerned with responding to the monopoly of members of the Indian community in cotton ginning and coffee processing.[12] Trade unions developed and gained recognition and momentum reaching a climax in 1945 when they organized a number of strikes and riots whose major grievances were largely economic albeit with hidden political motives.

Cooperatives worked underground as they were considered illegal and subversive by the colonial masters until 1946 when the Cooperative Ordinance was enacted.[13] Many other groups/organizations evolved to resist colonial rule and demand for reform in colonial policies on the pricing of agricultural produce. The birth of membership organizations such as the 'Young Men of Buganda' and the 'Uganda African Welfare

Associations' are cases in point.[14] The Bataka movement, the Uganda Farmers Union and the Bana ba Kintu were predecessors to the Uganda National Congress (UNC), the country's first political party established in 1952.[15] These emergent groups focused on unfair colonial taxation and unequal labour practices. Religious groups also emerged to counter the influence of Christianity by drawing on African cultural beliefs and traditional religion.[16] The colonial government responded by legislating tighter controls on African associations through registration. Statutes such as the 1946 Cooperative Act effectively placed the cooperatives under state supervision. Other laws were used to proscribe newspapers and arrest agitators.

For instance in 1956, the Uganda Express and Uganda Post were banned by the British colonial authorities for alleged sedition and the publisher, J.W. (Jolly 'Joe') Kiwanuka, was jailed.[17] Indeed, for most of the colonial period, vocal civil society groups were banned and suppressed, for example the political confrontation and crisis of 1945.[18]

As a result of the shrinking associational space, social organizations began to organize discreetly. The effort of CSOs partly contributed to the independence of Uganda. For example, in 1962, Kabaka Yekka, a pressure group, which became a political movement, formed to demand Buganda independence allied with Uganda People's Congress (UPC) to form the first independence government. Generally, trade Unions, ethnic groups and resistance movements mobilized supporters at both local and national levels, exerting pressure on the colonialists to relinquish power.[19]

The kind of civil society that enabled UPC/KY to come to power was suppressed once independence had been achieved. With the acquisition of power, UPC turned its attention to the practical aspects of economic development and started viewing CSOs as a potential source of opposition. Thus, in 1963, the Obote government nationalized the education sector with the state extending its monopoly over education through hierarchical and bureaucratized structures that were replicated within the schools. As Ssekamwa observes, Milton Obote's first step after independence was to enact the Education Act of 1963. The Act aimed at reducing the influence of religious foundation bodies in schools and to treat all teachers as government civil servants regardless of the foundation body of their schools. The Act also intended to 'depoliticize education'.[20] The un-pronounced intention was to undermine the involvement of parents, communities and religious bodies in schools, particularly at the decision-making level.[21]

The momentum of CSOs was significantly undercut by the single-party political structure following the political crisis of 1966/7 with the adoption of the pigeon hole constitution and the exiling of Kabaka Mutesa II, First President of Uganda and King of Buganda. From then on, until his overthrow in 1971, the Obote regime relied heavily on the support of the army; the military became partners of the government to the extent that no major political action could be contemplated without first ensuring the support of the military.[22] In the political changes that occurred 1966–7, Obote engineered military and constitutional manoeuvres that saw traditional leaders suppressed and removed from their seats.[23]

During the period 1971–79 of Idi Amin's rule, Uganda was characterized by dictatorship and the suppression of several freedoms including the right to associate which stifled the growth and activities of CSOs. Under Amin, the curtailing of CSOs assumed genocidal dimensions, or what some political commentators described as a 'reign of terror'.[24] Amin's government took over all the media, and some religious groups were outlawed.[25] For example, in September 1977, President Amin banned Pentecostal churches, and on 12 April 1978 armed soldiers stormed and desecrated the full gospel church, at Makerere arresting 200 believers.[26] Throughout Amin's period in power only a handful of faith-based organizations persisted in their work because of the terror meted out against them by the regime.[27]

From 1980 until 1985 the civil society sector grew steadily both in number and in activity.[28] NGOs developed specifically to participate in the reconstruction of the country following Amin's ousting and to offer social and welfare services. After a five-year guerrilla war in Greater Luweero, Museveni's fighters were warmly welcomed by the population when they removed the military junta that had overthrown Obote II. Museveni took the oath of office on 26 January 1986 promising that the occasion did not simply amount to another 'mere change of guard' but was a 'fundamental change'.[29]

Under pressure from the Bretton Woods Institutions, Structural Adjustment Programmes (SAPs) were introduced which had a telling impact on the operation of CSOs. While previously a strong state was considered crucial for economic growth, the 'Washington Consensus' that emerged in the 1980s prescribed a reduction of the state and an increasing role for civil society.[30] The state was perceived as bad and civil society as inherently good and it featured prominently in the discourse on good governance and major policy priority of donors. Government liberalized the economy and allowed competition against state-owned enterprises including cooperative unions. As a result, a number of these unions ran bankrupt and collapsed.

In the 1980s and 1990s, externally funded humanitarian NGOs were the dominant civic actors in Uganda, due to the near collapse of state authority after the rise of several armed rebellions. SAPs reforms were credited with restoring macro-economic stability; however, this was achieved at the cost of significantly reducing state capacity to provide public goods and services.

Poverty remained high and a shortage of social services made a case for the promotion of CSOs especially NGOs.[31] In this context, civil society in Uganda – largely equated with the activities of NGOs which frequently received aid from overseas donors – more often than not focused their work on delivery of services including health care, education and social welfare.[32] The 2000s witnessed an upsurge in advocacy and human rights organizations that entered Uganda in part as a condition for the receipt of donor aid.[33] This opened the way for CSOs that have dominated the civic space either as charities and development organizations or as human rights advocacy organizations. Donors have strongly favoured these CSOs, and indeed the latter are almost the result of donor conditions asking governments to open space for civil society development.[34]

The obstruction of civil society in Museveni's Uganda

NGOs

As CSOs and especially the NGOs proliferated, and their roles expanded beyond the traditional service delivery in relief and other humanitarian interventions, government responded with measures to regulate their activities. Government enacted the 1989 NGO Statute and later the Non-Governmental Organizations National NGO Policy-Uganda Act 2006. The willingness of donors, international NGOs and encouragement of government have contributed to the tremendous growth of the local voluntary sector. The main characteristic of local NGOs is that they are formed with the aim of addressing local issues but also, targeting funding by either foreign governments or international NGOs, which act as conduits of international finance to the local beneficiaries. This empowers them financially but also stifles independent decision-making. As some commentators have observed, local NGOs in Uganda suffer from a dependency syndrome and lack independent means of self-sustenance.[35] This has sometimes been attributed to the nature of the economic classes that exist in Uganda; that is, most people are poor and the middle class is economically weak.

However, government has accused some NGOs of acting as opposition political groups in many instances. With leading opposition political parties and their leaders highly restricted from operating freely, civil society actors have filled this gap which has resulted in the blurring of the lines between political opposition and civil society. NGOs have been regularly labelled as opposition groups during election periods. For example, in the period prior to the 2011 elections, the civil society groups came up with a document known as the *Citizens' Compact on Free and Fair Elections*.[36] The government received it with disdain, and shelved it. In attempting to control its critics, among them civil society, the regime of President Museveni has resorted to the use of state propaganda to tarnish the reputation and standing of NGOs with the hope of diminishing their influence in society.[37] Accusations such as being tools of foreigners and therefore serving the interests of aliens rather than the local citizens have been rampant,[38] the aim of the state being to cut off the support of the local citizens for these organizations.

As already mentioned, in 2016, the government of Uganda passed the 2016 Non-Government Organizations' Act (NGO Act, 2016), which was very restrictive on the operations of civil society actors. Section 44 prohibits NGOs from carrying out activities in any part of the country without approval from the District Non-Governmental Monitoring Committee (DNMC) and the local government, and a signed memorandum of understanding (MoU) to that effect. Additionally, NGOs may not extend their operations to new areas unless they have received a recommendation from the National Bureau for NGOs through the DNMC of that area. Section 5 establishes a National Bureau for NGOs that is granted broad powers, including to revoke an NGO's permit.

Besides the restrictive regulatory environment, NGOs in Uganda face other challenges including raids by security agencies, threats of deregistration, and break-ins during which office equipment and files are stolen.[39] Affected NGOs included Uganda Womens Network, Great Lakes Initiatives for Strategic Studies, Action Aid International-Uganda, National Coalition of Human Rights Defenders and many others. Moreover, in some instances, meetings by civic groups and human rights defenders have been stopped by police, which deemed them illegal.[40] In May 2019, a meeting to commemorate the International Day Against Homophobia, Transphobia and Biphobia (IDAHOT) was blocked on the orders of the Minister for Ethics and Integrity.

The Public Order Management Act (POMA), signed into law in October 2013, regulates public meetings which, according to the law, means a gathering, assembly, procession or demonstration in a public place or premise held for purposes of discussing acting upon, petitioning or expressing views on a matter of public interest.[41] This law has been used to limit civil society activities, to control civic and political space and gives the police broad powers to authorize or halt public gatherings. According to POMA, organizers of a public meeting must give at least three days' notice of the same to the police. If they fail to do so the event can be shut down, and the organizers held liable for a criminal offence. In December 2014, Phil Wilmot, an American living in Uganda and founder of Solidarity Uganda, was arrested and charged under POMA for holding a small meeting at a Guesthouse in Lira where he 'allegedly recruited people into activism'.[42]

While opposition politicians have been the primary targets of POMA restraints, CSOs working on contentious issues have also faced restrictions. In March 2014, the police dispersed a meeting of the Free and Fair Elections Campaign in Mbale by shooting into the air and using teargas. In Kabale, Zac Niringiye, an activist of the Free and Fair Elections Campaign and retired Assistant Bishop of Kampala, the number two in the Anglican Church hierarchy, was blocked on two occasions from addressing the public during a university lecture and radio interview for 'publicizing an illegal meeting [...] that may incite violence'.[43]

President Museveni and other government officials are sceptical of the self-arrogated claim of NGOs and other advocacy organizations that they represent the citizenry, the poor, the disadvantaged or any other specific constituency. NRM officials claim that they were elected in honest elections in which the whole citizenry participated and their behaviour is under the constant supervision of accountability agencies to assure that their policies and decisions are responsive to the public. In contrast, they argue that most CSOs are directed by a cadre of self-appointed leaders, many not even membership organizations, and are not subject – as politicians are – to the scrutiny of formal mechanisms of legal and political accountability.[44]

In 2017, a number of organizations including Action-Aid International-Uganda, Uhuru Institute and the Great Lakes Initiative for Strategic Studies were raided by the police which conducted a search with authorization to access computer accessories, mobile handsets, money transfer and bank-related transaction documents. The raid was followed by the freezing in October 2017 of the bank accounts of these organizations, which were accused of funding anti-government activities at a time the ruling party was driving a campaign to remove the presidential age limit provision from the constitution.[45] Also in October 2017, government directed twenty-five NGOs to declare their financial information to the national NGO bureau.

Later in July, 2018, the Electoral Commission (EC) suspended accreditation for election-related activities of the Citizens' Coalition for Electoral Democracy in Uganda (CCEDU). Without granting CCEDU the right to be heard, the group was accused of being partisan and failing to adhere to the legal framework and guidelines of the EC. Although the ban was eventually lifted, the suspension did not allow CCEDU to observe local elections, by-elections and elections in newly created districts. In effect, CCEDU was rendered ineffectual to the purpose for which it had been created.[46]

Media

State ownership of print and broadcasting media is considered to hamper a healthy civil society. Before the state liberalized Uganda's media landscape and privatised state media in the early 1990s, the media did not seriously function as a human rights champion and democracy watchdog. Privately owned media began to play a noticeable key role in the democratization process with the opening of privately owned television and radio stations, newspapers and social media platforms. However, state harassment of journalists and frequent closure of media houses mean the media cannot play a significant and positive role in the democratization process. Radio stations and newspaper houses have been closed several times.[47]

Muzzling political speech tends to be more pronounced in electioneering years. During periods of elections, broadcasts or new articles touching on sensitive issues, or providing a platform for the opposition, leave journalists at risk. For example, on 21 July 2015, three journalists in Jinja town, eastern Uganda, were suspended after hosting Kizza Besigye, the leading opposition figure, for a radio interview. The same day in Gulu, Bonny Payira of Jal Fresh Radio was arrested along with three of his talk show panelists for using language that allegedly insulted President Yoweri Museveni.[48] Just weeks later in early August, Eshato Publications Limited was forced to remove Mbabazi's congratulatory message from a consecration magazine of the new Bishop of North Ankole Diocese, Amama Mbabazi, an erstwhile confidant of Museveniwas opposing Museveni in 2016 elections. Two individuals (Pison Mugizi and Robert Baingana) were arrested for overseeing its sale. They allegedly printed the magazine with a congratulatory message of Mbabazi against the advice of the Diocesan Consecration committee allegedly because of pressure from State House.[49] During the 2020–1 campaign season where Mr. Robert Kyagulanyi popularly known as Bobi Wine emerged as the main opposition candidate, reports of obstructing journalists including arresting them became the order of the day.[50]

Similarly, the Uganda Communications Commission (UCC) on 6 March 2018 issued a one-month notice requiring all online data communication service providers, including online publishers, online news platforms and online radio and television operators to apply and obtain authorization from the commission with immediate effect. According to the notice, UCC based its decision on Section 5 of the UCC Act, which mandates the Commission to monitor, inspect, license, supervise, control and regulate all communications services. This mandate extends to audio, visual or data content production or dissemination through traditional broadcast media as well as internet-based platforms. The Commission indicated that measures would be enforced against non-compliant service providers and this 'may entail directing Internet Service Providers (ISP) to block access to such websites and/or streams'.[51]

A growing number of journalists and others have been charged in courts of law with defamation lawsuits. In 2015, journalists Madinah Nalwanga and Patrick Tumwesigye of Vision Group; Benon Tugumisirize and Ronald Nahabwe of *Red Pepper*; and Pidson Kareire of Drone Media were charged with criminal libel and defamation.[52] In 2017, eight managers and editors of *Red Pepper* were charged with libel, defamation, treason and computer misuse over a story which claimed Rwanda believed Ugandan President Yoweri Museveni was plotting to oust its leader, Paul Kagame.[53]

Criminal libel and defamation are usually preferred against journalists under Section 179 of the Penal Code Act. There are ongoing court actions such as that at the East African Court of Justice aimed at challenging sections 179 and 180 of the Penal Code Act. Other laws such as the Anti-Terrorism Act 2002, Anti-Pornography Act 2014, Regulation of Interception of Communication Act 2010, Computer Misuse Act 2011 and the Official Secrets Act 1964 have been used to restrict media freedom. Specifically, the Computer Misuse Act has been used to clamp down on social media critics like Dr Stella Nyanzi who was charged severally with cyber harassment and offensive communication. Other victims include MP Betty Nambooze who was also charged with cyber harassment and offensive communication.

On top of the restrictive legal and regulatory regime, journalists are facing various safety and security challenges as they are often targeted by security agencies through arbitrary arrest and harassment in the course of their duty. They are frequently victims of abuse by security forces especially the military and police. For example, the Human Rights Network for Journalists reported in 2016 that 2015 was a particularly bad year for journalists – some were shot while others suffered permanent injuries. Of 143 cases of press violations, 107 were committed by police, constituting 70 per cent.[54] In 2017, there were forty-five cases of arrests and detention of journalists, and twenty-seven cases of assault on journalists while eleven cases of blocking journalists from accessing news locations and ten of malicious damage to journalists' equipment and two cases of switching off radio stations on the orders of the UCC were also reported.[55] During 2018, the Press Index Report published by the Human Rights Network for Journalists (HRNJ)-Uganda documented 163 cases of violations and abuses, compared to 113 cases recorded in 2017. It reported that, for the tenth consecutive year, police was the leading offender of media rights (accounted for 53 per cent of all cases reported during the year), followed by the army (17 per cent).

Journalists who cover demonstrations have severally been arrested and detained. They were also forced to delete footage from their cameras and phones by soldiers and some media houses were forced not to live broadcast images of clashes between security agencies and protesting civilians in different parts of the country. In 2018, the UCC was at loggerheads with media houses, including Akaboozi FM, Beat FM, Capital FM, CBS FM, Pearl FM, Sapientia, Simba Radio stations, Bukedde, BBS, Salt, NBS, NTV and Kingdom Television requiring them to among others suspend them for covering arrests of Bobi Wine.

In September 2017, the UCC suspended the live broadcast of the parliamentary debate on the bill to remove the age limit provision from the constitution, claiming the broadcasts were inciting the public, stirring up hatred and promoting a culture of violence. In the last half of 2018, NTV journalists Herbert Zziwa and Ronald Muwanga were ambushed and assaulted by security officers as they reported live following the killing by shooting of Mr Yasin Kawuma, the driver of then MP Robert Kyagulanyi during the by-election campaigns for the MP for Arua Municipality, in the West Nile sub-region. The two journalists were later charged with inciting violence and malicious damage to property. In the same month, James Akena, a photographer working for *Reuters,* was assaulted by soldiers, arrested and detained for several hours as he covered the protests against the arrest of Robert Kyagulanyi in Kampala. His equipment was confiscated. NTV journalists Ronald Galiwango and Juma Kirya as well as *The Observer* photographer Alfred Ochwo were also assaulted during coverage of the same protests.

According to one academic and political analyst based in Kampala, 'the strategy of the NRM government in dealing with the independent press has been to use courts of law to pile pressure on nosy journalists and force them to self-censorship; and secondly, to target some media as a lesson to other publications and to the government's political opponents.[56]

The sum total of these actions has been to cow media practitioners and other actors from reporting or even commenting on key developments in the country, or holding leaders accountable. The threats of suspending broadcasting licences, coupled with the physical assaults on journalists and confiscation or destruction of equipment, have taken a toll on free expression. The media industry cannot retain its talent staff. Over the years, there has been an exodus from the country's leading newspapers, TV and radio stations as talented young journalists come to realize there is no future in the journalism profession. Journalist and media workers are not well-remunerated. Owners of media houses think that when a young person gets an opportunity to be on radio or TV, this is itself prestigious and perhaps it is the journalist or presenter who should pay the media company for giving that person a platform to shine and be famous! Some journalists have to depend on tips given by people they meet in the field, including news sources, which potentially compromises their professionalism yet it is something they do out of necessity for survival.

Worse is the ever greater constraints placed on the media industry by a dictatorial and increasingly authoritarian government on what can and cannot be reported. The interference by government on how media houses should operate, what to report and what not to report eventually cost media houses a lot as they lead to loss of viewership and readership. Media houses have been forced by the state to discontinue a popular programme and stop or drop a personality highly prized by the public. Once a station drops a popular programme and selling package it will lose listeners and thereby loosing advertisers which translates into financial loss.

According to Daniel Kalinaki,[57] the relatively small size of the market and the economy makes it difficult for media houses to train, pay and retain the best journalists but the inevitable departure of those journalists, often for better paying and less stressful communication jobs erodes experience and institutional memory.

The religious community

One of the oldest, most consistent and influential voices among civil society groups in Uganda is the religious community – comprising Christian, Islamic and other faiths. Uganda's religious community has been at the vanguard in the struggle for peace and social justice. Its role is inspired by values of morality which are also central to its teachings. The religious community attracts a huge following swelled by its work in providing relief services to communities throughout the country, as well as its provision of services in the fields of healthcare and education. Religious groups represent a tremendous source of moral authority, not only among their followers but also in the broader Ugandan society.

The Church recognizes its position within civil society and has, at times, joined in the struggle for justice, although at other times it either has opted to be supportive of the government in authority or has remained neutral with respect to political and socio-economic issues. In 1986, the coming to power of Yoweri Museveni's NRA/M government, which identified politicized ethnic and religious divisions as one of Uganda's key problems, led to notable changes in Uganda's religious field. Dismantling of multiparty politics weakened the old church-affiliated parties, while increased religious freedom led to a proliferation of Pentecostal-Charismatic churches.

Under the NRM, those clerics who have not openly opposed the government have found it relatively easy to operate without intervention or restraint, and those with large followings have also attracted state funding and presidential visits. Religious leaders critical of the government have been told by President Museveni and his confidants to stick to spiritual issues,[58] or have been dealt with decisively.[59] During the northern Ugandan war, clergy who spoke out about the government's mistreatment of Acholi civilians were imprisoned, harassed, and some missionaries also deported. Critical political statements by clerics have triggered reminders from the head of state and other top government officials that religion should not interfere with politics, while, somewhat paradoxically, religious leaders inclined towards the NRM have been appointed by the president to political positions and encouraged to speak.

In recent years, Museveni's critique of religion as a divisive factor has been increasingly coupled with his praise of religion as a benign collaborator. For instance, in a speech he gave at the born-again all-night New Year's prayers two months prior to the 2016 elections, Museveni declared that in coming years, religious groups would receive increased state funding, because they have helped the state to police the minds of its people instead of just depending on policing of the body. The fact that the statement was made at a born-again event was no mere coincidence. Ugandan religious and political discourse has in recent years become increasingly Pentecostalized, as seen for instance during debates about 'anti-gay' legislation.[60]

The Balokole/Born-again churches are very closely associated to the First Family. This association may be attributed to most members of the First Family being active in church and especially Pentecostal circles. For example, Patience Rwabwogo, daughter of President Museveni, is the founder of the Covenants Nations Church. There is an affinity between born-again churches and the First Family, which plays out in the political sphere. Since 1986, the population of born again churches has grown tremendously. Churches such as Rubaga Miracle Center of Robert and Jessica Kayanja, Namirembe Christian Fellowship of Pastor Kayiwa, House Prayer Ministries International of Pastor Bugingo and many others have large memberships and are very influential. President Museveni is quick to remind the Pastors of Pentecostal churches that despite pressure exerted on him to close the so-called 'biwempe' (make-shift buildings) churches, which is what many Pentecostal churches have been associated with, he did not see the need for that because Christians in those churches were not against government.

The Museveni regime has integrated religion into public affairs, but in quite different ways than previous post-independence Uganda governments, making particular groups allies of the government. In fact, it seems Pentecostal churches tacitly allied with President Museveni in exchange for protection against traditional church institutions and opportunities to express themselves and advance their agendas in the public space. Pentecostal pastors have also not only gained power and money but their churches have become centres of economic accumulation and navigating political networks for gaining visibility and getting access to several centres of political power.

In recent years, the state has established itself as a source of protection and provision of privileges for religious leaders – a strategy rendered all the more effective after cutbacks of donor funding.[61] Religious leaders have a choice to speak their mind and lose state resources or become agents of the government and continue enjoying benefits and privileges from state coffers. So the pragmatic value of a silent and diplomatic approach to governance issues in Uganda is a tactic that works for them, since confrontational clergy have often been openly condemned and side-lined by government. However, this position does not subdue and tame the excesses of political power that tends most times to be destructive. Remaining quiet so as to stay on good terms with an autocrat could also imply submission to autocracy.

The academia: Lecturers' associations and the student community

An engaged academia is one that fulfils broader societal role as independent actors, drawing on research and teaching to shape public discourse and civic engagement. The academia is often perceived as non-partisan, but can be far from neutral in the sense of being devoid of values, convictions and interests. Academics are supposed to be committed to the public good, to democracy and human rights, and to basing policies and decisions on facts established through study, research and critical reflection – as well as to challenging received wisdom based on new discoveries. However, the role of an engaged academic community in that theoretical sense has not been embraced by most academics. Low pay and poor working conditions have meant that academics are more engaged in part-time work and have not had time to engage policymakers and the wider public on critical societal matters. The state has also penetrated the academia with some being seen as cadres of the ruling party. In other words, the academia is not united in their mission of engaging the state in the pursuit of democracy and good governance.

The student community, on the other hand, has historically been one of the traditional advocates of democratic transformation in Uganda. It is one of the most vocal sectors of civil society in Uganda. The student community, largely represented by Makerere University, has spoken out on most key issues of national concern. The agitation by students has, on numerous occasions, incurred the wrath of the government. The security forces beat up students and several of them sustained injuries. The student lobby has, however, been effective in bolstering the debate on democratization and has also contributed to accelerating the public's demand for democratic change. However, the influence of students in promoting a civic culture is increasingly being undermined by the deliberate infiltration of the student population by mostly NRM cadres. This infiltration is supported by the regime as a way of weakening the radical sector of the student community.

In a nutshell, civic space in Uganda has been threatened at many levels including limitations on creation and registration, on functioning and freely engaging in activities, and on access to resources. We have seen that when some CSOs are considered too critical or too much of a nuisance, the Ugandan government has applied a range of measures under the guise of legality of existing rules, but which in effect descend into the grey zone between legal and extra-legal action. This has included arbitrary scrutiny of the governance of CSOs, de-registration, office closures, seizures of property, excessive fines, arrests and travel bans, among others.

Labelling has also been used to intimidate civil society actors as 'foreign agents' which directly impacts on their freedom, safety and potential to function. The rise of social media has given civil society more opportunities to make its voice heard but this rise has also increased the number of attacks by state agents inspired by governments to reinforce official propaganda. We have also seen increased attempts at the use of divide and rule tactics to disorganize the unity of CSOs. Government divides CSOs into polarized camps with one for and against the government. For instance, groups that focus on small-scale development or service delivery programmes are often promoted by government officials as examples to emulate, but some analysts point out that this category of CSOs 'ultimately end up compensating for government failure to deliver services in those sectors'.[62] Deeply divided, these CSOs never get the opportunity to know and see their real enemy. Instead of uniting to consolidate their position and use their combined brains, the government divides and exposes them. Government ensures the best brains of the country in CSOs are split into conflicting camps with one obsessed with working with government and conscripted to the networks and channels of exploitation.

Coping strategies

CSOs have adopted different coping strategies. Some CSOs decided to abandon pushing pro-democratization projects to shifting their focus towards politically neutral capacity-building and local service delivery programmatic activities in order to preserve their access to foreign support and government cooperation. Others have tried to raise money from domestic sources – often with limited success. Private sector donors remain reluctant to fund civic activities that could attract the ire of state authorities. Accepting state funding, if available, risks compromising organizational independence. The government has significantly expanded its support for domestic NGOs, yet the bidding process is opaque and generally favours apolitical or pro-government groups.

Faced with escalating restrictions, some traditional NGOs have begun moving towards alternative organizational structures. Organizations that were shut down have continued operating in a more informal and fluid manner. Groups are exploring new funding models that could generate greater community buy-in; some have transferred their advocacy activities to non-institutionalized initiatives. Operating without formal status creates new challenges. For example, it becomes more difficult to raise funding from international partners, build specialized expertise, or access public institutions and state authorities. This does not mean the end of civic engagement and mobilization. They can still have organized activities and virtual platforms around shared interests; however, these efforts often have remained divorced from larger policy discussions.

Other CSOs have practised self-censorship in fear of the repercussions of the law and state harassment which has implications in that the value of civil society in promoting democratic governance is progressively being eroded. Harassment of NGO leaders forced some to get out of their positions. For instance, Mr Godber Tumushabe, former Executive Director of Advocates Coalition for and Development Environment (ACODE), denied claims that his exit from his position was engineered by the government. Speaking after his farewell dinner in Kampala, Mr Tumushabe told *Sunday Monitor* that his exit was part of the transition process that had been on the table for long. He said, 'The pressure that came in at that point was just a matter of timing, otherwise ACODE was much ahead of government.'[63]

In mid-2013, ACODE was among the NGOs which President Museveni accused of funding members of parliament (MPs) to oppose the dust raising oil bill. ACODE was also part of the civil society efforts in opposing some of President Museveni's policies, including the controversial attempt to give away Mabira Forest. Mr Tumushabe said, 'At the time I left ACODE, government was uncomfortable with my work and particularly the work related to the oil and gas sector.' He further revealed, 'I think there is some truth in the perception that ACODE was under intense pressure [to get rid of me]. But what the public does not understand was that the ACODE [strategic] plan predates the government action. So, either way, this pressure was mounted at the time I was leaving.'[64]

During the 2021 electoral period, several organizations were raided by security agencies, and/or their bank accounts arbitrarily frozen by the Financial Intelligence Authority. There were arrests too. For example, Nicholas Opiyo, Executive Director of Chapter Four, a human rights advocacy organization, who was working on the November 2020 shooting of over 100 unarmed citizens by security forces, was abducted and a slew of charges eventually slapped on him. Consequently, Opiyo left for the United States after a difficult end of 2020 and tumultuous 2021.[65]

Despite a political and regulatory environment that in many respects is not supportive of a vibrant civil society, many of the organizations have shown considerable ingenuity in devising strategies to interact effectively with government and with society as well as to influence policy and public opinion. Civil society actors and observers agree that extensive cooperation between CSOs and local authorities is critical for grassroots impact and policy influence. There appears to be little concern that such cooperation with government might compromise an organization's integrity, in part because grassroots CSOs generally receive so little funding from government.

Where a CSO has worked for some time, typically, there is no friction with government because the organization's effectiveness is recognized. However, in new areas, there may be government resistance or friction. Some CSOs deal with this by emphasizing their own capacity, local grassroots support and appeals to higher levels or authority, if needed. When government suspends them from working, a top CSO leader noted in an interview, 'they appeal to their personal networks in government to bail them out'.

At times donors have not been spared by the government as they are also operating in the same environment like CSOs. The government threats to CSOs appear to have led donors to rethink their support to critical CSOs. So they shift to support local government and other agencies directly or they shift to other regions and countries. That is what we can call 'donor unpredictability' and the shifts in the funding models that have become rampant. This has led to CSOs change towards social enterprise as a window to financial sustainability. This is in realization that CSOs especially NGOs must get more knowledgeable, innovate using modern technology and find partners to collaborate with.

However, some CSOs struggle when it comes to entrepreneurship because the number of NGOs involved in social entrepreneurship remains low, so it is perhaps time for NGOs to diversify if they are to provide sustainable services and programmes. For example, the Uganda Health Monitoring Group (UHMG) has been heavily engaged in social marketing to increase access to health services and commodities with key funding from donors. But the organization has slowly pulled away from donor dependence to build a foundation that is able to sustainably fund its core functions without the input of donors. UHMG now runs its social goals as an enterprise and has become the largest distributor of health facilities, which among them include distributing more than 30 million condoms every month across the country.

Mildmay Uganda is another entity that is building a self-sustaining model. It was established about twenty years ago to provide HIV/AIDS care with 100 per cent of its funding from donors. However, the organization has been making deliberate plans to attain financial independence, which seeks to make it able to provide services even when donor funds shrink. They began a training institute that may grow into a university. There is a hospital under the same organization that provides paid for and non-paid for services to fill gaps. The lesson here is that for NGOs to search for financial independence, they should consider overhauling their systems to align them towards income generation.

Conclusions

We have seen that repressive tactics evidenced by the increasing regulation of civil society activities have become the order of the day in Uganda under President Museveni. The government has its own idea of a civil society that is loyal and works together with government to improve governance and not ask questions or provide civic platforms for public accountability. This is probably the reason why the current government loathes the idea of a critical civil society that is autonomous from the state and is seen as a threat to its power.

Apart from repression and intimidation, the government has a steady supply of resources available to get a section of CSOs including religious leaders that have a following countrywide in all corners. The CSOs manoeuvres are impacted by strategic considerations of how best to reach desired ends. The pragmatic value of a silent and diplomatic approach to governance issues is a tactic that works for them since confrontational activists in CSOs have been side-lined by government. However, this position does not subdue and tame the excesses of political power that tends most times to be destructive. Remaining quiet so as to stay in good books with an autocrat implies submissions to autocracy thus inadvertently contributing to the deepening of autocracy even when they are affected by it.

CSOs must speak out and mobilize all possible allies to add their voices to the condemnation of government transgressions. CSOs must make the painful choice of either keeping true to their mission of justice and defend the rights of those who may not have the space they occupy or to survive as any other Ugandan in the face of injustice, human rights abuse and declining democracy.

CSOs must continue to work together by creating sector-wide networks to avoid being isolated and becoming easy targets. In this way, the broader civil society will be able to strengthen their resilience to withstand the attacks through better collaboration; prediction of the realities ahead, adjusting their ways of operation to enable them deliver on their mandate in a complex and fragile political landscape. They should deepen the ownership of their work by the communities they serve. This way, those communities can put pressure on government whenever it clamps down on an organization in their locality. But this is only possible when communities appreciate the need to protect the whole CSO sector.

Relatedly, urgent means should be devised to help local communities understand their civic rights, responsibilities and value in demanding and protecting them. This way, citizens can offer some level of protection to these organizations from highhanded government institutions and officials. This is because, the continued lack of action against those cracking down on freedom of expression and civic space only emboldens the perpetrators to extend their boundaries of impunity.

Additionally, CSOs should continue to challenge and litigate against retrogressive provisions within national laws that infringe on the right to freedom of expression, assembly and association. CSOs should also challenge, in the courts of law, actions, especially the highhandedness with which state actors treat civil society actions, such as peaceful demonstrations. CSOs can do the above if they monitor, document and expose the illegalities in the laws, policies as well as actions by the state and state officials. The media as part of civil society could help to investigate and publicize the illegal actions and practices by the state that restrict civic space. CSOs embracing opportunities that social media provides as a tool for mobilization, and information dissemination is also key in protecting the precious CSO space.

Civil society needs to proactively develop and draw strategies to defend its image by telling its own story that protects its image and its role in deepening democracy. This should not only reach civil society but especially the general public especially on the positive contribution of civic space to building peaceful, stable societies, including inclusive and sustainable economic growth. The messaging should enable realization by the citizenry that an attack on civil society and independent media is intended to silence their voices and limit their rights to freely organize and challenge abuse and misuse of power by those in authority by criminalizing activism and dissent.

Lastly, civil society and their supporters need to become more political. Achieving social justice in a profound and lasting manner is fundamentally a political project. CSO being pushed to act as being nonpartisan and non-political will not work. Social, economic and political justice will be achieved when power shifts from the privileged few to the oppressed majority who directly bear the brunt of injustice. This power shift will not be delivered in meetings held in posh hotels but in freer, more creative, more inclusive spaces and theatres of nonviolent action.

CSOs must re-imagine their role and learn new, adaptive and creative ways of working. They must spell out more clearly how they believe change can happen through democratization and national reconciliation – through better theories of change and critical pathways to reform. And they must relearn the ethos and value of solidarity and collective action to withstand state harassment and other obstructions which are bound to continue.

Notes

1   Mucheak Bratton, 'Civil Society and Political Transition in Africa', Institute of Development Research, IDR Reports 11, No. 6 (1994).

2   Peter Lewis, *Political Transition and the Dilemma of Civil Society in Africa* (London: Routledge, 2018).

3   In Uganda, the NGOs are governed by the National Bureau for Non-Governmental Organizations under the Ministry of Internal Affairs, which registers and regulates NGOs.

4   Uganda NGO Forum, 'The Legal Environment for Civil Society in Uganda: Analyzing Options for How to Engage', Kampala (NGO Forum, 2021).

5   Laine Jusii, 'Debating Civil Society: Contested Conceptualizations and Development Trajectories', *International Journal of Not-for Profit Law* 16, no. 1 (September 2014): 59–77.

6   Arthur Larok, 'Uganda's New Activism: Beyond Egos and Logos', Carnegie Endowment for International Peace (24 July 2017). https://carnegieendowment. org/2017/07/24/uganda-s-new-civic-activism-beyond-egos-and-logos-pub-71600 (accessed 27 March 2020).

7   Mesharch W. Katusiimeh, 'Civil Society Organizations and Democratic Consolidation in Uganda', *African Journal of International Affairs* 7, no. 1&2 (2004): 99–116.

8   Michael Migisha, Yusuf Kiranda and Michael Mbate, 'Civil Society in Uganda: Broadening Understanding of Uganda's Civil Society Ecosystem and Identifying Pathways for Effective Engagement with Civil Society in the Development Process', Centre for Development Alternatives & Konrad Adenauer, Kampala (3 February 2020), 16.

9   Marvin Keith Mutebi, 'An Examination on the Role of Non-Governmental Organizations in the Democratisation Process of Uganda, 2005–2017: A Case Study of Africa Leadership Institute' (Masters Diss., Nkumba University).

10   Doyle Shane, 'Missionary Medicine and Primary Health Care in Uganda', in *Health for All: The Journey of Universal Health Coverage*, ed. Alexander James Medcalf, Sanjoy Bhattacharya, Hooman Momen, Monica Alexandra Saavedra and Margaret Jones (Hyderabad: Orient Blackswan, 2015).

11 Priscilla Wamucii, 'CSOs and the State in East Africa: From the Colonial to the Modern Era', in *Civil Society and Democratic Struggles in Africa*, ed. Ebenezer Obadare (New York: Springer, 2014).

12 Ibid.

13 Ministry of Trade, Industry and Cooperatives. www.mtic.go.ug/wp-content-/uploads-2019/9/Overview-of-cooperatives-in-uganda.pdf

14 Mahmood Mamdani, *Politics and Class Formation in Uganda* (Kampala: Fountain Publishers, 1990).

15 Wamucii, 'CSOs and the State'.

16 Akiki B. Mujaju, 'The Political Crisis of Church Institutions in Uganda', *African Affairs* 75, no. 298 (1976): 67–85.

17 Bernard Tabaire, 'The Press and Political Repression in Uganda: Back to the Future'? Journal of East *African Studies* 1, no. 2 (2007): 193–211.

18 GardnerThompson, 'Colonialism in Crisis: The Uganda Crisis of 1945', *African Affairs* 90, no. 365 (1992): 605–24.

19 Dan M. Mudoola, *Religion, Ethnicity and Politics in Uganda* (Kampala: Fountain Publishers, 1996).

20 J.C. Ssekamwa, *History and Development of Education in Uganda* (Kampala: Fountain Publishers, 1997).

21 Ibid.

22 A.G.G. Gingyera-Pinycwa, 'The Militarization of Politics in the African State: The Case of Uganda', in *Politics and Administration in East Africa*, ed. Walter O. Oyugi (Nairobi: East African Educational Publishers, 1994).

23 G.F. Engolm and A. Mazrui, 'Violent Constitutionalism in Uganda', *Government and Opposition* 2, no. 4 (1967): 585–99.

24 Henry Kyemba, *A State of Blood: The Inside Story of Idi Amin's Reign of Terror* (Kampala: Fountain Publishers, 1997).

25 Loyal N. Gould and James Leo Garrett Jr, 'Amin's Uganda: Troubled Land for Religious Persecution', *Journal of Church and State* 19, no. 3 (1977): 429–36.

26 Alex Kamoga, 'The Impact of the Pentecostal Movement on Christian life in Luweero Diocese', unpublished (2016). https://www.researchgate.net/publication/291320956_The_Impact_of_the_Pentecostal_Movement_on_Christian_life_in_Luweero_DiocesePentecostalMovement.pdffinal.pdf (accessed 18 May 2023).

27 *New York Times*, 'Amin Bans All but Christian Churches' (21 September 1977).

28 Abigail Barr, Marcel Fafchamps and Trudy Owens, 'The Governance of Non-Governmental Organizations in Uganda', *World Development* 33, no. 4 (2005): 657–79.

29 William Muhumuza, 'From Fundamental Change to No Change: The NRM and Democratisation in Uganda', *The East African Review* 41 (2009): 21–42.

30 Steve Kayizzi-Mugerwa and Arne Bigsten, 'On Structural Adjustment in Uganda', *Canadian Journal of Development Studies* 13, no. 1 (1992): 57–76.

31 Sabiti Makara, 'NGOs in Uganda: Their Roles, Typologies and Functions in Governance', Unpublished, Centre for Basic Research, Kampala (2000). https://www.eldis.org/organisation/A5492 (accessed 18 May 2023).

32 Barr et al., 'The Governance of Non-Governmental Organizations'.

33 Arthur Larok, Uganda's New Civic Activism'.

34 Ibid.

35 Barr et al., 'The Governance of Non-governmental Organizations'.

36 *Citizens' Compact on Free and Fair Elections in Uganda*. https:/www.academia.edu/12260723/citizens_compact_on_free_and_fair_elections_in_uganda

37   See, for example, Alex Gitta and Sella Oneko, 'Uganda: Museveni Blames Civil
     Society for Political Unrest', *DW* (9 October 2018). https://www.dw.com/en/ugandas-
     museveni-blames-civil-society-for-political-unrest/a-45432927

38   URN, 'Museveni Tells Foreigners to Back Off Uganda', *The Observer*, Kampala
     (10 September 2018). https://observer.ug/news/headlines/58627-museveni-tells-
     foreigners-to-back-off-uganda. In a warning against foreign interference, President
     Museveni claimed some unnamed foreign countries were determined to influence
     Uganda's politics by channelling financial assistance to the opposition through civil
     society organizations. See https://www.statehouse.go.ug/media/news/2012/12/13/
     president-museveni-condemns-ngos-and-agents-meddling-oil-production-
     programme

39   Emmanuel Ainebyona, 'Police on the Spot as Break-ins into NGO Offices Remain
     Uninvestigated', *Daily Monitor*, Kampala (9 March 2017). https://www.monitor.co.ug/
     uganda/special-reports/police-on-the-spot-as-break-ins-into-ngo-offices-remain-
     uninvestigated-1691384

40   The Independent, 'CSOs Report Pins Gov't for Interfering with Human Rights
     Defenders Work', Kampala (7 October 2020). https://www.independent.co.ug/csos-
     report-pins-govt-for-interfering-with-human-rights-defenders-work/

41   Public Order Management Act (2013).

42   Denis Olaka, 'Police Raids Solidarity Uganda Offices, Arrest Director', *URN*
     (27 September 2017). https://ugandaradionetwork.net/story/police-raids-solidarity-
     uganda-offices-director-arrested-over-presidential-age-limit

43   Anthony Katushaba, 'Police Storm Kigezi FM Studio, Switch off Political Program',
     URN (28 March 2014). https://ugandaradionetwork.net/story/police-storm-kigezi-
     fm-studio-switch-off-political-program?districtId=577

44   Ofwono Opondo, 'The Barking Dogs in NGOs Should Bow Their Heads in Shame',
     Uganda Media Centre (15 June 2019).

45   Sulaiman Kakaire, 'Why Police Raided NGOs, Froze Shs.7 Billion', *The Observer*,
     Kampala (23 October 2017). https://observer.ug/news/headlines/55568-why-police-
     raided-ngos-froze-shs-7bn.html

46   Elias Biryabarema, 'Uganda Suspends Work of 54 NGOs, Increasing Pressure
     on Charities', *Reuters* (20 August 2021). https://www.reuters.com/world/
     africa/uganda-suspends-work-54-ngos-increasing-pressure-charities-
     2021-08-20/#:~:text=Uganda%20suspends%20work%20of%2054%20
     NGOs%2C%20increasing%20pressure%20on%20 charities,-By%20Elias%20
     Biryabarema&text=KAMPALA%2C%20Aug%2020%20(Reuters),described%20
     as%20%22political%20persecution%22

47   Four radio stations were closed by government in September 2009. See Human
     Rights House Foundation, 'Four Radio Stations Closed in Uganda' (11 September
     2009). https//humanrightshouse.org/articles/four-radios-stations-closed-in-uganda

48   URN, 'Activist, Radio Manager Arrested for "Abusing" President Museveni', *The
     Observer*, Kampala (23 July 2015). https://allafrica.com/stories/201507231419.html

49   Human Rights Network for Journalists in Uganda, 'HRNJ-Uganda Alert, State House
     Orders Journalist to Delete Mbabazi's Congratulatory Message from Magazine
     and Apologize' (15 August 2015). https://hrnjuganda.wordpress.com/2015/08/05/
     hrnj-uganda-alert-state-house-orders-journalist-to-delete-mbabazis-congratulatory-
     message-from-magazine-and-apologize/

50   See, for example, Clare Muhindo, 'Eight Journalists Beaten on Orders of Military
     Officer at UN Human Rights Office', *African Centre for Media Excellency*, Kampala

(17 February 2021). https://acme-ug.org/2021/02/17/eight-journalists-beaten-on-orders-of-military-officer-at-un-human-rights-office/#:~:text=At%20least%20 eight%20journalists%20were,OHCHR%20in%20Kololo%2C%20Kampala.

51 Uganda Communications Commission, 'Registration of Online Data Communication Providers', Kampala (13 April 2019). https://uccinfoblog.wordpress. com/2019/04/13/registration-of-online-data-communication-providers/

52 ACME, 'Court Acquits Four Journalists of Criminal Defamation Charges', African Centre for Media Excellence, Kampala (17 March 2017). https://acme-ug.org/20 17/03/17/4345/#:~:text=This%20statement%20was%20first%20published,of%20 providing%20the%20defamatory%20information

53 Amon Katungulu, 'Red Pepper Publication Closed – Source', *NilePost*, Kampala (21 November 2017). https://nilepost.co.ug/2017/11/21/red-pepper-publications-closed-source/

54 Pascal Kwesiga, '215 Bad Year for Journalists in Uganda – Report', *New Vision*, Kampala (29 March 2016). https://www.newvision.co.ug/news/1420778/2015-bad-journalists-uganda-report

55 'Uganda Journalism under Attack', *Daily Monitor*, Kampala (2 May 2018). https://www.monitor.co.ug/uganda/news/national/uganda-s-journalism-under-attack-1754048

56 Interview in Kampala, 19 July 2019.

57 Daniel K. Kalinaki, 'Will the Last Journalist out Please Switch off the Newsroom Lights', *Daily Monitor*, Kampala (3 May 2017). https://www.monitor.co.ug/uganda/ oped/columnists/daniel-kalinaki/will-the-last-journalist-out-please-switch-off-the-newsroom-lights–1699480

58 'Museveni Says Religious Leaders Aren't Competent to Lecture Him on Politics', *SoftPower News* (11 February 2018). https://softpower.ug/museveni-says-religious-leaders-arent-competent-to-lecture-him-on-politics/

59 The Observer, 'Gov't Blocks Bishop Zac from Travelling', Kampala (5 April 2013). https://www.observer.ug/news-headlines/24603–govt-blocks-bishop-zac-from-travelling

60 Henni Alava and Jimmy Ssentongo, 'Religious (De)Politicization in Uganda's 2016 Elections', *Journal of Eastern African Studies* 10, no. 4 (2016): 677–92.

61 Ibid.

62 Yusuf Serunkuma, 'Democracy as Divide and Rule', *ROPE* (16 April 2021). https:// roape.net/2021/04/16/democracy-as-divide-and-rule/

63 I Was Not Forced Out – Acode Boss', *Sunday Monitor*, Kampala (23 November 2013). https://www.monitor.co.ug/uganda/news/national/i-was-not-forced-out-acode-boss-1559340

64 Ibid.

65 Nicholas Opiyo, the Executive Director of Chapter Four Uganda, confirmed his departure to the United States, saying the trip came at a time when he needed rest and respite following a difficult end of 2020 and tumultuous 2021. See 'Nicholas Opiyo: Let Me Take a Break', *The Independent*, Kampala (6 October 2021). https:// www.independent.co.ug/nicholas-opiyo-let-me-take-a-break/

6

Uncertainty, militarism and the politics of regime survival

Sabastiano Rwengabo

This chapter addresses the puzzle of militarism in Uganda and relates it to regime-survival imperatives of President Yoweri Museveni's ruling National Resistance Movement (NRM). After reviewing possible explanations for militarism, I develop conceptual and theoretical links between regime uncertainty and militarism, arguing that regime uncertainty creates incentives for relying on coercive state structures for the political and personal survival of regime elites. In the empirical section, I demonstrate regime uncertainty in Uganda during 1986–95, and its worsening trends in post-1995. Finally, I provide some concluding reflections as well as the theoretical and practical implications.

This chapter does not address debates on militarism across time and space, and theories of militaries as instruments of statecraft and foreign policy. Nor do I position myself on either side of the continuum: many societies detest being labelled 'militaristic' or associated with militarism. 'For the pacifist, everything military is equivalent to militarism. For the super-hawk, no amount of military power and influence would be too much.'[1] I focus on domestic militarism, not its international aspect as used in international politics and security studies. My argument focuses on the link between regime uncertainty and militarism, avoiding deep philosophical arguments about leadership behaviour and foundations of domestic Hobbesian sovereignty. Finally, I draw on the 'political uncertainty argument' in order to situate regime uncertainty within the broader debates on political development.[2]

The puzzle of militarism in Uganda

Scholarship on African politics underscores the persistence of militarism across the continent in form of *coups d'état*,[3] civil and transnational armed conflicts,[4] foreign military interventions amidst growing global militarism in the continent[5] and military roles in development.[6] In countries like Mali and Guinea-Conakry, recurrent coups reflect legacies of militaristic approaches to governance.[7] In others like Rwanda, Uganda, South Sudan, civil wars brought ruling regimes to power, causing militaries and militarism to dominate socio-political life.[8] In the Sahel and Gulf of Guinea, militaries remain central actors against drugs trafficking, violent extremism and multifarious non-traditional insecurities.[9] Such insurgencies divert militaries from their traditional defence roles to realms of internal policing. In Guinea and Cote d'Ivoire, armed forces are historical political interlocutors.[10] In troubled Somalia, Chad, and post-2012 Libya, the dangerously uncertain political-security environment forces armed actors to hold sway.[11] In these trouble-spots, militarism may be justified by prevailing, persistent insecurity. In relatively stable polities like Uganda, however, the military's ever-growing domestic influence – two-and-half decades since the 1995 constitution and holding of regular and periodic elections – sends worrisome signals of a militarized autocracy.

Yoweri Museveni crafted militarized rule through the veneer of electoral democracy. The Uganda People's Defence Forces (UPDF), together with equally militarized security and intelligence agencies, remains critical to electioneering, internal security and civil intelligence, partisan policing and governance of non-military affairs.[12] Beyond representation in parliament, the UPDF plays key roles in containing illegal fishing, civil registration and agriculture through 'Operation Wealth Creation' (OWC). Following a recent presidential directive to state ministries, departments and agencies (MDAs), the UPDF Engineering Brigade has appropriated infrastructure development as well.[13]

These developments are puzzling for three reasons. First, militarism undermines the 1995 constitutional promise that all power 'belongs to the people who shall exercise their sovereignty in accordance with this Constitution' and that all state authority emanates from *the people* who 'shall be governed through their will and consent'.[14] The Ugandan military, the UPDF, together with its intelligence wing, the Chieftaincy of Military Intelligence (CMI), is constitutionally required to submit to civilian authority.[15] The reality is different.

Parliamentary oversight remains lukewarm and military deployments rarely follow parliamentary approval. The military controls non-military spheres like policing.

In democratizing or democratic polities, civilian authority rests in civilian bureaucracies, judicial bodies, independent institutions or elected representatives who legislate on matters of state policy, including the establishment, constitution, functioning and deployment of armed forces. The UPDF shows limited respect for civilian state institutions. Several incidents have underlined the militarized autocracy of Museveni's regime including the 'Black Mamba' commandos' 'raping of the temple of justice' in 2005 and 2007,[16] and the Special Forces' violent entry into parliament and forceful eviction of opposition legislators during the 2017 constitutional amendment debate to lift presidential age limits.[17]

Third, democratizing societies expectedly avoid militarism as a step towards civilian control. In Uganda, however, the military, ruling party, government and the state are intricately fused despite the military's self-representation as a politically neutral 'people's army'. The UPDF is often poised against those who politically challenge the regime, which negates the nonpartisanship, political neutrality of the army, a key legal-constitutional principle of democracy. Both regime and military elites' behaviour naysay the constitutional promise that 'all power belongs to the people' for whom state authority is constituted and operationalized. Beyond the 1995 constitution, militarism also deviates from the democratic principles promised under the NRM's Ten-Point Programme and international rules.[18]

Existing explanations and alternative argument

Understanding persistent militarism amidst pretences of democratization is vital to unravelling the nuances of autocratic rule. The institutionalist explanation contends that weak institutions, such as political parties, legislatures, bureaucracies, judicial and conflict; resolution mechanisms; and civil society create governance lacunae in which militaries become gap-fillers. In much of Africa, 'the military is one of very few technically capable large institutions' with logistical, professional, and technical capabilities to contain daunting governance problems.[19] Accordingly, militaries are better structured, organized, with a more coherent ethos of respect for authority, vis-à-vis civilian institutions. When other state institutions fail, more organized institutions like armed forces claim both the legitimacy and organizational wherewithal to restore order in an otherwise disorderly governance space.[20]

This argument has merits. First, institutional weaknesses breed uncertainty, even anarchy, providing incentives for organized actors to seek to restore order. Second, militaries tend to perceive themselves as better organized than civilian institutions because of their rigid hierarchical structure and disciplinary nature, making it easier for them to impose order than the more competition-riddled civilian institutional actors. Third, militaries view themselves as relatively more cohesive because the nature of their work demands cohesion and unity. This creates incentives to impose unity and predictability to an uncertain socio-political space.

The institutionalist explanation, however, hardly reveals how and when civilian institutions acquire the wherewithal to replace militaries as embodiments of organized politics. It is unclear why it remains problematic to strengthen civilian institutions in militarized polities. The argument takes institutions as natural, not as evolving from deliberate and lengthy processes of socio-political transformation in which powerful actors' choices and behaviours inform institutional metamorphosis. Institutional weakness may result from regime uncertainty when regime elites fear, even work against, an established, elite-constraining, institutional order.

The second explanation, the personality thesis, avers that personal likes, dislikes and characteristics of an influential leader are key to understanding regime behaviour.

Accordingly, President Museveni is both a military leader and believer in militarism. Some analyses show that Museveni's personality, whims motives and interests tend to overrun the legal-rational rules and structures he has crafted.[21] Thus, rules-based structures become channels for pursuing leaders' interests not for establishing a rules-based order. For such a leader, rules are bendable; leasers' interests cannot be sacrificed.

Museveni's proclivity for seeking military solutions to most governance problems is seen in his consistent appointment of military officials to positions he considers critical to regime survival.[22] His might-is-right attitude is demonstrated in insistence on settling political questions of the 1970s and 1980s through armed rebellion,[23] militarily neutralizing armed opponents including the Allied Democratic Forces (ADF) and the Lord's Resistance Army (LRA),[24] militarized response to non-traditional security threats, terrorism, crime and urban riots,[25] and military presence in civilian state structures.

Against this bias on Museveni's part, the failure to strengthen civilian institutions like parliament and his tolerance for military corruption become comprehensible.[26] Recent research reveals tolerance for military corruption not as a sign of failure but as a means to regime sustenance.[27] While having some merit, this view fails to underline the basis and sources of leaders' preferences for militarism. Leaders are part of ruling-elite groups that constitute a regime. By interrogating the nature of regimes and conditions under which they rule we can uncover the motives and interests that hatch and nurture militarism.

Alternative argument

Regime Uncertainty breeds and/or perpetuates militarism. The growing military autocracy in Uganda is traceable to increasing regime uncertainty: the more the regime feels uncertain about its grip on power and safety of its leaders the more it resorts to militarism. This is especially after deviating from the 'Bush-War' promises, the 1995 constitution,[28] and amidst growing demands for accountability for abuses over the years and opposition to perpetual rule. Uncertainty stifles efforts to make Uganda's military politically neutral, and non-partisan, contrary to the promises and platitudes about professionalization. A politicized military helps to shock-absorb the uncertainties surrounding the regime, hence incentives for sustained militarized autocratization.

Regime uncertainty is a political-security situation *in which a ruling regime, in a given polity, lacks clarity about the political survival of its leaders and resilience of its public-ideological claims around which its rule has been justified.* Uncertainty creates incentives to forge and sustain overly coercive approaches to governance. While civilian society can behave militaristically, especially where counterinsurgency operations emphasize military solutions,[29] or where foreign policy is defined in terms of warfare, armed forces are the core embodiment of militarism. Since the military is the most coercive state organ, uncertain ruling regimes have incentives to exploit the institution as a cushion against uncertainty. This begets militarism, the tendency to rely on military solutions to political-governance problems.

In Uganda, the military's usurpation of civilian governance spheres, and the regime's reliance on military means to impose order, signifies political and personal uncertainty and indefensibility of the ideological claims of post-1986. Uncertainty inheres in the NRM's mistrust for civilian structures to maintain power, and in Museveni's deliberate subjection of state institutions to military influence. While focused on Uganda, this chapter reveals elite behaviour that is symptomatic of uncertain regimes in the developing world. The conceptual and empirical analysis here has important implications for framing the imperatives and motives of militarism, one of the major embodiments of autocratization and a persistent antidote to democratic developments in and beyond Africa.

Regime uncertainty and militarism:
Theory and practice in Africa

Militarism can be traced from regime uncertainty within domestic politics, in the context of national power struggles. The concept eludes unanimous definition. Any 'universal definition of militarism is likely to be meaningless',[30] for militarism entails and transcends 'acceptance of the theory of the inevitableness of warfare, and of the policy of military preparedness' for war as classically defined.[31] Philosophically, militarism entails 'glorification of military values, a propensity towards the use of force to solve problems, increases in the military apparatus', and definition of states as coercive Leviathans as cushions against war of man against man.[32] This 'exceptionalist militarism' implies the tendency of a state to stand the ultimate test of sovereignty: war.[33] Other dimensions also underscore the (re)production of justifications for,[34] as well as the creation and sustenance thereby, of military infrastructure (ideas, rules, processes, structures, technologies and practices of warfare) that typify intra- and inter-Leviathan relations.[35]

Practically, militarism involves deliberate *reliance on military structures and personnel to run most state affairs,* leading to 'the increasing influences of the military in civilian affairs'.[36] This tendency begets militarization, a process whereby militaristic traits are assimilated into social structures and individuals, leading to use of military strategies and actions, deployment of military weaponry and personnel, military involvement in internal security and policing, shoot-to-kill orders and attacks against perceived threats in non-war situations, and deployment of military officials in civilian bureaucracies. Thus, militarism creates incentives for militarization (the process), leading to what a 'Garrison State', in which specialists in violence become dominant actors in society.[37] A natural antonym of militarization is 'demilitarization', a process of shedding off militaristic traits, beliefs in military centrality and achieving civilian control over the military institution.[38]

Militarism is a practical phenomenon, part of everyday political practice. Both the tendency and practice give rise to: (a) *societal forces* – economic, political, cultural resources – being mobilized for military power (militarizing society); and relations of military power become recurrent and unambiguous;[39] (b) *Mobilization of social forces* and reproduction of social relations of military power enable the military to infiltrate, influence or usurp civilian governance realms; (c) The *military becomes the central locus* of political contests despite rules-based structures created to facilitate non-military political processes; (d) The *military's usurpation of civilian functions* does not "civilianize" the military; instead, it *militarizes civilians* by making them imbibe, adopt, military traits and attitudes.[40]

These features arise from regime uncertainty, which has both political and elite-security dimensions. Politically, regime uncertainty involves *lack of clarity* regarding power and the exercise thereof, power transitions, succession and continuity or change. Uncertainty can obtain about how long the ruling group will hold power or how it should exercise its power and the consequences thereof; the bases of its power and how they may be maintained, strengthened and/or consolidated; and how much power can be shared, diversified and/or decentralized to other entities and groups. Lack of clarity about these and similar concerns can lead to indecision, which cripples the exercise of power and could lead to regime collapse through counter-coup, armed rebellion or national crisis. It may also lead to excessive decisions and choices, such as purges, ethnic cleansing and other extremes of civil conflicts.[41]

Concerning elite security, regime uncertainty is about safety from harm and/or harassment of top regime leaders, their families and close allies. Political leaders can face serious personal and small-group challenges rooted in their conduct during power struggles, the individuals and groups they offended, the interests they negotiated, the alliances they betrayed and the pragmatic choices they made. A ruling group always pleases someone and displeases, even enrages, someone else. There is always a possibility for revenge by offended individuals, groups, criminal organizations, terrorist groups and even states. Revenge can be individualized (targeting specific leaders). It can be group-based (e.g. purges), or institutionalized through domestic or foreign alliances or organizations.[42]

Different factors – endogenous and exogenous, individuals and groups, deep-seated and immediate, material and non-material – combine to engender and inform the nature and extent of regime uncertainty. Articulating all of them here is impractical. What I surmise is that the nature of the ruling elite, the ways and means by which it acquired power, the immediate and long-term threats to its power, the ways in which it exercises/uses power, and the reactions of actors with which it relates determine the level of safety and security power-holders feel. Leaders facing less troublesome challenges, like negating agreed forms of local governance, may feel safer than those confronting the daunting task of pacifying a civil war-riddled country, clashes with neighbours or partners, extremist groups or geopolitical contenders. Similarly, regimes which ascend via armed conflict or coups d'état can be less certain than those which ascend via elections, though context determines whether or not rebels-turned-governors are more certain than elected leaders.

Regime uncertainty is a component of political uncertainty. Moses Khisa critiques the 'political settlement' argument with a conceptual articulation and evidence of 'political uncertainty', to explain Uganda's development malaise.[43] For Khisa, political uncertainty arises when there is 'absence of minimum and broad elite consensus on the overall framework for political engagement and economic management'.[44] Elites disagree on the type of government, state structuring, procedures for assuming office and overarching economic policy. For Khisa, political uncertainty manifests in key contentious issues: (i) the constitution, selfishly amended in 2005 and 2017, denying Uganda a peaceful presidential transition; (ii) *electoral disagreements* that hamper free and fair elections; (iii) the military's *ambivalent, controversial role* especially in civilian spheres; and (iv) the unsettled question of *presidential succession*, failure to peacefully change power. Together, these contentions constitute political uncertainty, and engender an environment in which government focuses on retaining power as opposed to transformation.

Drawing on Khisa's third element – the *role of the military* – I view the military's increasing role as a corollary of regime uncertainty. This uncertainty affects a small elite group. While these elites' concerns may be political, and impact national political-security certainty, the trepidations and fears are distinguishable from broad questions of national political certainty, hence the narrow conceptual and analytic lens of 'regime uncertainty' that offers an opportunity to unravel this group's militaristic tendencies.

Three aspects of regime uncertainty obtain in Uganda: (a) *weak social base* as the centre of gravity for the regime's power; (b) *fear of accountability demands* for possible abuses during civil wars, counterinsurgency operations since the 1980s; and (c) *promises not kept* in a rapidly changing society. On (a), Uganda's ruling elites lack deep-seated support from a clearly defined ideological group, social class or ethno-regional entity. On the second issue accountability, it is a problem not unique to Uganda; it afflicts war entrepreneurs. For example, Liberia's Charles Taylor faced domestic and regional pressure and was ejected from office in 2003 after leading one of Africa's most devastating civil wars.[45] Pressures against warlords like Bosco Ntaganda and Jean-Pierre Bemba of DRC and former Ivory Coast President Laurent Gbagbo, exemplify problems begetting accountability fears.[46]

The NRA militarily fought an elected government (treason), but once in power it conducted counterinsurgency operations in a nation-wide pacification campaign, the accountability for which remains elusive. Since 1995, the regime has violated constitutional and legal rules on domestic and foreign military deployments, and even excessively used armed forces against civilians, sowing seeds of possible accountability demands. Regime elites hardly state these openly, but 'Museveni and his close allies are fearful of being prosecuted under a new president for alleged wrongdoings'.[47]

On the third aspect of promises not kept, the NRM Ten-Point Programme articulated many promises which would have been realized within twenty years. Observers cautioned that the NRM's failure or success will be determined by how it tries to fulfil this promise. Doubts as to whether NRM could indeed bring about such a transformation 'were raised very early'.[48] Intra-regime self-awareness about unkept promises forces the NRM to rule through 'institutionalized arbitrariness' – whereby state institutions are unreliable, unpredictable and ultimately fragile. Unaccountable state violence, overconcentration of power in the executive and militaristic tendencies are familiar.[49] As foreseen in 1987, one of the issues 'that emerged early in the NRM strategy was the tendency towards militarism', the result of which was that 'the real political issues were not articulated'.[50] Overtime, the regime failed to consolidate legitimacy and support base, but, instead, faced accountability demands, transition pressures and internal fractures.

Regime uncertainty creates incentives to reconfigure state structures and processes in ways that serve regime interests at the expense of broader national goals. Reconfiguration may entail realignments in local governance, targeted 'engagements' with specific groups – ethnolinguistic, economic or geopolitical – believed to threaten the regime, or counterinsurgency operations in civil war contexts. Redistribution of political, economic, technological and coercive capabilities, advantages or disadvantages is also realignment. The core motive remains unchanged: secure the safety and power of regime leaders against perceived and/or real threats.

Uncertain regimes tend to rely on coercion to maintain power and/or enforce their ideological claims. Coercion need not entail the open, relentless, deployment of armed forces but it must consist in the ability to quickly and effectively deploy coercive instruments where needed and with resounding efficacy. To achieve/maintain this capability, an uncertain regime: (a) reconfigures the state's coercive machinery in such a way that loyalty from armed forces is assured for as long as is needed, where necessary by assuaging senior leaders within armed forces, employing various controls, and/or fusing the regime, armed forces and other governance structures;[51] (b) makes socio-economic and other changes unfolding within the polity to appear as inevitably resulting from fusion or interaction between armed forces and the regime, not the citizenry's enterprising exploitation of existing conditions; (c) subjects civilian structures on which regime elites depend most to armed forces even if other state institutions are reconfigured and made operationally capable of providing minimum developmental outcomes that can broaden legitimacy.[52]

Uncertain regimes are hesitant to allow democratic predictability regarding regime change or continuity. Such regimes tend to coercively impose their rule, whether or not they tolerate legal-constitutional and procedural practices like elections. Regimes with reasonable levels of legitimacy, based on their willingness to freely face competing ideas and groups or public scrutiny, through articulation of policy alternatives to the electorate, have less incentive to rely on military muscle. Since they respect constitutional and democratic processes, including electoral change of government, such regimes are more likely to rely on consensus, conversation and critical engagement with key stakeholders than regimes whose respect for democratic outcomes (e.g. electoral defeat) is minimal at best, or naught at worst. Instead, uncertain regimes strive to minimize the likelihood of electoral defeat.[53]

Uncertain regimes fear democratic processes which galvanize or strengthen opponents; demands for accountability; nondemocratic threats born of shrinking democratic space; and undemocratic means, such as coups d'état and armed rebellions. Such regimes may result from a fledgling coalition that wins an election at the margin, or one that splits after acquiring office.[54] A previously popular regime may also suffer uncertainty when it faces crisis, or backtracks on political promises: Cote d'Ivoire's president, Alassane Ouattara, instead of retiring in 2020, contested and won a controversial election after his party's presidential candidate, Amadou Gon Coulibaly, died suddenly in July 2020. His government faces serious uncertainty. Finally, regime uncertainty need not be a function of longevity. Its key feature is regime elites are unsure about their political and personal fate, which creates a fear of losing power.

To know that NRM elites fear losing power, we observe the ways in which power contestations, such as elections, constitutional amendments, anti-government demonstrations, are militarized, and regular references to the military's readiness to protect the regime in an unquestioned regime-preserving show of coercive power.

From the foregoing, regime uncertainty breeds militarism, first by reducing belief and confidence in civilian solutions to political problems, and second by reproducing or entrenching military ethos. Issues that affect the regime's survival – economic production, political negotiations, stateness and crisis response – are viewed through a military lens. This leads to militarization as observed in and beyond Uganda.

There are several implications of this theoretical framing. Methodologically, by revealing uncertainty in the triple forms of narrow support base, accountability fears and promises not kept, we are able to underscore the growing incentives to sustain rule militarily. By analysing how the regime crafts relations between the military, the government and other state institutions, we can tell whether uncertainty informed the choices and practices that engender military preponderance. Leaders' rhetoric reveals continuities in the military's centrality to regime survival. Evidence of the triple aspects of regime uncertainty – socio-political base, accountability fears and promises not kept – articulated as Uganda's real-world experiences provides sufficient empirical grounding for this analysis.

Through qualitative process-tracing, this chapter reveals that regime uncertainty remains a defining feature of NRM rule and creates incentives for regime elites to militarily surmount endogenous and exogenous threats. Second, by subjecting civilian authorities to military influences while reproducing the military ethos, regime uncertainty breeds continued reliance on the military for regime survival. Militarized governance increases with increased uncertainty.

Regime uncertainty and militarism in Uganda

Pre-1986 Uganda was not short of militarism. Colonial control had combined overt coercion during colonial pacification of especially recalcitrant areas (like Bunyoro-Kitara under Omukama Kabalega and later Buganda under Kabaka Mwanga), and other forms of colonial subterfuge. Later, three factors contributed to post-independence militarism: first, *post-colonial power relations*, between 1962 and 1964, show that leaders' choices were consequential. Following the 1964 mutiny among East Africa's armies,[55] Tanzania's leadership under Julius Nyerere disbanded the military, forged an anti-militarist ethos and reconstructed the military and its ethos. By contrast, in Uganda Prime Minister Apollo Obote brought the military closer during negotiations to end the mutiny, elevating Colonel Idi Amin to a position of strategic and decisive power.[56] This made Amin reliable during conflicts between Obote and President Edward Mutesa II, which informed Amin's central role in the 1966 attack on Mengo and later the 1971 coup d'état.

Second, *organization of post-independence state power*, especially during 1964–71, centred on means and instruments of violence. Unresolved conflicts, specifically between Obote and Mutesa, exposed intra-executive competition and created incentives for Obote to exploit the military's preponderant northern composition hitherto forged during colonialism.[57] He quickly outsmarted and militarily overthrew Mutesa in 1966, declared a state of emergency and imposed a republican constitution in 1967.[58] In turn, Obote fell to Amin's 1971 coup, replacing civilian-led militarism with *military dictatorship*.

Third, during military dictatorship, Amin relied on military instruments, military organization and military power.[59] Civilian institutions were subordinate to military authority and power. Simultaneously, Amin purged Obote's co-ethnic Langi and Acholi 'martial race', and entrenched militarized coercion.[60] Amin fell to the Tanzania-supported Uganda National Liberation Front (UNLF) – again militarily – which cemented the spectre of militarism.

Post-1986 promises: Origins and basis of uncertainty

During campaigns for the 1980 elections, Museveni of the Uganda Patriotic Movement (UPM) threatened armed rebellion if the process was rigged. His party was then new and insignificant. Even if elections were rigged, it was not UPM's/Museveni's victory at stake. The 1980 elections returned the UPC and Obote to power, against general expectations that DP would win. Chrispus Kiyonga of Bukonzo County, in Kasese district, won the only UPM seat. Museveni contested in Mbarara North and lost to DP's Sam Kahamba Kutesa. Museveni claimed a rigged national election, that DP's victory had been snatched. He declared war in 1981 without DP's official sanctioning, and captured power in 1986. In a 1997 autobiography, Museveni called his armed contestation against an elected government a 'struggle for freedom and democracy in Uganda'.[61]

Between 1986 and 1995, Uganda was under a government by a former rebel group. As early as 1987, keen observers decried creeping militarism in Uganda.[62] The NRM promised several changes, including the return to democracy.[63] Following countrywide consultations and Constituency Assembly (CA) elections in 1993, a new constitution came into force in 1995, which, inter alia, provided for presidential age and term limits and subjection of the military to civilian authority. In 2006, Museveni's constitutional two five-year terms were to end, but the 2005 constitutional amendment removed presidential term limits, allowing him to contest in 2006. Museveni would have reached the constitutional age limit of seventy-five years, but in 2017, a controversial constitutional amendment, during which the military forced opposition legislators out of parliament, allowed him to contest the 2021 elections.[64]

During 1986–95, regime uncertainty was evident in several respects. First, several armed groups challenged the NRM, diverted policy attention from pursuing socio-economic recovery and development to managing counterinsurgency operations and containing insecurity.[65] Second, misconduct of security forces during counterinsurgency operations, such as in northern and eastern Uganda, contributed to eroding the regime's nascent legitimacy.

The Mukura massacres,[66] for instance, naysaid the NRA's promise of disciplined conduct. The Namu-Okora incident contributed to more young Ugandans joining the nascent LRA rebellion.[67] Third, despite the so-called broad-based government, intra-NRM opposition to Museveni grew. Museveni's foreign minister, Paul Kawanga Ssemwogerere, challenged him in the 1996 elections. From 2001 to 2016, Kizza Besigye, Museveni's former personal doctor and 'bush-war' comrade, challenged the incumbent in successive elections.

Alongside unresolved pre-1995 conflicts in northern Uganda, new armed groups emerged after 1995 and threatened the regime. The ADF attacked western Uganda in November 1996, and a serious war raged for many years as was the case in northern Uganda. In responding to internal challenges, regime elites, including Museveni, were accused of serious abuses, inhuman and degrading treatment of opponents and suspects,[68] even worse wrongdoings like genocide claims.[69] To repair its image and legitimate its rule, the NRM employed many different methods, such as periodic elections, clientelist expansion of social base, improving peace and security in most parts of the country, and sustained economic development.

By the year 2000, the regime had internal discontent over clientelism, personalist rule and impunity.[70] As other legitimation efforts tended to fail, the regime intensified its best method: militarism. Internal controls became militarized. Unaccountable, unadjudicated killings became rampant via shoot-to-kill orders, for example as executed by the Colonel Elly Kayanja who headed Operation Wembley in Kampala in the early 2000s.[71]

Post-1995 uncertainty and militarism

Regime uncertainty has been increasing since 1995. The LRA and ADF wars raged on. Within the NRM, misrule incubated internal opposition, which led to defections and sustained opposition. Unwilling to peacefully leave power, ruling elites combined militarism with constitutional manipulations. Museveni overcame initial constitutional constraints to autocratic backsliding, like presidential term and age limits, by maintaining his stranglehold over political processes, mainly through militarized elections; tolerance for military corruption; and protection for himself and his family via an elite section of the army.[72]

As uncertainty increased the military-elite group expanded, from a Presidential Protection Unit (PPU) to a Presidential Guard Brigade (PGB) and to Special Forces Command (SFC) under the command of Museveni's son and other specially selected loyal officers. The NRM's 'struggle for democracy' has become a pursuit of militarized personal and family rule. Since the 'Black Mamba' commandos' attack on the judiciary in 2005 and 2007,[73] the militarized killings surrounding Kyagulanyi since 2017 (shooting of his driver, Yasin Kawuma, on 12 August 2018) and Special Forces' violent eviction of opposition Members of Parliament in 2017,[74] militarized autocracy has intensified.

Militarism in post-1995 Uganda naysays the 1995 constitutional promises, the NRM/A Ten-Point Programme,[75] the nation-wide constitution-making process, 'mustard seeds' of democracy as seen in regular elections and attempts at professionalization of the UPDF. The constitution stipulated boundaries for the national army; respecting these limits would have addressed the historical civil-military problem and strengthened civilian control. But the military still influences civilian processes – legislation, elections, policing and civil service.

The nation's coercive machinery for addressing mainly military problems has evolved as a regime-centred structure when one considers provisions on the High Command and National Security Council in the 2005 UPDF Act, the UPDF's involvement in partisan politics, and militarization of intelligence services and civilian state institutions.[76] The regime's narrow base, accountability fears, and unkept promises, begot this phenomenon.

Weak centre of gravity: Narrow regime base and militarism

Uganda's regime consists of politician-and-soldier Museveni, his family and their close allies who retain primacy in security services. Baligidde sums up this regime:

Some are individuals, groups of individuals, or *a Cabal consisting of a few 1980s NRA bush war historicals, who exercise ultimate decision-making power and authority* ... They include the President as the predominant leader at the State level, the Cabinet, and the [UPDF] High Command. They have the ability to commit the resources of the State and with respect to a particular problem, with the authority to make a decision that cannot be easily reversed.[77]

This makes the UPDF High Command a regime structure, not a state one. The NRA 'cabal', or inner circle, calls themselves 'Bush War Heroes'. Museveni recently added the first "Descendants' Resistance Army" (DRA I) – children and grandchildren of these 'liberators' – during a State of the Nation Address on Friday, 4 June 2021. He sugar-coated the DRA I as young Ugandans without 'home poverty pressures' and better positioned to fight corruption when they occupy senior government positions.[78]

Ironically, the NRM thrives/survives on corruption.[79] Clientelism, patronage, nepotism overshadow other accomplishments like 'political and infrastructural rehabilitation coupled with an economic renaissance' by 1995, a strict code of conduct for military elites that differed from previous regimes, and popular democracy via Resistance Councils (RC).[80] The regime restored peace in many parts of Uganda, built a regional and international image vide regional integration, military interventions, liberalization of the economy and joining the global war on terror. These accomplishments, however, are overshadowed by growing youth unemployment, socio-economic and political uncertainty, and recurrent insecurity in areas like Rwenzori region since 2012 due to regime-survival politics of fragmentation.[81]

Non-consensual politics inheres in degenerate intra-NRM rule exemplified by growing illiberalism and intolerance for dissenting views, subordination of 'formal/legal state structures to the informal, patron-client networks of power', marginalization of NRM veterans, concentration of power in the office of the president,[82] and growing corruption and impunity. These deviations generated intense intra-NRM opposition, eroded the regime's evolving social base and forced it to resort to dynastic rule through regime-elites' children codenamed DRA.

Museveni discussed the DRA issue with his children. He asked them 'to take forward the work of the original NRA of their parents', and appointed one of them, 'Ms. Irene Kaggwa, to manage Uganda Communications Commission' whom he praises for going a 'good job'.[83] National issues, appointments to state positions, are reduced to family talk, not engaged via formal state institutions, like cabinet, Public Service Commission or anti-corruption agencies. Museveni claims NRM descendants, appointed akin to nepotism and dynastic rule, can end corruption which has co-constituted his rule. Dynastic rule is far from democratic. It can best be imposed militarily. Because DRA hardly represents the broad Ugandan society. It embodies NRA-elite families. This class metamorphosis – breeding of an exclusive, non-meritocratic, elite class – incubates a group akin to an Americo-Liberian masterclass whose misrule and exclusive governance sowed seeds of Liberia's protracted fragility.[84]

Baligidde's specification underscores Museveni's proclivity for close-family rule. This element of personalized rule is maintained through excessive powers concentrated in the presidency. Uganda's Cabinet theoretically makes policy but not all ministers wield actual power. Some are position-holders appointed to assuage some groups, social, regional, political or otherwise. Others may be appointed to implement assignments for regime elites. NRA 'bush war historicals', like Moses Kigongo, Salim Saleh or Kahinda Otafire, wield more power than non-bush-war ministers. The president's revelation about DRA-I highlights the regime's loci of power and decisional processes beyond the purview of formal state structures. This explains why violence and threat of violence are key for regime survival. The DRA-I underscores elites' confidence in the engineered fusion between themselves, the military, government and the state. Impunity regarding personal rule and/or family power requires coercive capability to sustain it, hence militarism.

Countless examples of militarized impunity can be cited. But one recent instance suffices. In 2019, Maj Gen Matayo Kyaligonza, a 'Bush War Hero' and Uganda's ambassador to Burundi, was accused, together with his bodyguards, of assaulting a female traffic police officer during a stop for making an illegal u-turn in the road. He got out of the car and assaulted the officer right on the road. No disciplinary action was taken, instead the then internal affairs minister, Gen. Jeje Odongo, described it as 'most regrettable and detestable'. Kyaligonza was neither recalled from diplomatic, per a parliamentary resolution,[85] nor prosecuted in court, as the policewoman reportedly sued.[86] While his bodyguards, Cpl Peter Bushikindi and Pte John Robert Okurut, were supposed to be subjected to the military judicial process, there was no evidence they were charged or sanctioned accordingly.

Kyaligonza was reportedly 'summoned by the police to make a statement that will be used to process this matter to its logical conclusion',[87] but on 2 April 2019 the Deputy Prime Minister, Gen Moses Ali, advised parliament to 'leave Kyaligonza issue to Generals'.[88] During a parliamentary debate to sanction Kyaligonza, Ali stated that the submitting MP, Roland Mugume, was not in order to claim that generals need medical attention. Mugume sought parliamentary sanctioning of Kyaligonza for contempt of parliament following parliament's call upon the executive to expedite the implementation of the resolution by parliament to recall him from diplomatic posting. For Gen Ali, MP Mugume was 'wrong to say that Generals need medical attention. *He is not a General and so I do not think he has the ability to assess this'*.[89]

Neither the general-turned-ambassador nor Ministry of Foreign Affairs nor UPDF publicly apologized over the incident. This incident highlighted elite impunity, negation of the principle of separation of powers and disregard for democratic checks. Above-the-law individuals and family members of the cabal disrespect state accountability demands. Kyaligonza was a member of the NRA High Command as of 26 January 1986 and remains a member of the Defence Forces Council and UPDF High Command after to date.[90] He, like other NRA commanders, if they cross to civilian roles, or retire from the military, they retain 'ultimate decision-making power and authority'.[91]

Narrow social base of the regime

The NRM's social-group base, as the regime's centre of gravity, is weak. This weakness creates incentives for imposition of militarized rule. The regime lacks deep-seated support from a clearly defined ideological group, social class or ethno-regional entity. Second, legitimacy hitherto acquired through post-1995 constitutional politics, expansion of a social base through clientelism and patronage, and middle-class socio-economic progress, has been diluted by corruption, impunity, nepotism, constitutional u-turns, resurgence of insecurity and militarization of civilian institutions like elections and the public service.

Because of generational change, young Ugandans are not convinced by appeals to previous brutal regimes as justifications for perpetual NRM rule. The NRM's initial popular support especially in central and southwest regions, which helped overcome this weak base, has dwindled over time. This is reflected in Museveni's declining official electoral performance since 2011, the tendency to manipulate electoral processes, revelations by Supreme Court rulings on election petitions of 2001 and 2006 and the opposition's loss of trust in the judiciary to adjudicate electoral conflicts.

The issue of lacking a clearly defined ideological group, social class or ethno-regional base may sound counterintuitive for critics who think south-westerners rule Uganda.

Besides, the regime initially enjoyed support from west/southwest and central Uganda, which may make one cautious about this assessment. The regime has also enabled the middle class to enjoy some level of socio-economic progress, contained armed insecurity, presided over a growing economy and improving infrastructure landscape and opened the country to regional-economic opportunities. But close examination reveals a weak social-group base – because many parts of western Uganda (including Ankole, from where Museveni hails) were strongholds of the UPC government which the NRM/A fought.

In Ankole, Museveni/UPM scored miserably during the 1980 elections. He lost to Kuteesa in Nyabushozi County, indicating lack of a home-support base. Museveni identifies himself with Ankole's subethnic Bahima, who were mainly DP supporters. But he did not base his bush-war there possibly because his people disapproved of his militarism. DP party did not endorse the post-1980 elections war. Museveni relied on Rwandese refugees for command and combat operations; these later became the core of Rwandese Patriotic Front (RPF) that overthrew President Juvenal Habyarimana's government in 1994. Some of the commanders and core supporters during the war have defected. Between the late 1990s and 2010s, Museveni's strongest opposition has come from southwestern Uganda, revolving around former comrades like Kizza Besigye, John Kazoora, Mugisha-Muntu and Amama Mbabazi.[92]

The NRA's rebel tactics, such as protecting civilians, disciplined conduct, propaganda and avoidance of open terrorism, may have improved its reputation.[93] The merger between Museveni's Popular Resistance Army (PRA) and former president Yusuf Lule's Uganda Freedom Fighters (UFF) to form the NRA/M served to secure critical support in Buganda where UFF federalists could have allied with Kayiira's UFM, Buganda DP members and other Buganda-based groups, against Museveni's PRA. Without DP, Buganda's and western-Uganda's endorsement, the PRA would have been in oblivion.

Regime elites retain awareness about this historical weakness. People's cooperation followed signals that the NRA merged interests of militarists like Museveni/PRA and Lule who was perceived to represent Buganda's interests.[94]

Political-security volatility and disillusionment forced Ugandans to support the NRM/A. 'Ugandans in the political south of the country provided the regime with overwhelming popular political legitimacy for bringing to an end the atrocities, plunder and systematic torture and rapes they had suffered at the hands of the previous two regimes.'[95] Support was driven by the need for basic human survival and dignity. Despite tensions between the NRM, UFM, some UFF federalists, and DP supporters, support increased after government restored kingdoms in 1993, which was Buganda's interest. The regime still sought to disempower kingdoms by legislating that kingdoms remain de-politicized.[96] Over this demand, contentions with kingdoms increased and vestiges of support waned. This has bred militarized, deadly, clashes between government and kingdoms, with Buganda in 2009 and the Rwenzururu in 2016.[97]

To neutralize the threat of organized politics, NRM elites espoused the politics of individual merit. From 1986 to 2005, political parties were banned; despised as divisive, based on sectarianism and responsible for past political instability and crises. Cooperative societies were killed. Traditional authorities like kingdoms, and powerful districts, were split to create new/weak ones. Group unity was discouraged, divisions within armed forces fuelled. The NRM converted to a political party in 2005 with the message that it was getting rid of pro-multiparty members.[98]

Organized political interests or collective power struggles were reduced to atomized, individualized political engagements in which personality, as opposed to group synergy, reigned. Charismatic individuals may not represent diverse interests of professional associations, trade unions, farmers' groups, cooperative societies, industrialists and trader associations, ethnic and regional forces and traditional authorities. When power is individualized, fragmented, it scatters, as Obote's and Amin's experiences show.[99] Increasingly, individual-merit politics lacked legitimacy and bred intra-NRM fractures that contributed to regime uncertainty. Consequent to a weak social base, the crisis of legitimacy bred violence-centric rule under Museveni's NRM.[100]

The NRM was neither a mass party nor a nation-wide liberation movement owing to opposition from northern and eastern Uganda. It was bereft of a clear social and ideological base, thus reducing itself to personal and family rule. Entangled in pacification campaigns and counterinsurgency operations, the NRM/A could not avoid abuses,[101] the accountability for which hovers over regime elites. Parties like UPC and DP, which however sectarian, had ideological foundations and social-group support bases, were replaced with two decades of 'No-Party Democracy', or *Movementocracy*.[102]

This de-institutionalization of democracy meant that Museveni relied on clientelism, cooptation and neopatrimonialism,[103] concurrent with weakening of government organs, erosion of checks and balances, and slumping of civilian state institutions, and fusing the NRM politburo with UPDF decision-making echelons and government. Moderating voices, from political parties, civil society, socio-cultural structures and civilian institutions, are silenced through corruption or coercion. As electoral success depends on appropriation of state resources, not on societal and organized-group support, elections are also militarized.

Declining *regime legitimacy*, especially since the 2005 constitutional u-turn and accompanying defections by former regime insiders, continues to worsen regime uncertainty, correspondingly exacerbating militarism. Legitimacy had been forged by presenting the NRM as a liberation movement. But anti-Museveni rebel movements were aware that NRM's legitimacy depended on 'government's capacity to restore law and order', and thus became the 'most immediate, and perhaps the greatest, threat to NRM legitimacy'. [104] Civil wars become a 'widespread threat of insecurity ... around the country'; as the LRA conflict persisted in the north, the ADF 'gathered ominous momentum in the west' in a similar strategy aimed at denying NRM 'a basis for legitimacy by preventing peace and stability'.[105]

Not surprisingly, Museveni's electoral support in western districts like Kasese, the epicentre for ADF war, declined in 2001. By 2006, Kasese had become a stronghold for opposition Forum for Democratic Change (FDC). Legitimacy crises appeared during the late 1990s when Besigye authored 'An Insider's View of How the NRM Lost the Broad Base', a critic of regime deviation from the cause of the 1981–6 war. This 'Insider's View' later informed Besigye's '*The Democratic Reform Charter*' for the 2001 and 2006 elections.[106]

Besigye highlighted growing autocratization within the NRM.[107] He was retired from the army and challenged Museveni in hotly contested elections in 2001, 2006, 2011 and 2016. Possibly fearing possible prosecution after regime change, Museveni reversed his constitutional promises against internal and external opposition. The 2005 amendments removed presidential term limits. During the 2017 constitutional amendments, no organized group openly backed removal of presidential age limits; instead, there was wide opposition in and outside parliament. During debate in parliament, the military entered parliament chambers and roughed up opposition MPs.

The method by which parliament voted on these amendments remains dubious. Anti-amendment protests and demonstrations often turned violent as more than 70 per cent Ugandans reportedly favoured retention of presidential age limits.[108] Opposition to lifting presidential term limits, within the NRM, opposition groups, Ugandan society and international community worsened regime uncertainty. The 2017 amendment eroded the remaining iota of legitimacy.

Current indications of regime support are based on benefits or hopes to benefit from neopatrimonial access to state resources, appointments and corruption, and lack of a strong opposition alternative, not on ideological and/or organized-group convictions. Political corruption 'has enabled the government to cement the loyalty of individual state leaders as well as to mobilize political support for maintaining the regime in power'.[109]

As it strives 'to curb practices that could affect their political support',[110] the regime lacks a support base to equipoise dwindling legitimacy but manipulates state-market relations out of fear of possible opposition from economically powerful groups. As socio-economic progress failed to expand the regime's middle class support, 'the executive has denied public resources to entrepreneurs deemed too close to political opponents as well as used preferential resource allocations to weaken collective action by organised business'.[111] These measures 'maintain the patrimonial character of government-business relations',[112] while providing resources for militarized response to changing fortunes amidst generational changes.

Generational change and a restive burgeoning youth further increase regime uncertainty, forcing the regime to resort to militarism. Young Ugandans, save for direct regime beneficiaries or DRA-I members, are not convinced by appeals to

Amin-Obote misrule. These 'Movement Babies', more than 78 per cent below thirty years of age and 'therefore born during the NRM regime',[113] are sceptical of liberation rhetoric and fears about previous governments. As some NRM leaders defected (e.g. Mbabazi, Besigye, Sejusa, Muntu), grew old (most of them) or died (e.g. Eriya Kategaya, Kirunda Kivejinja, Elly Tumwine), ruling elites are uncertain about their political and personal fate in a country where young citizens can demand for historical and contemporary accountability. 'Fearful of being prosecuted under a new president for alleged wrongdoings',[114] including mistreating former comrades-at-arms and fomenting divisive intrigue in state institutions,[115] Museveni, his family, other NRA elites and their DRA descendants, have crippled civilian institutions and militarized others. Thus, youthful opponents like Bobi Wine face militarized repression and harassment, turning the military into a political-negotiation tool.

The foregoing illustration of the link between narrow social base and militarism clarifies that amidst a shrinking support base, Uganda's increasingly uncertain regime faces strong incentives to sustain rule through coercion. Elections are preceded by strategies 'to minimize the likelihood of losing to any competitors'.[116] Intra-NRM rifts and fear of electoral defeat force manoeuvres that enhance prospects for ruling elites to retain power, all of which imply that election-related coercion/repression is employed.[117] Further intra-NRM defections, as seen in Mbabazi's challenge to Museveni during the 2016 elections, meant that the 2017 lifting of presidential age limits was so critical that the Special Forces were deployed to invade parliament, and the subsequent 2021 elections were highly militarized amidst the Covid-19 pandemic. The post-2021 era is even more uncertain following accountability demands for the 2016 attacks on Rwenzururu and the 2020–21 election-related killings by state security forces,[118] adding salt to wounds of previous wrongdoings. Thus, the regime is hell-bent on retaining power either with Museveni in chair till death or with his son, General Muhoozi Kainerugaba, succeeding his father.

Fear of accountability and militarism

Museveni's regime seems to fear political and personal accountability due to some wrongdoings, unkept promises, coercive rule and generational changes that render liberation rhetoric stale. Imposing order in a state of disorder, such as Uganda was by 1986, can be problematic. The order-imposing political force compels those it accuses of disorder to succumb to its newly imposed order. Initially, Hobbesian Leviathans must subdue opposing groups, or prevent emergence of such opponents, to impose themselves upon societies.

Plato's philosopher king – Museveni considers himself the only one with the 'vision' to transform Uganda – is not always universally acceptable. The socio-political order imposed by philosopher kings, Leviathans and visionaries is a one-sided order defined and determined by the ordering individual or group. Yet, disorder itself benefits its practitioners. Instances of beneficial disorders are numerous – from drug cartels in Colombia complicating orderly governance to benefit from semi-anarchic landscapes, to terrorist groups like al-Shabaab in Somalia seeking to impose their order after displacing the state, to Islamic State seeking to impose a global Caliphate, to Chinese communists demanding unquestioned civilian obedience in a dramatic process ending in the Tiananmen debacle. Brutally imposed orders, however, can boomerang following demands for accountability. The fear of accountability seems to be intense among NRM/A elites.

Some actors accuse the NRM of serious crimes, not just during counterinsurgency operations but also against political opposition since 2001. Some analysts go as far as raising alarms of genocide in northern Uganda, arguing that Acholiland was 'ravaged by a genocidal war' and other 'forms of systematic violations of human rights', specifically when NRA forces 'began to arrest, detain, beat, rape, and murder unarmed civilians in Acholiland'.[119] These accusations create a spectre of accountability demands should the NRM lose power or allow state institutions to function independent of regime-elites' underhand control.

Post-1986 Uganda witnessed the imposition of a Musevenic order, characterized by all-powerful presidency, erosion of organized groups, absolute power of NRA/M 'historicals', disrespect for civilian institutions and human rights abuses.[120] Militarism, domestic and regional,[121] served to impose Musevenic order through suppressing political dissent within NRM and broad Ugandan society; fusion of state, NRA/M and government; neopatrimonialism; political and military corruption; and regional military adventurism.

Apprehensions about accountability demands increase with autocratic tendencies and war rhetoric. Those who joined Museveni to fight for the Ten-Point promises feel betrayed. To them, human blood, the ultimate cost of war, was shed to enthrone autocratic rule without transforming Uganda's socio-political landscape to make it amenable to consensual politics and state autonomy.[122]

The cost of counterinsurgency operations by and against Museveni's opponents is directly linked to militarism. Between 1972 and 1986 when Uganda was at war, Museveni was one of the main leaders during the 1972–80 anti-Amin, and 1980–6 Anti-Obote wars. The 1981–86 'Bush War' was very costly due to the Obote government's counterinsurgency efforts and the changing dynamics of civilian involvement.[123] After 1986, more than ten armed rebellions opposed Museveni.[124] Some erupted soon after Museveni captured power; others, like UFM, FEDEMU and Uganda National Rescue Front (UNRF), had separately fought Obote. UFM and FEDEMU joined NRM as a time-buying strategy only to be outsmarted.[125]

While 'Museveni Wars' have background causes and drivers predating NRA/M, after 1986 they were indubitably armed contestations against Museveni's rule. Within Kampala, the Force Obote Back Again (FOBA) forces were active and threatened the new regime.[126] The National Democratic Alliance (NDA), led by one of Museveni's rebel soldiers, Maj. Herbert Kikomeko-Itongwa (RO 100), fought Museveni's government.[127] Disputes between NRM/A, FEDEMU and UFM were never resolved until Dr Andrew Lutaakome Kayiira (appointed Energy minister in 1986) mysteriously died in March 1987 shortly after he was acquitted of treason charges.[128] In northwestern Uganda, the West Nile Bank Front (WNBF) and UNRF actively opposed Museveni.

Leaders of the WNBF and UNRF I were linked to the defunct Amin regime (which Museveni militarily opposed), and opposed Obote II government. Moses Ali (UNRF 1), a minister under Amin; Juma Oris (WNBF); Ali Bamuze (UNRF 2); and Former Uganda National Army (FUNA) forces, were invited to join Tito Okello's government after the 1985 coup but Museveni overthrew Okello shortly thereafter. Ali later joined Museveni, and remains one of Uganda's longest-serving ministers. Bamuze and some of his UNRF 2 received amnesty and joined the UPDF. Former government forces and leaders displaced by Museveni/NRA feared a possible NRA/M's revenge campaign, regrouped and attacked NRA-UFM forces. The ensuing pacification campaign involved abuses in northern Uganda.

This state of affairs led to the emergence of armed resistances like Holy Spirits Movement (HSM) led by Saverino Lukoya and later Alice Auma Lakwena, and later LRA led by Joseph Laor Kony.[129] In managing these tensions, NRA forces often slipped out of their otherwise disciplined conduct: activist-rebel-forces were hardly groomed in professional military conduct and may have been initially angry against various social forces that supported or constituted their political-military foes during the 1980s. NRA leaders displayed mistrust and suspicions against other forces whose cooperation they needed. One such a group is the Okello junta. Soon after Gen Tito Okello and Bazilio Okello overthrew Obote in 1985, Kenya's President Daniel Arap-Moi mediated a power-sharing agreement.

In December 1985, Okello, Museveni and Moi signed the deal to form a seventeen-member military council to govern Uganda. The Military Council, to be chaired by Okello, deputized by Museveni, would comprise seven UNLA members, seven NRA members and representatives of other smaller factions (UNRF, FUNA and FEDEMU). The NRA and UNLA would constitute 42 and 44 per cent of the national army respectively, other groups taking 14 per cent. 'Just one month after the execution of the Nairobi power-sharing agreement, the NRA unilaterally abrogated the treaty and proceeded with the military capture of Kampala.'[130]

Whatever reservations Museveni had about power-sharing, this unilateral abrogation of the Nairobi Peace Deal signalled to UNLA leaders that the NRM/A was untrustworthy. Thus, after the NRA took over, fear of the new regime bred warnings of impending danger to northern Uganda. The retreating UNLA forces and leaders attracted some young people and crossed into southern Sudan. There is a justified belief that while the Okellos paved way for Museveni by overthrowing Obote in 1985, Museveni betrayed them militarily. This feeling of betrayal largely informed the formation of Uganda People's Democratic Army (UPDA), in Juba, March 1986, led by Brigadier Odong Latek.

The NRA/FEDEMU unit in Namu-Okora, Tito Okello's home area, carried out abuses amounting to war crimes in May–July 1986.[131] Museveni reportedly reacted angrily to these abuses, but the incident signalled the ferocity of NRA/FEDEMU forces towards civilians.[132] In northeastern Uganda, the rebel Uganda People's Army (UPA) formed there following general insecurity. In June–July 1989, the NRA's 106th battalion soldiers, under Maj Chris Bunyenyezi (a Rwandan-refugee-turned-NRA-soldier), arrested suspected UPA collaborators in Kapir and Mukura sub-counties, Kumi district, confined them in a train wagon wherein more than sixty suffocated to death. Justice after this incident remains fuzzy.[133]

The link to militarism is three-pronged. First, Museveni insisted on militarily suppressing armed opposition, instead of serious pursuit of negotiated settlements. The more he militarily confronted armed opponents the more the military became drawn in internal politics, partly prolonging civilian suffering. Second, accountability for abuses during counterinsurgency operations remained elusive, which increased incentives for further militarism. Militarized abuses have increased with increasing uncertainty exacerbated by constitutional betrayals and stifling of intra-NRM transition. Hence, militarized abuses recur across Uganda since regime elites seek perpetual rule. Finally, unarmed opposition, crime and inter-institutional disagreements are confronted with military power, as seen in the 2016 attacks on Rwenzururu, the 2005 and 2007 attacks on the judiciary, the 2017 attack on parliament, and militarization of elections and the Covid-19 pandemic.[134]

Promises not kept – the Ten-Point Programme and militarism

Governments maintain power by offering political goods (e.g. security), satisfying people's needs (development, social services) and keeping promises. Where political promises remain unkept, governments resort to coercion, non-coercive self-justification, ideological manipulation or corruption. The Ten-Point Programme sounded as a promising transformation agenda in a country afflicted by the 1966–71 crises and 1971–79 Amin dictatorship. Despite claims that UPC had manipulated the 1980 election results, the rigged election cannot have reasonably justified war by an insignificant party/candidate. Rigging was used to woo disgruntled Ugandans into Museveni's war. This may explain why other equally disgruntled groups, like FUNA, UNRF, UFF and FEDEMU, initially chose to fight separately instead of joining Museveni's PRA. In the end, groups which joined the PRA, such as Lule's UFF and Kayiira's FEDEMU, were edged out, rendered inexistent.

The NRA used guerrilla tactics Museveni had learned from liberation movements in Mozambique, to politically conscientize rebel soldiers and civilians. A secret structure, the RC system, was instituted in NRA-controlled areas.[135] The Ten-Point Programme served to discipline the rebel army, mobilize popular support and construct a cogent political and economic justification for Museveni's war.[136] The Ten-Point promises have not been kept. Despite modest efforts, such as political stability, restoration of the economy and periodic elections, the very problems the Programme promised to address persist.

One cannot attempt a would-be encyclopaedic assessment of NRM performance regarding the Ten-Point Programme for almost forty years. Both regime enthusiasts and critics alike can pin-point success and failure. Beyond political stability, achieved not through peaceful transition but single-rule regime longevity and an elusive presidential succession, the Programme was mainly dishonoured. The problems it sought to address still haunt Uganda. This has bred new complications the enumeration of which is constrained for space reasons. Politically, the promise of democracy has been sacrificed at the altar of autocracy, via the removal of presidential term and age limits; stifling hopes of peaceful transition; use of armed forces to suppress political dissent; and weakening of civilian institutions.

Economically, youth unemployment, persistent urban and rural poverty, weakening of indigenous private sector, donor dependence, weak manufacturing sector, weak indigenous and foreigner-dominated banking sector and infrastructure underdevelopment all render Uganda economically fragile. Socially, nation-building failures, partly due to sectarianism and nepotism, and avoidance of processes like National Dialogue means that national cohesion eludes Uganda. Fragmentary governance, practised via multiplication of government agencies, creation of districts and kingdoms and other authority structures, means that intra-country bonds of cohesion have been torn asunder through subnational and intra-state divisions.

Explaining these unkept promises, though analytically useful, would require ample space but a summation linking them to militarism should suffice. In the main, these promises would have informed non-sectarian governance, and multidimensional security, but were not be kept. The promises seem to have been intended more to achieve the PRA/NRA's survival in an uncertain environment,[137] and later for power consolidation, than for holistic transformation of state-society relations.

Over-emphasis on military solutions to governance problems, and growing military preponderance in civilian governance realms and foreign policy, undermines the development of requisite institutional capabilities for non-militarized governance. The military gap-fills for hollowed-out civilian structures, and has become complicit in, and shares, the regime's corrupt siphoning of public resources.[138] This gnaws at the marrow of state capacity and effectiveness. Sacrificing peaceful democratic transition and presidential succession (2006 and 2021) at the altar of Museveni's continued rule rendered militarized coercion a critical toolkit on his power politics and regime survival.

Conclusions and implications

Regime uncertainty, which confronts Uganda's ruling elites, creates incentives for militarism. Uncertainty, about the political and personal fates of Uganda's regime elites and their cronies, rooted in promises not kept, accountability fears and weak socio-political base, renders Uganda beholden to coercive governance logics. Increasing uncertainty informs growing incentives to weaken civilian institutions and rely on military coercion. Uncertainty increased over time owing to deviations from political and constitutional promises, forcing the regime to militarily face the changing regime-survival exigencies.

The NRM's ideological claims about individual merit politics, democracy, self-sustaining economy and national unity are no longer defensible; instead, corruption, impunity and elite control over the military animate rule. Regime uncertainty is especially common with regimes which acquire power through armed violence, and the NRM's reliance on the military underscores its self-awareness that its promises were not kept, that its legitimacy is dwindling, that processes of imposing its rule caused serious concerns that may ignite anti-elite demands for political and personal accountability.

These findings reveal elite behaviour that is symptomatic of uncertain regimes in developing-world polities, which has important implications. First, protracted rule requires not just ideological metamorphosis and programmatic change, such as happened in Tanzania and Singapore under CCM and People's Action Party (PAP) respectively, but peaceful intra-party power transitions. Such regimes can avoid militarism because the ideological, nation-building, and developmental changes they wrought upon society render militarized rule unnecessary. Lack of intra-NRM transition, presidential succession and national cohesion force NRM elites to rely on militarized coercion, cooptation and corruption. These strategies are typical of long-personalized rules in countries like Cameroon under Paul Biya and Zimbabwe under Robert Mugabe.

Second, while militarism is not atypical of civilian leaderships, it is commonplace with military leaderships, which Museveni's NRM typifies – hence a possible positive correlation between the presence of military leaderships and militarism. Finally, militarism tends to erode civilian state-institutional capacity, which sows seeds of long-term uncertainty and fragility. This is because the would-be moderating forces and processes are diluted or eroded, which weakens the foundations for negotiated settlement of post-regime raptures such as obtain in post-Qaddafi Libya.

Methodologically, a regime-type approach is useful for predicting the trajectory of rule in a given polity. As a military regime, the NRM entrenched specific personalities – the bush-war historicals – in the UPDF Act, implanting militarism that tightened multifaceted elite control. Since 2005, legally, specific NRA individuals, not institutional role-holders, dominate the UPDF High Command, Military Council and National Security Council. The nature of the regime and trajectory of rule may be correlated.

Second, support bases for rebel-movements-turned-state-governments demand conceptual and methodological innovation. It is easy to conflate public support for regime legitimacy. But support absent viable alternatives in a crisis-riddled socio-political landscape, much like protest votes, ought not to be conflated with legitimacy. It is useful to seek explanations for why regimes acquire support despite lack of a strong social-class or ideological base (e.g. NRM) while regimes with clearly-defined ideological and identity support base (like UPC) lose support.

Practically, Uganda's political-security future is uncertain. Militarism has neither widened nor deepened NRM support base. It has not erased accountability fears related to the regime's coercive practices. Consequently, political and personal insecurity for NRM elites exacerbates political uncertainty. Perhaps intra-NRM and inter-party elite consensus leading to amnesty for NRM elites can help attenuate this uncertainty and facilitate peaceful transition. Second, the NRM suffocates organized political and nonpolitical interests. This may force post-NRM Uganda to succumb to unclear political-ideological groups, instead of clearly articulated and organized interests. This de-institutionalization of politics renders armed forces critical for post-NRM rule. Finally, post-1986 generational changes imply that post-NRM

Uganda shares little with militarism and pre-NRM failures. This necessitates outliving current tendencies, like creating a DRA-style exclusive masterclass and positioning military personnel in critical governance positions, in order to reverse present-day autocratization.

Notes

1 Kjell Skjelsbaek, 'Militarism, Its Dimensions and Corollaries: An Attempt at Conceptual Clarification', *Journal of Peace Research* 3, no. XVI (1979): 216.

2 Moses Khisa, 'Political Uncertainty and Its Impact on Social Service Delivery in Uganda', *Africa Development* XL, no. 4 (2016): 159–88.

3 Patrick J. McGowan, 'African Military Coups d'État, 1956–2001: Frequency, Trends and Distribution', *The Journal of Modern African Studies* 41, no 3 (2003): 339–70.

4 Eboe Hutchful and Abdoulaye Bailey, *The Military and Militarism in Africa* (Dakar: CODESRIA, 1998).

5 Rita Abrahamsen, 'Defensive Development, Combative Contradictions: Towards an International Political Sociology of Global Militarism in Africa', *Conflict, Security & Development* 19, no. 6 (2019): 543–62; Horace G. Campbell, 'The Quagmire of US Militarism in Africa', *Africa Development* 45, no. 1 (2020): 73–116.

6 Nils Zimmermann and Jahara Matisek, 'A Developmental Role for Militaries in Africa: The Peace Engineering Corps Solution?' *Beiträge aus Sicherheitspolitik und Friedensforschung* 38, no. 2 (2020): 112–17; Rita Abrahamsen, 'Return of the Generals? Global Militarism in Africa from the Cold War to the Present', *Security Dialogue* 49, no. 1–2 (2018): 19–31.

7 Juliette Gallo, 'Breaking the Cycle: Military Coups in West Africa', Washington DC: Fragile States Index, Friday (8 July 2022). https://fragilestatesindex.org/2022/07/08/breaking-the-cycle-military-coups-in-west-africa/ (accessed 13 April 2023).

8 Gilbert M. Khadiagala, ed., *War and Peace in Africa's Great Lakes Region* (New York: Palgrave Macmillan, 2017).

9 Linnéa Gelot and Adam Sandor, 'African Security and Global Militarism', *Conflict, Security & Development* 19, no. 6 (2019): 521–42; UN Security Council, *Activities of the United Nations Office for West Africa and the Sahel* (New York: UNSC, S/2022/1019 2022).

10 Gelot and Sandor, 'African Security and Global'.

11 Ibid., 521–2.

12 Rebecca Tapscott, *Arbitrary States: Social Control and Modern Authoritarianism in Museveni's Uganda* (Oxford: Oxford University Press, 2021).

13 'Engineers up in Arms over Projects Ring-Fenced for UPDF', *The Independent*, Kampala (10 October 2021). https://www.independent.co.ug/engineers-up-in-arms-over-projects-ring-fenced-for-updf/).

14 Republic of Uganda, *Constitution of the Republic of Uganda*, 1995 (as amended), (Entebbe: UPPC), Art. 1.

15 Ibid; Republic of Uganda, *The Uganda People's Defence Forces Act 2005* (Entebbe: UPPC, 2005).

16 Moses Khisa, 'The Making of the 'Informal State' in Uganda', *Africa Development* XXXVIII, no. 1–2 (2013): 203; Albert Gomes-Mugumya, 'Reflections on Rights and Conflict from Uganda', in *Human Rights and Conflict Transformation: The Challenges*

of Just Peace, ed. Véronique Dudouet and Beatrix Schmelzle (Berlin: Berghof Handbook Dialogue Series, 2010), 80.

17   Pius Gumisiriza, 'Human Rights Practices in Uganda', in *Global Encyclopedia of Public Administration, Public Policy, and Governance,* ed. Ali Farazmand (Cham: Springer, 2019); James Tonny Dhizaala, 'Presidential Politics in Uganda: Driving Democracy Underground', *Australasian Review of African Studies* 41, no. 1 (2020): 70–85.

18   This *Program* promised: (1) democracy, (2) security, (3) national unity, (4) independence, (5) constructing an independent, integrated and self-sustaining national economy, (6) restoring and rehabilitating social services,(7) ending corruption and misuse of power, (8) addressing the plight of displaced/war-affected people, (9) pan-African cooperation and (10) pursuing a mixed economy. Joanna R. Quinn, 'Constraints: The Un-Doing of the Ugandan Truth Commission', *Human Rights Quarterly* 26 (2004): 401–27. At p. 403.

19   Zimmermann and Matisek, 'A Developmental Role', 112.

20   Samuel P. Huntington, *Political Order in Changing Societies* (Cambridge, MA: Harvard University Press, 1968); Abdul BK Kasozi, *The Social Origins of Violence in Uganda, 1964–1985* (Montreal, Buffalo: McGill- Queen's University Press, 1994); Sabastiano Rwengabo, 'Regime Stability in Post-1986 Uganda: Counting the Benefits of Coup Proofing', *Armed Forces and Society* 39, no. 3 (2013): 531–59.

21   Joshua B. Rubongoya, *Regime Hegemony in Museveni's Uganda: Pax Musevenica* (New York: Palgrave Macmillan, 2007); Aili Mari Tripp, *Museveni's Uganda: Paradoxes of Power in Hybrid Regime* (Boulder, CO: Lynne Rienner, 2010); Joe Oloka-Onyango and Josephine Ahikire, eds., *Controlling Consent: Uganda's 2016 Elections* (Trenton, NJ: Africa World Press, 2017).

22   Haggai Matsiko, 'Museveni and the Army', *The Independent,* Kampala (27 November 2017). www.independent.co.ug/museveni-and-the-army/ (accessed 15 March 2019); James Nkuubi, 'Of "Yellow" Police, a Cadre Army and the Liberation War Psychosis: The Question of Electoral Security' in *Controlling Consent: Uganda's 2016 Elections,* ed. Joe Oloka-Onyango and Josephine Ahikire (Trenton, NJ: Africa World Press, 2017), 401–30.

23   Yoweri K. Museveni, *Sowing the Mustard Seed: The Struggle for Freedom and Democracy in Uganda* (London: Macmillan Education, 1997); Daniel Wadada Nabudere, "The Uganda Crisis: What Next?" *Ufahamu: A Journal of African Studies* 15, no. 3 (1987): 54–78.

24   Tripp, *Museveni's Uganda*; Robert Gersony, *The Anguish of Northern Uganda: Results of a Field-Based Assessment of the Civil Conflicts in Northern Uganda* (Kampala: USAID Mission, 1997); Sabastiano Rwengabo, *Security Cooperation in the East African Community* (Trenton, NJ: Africa World Press, 2018).

25   Nkuubi, 'Of "Yellow" Police'.

26   Roger Tangri and Andrew M. Mwenda, 'Elite Corruption and Politics in Uganda', *Commonwealth & Comparative Politics* 46, no. 2 (2008): 177–94; Roger Tangri and Andrew M. Mwenda, 'Military Corruption and Ugandan Politics Since the Late 1990s', *Review of African Political Economy* 30, no. 98 (2010): 539–52.

27   Gerald Bareebe, 'Predators or Protectors? Military Corruption as a Pillar of Regime Survival in Uganda', *Civil Wars* 22, no. 2–3 (2020): 313–32.

28   Sabiiti-Makara, Lise Rakner and Lars Svasand, 'Turnaround: The National Resistance Movement and the Reintroduction of a Multiparty System in Uganda', *International Political Science Review* 30, no. 2 (2009): 197–8.

29   See, e.g. Saul M. Rodriguez, 'Building Civilian Militarism: Colombia, Internal War, and Militarization in a Mid-Term Perspective', *Security Dialogue* 49, no. 1–2 (2018): 109–22.

30   Skjelsbaek, 'Militarism, Its Dimensions and Corollaries', 213.

31   Albert T. Lauterbach, 'Militarism in the Western World: A Comparative Study', *Journal of the History of Ideas* 5, no. 4 (October, 1944): 446.

32   Thomas Hobbes, *Leviathan: Or the Matter, Form and Power of a Commonwealth, Ecclesiasticall and Civil* (Oxford: Clarendon Press, 1651/1965), 8; Rodriguez, 'Building Civilian Militarism', 112.

33   Bryan Mabee and Srdjan Vucetic, 'Varieties of Militarism: Towards A Typology', *Security Dialogue* 49, no. 1–2 (2018): 96–108.

34   Skjelsbaek, 'Militarism, Its Dimensions and Corollaries', 220.

35   On when and why violence can erupt between Leviathans, See Robert Powell, 'Anarchy in International Relations Theory: The Neorealist-Neoliberal Debate', *International Organization* 48, no. 2 (Spring, 1994): 313–44; Kenneth N. Waltz, *Theory of International Politics* (Reading, MA: Addison-Wesley Publishing Company, 1979).

36   Marek Thee, 'Militarism and Militarization in Contemporary International Relations', *Security Dialogue* 8, no. 4 (1977): 296.

37   Harold D. Laswell, 'The Garrison State', *The American Journal of Sociology* 46, no. 4 (1941): 455–68.

38   Ali A. Mazrui, 'Anti-Militarism and Political Militancy in Tanzania', *The Journal of Conflict Resolution* 12, no. 3 (1968): 269–84.

39   Mabee and Vucetic, 'Varieties of Militarism'.

40   Moses Khisa, 'Politicisation and Professionalisation: The Progress and Perils of Civil-Military Transformation in Museveni's Uganda', *Civil Wars* 22, no. 2–3 (2020): 289–312.

41   Donald L. Horowitz, *Ethnic Groups in Conflict* (Berkeley and Los Angeles: University of California Press, 1985).

42   Liberia and Sierra Leone come to mind here. See: Amadu Sesay, Charles Ukeje, Osman Gbla and Olawale Ismail, *Post-war Regimes and State Reconstruction in Liberia and Sierra Leone* (Dakar: CODESRIA, 2009).

43   Khisa, 'Political Uncertainty'.

44   Ibid., 165.

45   Sesay et al., *Post-war Regimes*.

46   On Ntaganda, See Amissi M. Manirabonaa and Jo-Anne Wemmers, 'Specific Reparation for Specific Victimization: A Case for Suitable Reparation Strategies for War Crimes Victims in the DRC', *International Criminal Law Review* 13 (2013): 977–1012. Bemba Was Acquitted By The Icc. See 'ICC Appeals Chamber Acquits Mr Bemba from Charges of War Crimes and Crimes against Humanity', *The Hague: ICC* (8 June 2018). https://www.icc-cpi.int/Pages/item.aspx?name=pr1390 (accessed 21 October 2021). On Gbagbo, see *The Prosecutor v. Laurent Gbagbo and Charles Blé Goudé*, *The Hague: ICC*. https://www.icc-cpi.int/CaseInformationSheets/gbagbo-goudeEng.pdf (accessed 21 October 2021); Also, see Giulia Piccolino, 'David against Goliath in Côte d'Ivoire? Laurent Gbagbo's War against Global Governance', *African Affairs* 111, no. 442 (2012): 1–23.

47   Roger Tangri and Andrew M. Mwenda, 'President Museveni and the Politics of Presidential Tenure in Uganda', *Journal of Contemporary African Studies* 28, no. 1 (2010): 31.

48 Nabudere, 'The Uganda Crisis', 55.

49 Tapscott, *Arbitrary States*.

50 Nabudere, 'The Uganda Crisis', 56.

51 Rwengabo, 'Regime Stability'.

52 Matsiko, 'Museveni and the Army'.

53 Makara et al., 'Turnaround', 194.

54 Uganda's KY-UPC alliance of the 1960s is an example. Kasozi, *The Social Origins of Violence*; Tarsis B. Kabwegyere, *The Politics of State Formation and Destruction in Uganda* (Kampala: Fountain Publishers, 1995).

55 Mazrui, 'Anti-militarism and Political Militancy'.

56 Ibid.

57 Sabastiano Rwengabo and Julius Niringiyimana, 'Colonial Origins of the Lord's Resistance Army Conflict in Northern Uganda', in *Civil Conflicts and Peace Building in Africa*, ed. George Kieh and Kelechi Kalu (Lanham, MD: Rowman & Littlefield, 2022), 281–309.

58 Kasozi, *The Social Origins of Violence*.

59 Ali A. Mazrui, 'Between Development and Decay: Anarchy, Tyranny and Progress under Idi Amin', *Third World Quarterly* 2, no. 1 (1980): 44–58.

60 Rwengabo, 'Regime Stability in Post-1986 Uganda'.

61 Museveni, *Sowing the Mustard Seed*.

62 Nabudere, 'The Uganda Crisis'.

63 Khisa, 'Political Uncertainty'.

64 Dhizaala, 'Presidential Politics in Uganda'.

65 Erin K. Baines, 'Uganda: In-between War and Peace', *African Studies Review* 53, no. 1 (2010): 143–8.

66 Justice and Reconciliation Project, *The Mukura Massacre of 1989* (Gulu: JRP), RP Field Note XII, (March 2011). http://justiceandreconciliation.com/wp-content/uploads/2011/03/JRP_FNXII_Mukura-Massacre.pdf (accessed 25 October 2021).

67 Ogenga Otunnu, 'The Path to Genocide in Northern Uganda', *Refuge* 17, no. 3 (1998): 4–13.

68 See, e.g. Nannozi Susanie Ggoobi, Vicent Kibira, Jonah Kiberu and Joseph Kayemba, 'Brutal Arrests, Illegal Detention and Torture: A Failed Test for Rule of Law in Uganda', Kampala, GRC Policy Brief 010, December 2021.

69 Otunnu, 'The Path to Genocide'; Todd David Whitmore, 'Genocide or Just Another "Casualty of War"? The Implications of the Memo Attributed to President Yoweri K. Museveni of Uganda', *Practical Matters* 3 (Fall 2010): 1–49.

70 Kiiza Besigye, 'An Insider's View on How NRM Lost the "Broad-Base"', *Sunday Monitor*, Kampala, 7 November 1999.

71 Bruce Baker, 'Multi-Choice Policing in Uganda', *Policing and Society* 15, no. 1 (2005): 25–8.

72 Rwengabo, 'Regime Stability in Post-1986 Uganda.'

73 Moses Khisa, 'The Making of the "Informal State"', 203; Gomes-Mugumya, 'Reflections on Rights and Conflict, 80.

74 Gumisiriza, 'Human Rights Practices'; Dhizaala, 'Presidential Politics'.

75 Museveni, *Sowing the Mustard Seed*, 217.

76 Fredrick Golooba-Mutebi and Sam Hickey, 'The Master of Institutional Multiplicity? The Shifting Politics of Regime Survival, State-Building and Democratisation in Museveni's Uganda', *Journal of Eastern African Studies* 10, no. 4 (2016): 601–18; Privacy International, *For God and My President: State Surveillance in Uganda* (London: Privacy International, 2015).

77 Samuel H. Baligidde, 'Diplomacy for Development or Doom? Epistemological Reflections on Uganda's Recent Foreign Policy Achievements and Blunders', *Estudios Internacionales* 44, no. 171 (2012): 36.

78 Yasiin Mugerwa and Franklin Draku, 'Museveni Talk on Rich NRA Children Sparks Uproar', *Daily Monitor*, Kampala (6 June 2021). https://www.monitor.co.ug/uganda/news/national/museveni-talk-on-rich-nra-children-sparks-uproar–3427718 (accessed 5 September 2021).

79 Tangri and Mwenda, 'Elite Corruption and Politics'; Tangri and Mwenda, 'Military Corruption'; Bareebe, 'Predators or Protectors?'

80 Rubongoya *Regime Hegemony*, 59.

81 Moses Khisa and Sabastiano Rwengabo, 'The Deepening Politics of Fragmentation in Uganda: Understanding Violence in the Rwenzori Region', *African Studies Review* 65, no. 4 (2022): 939–64.

82 Rubongoya, *Regime Hegemony*, 131.

83 Republic of Uganda, 'State of the Nation Address by H.E. Yoweri Kaguta Museveni, President of the Republic of Uganda, at Kololo Indepndence Grounds', 4 June 2021.

84 Sesay et al., *Post-war Regimes*, 19–54.

85 Republic of Uganda, 'Parliament Hansard, 27 February 2019', Parliament of Uganda, Kampala (2019).

86 'Assaulted Traffic Officer Sues Gen Kyaligonza, Wants Shs. 200m Compensation', *Daily Monitor*, Kampala (10 June 2019). https://www.monitor.co.ug/uganda/news/national/assaulted-traffic-officer-sues-gen-kyaligonza-wants-shs200m-compensation-1831124 (accessed 6 September 2021); 'MPs Resolve to Recall Ambassador Kyaligonza from Burundi', *The Observer*, Kampala (28 February 2019). https://observer.ug/news/headlines/59992-mps-resolve-to-recall-ambassador-kyaligonza-from-burundi (accessed 6 September 2021).

87 Republic of Uganda, 'Parliament Hansard', 7.

88 'Leave Kyaligonza Issue to Generals – Moses Ali', *Daily Monitor*, Kampala (3 April 2019). https://www.monitor.co.ug/uganda/news/national/leave-kyaligonza-issue-to-generals-moses-ali-1817504 (accessed 6 September 2021).

89 Republic of Uganda, 'Parliament Hansard, 2 April 2019', Parliament of Uganda, Kampala (2019), 8 (emphasis added).

90 Republic of Uganda, *The UPDF Act*, Sec. 14 and Third Schedule.

91 Baligidde, 'Diplomacy for Development', 36.

92 See, e.g. John Kazoora, *Betrayed by my Leader: The Memoirs of John Kazoora* (Kampala: Self-Published, 2012).

93 See, e.g. Stephen Arves, Kathleen Gallagher Cunningham and Caitlin McCulloch, 'Rebel Tactics and External Public Opinion', *Research and Politics* 6, no. 3 (2019): 1–7.

94 Ogenga Otunnu, *Crisis of Legitimacy and Political Violence in Uganda, 1979 to 2016* (New York: Palgrave Macmillan, 2017), 30–55, 181.

95 Ibid., 180.

96 Republic of Uganda, *Constitution of the Republic*, Article 246; Republic of Uganda, *The Institution of Traditional or Cultural Leaders Act, 2011* (Entebbe: UPPC, 2011).

97 Tapscott, *Arbitrary States*; Khisa and Rwengabo, 'The Deepening Politics'.

98 Makara et al., 'Turnaround'.

99 ABK Kasozi, *The Social Origins of Violence*.

100 Otunnu, *Crisis of Legitimacy*, 179–314.

101 Ibid., 218 ff.

102 Aaron K. Mukwaya, 'Movementocracy and the Challenges Facing Political Parties in Uganda: Fundamental Right to Political Participation', *Mawazo* 9, no. 1 (2010): 197–207.

103 Charles N. Bwana, 'The De-Institutionalization of Democracy and the Rise of Neo-Patrimonial Politics in Uganda', *Mawazo* 10, no. 1 (2011): 161–72.

104 Rubongoya, *Regime Hegemony*, 132.

105 Ibid.

106 'Movement Rejects Besigye Reform Proposals', *New Humanitarian* (6 August 2001). https://www.thenewhumanitarian.org/report/24593/uganda-movement-rejects-besigye-reform-proposals (accessed 5 September 2021); 'The Democratic Reform Charter', *The Monitor*, Kampala (24 July 2006). https://allafrica.com/stories/200607250518.html (accessed 5 september 2021).

107 Besigye, 'An Insider's View'. Also see: https://allafrica.com/stories/199911070045.html (accessed 2 February 2022).

108 Economic Intelligence Unit, 'Age Limit Protests Turn Violent', *The Economist*, London (23 October 2017). http://country.eiu.com/article.aspx?articleid=786012662 (accessed 5 September 2021).

109 Tangri and Mwenda, 'Elite Corruption and Politics', 177; Bareebe, 'Predators or Protectors?', 313.

110 Roger Tangri and Andrew M. Mwenda, 'Politics, Donors and the Ineffectiveness of Anti-Corruption Institutions in Uganda', *The Journal of Modern African Studies* 44, no. 1 (2006): 101.

111 Roger Tangri and Andrew M. Mwenda, 'Change and Continuity in the Politics of Government-Business Relations in Museveni's Uganda', *Journal of Eastern African Studies* 13, no. 4 (2019): 678.

112 Ibid., 678.

113 Anna Reuss and Kristof Titeca, 'When Revolutionaries Grow Old: The Museveni Babies and the Slow Death of the Liberation', *Third World Quarterly* 38, no. 10 (2017): 2347.

114 Tangri and Mwenda, 'President Museveni and the Politics', p. 31.

115 See, for example, 'Maj. (Rtd) John Kazoora's Memoirs: How I Fell Out with Museveni', *Daily Monitor*, Kampala (11 August 2012). https://www.monitor.co.ug/uganda/magazines/people-power/maj-rtd-john-kazoora-s-memoirs-how-i-fell-out-with-museveni-1522996 (accessed 25 October 2021).

116 Makara et al., 'Turnaround', 194.

117 Ibid., 198–9.

118 Oxford Analytica, 'Uganda Campaign Clashes Presage Post-Election Unrest', Expert Briefings (4 December 2020). https://doi.org/10.1108/OXAN-DB257996

119 Ogenga Otunnu, 'The Path to Genocide'; Whitmore, 'Genocide or Just Another'.

120 Daily Monitor, 'Maj. (Rtd) John Kazoora's memoirs'; Gumisiriza, 'Human Rights Practices'.

121 On regional militarism and regime survival, see: Martijn Engels, *Museveni's Wars: Military Interventions as a Tool of Regime Stability*, MA Dissertation (Ghent: University of Ghent, 2016); Jonathan Fisher, 'Managing Donor Perceptions: Contextualizing Uganda's 2007 Intervention in Somalia', *African Affairs* 111, no. 444 (2012): 404–23.

122 Kazoora, *Betrayed by my Leader*; Miria R. K. Matembe, *The Struggle For Freedom and Democracy Betrayed: Memoirs of Miria Matembe as an Insider in Museveni's Government* (Kampala: Self-Published, 2020).

123 Museveni, *Sowing the Mustard Seed*; Ondoga Ori Amaza, *Musevenis Long March: From Guerrilla Statesman* (Kampala: Fountain Publishers, 1998); Nelson Kasfir,

'Guerrillas and Civilian Participation: The National Resistance Army in Uganda, 1981–1986', *The Journal of Modern African Studies* 43, no. 2 (2005): 281.

124 'Herbert Itongwa: A Soldier Who Turned Guns on His Own Govt', *Daily Monitor*, Kampala (23 April 2013). https://www.monitor.co.ug/uganda/lifestyle/reviews-profiles/herbert-itongwa-a-soldier-who-turned-guns-on-his-own-govt-1541122 (accessed 24 September 2021).

125 Yash Tandon, 'Elements of Continuity and Change between Obote and Museveni: Some Lessons from Obote's Rule for Museveni's Government', *Ufahamu* XV, no.3 (1986/87): 87–8.

126 Nabudere, 'The Uganda Crisis'.

127 Daily Monitor, 'Herbert Itongwa'; Julius Odeke, 'Ex-Rebel Leader Itongwa Dies in Germany', *The Independent*, Kampala (26 April 2013). https://www.independent.co.ug/ex-rebel-leader-itongwa-dies-germany/ (accessed 25 September 2021).

128 Henry Gombya, 'The Forgotten Hero – Remembering Dr Kayiira', *The Uganda Citizen* (13 March 2010). https://web.archive.org/web/20120426084313/http://www.theugandacitizen.com/news/93-henry-gombya.html (accessed 25 September 2021).

129 Robert Gersony reported that former soldiers and leaders told communities that the NRA/M was led by Banyarwanda who were out to decimate people of northern Uganda. Rwandese refugees, like Fred Rwigema, Paul Kagame, Chris Bunyenyezi, Peter Baingana and others, had joined NRA and were in Museveni's state infrastructure. See Gersony, *The Anguish of Northern Uganda*.

130 Ibid., 12, emphasis added.

131 Otunnu, 'The Path to Genocide', 5–6.

132 Gersony, *The Anguish of Northern Uganda*, 22–3.

133 'Revisiting the Mukula Massacre 28 Years Later', *Daily Monitor*, Kampala (15 July 2017). https://www.monitor.co.ug/uganda/magazines/people-power/revisiting-the-mukura-massacre-28-years-later-1710750 (accessed 25 October 2021); Justice and Reconciliation Project, *The Mukura Massacre of 1989* (Gulu: JRP), RP Field Note XII (March 2011). http://justiceandreconciliation.com/wp-content/uploads/2011/03/JRP_FNXII_Mukura-Massacre.pdf (accessed 25 October 2021); Chris Obore, 'The Untold Story of the 1989 Mukura Massacre', *Daily Monitor*, Kampala, 21 January 2007.

134 See, for example, Privacy International, *For God and My President*; James Nkuubi, 'When Guns Govern Public Health: Examining the Implications of the Militarised COVID-19 Pandemic Response for Democratisation and Human Rights in Uganda', *African Human Rights Law Journal* 20 (2020): 621–38.

135 Kasfir, 'Guerrillas and Civilian Participation'.

136 Rita M. Byrnes, ed., *Uganda: A Country Study* (Washington, DC: FRD, Library of Congress, 1992).

137 Kasfir, 'Guerrillas and Civilian Participation', 281–5.

138 Bareebe, 'Predators or Protectors?'

7

The military as an instrument of regime survival

Gerald Bareebe

Regardless of the political turbulences it has encountered, the Museveni regime in Uganda is much more entrenched than many of its foes had anticipated. The main question of concern that arises from this situation *how has the NRM government managed to maintain power for almost four decades*? In answering this question, this chapter focuses on three elements that epitomize the instrumental use of the military to guarantee the survival of the Museveni regime in Uganda. The first is the use of the army to halt attempts by opposition groups to mobilize dissent, and to enforce cohesion within the ruling party. The second is the discrete cultural domain of military operations and procedures gyrating around familial relations and close family ties. The third is the ability of President Museveni to out manoeuvre and prevent military officers from acquiring sufficient political power to challenge his authority. The regime feels secure because it is firmly protected by the military from its opponents, but also relies on ethnic and family ties to prevent dissent within the army ranks.

Uganda has had a turbulent history characterized by civil wars and military overthrow of democratically elected governments. The army in Uganda has historically been divided along ethnic and geographical lines, which is partly responsible for past political volatility such as the 1964 mutiny and the 1971 coup d'état against President Milton Obote's government. Since gaining independence in 1962, Uganda's army has been afflicted by political factionalism, ethnic divisions, corruption and a lack of professionalism. Yet still, the military remained the most powerful political institution in the country because of its willingness to employ violence to protect a specific regime in power or influence political developments. As a result, army officers became infamous for committing heinous crimes including political assassination, torture, armed robbery and the mass incarceration of innocent civilians.

When President Yoweri Museveni came to power in 1986, he promised to establish a professional and nonpartisan army that would be subordinate to a democratic civilian authority. Museveni also promised to curb the military's political influence which had led to the ouster of previous regimes. Charmed by Museveni's idealistic promises, many Ugandans and the international donor community expressed hope that a professional military institution could help the country overcome the tumult of past years that were marked by sporadic violence and socio-economic collapse.

Museveni's vision of the army, the donors contended, was impressive and so it was said that Uganda had become a successful case of post-conflict state reconstruction.[1]

However, more than three decades later, Museveni has resisted both internal and external pressure to depoliticize and de-ethicize the army. He tightly controls the country's armed forces and employs the military for regime survival projects. As a result, the Ugandan army has maintained a controversial place in the country's politics because of the way it is used to stifle political dissent. Despite the 2002 defence reform programme that was intended to create a professional and well-disciplined national army, Ugandan soldiers have remained both the perpetrators and victims of Museveni's political agenda built on the use of violence.

Between 2002 and 2004, Uganda undertook an ambitious defence review process intended to establish structures that would facilitate the depoliticization, de-ethnicization and depersonalization of the army. It was argued that, if well implemented, the reforms could allow the army to play its conventional role of defending the country's territorial sovereignty and not be involved in partisan politics. A deep evaluation of the impact of these reforms shows that they have had a double-edged impact. On the one hand, they have successfully strengthened the UPDF's effectiveness which has allowed the army to play coercive roles, both domestic and foreign, demonstrated by successful military interventions in countries like Somalia and South Sudan. On the other, the reforms have failed to transform the UPDF from a partisan force into a true national army. Instead, the President has exploited the new reform structures to tighten his grip on the army by further personalizing and politicizing the army.

As a result, the UPDF remains a highly personalized army whose character is tied to the person of President Museveni to a significant degree. In what follows, I start by examining the literature on the instrumental use of the army through nepotism and patronage. I then proceed to explore Uganda's defence review process of 2002–04 whose aim was to create a professional and non-partisan military institution. Finally, I show how, as an institution, the UPDF has remained highly partisan and personalized and the ways in which it is used to safeguard the survival of President Museveni's regime.

Conceptualizing the instrumental use of the army

Several scholars have shown how the army can be an important tool for the consolidation of autocratic governance.[2] Non-democratic regimes essentially depend on the military to suppress opposition parties, subdue civil society and curtail mobilization against the regime.[3] To survive long in power, autocratic leaders require loyal security organizations that are willing to employ violence against regime opponents.[4] However, autocratic leaders are often careful not to allow the military to acquire sufficient power and autonomy to threaten their rule.[5] The control of armed forces is thus a matter that concerns autocratic leaders, forcing them to employ a range of strategies to regulate, contain or subdue security organs. These strategies include, military purges targeting top-ranking officers, rewarding loyal officers with positions of power, as well as allowing corruption to flourish and offering bribes to military leaders.[6] The aim is to bind the military to the ruling regime making the two mutually dependant on each other.

There has been a recent surge in scholarly accounts of autocratization, focusing on the imperfections of political institutions,[7] and how they are troubled by bad governance practices such as political exclusion, the personalization of power and human rights abuses.[8] Other studies have focused on how power in autocratic regimes is consolidated and employed to repress competing groups.[9] This implies that the ruler has marginalized all institutions and processes in the defence sector and has total control of all aspects of military policy including appointments, promotions, budgeting, recruitments and retirements. For repression to be successful, the autocratic ruler must create powerful security and intelligence organs which are well-organized and sufficiently equipped with instruments of coercion.

However, a powerful military can be a double-edged sword. On the one hand, a strong army is necessary for autocratic consolidation through coercion and intimidation. On the other, a powerful military can force the autocratic ruler to make greater concessions to elites in the armed forces which could raise the possibility of a coup d'état. The fear of a coup leads autocrats to place great emphasis on tight control over their armed forces. Such an objective is achieved by employing a range of strategies including purges and appeasements – e.g. promotions and paying high wages to army officers. In many poor autocratic countries, the military contributes to the high echelons of economic elites because of the wealth it accumulates through high wages, corruption and benefits from classified funding sources.

Understanding how security forces are organized and how they are employed to support regime consolidation is important for our comprehension of the distinct behaviour and nature of autocratic regimes. This is so because the ways in which autocrats organize their security forces has a bearing on internal conflicts, repression, defection, regime change and military effectiveness.

Writing about the experience of many post-independent African countries, scholars such as Samuel Decalo,[10] Fjelde Hanne,[11] Volker Krause and Susumu Suzuki[12] link autocracy with the outbreak of armed conflict on the continent. They have broadly argued that autocratic regimes are more likely to experience civil wars than democracies. Likewise, Daniel Stockemer argues that autocracies have a significantly higher probability of experiencing intrastate warfare.[13] Many autocratic regimes practise political and social discrimination which creates tension between citizens who prefer democracy versus the regime that feels threatened by the forces of democracy. As of 2021, twelve out of sixteen countries in Africa that were facing civil violence have either autocratic or illiberal governments. A large majority of these conflicts were taking place in countries where leaders had come to power through a coup or had changed their constitution to remove term limits.

Sub-Saharan Africa has been particularly prone to exclusionary politics, coups and civil wars.[14] Most of the conflicts in post-independent Africa are fundamentally linked to the abuse of power, ethno-political disagreements and a lack of sufficient checks and balances against executive power.[15] Afrocentric scholars have highlighted the growing cases of groups that are excluded from politics based on religion, ethnicity, gender, class and ideological beliefs.[16] Autocratic regimes are inherently unstable because they essentially depend on political coercion which comes with the risk of coups,[17] civil war and social discontent.[18] In most African autocracies, those in power exploit their access to power to accumulate ill-gotten wealth through corruption, bribery and pillage at the expense of groups that are excluded from government.[19] The military has become an important factor for maintaining and reinforcing socio-economic and political inequality as it is used by autocracies to perpetrate violence, intimidate citizens and enforce acceptance and compliance.

In addition, autocratic regimes practise ethnic exclusion which further increases the risk of civil war.[20] The use of ethnic exclusion as a governance strategy is driven by the fear that rival ethnic groups could exploit their violent capabilities to overthrow the autocrat from power. He is thus forced to manoeuvre to protect his rule by deterring threats through eliminating his rivals from key positions and replacing them with those with blind loyalty to his rule. When this is carried out along ethnic lines, it increases the risk of coups and civil war.[21] Indeed, an examination of the governance practices of autocratic regimes points to the repeated elimination of rivals through military purges[22] and assassinations[23] in the process of consolidating power. Military purges help to prevent domestic rivals from political mobilization because it shows the strength of the regime,[24] – that is, its ability to eject undesired officers including those revered as powerful.[25] This is particularly prevalent in countries where political power is concentrated in the hands of a single ruler.[26]

In Africa, autocratic regimes practise military purges in two ways. The first is the instrumental use of corruption where military officers are allowed and sometimes encouraged to engage in corrupt deal-making by autocrats because it serves as a tool of political control.[27] Having a cadre of corrupt army generals leaves such officers beholden to the regime leader who can arrest and charge them with corruption in the event they choose to challenge his grip on power. Second, rather than pay soldiers well or allow them to accumulate wealth through corruption and pillage, African autocratic rulers can use military purges, especially arrest and incarceration of errant army officers as a way of spreading fear, enforcing loyalty and assuring compliance. Soldiers are thus coerced to support the incumbent leader and regime fearing the consequences of being perceived to be against the status quo.

Autocratic governance varies and is highly contingent on many factors. For instance, some autocratic regimes prefer to integrate civilian technocrats into their governments as was the case in Brazil in the1970s and Argentina in the 1960s.[28] Others form political parties and nurture dominant ruling coalitions as in Cuba under Colonel Fulgencio Batista Zaldívar. They organize elections, solicit civilian support and establish stable governments with a vested interest in socio-economic transformation. Available data indicate that approximately three-quarters of autocrats who lose power do so through coups d'état.[29] To contain this threat, autocrats tend to staff the army with a small group of trusted acolytes consisting of friends, tribemates or relatives.[30]

In Africa, this problem has been exacerbated by the mixture of ethnicity and nepotism as a strategy for regime consolidation.[31] Kristen Harkness has, for example, argued that most African armies are afflicted by nepotism, patronage and ethnic divide.[32] In her study of the Congolese military, Judith Verweijen argued that patronage networks have led to problems of parallel command structures, unnecessary competition for positions, resources and interests.[33]

Scholars such as Paul Brooker,[34] Amos Perlmutter[35] and Eric Nordlinger[36] have emphasized that social control is a common occurrence in autocratic regimes where the army or a clique of military officers is in direct control of all aspects of citizens' lives. However, total control of the army does not necessary guarantee survival of autocratic regimes if other aspects of society are hostile to their rule. Thus, autocrats seek social control and engage in activities designed to engineer new social identities by using mass media and clandestine propaganda to brainwash citizens into supporting their rule. The society is both suppressed and indoctrinated into believing that the autocratic regime works in the best interest of citizens.

Since gaining independence in 1962, Uganda has not had a professional and permanent army. This chapter examines the instrumental use of the army through nepotism and patronage under the Museveni regime. Each of the previous Ugandan presidents tried to dismantle the army and re-constitute one loyal to their rule. Having an army that is loyal to the regime leader was considered significant for the consolidation of power. Indeed, the principal threat that previous Ugandan autocratic leaders faced came from within the army rather than from outside. Past leaders were ousted from power after they lost the support of the army. However, after capturing power in 1986, President Museveni promised to end this phenomenon by establishing a national army that was professional and permanent.

In 2002 Uganda embarked on ambitious defence reforms with the sole aim of transforming the NRA (renamed UPDF) – a ragtag rebel group that captured power after years of armed insurgency – into a professional national army embodying the aspirations of majority Ugandans. In the next section, I examine the defence reforms that were introduced after 2002. I argue that these reforms have not led to the desired outcome largely because of the actions of President Museveni who sees a professional army as a threat to his rule. Thus, in the same way as previous leaders, President Museveni has worked to encourage partisan allegiances, nepotism and cronyism in the army as a way of consolidating power and deterring threats to his rule.

Military reforms and professionalization

Six years after capturing and consolidating power, NRA elites sought to change the ideological orientation and strategic vision of Uganda's national army. They argued that, having seized power through guerrilla warfare, the Ugandan army essentially remained a guerrilla outfit with limited appeal among Ugandans beyond the former bush war networks.[37] The NRA systems were deemed obsolete because they sprung from a guerrilla mind-set.[38] In their interactions with citizens, NRA soldiers continuously exhibited a guerrilla-like mentality which was considered counterproductive for the sustainability of the newly achieved peace. Aggravating this problem was the scale of atrocities committed by the NRA in its pacification of the northern and eastern parts of the country.

The NRA's brutal counterinsurgency tactics raised doubts among Ugandans over the army's commitment to democracy and the respect for human rights. Likewise, the government continued to spend the largest part of its budget on unnecessary military expenditure and lost part of its budget through corruption and pillage.[39] To address these challenges, the government searched for policies that would transform the military from a rag-tag rebel outfit into a modern, professional and accountable defence force.

By the early 2000s, the Ugandan government and its major donors started developing an agenda that linked security and development. Hence, the focus of investment shifted to Security Sector Reform (SSR), which was considered an important tool for fighting inefficiency and corruption in the army. Furthermore, Uganda's major donors were constantly expressing concerns that the country's defence spending as a percentage of GDP was unsustainably rising annually amidst mounting socio-economic problems.[40] The country's limited financial resources, the donors contended, were being spent on salaries for redundant soldiers and the purchase of expensive military hardware at the cost of other important matters like health, education, poverty alleviation and infrastructure development. As a result, international financial institutions like the World Bank and the IMF decided to peg their financial assistance to Uganda to cuts on military expenditure until the government achieved the required defence spending level of 2 per cent of GDP.[41] This attracted the ire of the ruling elites, who accused the donors of being indifferent to Uganda's security concerns.

The Museveni government maintained that high military expenditure was necessary to improve security and to create a favourable environment for trade, investment and eventual economic growth.[42] Museveni himself warned donors that cutting defence spending posed a threat to the security of Ugandans, particularly in the north where the army was battling the LRA insurgency. His objection to cuts on defence spending was also based on the understanding that Uganda was sandwiched between hostile neighbours like Congo and Sudan who were allegedly supporting the ADF and LRA insurgencies. As a UPDF Political Commissar explained:

> The donors, particularly the World Bank, were very wrong in forcing us to cut military spending. They forced us to retire many of our soldiers, thinking that there won't be more wars. The outcomes were terrible for Uganda. You had many individuals who had spent their entire lives in the army being sent home (without) any retirement package. The result was prolonged insurgencies like LRA and ADF because we ran short of manpower.[43]

Advancing the notion of state fragility, the Ugandan government looked for ways to persuade donors to continue supporting its defence budget. Hence, a defence review process was launched to assess the prevailing security threats and the necessary resources required to defend the country. The UK's Department for International Development (DfID) agreed to fund the entire process with the aim of getting clarity on the threats to Uganda's security.

Although the process was led by the Ministry of Defence, the review committee consisted of multiple government departments and agencies, including parliament, members of academia and civil society groups. It was led by the Defence Reform Secretariat in the Ministry of Defence. The key players in the review process included the Commander-in-Chief, Yoweri Museveni; Defence Minister Amama Mbabazi, Deputy Defence Minister Ruth Nankabirwa; Ministry of Defence Permanent Secretary Gabindadde Musoke; Army Commander Gen. Aronda Nyakairima; UPDF Chief of Staff Maj. Gen. Joshua Masaba and the donor community led by the UK.[44] The main focus was on the 'hardware' and 'software' needs of the military – that is, to provide the soldiers with the necessary armaments to defend the country but also to change the mind-set, beliefs and personality traits of soldiers so that they can see themselves as a national army representing the interests and aspirations of all Ugandans irrespective of political affiliation and ethnic identity.

The review proposed measures for building the army's internal systems and processes to support the creation of a national army. The 1995 Constitution had facilitated the transformation of the Ugandan army from a rebel outfit into a much broader Uganda People's Defence Forces. This transformation, it was argued, would facilitate the creation of a national army, representing all aspects of Uganda's socio-economic and spatial dimensions.

Thereafter, attention shifted to addressing Uganda's long-term and immediate security needs and the size of the force needed to confront such threats. The government reduced the size of the military from 60,000 to 48,000 soldiers. This was meant to lay a foundation for long-term effectiveness in the conduct of the military. A small force, it was argued, would be less of a burden to the economy, easy to train and equip, and able to carry out its operations efficiently. The demobilized personnel were enrolled in a reserve force that was under constant surveillance in the event they engaged in destabilizing activities.

In executing the demobilization process, Uganda kept a keen eye on its key security threats. These were identified in the defence review white paper as: (1) border insecurity, including covert and overt invasion, illicit trade and illegal crossing; (2) external influences, specifically threats from outside Uganda's borders such as hostile policies/actions of neighbouring states; (3) political instability, especially tensions emerging from internal governance challenges, weak state institutions and political competition; (4) environmental stress and resource challenges; (5) social polarization; and (6) civil disasters.[45]

Among the internal reforms that were introduced was the re-organization of the army into two service forces. The military was to be segmented into the Land Forces, the Air Force and any other service force prescribed by parliament. Since then, the president has added the Reserve Force and the Special Forces Command (SFC), all of which function as fully fledged service forces. Furthermore, within the service forces, there were other strategic sub-divisions, including the infantry division, the armoured brigade, the air defence division, the artillery division, the engineering brigade, the service battalion and the field hospital.

These divisions are now strategically and geographically stationed in different parts of Uganda, ready to respond to any threat to the country's sovereignty. For instance, the first division is located at Kakiri, a small town near the capital, Kampala. It oversees security for central Uganda. The second division is headquartered in Mbarara and oversees security in western Uganda. The third division is headquartered in the eastern town of Moroto and oversees security in eastern

Uganda and the restive Karamoja region. The fourth division is headquartered in the northern town of Gulu and oversees security in the north and the West Nile sub-region. The fifth infantry division is stationed at Acholi Pii in Pader district and, together with the fourth division, oversees security in the Acholi region and the porous border with South Sudan. Each division is headed by a division commander who is assisted by several structures like the division intelligence unit and the division court martial.

Since 2004, the Ugandan government has spent considerable resources on various initiatives designed to facilitate the professionalization and modernization of the army and to enhance the capacity of its intelligence agencies. As recommended by the review, the government has established a well-trained and well-equipped force ready to respond to sudden events like insurgencies. New organs like the Joint Intelligence Committee (JIC) and the National Security Council (NSC) were created in 2003 to streamline the command-and-control systems of the army. The president officially chairs the NSC. The council has broad representation that includes the ministries of Internal Affairs, Foreign Affairs, Defence and Security and the Office of the Attorney General. All heads of security organs were also given a seat on the NSC. These include: The Inspector General of Police, the Chief of Defence Forces, the head of Internal Security Organization (ISO) and the head of the External Security Organization (ESO). Among its roles, the NSC advises the president on security matters, coordinates intelligence and reviews from JIC. At local government levels, new structures like the District Security Committees (DSC), the District Intelligence Committees (DIC) and Sub-County Security Committees were created, each headed by military intelligence officers.

Whereas the UPDF's successful internal restructuring cannot be overlooked, it is imperative to question whether the Ugandan army has been transformed into a non-partisan army embodying the broad interests and aspirations of Ugandans. A critical examination of the UPDF shows that this aspiration remains a pipe dream. What is clear is that – as the regime continues to face mounting social and political upheavals – the UPDF has become an important force for guaranteeing Museveni's survival. The next section of this chapter turns to a consideration of the manner in which the military has been used to entrench Museveni's rule by curtailing activities that challenge the status quo.

From professionalization to personalization

Museveni has consistently argued that his dream is to build an army that can form a foundation for Uganda's democracy and socio-economic transformation. To this end, he has emphasized the point that the Ugandan army should not be simply restricted to fighting wars but should also become an engine for socio-economic development. In his speeches after coming to power, Museveni often argued that once internal peace and stability had been achieved, the military would divorce itself from politics and allow democracy to take root in all institutions of the state.[46]

Early in his rule, sections of Ugandans praised President Museveni for his good management of the army and for heralding a departure from the country's previous crises of coups and military-orchestrated violence.[47] Museveni was quick to blame previous regimes for personalizing the military. To him, the regimes of Obote and Amin had failed to curb the interests of armed elites or to subordinate the military to civilian authority, which led to years of violence and bloodshed. He writes in his memoir that:

> In the past armies belonged to individuals and not to Uganda. We believe that armies should be national and nationalist. They should not be swept away by the changes of the government or by the exit of individuals from power. This is why we attach the greatest importance to the politicisation of our soldiers. They must assimilate the aspirations of all the citizens of Uganda so that they can learn to serve them all, and not just individuals or a section of the community.[48]

The Ugandan government has introduced several programmes and initiatives which it claims are aimed at creating an inclusive military force. For instance, recruitment of new soldiers currently takes place at district level which allows all regions of the country to have some form of representation in the army. Because of this policy, the Uganda army has a fair ethic representation at the rank-and-file level and in the lower structures of military leadership.

However, the topmost leadership of the army has essentially remained a preserve of Museveni's home region of western Uganda.[49] For instance, until 2010, all the officers at the rank of full General, the top echelon of the UPDF, hailed from western Uganda. They included: the president himself; his brother, Gen. Caleb Akandwanaho (a.k.a. Salim Saleh); Gen. David Tinyefuza; Gen. Elly Tumwine; and Gen. Aronda Nyakairima. The president faced a barrage of criticisms from the press, the opposition and from civil society organizations over his failure to guarantee ethnic representation in the army's top echelons. Hence, he responded to his critics in 2010 by promoting Jeje Odongo to full general, becoming the first officer outside the President's home region to attain such a position. Yet, surprisingly, Museveni instantly retired General Odongo from the army after his promotion, a decision critics considered a well-calculated attempt to make his promotion redundant. Subsequently, Museveni promoted Moses Ali, an officer from the West Nile-sub-region, to the rank of full General. However, his promotion was considered inconsequential since Ali had already been retired from the army and was well over seventy years of age and serving in a civilian position as a deputy prime minister.

An examination of President Museveni's actions and policies towards the army shows that he has failed to create a professional army that is non-partisan and accountable to Ugandans. First, he has failed to separate the army from himself. He treats the UPDF as his personal product and views it as his personal army. Second, he has undermined the professionalization of the army by embedding the military within the ruling party. The military now sees itself as an extension of the ruling party and works vigorously to safeguard the subjective interests of the party and its elite. Likewise, the personalization of the UPDF is evident in how Museveni handles appointments and promotions in the army and how he deploys the military to secure his political position. The personalization of the army is also evident in the way he employs informal procedures to deal with divisions and disagreements in the army.

The informal criterion for promotion and appointment to top positions in the UPDF is based on how loyal an individual is to the President and the ruling party. This means that the President must engage in secretive surveillance of his top lieutenants in order to establish who deserves a promotion and who should be purged from the corp. Given Uganda's history of military generals overthrowing political leaders, Museveni is said to value loyalty and trust among officers who are close to him. Hence, in his attempt to recruit trusted officers, he often turns to his blood relatives, tribesmen and his 'bush war' network.[50]

Transparency and meritocracy have been sacrificed at the altar of tribalism and nepotism. A 2008 survey carried out by *The Independent* magazine indicated that 75 per cent of the twenty-three top positions in the army were held by officers from Museveni home region. The central region (Uganda's largest region by population) held only 17 per cent, the north 9 per cent and the east zero.[51] Among the current and retired top military officers with blood connection to the President include: the president's son Gen. Muhoozi Kainerugaba (who has served as commander of Special Forces, commander of the Land Forces and currently as Senior Presidential Advisor), Caleb Akandwanaho, the president's younger brother (who served as army commander and now Presidential Advisor on Security), Maj. Gen. Sabiiti Muzeyi, cousin to the President (who has served as commander of Military Police, Deputy Inspector General of Police and currently general manager Luwero army industries).

Others include Col. James Kateera, cousin to First Lady Janet Museveni (who has served as deputy commander of the UPDF fourth division); Lieutenant Gen. Henry Tumukunde (Retired), the president's in-law (who has served as security minister and director of spy agencies); and Lieutenant Colonel (Retired) Bright Rwamirama, a cousin to the president (who has served as State Minister for Defence and Veteran Affairs and currently is the minister in-charge of animal industry).

Time and again the President has tried to rationalize this imbalance, arguing that it is logical for his ethnic and home region to dominate military positions because when he launched his rebel insurgency in the early 1980s, he was first joined by people from his ethnic group. But this explanation does not stand up to scrutiny. It is now almost four decades since Museveni captured power, but the imbalance remains. Indeed, an examination of his recent appointments doesn't reveal any attempt to correct the imbalance. Instead, the President has entrenched this imbalance even further viewing it as necessary to his survival in power. This is apparent because he often finds himself reliant on his relatives and in-laws in the military to get intelligence information and to execute special political assignments.

The above discussion underlines an obvious fact that for Museveni's regime, family and ethnic ties matter a lot. For regime critics, this blatant nepotism is detrimental to Uganda's democratic progress because it promotes one-man rule. For regime insiders however, it is the most rational mechanism for promoting trust and comradeship. And, it is necessary for regime continuity. Whereas Museveni's nepotistic tendencies have been widely denounced, such family-based appointments are beneficial to him in several ways.

First, when his relatives are at the helm of the army, it makes it easy for him to use the military for repression and coercion because it is under the control of individuals with blind loyalty to him and can serve his interest unquestioningly. Second, because top army officers have blood relations with the President, they have a subjective interest in his hold on power. They see him as guaranteeing the protection of their wealth, power and status. A threat to Museveni is, therefore, construed as a threat to their own privileges. More than anything else, this power dynamic has allowed Museveni to rule Uganda for longer than all other post-independence leaders combined.

Nonetheless, the consequence of this family and ethnic-based rule is that Uganda is still far behind in its efforts to build a genuinely professional army. In the same way as Obote and Amin who saw the military as an extension of their power, Museveni also sees the UPDF as an integral part of his regime which can be deployed against political rivals. This has affected Uganda's democratization in two ways. First, it has resulted in the militarization of politics as the army is at the forefront of purging Museveni's opponents. Secondly, it has affected civil-military relations as many Ugandans see the army as a partisan force. Independent voices inside the army are silenced and army officers often make decisions based on how it helps the ruling party maintain power. How does Museveni handle dissent and disagreements in the army?

Dealing with dissent and rewarding loyal army officers

Whether in the army or the ruling party, expressing views that disagree with the President or the official position of the ruling party is severely punished, while blind loyalty is rewarded. This encourages NRM party members to become more devoted to the President and his regime hoping to be rewarded with lucrative positions in government. For instance, in 2017, members of parliament who led a controversial campaign to remove the age-limit provision from the constitution were rewarded with ministerial appointments, while those who opposed the amendment were side-lined or violently arrested by the army on orders of the President.[52] For example, MP Raphael Magyezi was rewarded with a ministerial position in 2021 for spearheading a controversial amendment to remove the age limit close from the constitution which allowed Museveni to run for re-lection. The bill was challenged by the opposition and civil society organizations, but the ruling party passed it using its super majority in the national assembly. The same scenario played out ahead of the 2016 general elections when Museveni gave ministerial posts to loyalist MPs like Evelyn Anite, who championed a proposal to change the ruling party's constitution to block former Prime Minister Amama Mbabazi from competing against Museveni for party flag bearer in the presidential election.

Although the constitution bars the military from engaging in partisan politics, high-ranking officers maintain close ties with the ruling party and often make public statements in support of the regime. Other officers openly participate in activities that are designed to sabotage opposition mobilization against the regime. As with the ruling party, Museveni uses the strategy of rewarding loyal army officers, especially those who oversee violent crackdown of anti-regime protests. For instance, in 2016, long-standing tensions and grievances by ethnic Bakonzo against the central government boiled over leading to sporadic violence between government and the Rwenzururu kingdom. In response, Museveni deployed the military commanded by then Brig. Peter Elwelu. More than 100 local people were killed in this operation, including women and children.[53] To date, about 167 civilians who were charged with terrorism, treason and murder remain in pre-trial detention.

The international donor community and civil society organizations have consistently called for an independent investigation to establish the number of death and to prosecute army offers responsible for killing civilians, but the Ugandan government has rejected these calls. Instead, Museveni publicly applauded Elwelu for commanding a deadly operation which he claimed had 'taught a harsh lesson' to the Rwenzururu king and his subjects. Subsequently, Museveni promoted Elwelu through the ranks (from Brigadier to Major General and Lieutenant General) within a period of five years. He has further elevated him from his previous position of commander of the second division to commander of Land Forces and later to a higher position of Deputy Chief of Defence Forces.

Critics have argued that Museveni's strategy of rewarding loyalists and punishing those who express dissenting views breeds impunity and affects military professionalism. While this may be true to an extent, there are several political benefits of this strategy that are often overlooked. In the first instance, it has allowed Museveni to create fear within the army and the ruling party and threaten those who may wish to challenge him. Punishing errant army generals sends a clear message about the consequences of expressing disagreements with the President and signals to his generals that he is the person in-charge of their fate.

Second, it creates a belief among ruling party elites that they are better off with him – that is, nobody can challenge him since top army Generals value and unquestionably follow his leadership. This, in turn, cements the 'big man' syndrome as everything runs at his discretion. Inside the ruling party, the strategy helps Museveni to create pluralistic ignorance (i.e. a situation in which a majority in the regime feel that the decisions they have taken are wrong but fear to raise objections, believing that others accept them). Raising an objection is equated to challenging the regime leader which is taboo. This has further allowed Museveni to cultivate a cult-like status by positioning himself as a selfless and benevolent leader fighting for the survival and wellbeing of Ugandans while casting his critics as motivated by self-interest. For instance, Museveni has consistently described the country's opposition groups as 'wolves lurking around to tear Uganda apart' and says he will not hand over power as long as 'I have support of my army'.[54] Finally, because he knows his own party cannot internally challenge him, he acts decisively and with overreaching authority.

Despite enjoying unrivalled loyalty among top military officers, there is evidence to suggest the existence of power struggles between the President and certain military officers who express views considered 'unpleasant'. Where this situation has arisen, Museveni mainly relies on three strategies to deal with critical military officers. First, he uses informal mechanisms like *katebe* (non-deployment) to punish independent-minded army officers.

Given the relatively low salaries earned by military officers in Uganda, spending years undeployed is deemed a punishment from the Commander-in-Chief because it denies that army officer the lucrative financial benefits that come with military deployment. Second, he uses formal institutions like the court martial to prosecute critical army officers. Where the regime leader is not certain of winning a case in civilian courts, the state engages in tactics like deliberate delay of trials to frustrate officers hoping for a speedy trial.

Third, the president also engages in negotiations with army officers who have fallen out with him. He has shown a willingness to forgive officers if they 'repent' and seek his forgiveness. Such officers are mostly sent for further training, to undergo some sort of rehabilitation, before being returned to the fold. As a result, elites in the armed forces understand that they have to deal with a powerful president who has the army under his full control.

In contrast to the Ugandan parliament, which has proven woefully inept at asserting its constitutional right to check the President's overreach, some military elites often use courts of law to challenge some of the President's decisions. The concern stems from the fact that the President wields supreme power to punish, demote or order the arrest of any serving or retired army officer suspected of wrongdoing. Some army officers prefer to use civil courts because the legitimacy and independence of the court martial are questionable as it works at the whim of the Commander-in-Chief, who appoints and dismisses at will the officers who constitute the court martial.

The battle between the regime and critical army officers such as Maj. Gen. James Kazini, Lt. Gen. Henry Tumukunde and Gen. David Sejusa shows that army officers do not expect justice in the court martial, especially in cases that involve policy disagreement with the President. They are quick to appeal decisions of the court martial in the High Court. The trial of Gen. Sejusa (formerly Tinyefuza) perfectly captures the lack of confidence in the court martial by military officers. Sejusa held the position of Coordinator of Intelligence Agencies until 2013 and was one of the most influential commanders in the UPDF. He had been a formidable leader in the civil war that brought Museveni to power, held senior positions in the army and sat on the UPDF High Command, the supreme decision-making body of the army.

Gen. Sejusa's disagreement with Museveni first became public in 1996, when he stunned the military hierarchy by giving testimony before a parliamentary committee in which he castigated the regime's handling of the LRA insurgency in northern Uganda. Since Sejusa was the overall commander of the counterinsurgency campaign against the LRA rebels, his testimony rattled the regime and the military hierarchy. He was quickly summoned to the High Command for a dressing-down. However, prior to his appearance, he wrote a surprise letter to Museveni requesting to resign from the army. In his letter, he noted: 'I find it unjustified to continue serving in an institution whose bodies I have no faith in or whose views I do not subscribe to ... I know my own faults very well and I do not suppose I am an easy subordinate; I like to go my own way.'[55]

The President, however, rejected Sejusa's retirement plans, telling reporters on 17 December 1996 that Sejusa cannot be allowed to retire because he still has 'problems' to sort out.[56] Although the President did not specify which kind of problems he was referring to, several media outlets and political analysts indicated that the regime had long suspected Sejusa of harbouring political ambitions.[57] As one of the founding members of the NRA and one of its most gifted fighters during the bush war, Sejusa had built a reputation that was rivalled by few inside the military. A political contest between Museveni and Sejusa would come with serious ramifications for the regime.

Subsequently, the regime developed a strategy of containing Sejusa's political ambitions. The strategy involved the use by all means possible, legal or illegal, to deny him retirement from the army given that serving officers are constitutionally barred from active politics. For an outsider, a decision not to fire a critical army officer seems counterintuitive, but for regime insiders, it was the most rational strategy to guarantee regime survival as a political contest between Museveni and Sejusa, a revered regime insider, would bring unpredictable consequences.

Nonetheless, the regime underestimated how far Sejusa was willing to go to force his retirement from the army. In a twist of events, he filed a petition in the Constitutional Court in 1996 challenging the decision to deny him retirement. The court ruled in his favour and approved his retirement, but the state appealed to the Supreme Court, the highest court in the land. The Supreme Court has been at fault for making controversial pro-regime decisions.[58] It overturned the decision of the Constitutional Court, concluding that Sejusa's quest for retirement from the army did not comply with formalities and procedures prescribed by the law.[59]

President Museveni praised the decision of the Supreme Court as important for the country's stability. At the time, both the Constitutional and Supreme Courts were considerably independent, and their conflicting rulings show how they weighed the implications of Sejusa's retirement. In Sejusa's case, it is believed that the Supreme Court considered the political implications and the precedent it would set if Sejusa had been allowed to retire in those circumstances. It is the same political and practical implications the

Supreme Court based on not to annul the presidential elections in 2001 and 2006 even after the court found widespread cases of rigging and falsification of results.

Accordingly, Sejusa was placed on katebe (non-deployment) for many years as punishment for his bellicosity. During this period, press reports talked of prolonged negotiations involving senior military officers who tried to reconcile the President with Sejusa. The result of this rapprochement became public in 2004 when, in a surprise move, Sejusa publicly apologized to Museveni for the 1996 fallout. He claimed that he had been misled by certain forces and asked the President for forgiveness because he had seen the 'light'.[60] Sejusa's 'sincere apology' earned him the temporary trust of the President, who later appointed him the Coordinator of Intelligence Agencies. By virtue of this position, Sejusa was placed at the forefront of processing sensitive intelligence information about the regime's enemies – both internal and external. This explains why he was accused of having played a role in several controversial incidents like the arrest of opposition figure Kiiza Besigye in 2005, the military raid on the High Court in 2005 and the closure of independent media houses during the Buganda protests in 2009.

It was not until 29 April 2013 that Sejusa issued a letter containing bombshell revelations that shocked the nation and sent shivers down the spine of the top military elite.[61] In the letter, Sejusa asked the director of ISO to conduct a systematic investigation of allegations that top officials, including the chief of police, plotted to either assassinate or frame their colleagues who were perceived to be against the so-called 'Muhoozi Project',[62] an alleged plot by Museveni to have his son, Muhoozi Kainerugaba, succeed him as president.

Sejusa's suggestion that Museveni's son was being groomed to take over from his father was bolstered by Kainerugaba's meteoric rise through the military ranks to become a two-star general and commander of the Special Forces, the presidential guard, at that time – in 2013. Sejusa further alleged that those targeted for assassination due to their opposition to the 'Muhoozi Project' included himself, then-Prime Minister Amama Mbabazi and then Chief of Defence Forces, Aronda Nyakairima. He wrote:

Intelligence has picked some clandestine actions by these reckless and rather naïve actors to have some youth recruited as rebels and then frame some members of security services and key politicians perceived as anti-establishment. … You need to investigate the very serious claims that the same actors are re-organising elements of former Wembley under one police officer Agasirwe Nixon to assassinate people who disagree with this so-called family project of holding onto power in perpetuity.[63]

Although many Ugandans had long suspected the existence of the 'Muhoozi Project', Sejusa's revelation added a new twist because it was the first time Ugandans learnt that the succession debate was generating serious anxieties inside the military. Afterwards, the media published reports about the alleged assassination conspiracies, raising questions about the safety of those seen as opposed to the project. The mysterious death of Gen. Nyakairima, less than a year after Sejusa had written his controversial letter, raised more questions about the issue. Moreover, the speed with which the regime's backers publicized the cause of Nyakairima's death even before a post-mortem had been carried out, raised concerns which played out in the media, with many Ugandans speculating about what, and who might have, killed Nyakairima.[64]

To curtail mass circulation of the contents of Sejusa's letter, the government launched a media crackdown and closed two newspapers, *Daily Monitor* and the *Red Pepper*, as well as two radio stations, KFM and Dembe FM, for publishing contents of the letter. Sejusa himself fled to exile in London. A few months after arriving in the UK, he told journalists that Museveni had rigged the 2006 election. He further revealed that he was part of a high-level intelligence group created by Museveni to rig the election in his favour. He argued that the official results this intelligence group obtained showed that Museveni got only 30 per cent of the total vote and the opposition candidate – Kizza Besigye – got 69 per cent. According to Sejusa, the regime falsified election results. Invariably, the ruling party disputed this claim.[65]

Sejusa's case reveals the intricacies of power in a hybrid authoritarian system in which the regime relies on both political plurality and military coercion for survival. The military may be a strong actor in the political system, but its actions also reveal an institution that is itself constrained by the political system in which it is deeply embedded and of which it is a part. It is also true that whereas the President retains unrivalled power, some military officials have not been afraid to challenge his authority through both formal and informal institutions. For instance, when the President publicly called for the court-martial of Colonel Besigye after he criticized the NRM government in 1999, Besigye quickly mobilized Bahororo elders' councils of his ethnic group who protested his impending trial and convinced the President to drop the idea, which again demonstrates the power of social, and especially ethnic, elites.

Conclusion

What has emerged with the Museveni regime are two contradictory tendencies: on the one hand Museveni sees the military as a key ingredient for political stability and power retention. Paradoxically, stability is dependent on political loyalty. Embodied in the controversies explored above is a struggle for power between the leader of the regime and certain institutions of the state as well as individual actors. Although parliament is too weak to effectively provide checks and balances against the regime, some vibrant members of the ruling party and the courts of law are willing to fight for the right to exercise their authority.

To survive in power, Museveni wants political elites and military officers to be blindly loyal to him and should accept his decisions, irrespective of whether they are unlawful or illegitimate. On the other hand, is the impulse of a military institution keen to develop professional norms and process as a foundation for peace and stability. This explains why some army officers have been willing to go to courts of law to challenge controversial decisions taken by the regime leader, although admittedly only a few have done so. Amidst such challenges, the regime leader is still able to make manoeuvres that, taken together, help cement his control of the army. One such manoeuvre has been creating multiple auxiliary military units, stuffing them with individuals with blind loyalty to his regime, providing them with sufficient resources and then deploying them on important missions intended to facilitate the broad regime survival project.

The literature on military purges has largely focused on the elimination,[66] and assassination of rivals.[67] However, the action of Museveni shows that there is a wide range of strategies that autocratic leaders use to control the army. Museveni hardly engages in acts of assassination against his rivals. Instead, he has skilfully used corruption, ethnicization and nepotism to manage the army. While the military in Uganda does not enjoy high salaries and attendant benefits, top army officers are nevertheless allowed to gain wealth through corruption and deal-making. In return, they feel compelled to support the regime because those who are perceived to be critical of the regime are often arrested and charged with corruption while corrupt but loyal officers get off scot-free.

Scholarly accounts of autocratic regimes point to the ways in which they use mass incarceration of military officers as part of a purge strategy. However, a study of Museveni's regime shows that military control can be achieved without necessarily engaging in risky mass incarceration of errant army officers. While Museveni sometimes engages in the arrest and prosecution of generals who turn critical of his rule, he does not do so on a mass scale.

As highlighted in the chapter, even though Museveni's regime has prosecuted several errant army officers, many of them seldom get convicted and some have successful challenged their trial in civil courts.

Although Museveni has faced powerful critics within the army who possess enough clout to threaten his grip on power, he has successfully weakened his rivals' capability to mobilize against his rule or stage a coup. Scholars such as Roessler have argued that autocrats who face threats to their power will use coercion and assassination to eliminate the elites who threaten their power.[68] However, using such a punitive approach can prompt a strong response from entrenched military elites to overthrow the regime before they lose their power and privileges. This precisely is what forces Museveni to exercise some level of restraint against errant but powerful military generals.

Notes

1   Kreimer Alcira, 'Experience with Post-Conflict Reconstruction: Uganda Case Study' (The World Bank Volume VI, Washington, DC, 2000).

2   Gobel Christian, 'Authoritarian Consolidation', *European Political Science* 10, no. 2 (2011): 176–90.

3   Ibid.

4   Kailitz Steffen and Daniel Stockemer, 'Regime Legitimation, Elite Cohesion and the Durability of Autocratic Regime Types', *International Political Science Review* 38, no. 3 (2017): 332–48.

5   Acemoglu Daron, Davide Ticchi and Andrea Vindigni, 'A Theory of Military Dictatorships', *American Economic Journal: Macroeconomics* 2, no. 1 (2010): 1–42.

6   Gerald Bareebe, 'Predators or Protectors? Military Corruption as a Pillar of Regime Survival in Uganda', *Civil Wars* 22, no. 2–3 (2020): 313–32.

7   Peceny Mark, Caroline Beer and Shannon Sanchez-Terry, 'Dictatorial Peace'? *American Political Science Review* 96, no.1 (2002): 15–26.

8   Caitlin Talmadge, 'Different Threats, Different Militaries: Explaining Organizational Practices in Authoritarian Armies', *Security Studies* 25, no.1 (2016): 111–41.

9   Jessica Weeks, *Dictators at War and Peace* (Ithaca: Cornell University Press, 2014).

10 Samuel Decalo, 'African Personal Dictatorships', *The Journal of Modern African Studies* 23, no. 2 (1985): 209–37.

11 Fjelde Hanne, 'Generals, Dictators, and Kings: Authoritarian Regimes and Civil Conflict, 1973-2004', *Conflict Management and Peace Science* 27, no.3 (2010): 195–218.

12 Krause Volker and Susumu Suzuki, 'Causes of Civil War in Asia and Sub-Saharan Africa: A Comparison', *Social Science Quarterly* 86, no. 1 (2005): 160–77.

13 Daniel Stockemer, 'Regime Type and Civil War – A Re-evaluation of the Inverted U-Relationship', *Global Change Peace & Security* 22, no. 3 (2010): 261–74.

14 Kieh Klay and Kelechi Kalu, *Democratization and Military Coups in Africa: Post-1990 Political Conflicts* (Maryland: Lexington Books, 2021).

15 Jack Paine, 'Ethnic Violence in Africa: Destructive Legacies of Pre-Colonial States', *International Organization* 73, no. 3 (2019) 645–83.

16 Edwin Etieyibo, Mucha Musemwa and Obvious Katsaura, 'Identities, Exclusionism and Politics in Africa', *African Studies* 79, no.4 (2020): 361–6.

17 Kristen A. Harkness, 'The Ethnic Army and the State: Explaining Coup Traps and the Difficulties of Democratization in Africa', *Journal of Conflict Resolution* 60, no. 4 (2016): 587–616.

18 Victor Asal, Michael Findley, James A. Piazza and James Igoe Walsh, 'Political Exclusion, Oil, and Ethnic Armed Conflict', *The Journal of Conflict Resolution* 60, no. 8 (2016): 1343–67.

19 Mwangi Kimenyi, 'Ethnicity, Governance, and the Provision of Public Goods', *Journal of African Economies*, 15 no.1 (2006): 62–99.

20 Roessler Philip, 'The Enemy Within: Personal Rule, Coups, and Civil War in Africa', *World Politics* 63, no. 2 (2011): 300–46.

21 Ibid.

22 Jun Koga Sudduth, 'Purging Militaries: Introducing the Military Purges in Dictatorships (MPD) Dataset', *Journal of Peace Research* 58, no. 4 (2021): 870–80.

23 Kerata B. Chacha, 'Scars of Memory and Scales of Justice: Rethinking Political Assassinations in Post-Colonial Africa', *CODESRIA Bulletin* 3, no.4 (2015): 94–8.

24 Sudduth, 'Purging Militaries'.

25 Maves J. Braithwaite and Jun Koga Sudduth, 'Military Purges and the Recurrence of Civil Conflict', *Research & Politics* 3, no. 1 (2016): 1–6.

26 Jun Koga Sudduth, 'Strategic Logic of Elite Purges in Dictatorships', *Comparative Political Studies* 50, no.13 (2017): 1768–801.

27 Bareebe, 'Predators or Protectors'?

28 Guillermo O'Donnell, *Modernization and Bureaucratic-Authoritarianism: Studies in South American Politics* (Berkeley: Institute of International Studies, University of California, 1973).

29 Milan W. Svolik, 'Power Sharing and Leadership Dynamics in Authoritarian Regimes', *American Journal of Political Science* 53, no. 2 (2009): 477–94.

30 Abel Escribà-Folch, Tobias Böhmelt and Ulrich Pilster, 'Authoritarian Regimes and Civil–military Relations: Explaining Counterbalancing in Autocracies', *Conflict Management and Peace Science* 37, no. 5 (2020): 559–79.

31 George Dev, 'Democracy and Tribalism in Africa', *Offshore (Conroe, Tex.)* 56, no. 6 (1996).

32 Harkness, 'The Ethnic Army'.

33 Judith Verweijen, 'Soldiers Without an Army? Patronage Networks and Cohesion in the Armed Forces of the DR Congo', *Armed Forces and Society* 44, no. 4 (2018): 626–46.

34 Paul Brooker, *Non-Democratic Regimes: Theory, Government, and Politics* (New York: Palgrave Macmillan, 2000).

35 Amos Perlmutter, *Modern Authoritarianism: A Comparative Institutional Analysis* (New Haven, CT: Yale University Press, 1981).

36 Eric A. Nordlinger, *Soldiers in Politics: Military Coups and Governments* (Upper Saddle River, NJ: Prentice-Hall, 1977).

37 Joshua Rubongoya, *Regime Hegemony in Museveni's Uganda: Pax Musevenica* (New York: Palgrave Macmillan, 2007).

38 Interview with Hon. Muwanga Kivumbi, a Member of Parliament who sits on the Parliamentary Defence Committee, 3 June 2016.

39 Roger Tangri and Andrew M. Mwenda, 'Military Corruption & Ugandan Politics since the Late 1990s', *Review of African Political Economy* 30, no. 98 (2003): 539–52.

40   Ibid.
41   Andrew M. Mwenda and Roger Tangri, 'Patronage Politics, Donor Reforms, and Regime Consolidation in Uganda', *African Affairs* 104, no. 416 (2005): 449–67.
42   Interview with Colonel Shaban Bantariza, 5 July 2017.
43   Interview with Colonel Felix Kulayigye, 27 July 2017.
44   Uganda Government White Paper on Defence Transformation, June 2004.
45   Ibid.
46   Professionalizing the army has been a common topic in many speeches of President Museveni available online: http://www.statehouse.go.ug
47   Joe Oloka-Onyango, 'A Sociopolitical Biography of Uganda's Yoweri Kaguta Museveni', *Africa Today* 50, no. 3 (2004): 28–52.
48   Yoweri Museveni, *What Is Africa's Problem?* (Kampala: NRM Publications, 1992), 79.
49   International Crisis Group report, 2012.
50   Interview with Hon. Kaps Fungaroo, a Member of Parliament and former Shadow Minister for Defence.
51   'Family Rule in Uganda', *The Independent*, Kampala (11 March 2009). https://www.independent.co.ug/family-rule-uganda/
52   Ibrahim Ssemujju Nganda, 'The Day Museveni's Guards Invaded Parliament', *The Observer*, Kampala (4 October 2017). https://observer.ug/viewpoint/55238-the-day-museveni-guards-invaded-parliament.html (accessed 12 February 2019).
53   Human Rights Watch, 'Uganda: Ensure Independent Investigation into Kasese Killings' (15 March 2017). https://www.hrw.org/news/2017/03/15/uganda-ensure-independent-investigation-kasese-killings#:~:text=Human%20Rights%20Watch%20found%20the,palace%20compound%20on%20November%2027 (accessed 31 May 2023).
54   Daily Monitor, 'I Cannot Leave Power to Wolves, Says Museveni' (18 January 2015). Available online: http://www.monitor.co.ug/News/National/I-cannot-leave-power-to-wolves--says-Museveni/688334-2592430-11wm4baz/index.html (Accessed 19 May 2016).
55   Gen. David Sejusa's letter to Museveni. https://niyibizi.wordpress.com/2016/02/07/ (accessed 21 April 2017).
56   Interview with Kulayigye.
57   Faustin Mugabe, 'When Soldiers Were Accused of Making Political Statements', *Daily Monitor*, Kampala (22 May 2022).
58   Recently, Justice George Kanyeihamba, a retired member of the Uganda Supreme Court, criticized his colleagues on the bench for changing their rulings after phone calls with the President in 2006 when they handled a petition challenging Museveni's electoral victory.
59   The Eagle Online, 'Museveni vs Sejusa: The Three-Decade Battle between Uganda's Two Most Prominent Generals' (30 May 2016). http://eagle.co.ug/2016/05/30/museveni-vs-sejusa-three-decade-battle-ugandas-two-prominent-generals.html
60   'David Sejusa – the Daring General', *Daily Monitor* (7 February 2016). http://allafrica.com/stories/201602081316.html
61   Gen. David Sejusa's full letter is available online: http://www.monitor.co.ug/News/National/Gen–Sejusa-s-letter/688334-1681866-2ejfglz/index.html (accessed 14 May 2015).
62   Tom Rhodes, 'In Uganda, Media Muzzled over Alleged Muhoozi Project', *Committee to Project Journalist* (15 May 2013). https://cpj.org/blog/2013/05/in-uganda-media-muzzled-over-alleged-muhoozi-proje.php (accessed 3 May 2018).

63   Sejusa's letter, 26.

64   'Nyakairima's Death: Radio Katwe, Social Media Explode with Conspiracy Theories',
     The East African (19 September 2015). http://www.theeastafrican.co.ke/news/
     What-really-killed-Gen-Aronda-/-/2558/2876782/-/99w04v/-/index.html (accessed
     3 May 2018).

65   'Exiled Ugandan General Says Museveni Stole 2006 Elections', *African Review*
     (17 December 2013). http://www.africareview.com/news/Exiled-Uganda-general-
     says-Museveni-stole-election/979180-2115434-10ah9y9/index.html (accessed
     17 May 2018).

66   Stephen McLoughlin and Maartje Weerdesteijn, 'Eliminating Rivals, Managing
     Rivalries: A Comparison of Robert Mugabe and Kenneth Kaunda', *Genocide Studies
     and Prevention* 9, no.3 (2016): 116–36.

67   Zaryab Iqbal and Christopher Zorn, 'The Political Consequences of Assassination',
     The Journal of Conflict Resolution 52, no. 3 (2008): 385–400.

68   Roessler, 'The Enemy Within'.

8

Institutionalized arbitrariness as autocratic adaptability

Rebecca Tapscott

What is the role of unpredictability in autocratic adaptability? In particular, how can a regime undermine the very institutional resources it relies on to govern and procure legitimation?[1] This chapter engages these questions by drawing on the concept of 'institutionalized arbitrariness' – an approach to governance that is defined at its core by political unpredictability.[2] Institutionalized arbitrary rule departs from traditional notions of personalized autocratic rule in that it relies more heavily on impersonal institutions to regularize unpredictability into a broader system of governance. This type of governance flourishes with the spectre of unaccountable and unproportioned state violence, and the perception of widespread state surveillance.

In regimes typified by institutionalized arbitrariness, rulers emphasize fragmenting opposition even more so than monopolizing control. This approach fosters an unstable political environment in which it is difficult for anyone to consolidate a political constituency. As a result, institutionalized arbitrariness allows authoritarians to tolerate limited spaces of dissent and democracy – and potentially even leverage them to extend autocratic legitimacy and longevity.

Many have described Uganda under President Yoweri Museveni as a place where 'confusion' and 'uncertainty' are central to everyday life and especially encounters with the state.[3] The regime is known for accommodating unaccountable state violence, and fostering cadres to engage in local human surveillance as part of a nation-wide intelligence system.[4] A porous distinction between citizen and state on the one hand, and state and regime on the other, has helped the ruling party to frame its opponents as enemies of the state. At the same time, some elements of a democratic system have been implemented over the years and still endure, and legal order remains important especially for the resolution of mundane disputes in everyday life.[5] Combined, we observe a state that has outsourced responsibility for many aspects of governance with citizens, while at the same time preserved a degree of democratic legitimacy for the regime.

Museveni's earlier years in power are often narrated as a time of opportunity and promise. Uganda was known as a donor 'darling' and a fledgling democracy.[6] With steady economic growth came the view that the country was consolidating and developing in line with goal posts set by international development agencies. Yet, as this chapter outlines, the roots of institutionalized arbitrary rule arguably were already in place, set in motion through key historical junctures including British colonial intervention and the rebel origins of Museveni's political party. I propose that these significant historical events shaped the relationship between governing institutions and the state's enforcement capacity with long- term consequences – chiefly, they provide the backdrop for Museveni's autocratic adaptability, and shape how it plays out in practice and in the everyday lives of ordinary Ugandans.

The chapter first sets out the theory of institutionalized arbitrariness and its manifestations in Uganda, highlighting how it relates to autocratic adaptability. It then turns to two historic junctures and their implications. First, it reflects on how colonial intervention may have set the groundwork for a system of governance in which jurisdictional claims are both plural and fluid. Second, it considers how the origins of the local governance structure in post-1986 Uganda as part of a system of rebel rule during insurgency may have further embedded this jurisdictional fluidity. In this sense, I propose that the structure of local governance limited the NRM's accountability while at the same time establishing its authority. The chapter then reflects on two dynamics that have helped co-opt and defang political opposition under the NRM: fragmentation and incorporation on the one hand, and threat and protection on the other. The chapter concludes with a case study of Uganda's Crime Preventer programme to illustrate the implications of this argument, and how institutionalizing arbitrary rule has contributed to autocratic adaptability in Uganda in recent years.

Theory and history of institutionalized arbitrariness

Though Uganda's ruling regime under Museveni and his NRM party has been increasingly described as authoritarian, it nonetheless has both introduced and maintained elements of democratic rule. Museveni came to power calling for democracy and made numerous important institutional reforms, some of which decentralized power and increased citizen participation, and others of which weakened and removed checks on executive power.

Alongside and through different processes of democratic and autocratic governance, Museveni has managed to consolidate his hold on power and develop a governing system that has allowed for manifestations of free speech and civic organization, while at the same time preventing organized political opposition from removing him and his party from power through traditional democratic methods.

Here, I propose that these seeming contradictions are upheld through a system of political unpredictability that I call 'institutionalized arbitrariness'.[7] Institutionalized arbitrariness is characterized by a multiplicity of governance actors, who have overlapping and at times contradictory mandates that are often redefined, sometimes *post hoc*. The result is that though these actors and associated institutions can and do sometimes function as expected, citizens can rarely trust that they will provide authoritative decisions; or that they will enforce decisions subsequently. This creates political unpredictability, such that citizens engage cautiously with governance actors and – though they may attempt to make claims on them – have little ability or recourse to demand accountability if those claims remain unfulfilled.

Institutionalized arbitrariness is by definition anti-democratic because it weakens civic organization and collective action. Rather than working through direct repression and demobilization, this approach to governance can accommodate some democratic spaces. In turn, these democratic spaces help reproduce and legitimate the regime. However, these spaces are fragile, because they can be side-lined, redefined or collapsed with little or no warning. As a result, citizens seek to mitigate or manage this uncertainty themselves. Many respond by self-policing, curating their opinions and actions in a way that they believe will reduce their risk of facing potentially costly repercussions.

The regime can thus leave in place and even introduce certain democratic features, like an independent (if at times compromised) judiciary, media and elections. In turn, this has left seeds of hope in society that the regime is not repressive in the first instance, and indeed that there are avenues for inclusion and participation that set this regime apart from its predecessors.[8] Some have described a resulting 'subjunctive' subjectivity, in which political engagements are 'conditioned by pragmatic considerations made in light of simultaneously doubtful and hopeful expectations of the future'.[9] This approach to governance also helps the regime maintain positive relations with the international community, whether authentically so, or by providing avenues for more democratic states to claim plausible deniability of the Ugandan state's authoritarian tendencies.

Scholars Frederick Golooba-Mutebi and Samuel Hickey have advanced a related argument about pockets of bureaucratic effectiveness in Uganda, in which hard and soft power are combined to uphold personalized rule, while at the same time formal rules-based governance is also permitted.[10] These pockets of effectiveness do not reflect a trajectory towards a more impersonal or democratic state form, but rather have sustained an image of 'stateness' that has garnered both domestic and international support – albeit a support that has waned in recent years with the deterioration of electoral quality and increasingly blatant human rights violations. Their insights draw on the concept of institutional multiplicity: 'Unlike the notion of hybridity, which assumes a direct mixing and melding of institutional arrangements into new and distinct forms, institutional multiplicity allows for the relatively discrete operation of different rule systems in a given context and draws attention to the significance of achieving some sort of balance between alternative institutional forms and political strategies of rule.'[11] These rule systems can be concordant or discordant, creating a stable or volatile political system respectively.

Examples of these dynamics are widespread. As one Community Liaison Officer explained:

> The law is made by people to guide. But you find that there are some situations that really don't need you to apply the law … Even a criminal case, they [the community] want to solve it like it's civil. There are some cases which are on the border. They are not really legal issues, but they come to police. Like land disputes.

In Uganda, land is a civil matter, but they would rather have police intervene when they are negotiating, when they feel it requires force.

He continued:

> The criminal cases which probably are not really intended, like manslaughter, the victim could have gotten in a fight at a drinking place that results in a murder. The community agrees: let us resolve it. If we take the man without addressing [the underlying cause of the fight], it might result in more disputes. Instead of taking that man to court we say, 'Why don't we sit together. You were both wrong, but do two wrongs make a right? So let's solve the [underlying] dispute' ... [12]

While legal pluralism and multiplicity have been well elaborated in scholarly works, as well as by my interlocutors, a less well understood component of institutionalized arbitrariness is fluid and changing jurisdictional claims. Here, I understand jurisdiction as the things over which an actor can claim legitimate authority. Starting from the premise that jurisdictional boundaries are socially constructed, it is evident that they are also inherently dynamic, contested, negotiable and permeable. However, in many societies, they have nonetheless stabilized to the extent that citizens can establish shared expectations of authorities, formal and informal agreements yield expected results, and citizens can strategically select the best forum for their case (known as 'forum shopping').

By contrast, in a system of institutionalized arbitrary rule, jurisdictional boundaries can be repeatedly redefined. For example, a person, place or event can be brought into the state's jurisdiction, and thus be subjected to formal state law – or alternatively individuals or institutions may redefine state's jurisdiction more narrowly, casting the issue into the realm of other non-state authorities, and denying the ability to make legitimate claims on the state.

A clear illustration of this from my research is the role of local vigilantes and citizen community policing initiatives, whom the Ugandan state occasionally claims as an extension of state authority and at other times relegates to the role of civilian volunteer.[13] At times, public officials give these actors authority to use violence to police and punish; at other times, officials punish citizen-police for overstepping the law. They thus serve a purpose for the state, but they are also conveniently disowned. Jurisdictional fluidity characterizes many sectors in Uganda, not just security, policing and justice. For example, Ugandan land law has been described as a 'grey zone', in which law is vague and malleable, remaining open to interpretation.[14] As noted by Anne Mette Kjaer, 'when land institutions are left in flux, land can better be used as a political resource to appeal to landless voters, to maintain support of political cronies, or to attract large investors in land'.[15]

Where does institutionalized arbitrary rule come from? And how 'new' or 'modern' is it? The following two sections situate and contextualize this mode of governance in Uganda's political history. The discussion highlights a longstanding tension between unity and fragmentation (often along ethnic, religious, and regional lines) with which Uganda's rulers have had to engage and recon – with varying degrees of success.

British colonialism and jurisdictional politics

Ugandan political scientist Mahmood Mamdani has long shown how legacies of British colonial intervention have gone on to shape how power is organized and how it continues to fragment resistance in post-colonial Africa.[16] Mamdani describes the colonial state as 'Janus-faced'. One face was that of a state governed by and for rights-bearing colonizers, characterized by the rule of law, civil society and checks on concentrated power. The other face ruled the 'subject peasantry', and – using a language of community, culture, tradition and unitary authority – was characterized by 'extra-economic coercion and administratively driven justice'.[17] These two forms of power worked together to support a hegemonic colonial authority. Their legacy was constituted as a longstanding obstacle to democratic governance by embedding tribal and ethnic divisions into the structure of the post-colonial state.[18]

In Uganda, this embedding of ethnic power in the state began in the early days of colonial intervention. Colonially appointed chiefs were tasked with tax collection, passing local ordinances and determining punishments for violations of colonial laws. These chiefs were accountable to British colonizers. In Mamdani's terms, the chiefs represented 'decentralized despotism', employing authoritarian and unaccountable power in their colonially defined jurisdictions. Chiefs were appointed across the colony, creating new structures of authority especially in regions that had no pre-colonial tradition of chiefly structure.[19]

The chiefly structure both organized the polity along regional and ethnic lines, and at the same time, used fragmentation between and within different ethnic and regional groups to stave off collective political dissent.[20] For instance, the British colonial system relied on migrant labour within the country. To prevent collective action among this new class of young workers, the British reinforced the gerontocratic authority of localized elders.[21] The British further nominated youth activists to the Native Council to 'satisfy' their political aspirations in the short term.[22] In this way, the British leveraged regional fragmentation and ethnic divisions to thwart organized political dissent.

In many contexts, colonial subjects were aware of the confusion and contradictions inherent in plural legal environments, and sought to use these strategically to achieve more desirable outcomes. Lauren Benton calls this 'jurisdictional politics' and describes how it produced a type of patterned jurisdictional fluidity that supported an evolving colonial authority. 'Colonizers erected jurisdictional boundaries that were precise but inherently unstable and, therefore, subject to frequent revision.'[23] While Benton's study focuses on India, she notes 'Similarities in the dynamics of jurisdictional disputes in colonial settings over the course of the long nineteenth century are striking. In all cases, the colonizers themselves introduced jurisdictional ambiguity into the colonial legal order.'[24]

The anticolonial struggle and independence for African states left in its wake a state apparatus that had been upheld by racial distinctions on the one hand, and the distinction between the civilized urban centre and the traditional rural periphery on the other. While independence ended the racial divide, not so with the distinction between civil society and peasant society. This legacy left a state structured to accommodate customary law, defined by its plurality and coercive enforcement. In Uganda, Rubongoya has argued that 'the absence of a nationalist struggle [preceding independence] denied the Ugandan people a chance to see beyond their ethnic, religious, and regional differences most of which had been disproportionally magnified by colonial state politics'.[25] The results were both unifying and fragmenting. While 'the dismantling of colonial racism ... [unified] victims of colonial racism ... the question of redistribution ... divided that same majority along lines that reflected the actual process of redistribution: regional, religious, ethnic and at times just familial'.[26] In this context, Uganda's post-independence rulers relied on ethnic alliances and military force to control a fragmented country, resulting in neopatrimonial politics as a form of indirect rule called the 'bifurcated state'.

This legacy of plural and jurisdictionally fluid legal order, paired with coercive implementation, helps us understand many aspects of post-independence Ugandan politics, where rulers have sought to work with and around existing regional, ethnic and religious divides. As Mamdani notes, 'every movement against decentralized despotism bore the institutional imprint of that mode of rule. Every movement of resistance was shaped by the very structure of power against which it rebelled'.[27] This is true not only for civil society, but also those who have sought to govern Uganda. Both those who resist and embrace despotism have been constrained to varying degrees by pre-existing and embedded power structures.

Many of Uganda's rulers have worked directly with the grain of such divisions, bringing co-ethnics into the military and state apparatus alongside a strategy of divide and rule. While these patterns can also be seen under Museveni's tenure,[28] Museveni clearly also saw ethnic and other identarian divisions as a potential source of political instability. His early political platform prioritized anti-sectarianism, calling tribalism 'backward' and emphasizing 'the unity of our people as a sine qua non for lifting themselves out of their miserable living conditions'.[29]

Another important legacy that Museveni inherited was the role of the military in governance. Obote, and especially Amin, instrumentalized state militarism in ways that both helped Museveni justify his guerrilla war, but also set the contours for Museveni's future rule. From the beginning, then, Museveni sought in various ways to limit the influence of and gain control over ethnicity, religion and regionalism as potential sources of political organization and mobilization outside of the NRM. At the same time, he has also come to reproduce and rely on these very forms of political organization and control.

The following section moves directly to Museveni's rise, starting with his 'Bush War' waged in the 1980s in order to highlight how early governance choices were both informed by pre-existing divisions and modes of political organization, and how those decisions have arguably gone on to set a pathway for the emergence of institutionalized arbitrariness as a particular and contingent form of illiberal rule that we see in Uganda today. Given the book's stated focus on understanding the development of authoritarianism under Museveni, I do not elaborate on other key figures in Ugandan history, including Milton Obote, Idi Amin, and Kabaka Edward Mutesa of Buganda.

The Bush War and movement politics

The National Resistance Movement emerged as the political wing of a rebel insurgency that Museveni launched in 1981. It fought the governments of Milton Obote and later Tito Okello over five years, before taking power in 1986. Museveni described his movement as 'fighting for a just cause – for the democratic rights and human dignity of our people which have been trampled on for two decades –,'[30] a war waged to free Uganda from tribalism, dictatorship and foreign domination.[31] Much of the history of this war narrates the NRA as a disciplined military that paired guerrilla tactics with an ideology of democracy and inclusion;[32] others have depicted a starker view that emphasizes the coercive nature of war, and the violence and suffering experienced by the civilian population.[33]

In his 1981 speech 'Why We Fought a Protracted People's War', Museveni emphasized his decision to wage a 'people's war'. In his own words, a people's war is 'a strategy where popular forces, namely, those forces supported by the masses, wage a protracted war against those in power ... The basic weapon ... is the support of the people and their political consciousness' ... ' According to Museveni, a protracted people's war is governed by the following principles: 'When the enemy attacks, we withdraw; when he encamps, we harass him; when he retreats, we attack ... above all, integrate yourself to become one with the people in order to ensure support.'[34] As I will suggest, this set a pathway for blurring the line between party, state and populace, setting the scene to make ordinary Ugandans responsible for peace and stability through their allegiance to the NRM.

Museveni launched his war from the Luwero Triangle, north of Kampala. He and many of his compatriots were from the southwest of the country, and this meant that he had to build alliances along non-ethnic lines. In part, he achieved this by eliminating the authoritarian chiefly structure and replacing it with a democratic system of resistance councils and committees.[35] However, as Branch elaborates, 'The NRA did not go to the bush to effect a reform of the local state but, instead, to carry out a revolution in the national state; local reform was hit upon as an instrument for building support for its national struggle.'[36] While tribalization represented an obstacle to political mobilization for the rebels at a local level, it was an opportunity at the national level. Some have linked the entrenchment of a north-south divide to NRA's politics of mobilization, which framed the revolution in regional terms, 'as a struggle to throw out the north in favour of the south'.[37]

To replace chiefly authority, the NRA/M established wartime Resistance Councils (RCs, renamed Local Councils in 1995). These were initially established to provide resources and intelligence to Museveni's rebels, and also allowed the rebels to communicate their ideology with civilians.[38] RCs were given wide-ranging responsibilities over local governance, including in the areas of security and justice. As Museveni explained in his autobiography:

When we started the bush war in 1981, we had secret committees of volunteers who banded together as support groups for fighters, to mobilise food, recruits and intelligence information. From 1982, beginning in the liberated zone near Semuto, we started holding elections to these committees and formalising them as 'Resistance Councils' (RCs). Their brief was extended to controlling crime and to generate administration in their areas. After our victory in 1986, we spread the concept and practice of Resistance Councils through the country.[39]

Mamdani notes that the NRA/M secured popular support in part by abolishing the position of chief – and thus the chief's unchecked power.[40] RCs were elected by all residents of an area, and in this sense, they both helped illustrate the NRM's commitment to democracy and represented a substantial shift to a more inclusive approach to governance.[41] At the same time, because the NRA/M did not interfere in the people's selection, it limited the rebels' responsibility for and involvement with local governance decisions. In this sense, RCs both localized and extended rebel control without the rebels taking on direct governance responsibilities.

After the NRA seized Kampala in 1986, RCs were established across the country in a five-tiered structure, with elected representatives at the village, parish, sub-county, municipality and district levels. By the end of 1986, RCs were established in most villages across Uganda,[42] and countrywide elections were held in 1989 and 1992.[43] In 1995, RCs were enshrined in the constitution as the backbone of local government and renamed 'Local Councils' (LCs). Many lauded RCs, as they offered an alternative structure to kingdoms, regions, chiefs and political parties. However, tensions emerged early on between old and new systems. On the one hand, RCs warned chiefs against 'mistreating' people; on the other, democratically elected RCs sometimes had difficulties establishing their authority.[44] For example, Golooba-Mutebi quotes one sub-county chairman explaining why he did not enforce local bylaws in his area:

> It is very difficult to do that sort of thing. People may know that what they are doing is wrong, but if you punish them or report them to higher authorities, they will hate you. Some may even start plotting to harm you. I don't want to create enemies for myself. If I ask them to do something and they refuse, I just leave them.[45]

Chiefs and other local authorities were permitted to contest for RC positions; in theory the electoral process would facilitate the removal of unpopular leaders, and unsatisfactory members could be recalled between elections.[46] At the same time, the RC system offered no mechanism to organize civic action. Mamdani suggests that, as a result, those 'who were better organized outside the RC came to dominate the RC. A consistent feature of the RC system was that it came to stabilise peasant communities on the basis of leadership by its more prosperous members. Political reform went hand in hand with social conservatism.'[47]

RCs also provided a pathway for information and resources to flow more easily between Kampala and villages across the country. In addition to providing a structure for the government to share information on policies and developmental programmes with the populace, they allowed intelligence to flow to Kampala. RCs were also a conduit for government-directed resource distribution, including staple goods such as paraffin and sugar.[48] In later years, they directed the distribution of development aid and other commodities.[49] Some people describe today's LCs in similar terms. For example, a women mobilizer for the NRM commented, if political opposition were to occupy elected positions in the LC1, LC2 and LC3 (local councils from the village, parish and sub-county levels, respectively), while the NRM remains 'at the top, how can any resources get down to the communities? It's better to have NRM all the way down'.[50] In this way, the NRM fused its party structure to the state structure all under what was called the Movement system.

For years, RCs functioned in a legally ambiguous space, leading to conflicts between RCs and other state authorities.[51] As noted by Mamdani, RCs simultaneously represented state and regime power alongside local democracy, making them difficult to pin down:

> The bureaucratic point of view sees the RCs as no more than appendages of the civil service, created to implement government policy more effectively – in other words, as organs of the state. The democratic point of view, on the other hand, sees the RCs more as popular organs created to counter and hold in check abuses of the civil service and all other state functionaries; as organs of the people, whereby RCs could legitimately be the site of a healthy debate between points of view that cover the whole range of ideological positions within Ugandan society. The third point of view, which may be termed sectarian, sees RCs as organs of one single political group, the NRM.[52]

RCs thus played multiple roles. Having been founded by the NRM and functioning in part as a patronage system connecting the resources of the central state to the grassroots, they are in some ways intrinsically linked to the state (which, as discussed, is itself merged with the regime). In other ways, as locally elected actors who reside in the community and depend on localized and personalized social networks for survival, they are very much local community members. Many have proposed that this accounts for the widely held view that they are legitimate and helpful governance actors, even in areas of the country that have a mixed track record of supporting the NRM.[53]

The structure of RCs, and their implementation in the context of a successful vanguardist liberation movement, introduced certain institutional arrangements that were favourable to the development of institutionalized arbitrary rule. RCs may have been designed and adopted with largely strategic and ideological interests in mind (e.g. allowing the NRA to hold ground without taking on burdensome administration of civilians, while enacting the NRA commitment to democracy).[54] However, they nonetheless established a system that placed responsibility for administering governance with citizens, while granting the regime authority to rule – and even implying some democratic legitimacy for this authority. In this sense, they helped elide the division between civilian and state. In a context where the ruling regime also merged itself with state institutions through the liberation movement, this fuzzy divide has arguably laid the groundwork for a narrative that political opposition to the NRM is never legitimate.

Fragmentation and incorporation; sword and shield

Two other dynamics have helped the NRM manage its political opposition: first, fragmentation and incorporation have created a context where many competing factions are indebted to the regime. Second, threat and protection have ensured that much as people might fear the regime; they also dread its demise. While the first dynamic helps understand how fragmentation contributes to institutionalized arbitrary rule, the second highlights the important and nuanced role that state violence and memory thereof play in sustaining this regime.

As noted in the earlier sections on colonial intervention and the 'Bush War', fragmentation and incorporation are evidenced in other major reforms of the new NRM regime.[55] These include implementation of so-called 'no-party' Movement system of politics, the formation of special interest groups (notably for women and youth), as well as the processes of creating new districts. In the no-party system, there were nominally no political parties and politics proceeded on the basis of individual merit. In theory, politicians would campaign on ideas rather than as part of parties, and all citizens would be considered de facto members of the 'Movement'. While this approach was advertised as a way to limit sectarianism and ethnic conflict, it also helped fuse the NRM party with state institutions.

The creation of new special interest groups also illustrates how the NRM has combined processes of fragmentation and incorporation in order to mobilize and engage citizens while limiting broad-based political action. Quota systems for women and youth were established as part of the first RCs, and were later implemented across levels of government, from national parliament to village councils. Though lauded as democratic and progressive, others have noted that over time, these policies had the effect of co-opting particular groups by first defining interests around identarian politics, and then by providing avenues for patronage to placate these groups.[56] This 'special interest logic' frames youth and women as marginalized and in need of special interest representation, even while both are majority groups in their own right.

The centralization and standardization of channels for engagement in political and policy processes have provided fertile ground for NRM patronage and agenda-setting among youth and women.[57] As explained by former government minister, parliamentarian and women's rights activist Miria Matembe:

> … affirmative action has been patronized. It is now being looked at as a way of securing jobs … Women have been co-opted in state structures. They have been compromised and lost their ability to challenge state structures, which are undermining their rights … For instance, every time the elections – new districts are created. Why are they created? To give opportunity for more women to come in. Women don't think they have done it on their own. They see it as a favour from government. So then they do nothing else but support [government] interests.[58]

As noted by Matembe, the continued creation of new districts feeds into processes of fragmentation and co-optation. Since 1986, the number of districts in Uganda has increased from 33 to 136 in 2020. New districts help the regime build electoral alliances with new jurisdictions and extend patrimonial networks by creating new administrative and political positions.[59]

Additionally, the NRM has built its authority on the back of both promises of protection and threats of violence – whether instigated by the regime itself or by withdrawing protection. From the outset, Museveni's decision to use a protracted people's war, paired with the unrestrained violence of Obote's military, resulted in significant civilian casualties. As Bernard writes:

> Museveni's writings made clear the strategy of the guerrilla: to push the regular army, by harassment, to reveal its real nature to the citizens. The corollary of this is that the struggle will certainly cause a massive number of civilian casualties, which will provoke the support of the masses. For him, the aim of such warfare was to defend neither territory nor population, but rather to engage the state in a paroxysm of violence and turn it over on the state.[60]

During Museveni's 'Bush War', Obote's army terrorized the civilian population, resulting in an estimated 30,000 to 500,000 deaths.[61] The violence of this war continues to be an important reference point for the NRM regime; the NRM has, for example, reproduced images of the skulls and bones of civilians killed in the conflict as part of political messaging campaigns, warning Ugandans of the violence that could unfold in the case of regime transition.[62] The government's power to harm and protect takes on further salience in the context of widespread poverty and unemployment combined with a patrimonial system of resource distribution that is also highly militarized. The NRM's 'big tent' philosophy heightens the potential costs of exclusion.

Finally, it is important to note that political systems in Uganda are tightly linked to military power. One illustration of this is that government resources are often distributed through the security sector. Examples are widespread. Take the state's decision to bring its massive agricultural extension programme under the military.[63] At the time, Museveni argued that the programme had suffered from corruption under civilian management, and that the military would be more disciplined in implementation.[64] He also noted that it would help create jobs for veterans. Similarly, the military has been deployed in recent years to respond to crises including the 2020 locust outbreak and Covid-19 relief.[65] As I discuss in the next section, the role of the military and security services in the political economy helps to understand the dynamics of local and often informal security sector activities – young people, mainly men, join local defence units, vigilante groups and local policing efforts with the hope of gaining access to livelihood options.

Such programmes are often organized to encourage young people's aspirations, for example, combining livelihood trainings with military trainings, and then draw on the resulting networks to distribute development opportunities and access to loans and credit. The regime has also long offered free military trainings, like *chakamchaka*, which sought to instil patriotism while also claiming to improve employment prospects. These programmes follow logically from the NRA's people's movement, and the ensuing constitutional provisions that call on all Ugandans to mobilize to protect the state in times of crisis.[66]

Crime preventers and institutionalized arbitrariness

To elaborate how institutionalized arbitrary rule works in practice, and shapes the way that citizens can mobilize collectively, I present a brief discussion of Uganda's Crime Preventer programme.[67] A closer look at the initiative illustrates how changing jurisdictional claims in a context of institutional multiplicity made achievable two seemingly contradictory goals: on the one hand, the regime was able to establish a new organization to mobilize and placate a large and potentially volatile population; on the other, it was able to destabilize and fragment local collective action – both within civil society and among Crime Preventers themselves – for the benefit of the status quo.

Community crime prevention has existed as a concept in Uganda since at least 1989, when the Ugandan police introduced community policing.[68] These included 'Crime Prevention Panels', with the first crime preventers 'passed out' in 1994 at Katwe Police Station in Kampala.[69] A decade later, African security scholar Bruce Baker noted that Crime Prevention panels were planned for every sub-county, but at the time only operating in a few districts. Baker elaborates that these panels 'consist of local residents trained in crime prevention with a view, not only to empowering people about crime prevention and the requirements of the law, but to facilitating acceptance of responsibility for law and order in their locality'.[70]

In addition to training citizens and members of professional associations on community policing, law and the justice system, annual functions and competitions were organized to maintain 'motivation, functions, and competencies'.[71] Crime Prevention Panels were not implemented in the north due to the insurgency, and Community Policing was only initiated in Gulu a few years after the tentative peace agreement was reached in 2006.[72]

From the earliest days, some citizens refused to engage with the programme, viewing it as a 'ruling party project'.[73] These doubts were confirmed with the appointment of General Kale Kayihura as the Inspector General of Police in 2005. Kayihura was a longtime ally of the regime, having joined the Bush War in its earliest years.[74] A *Daily Monitor* article quotes Kayihura as saying: 'I found the police on one side and the people on the other. But when I looked around, there was a programme that could bring the two together and the programme was community policing.'[75] He quickly reformed the Crime Preventer programme to serve more blatantly political ends.

In 2011, Crime Preventers were recruited to support police efforts to manage national election processes. In 2015, Kayihura massively ramped up those efforts with a plan to recruit thirty Crime Preventers in every village.[76] The programme was organized to mirror existing governance structures, with a tiered system of 'commanders' at the village, sub-county, district and regional levels reporting to a National Crime Preventer Forum based in Kampala and run by young elites with ties to the NRM. Crime Preventers received a variety of trainings, ranging from *ad hoc* village or sub-county level trainings often run by current or former police or military officers, to regional and national-level trainings held at the police training school. These iterative trainings helped build a network of crime preventers, inculcate a sense of commitment to the programme, and extract out those who were not sufficiently committed to the programme – and by implication, to the NRM.

When the government first declared its intentions for a massive recruitment of crime preventers, many feared that they would be used to as a political militia. These fears appeared warranted, given the tense political climate. The Secretary General of the NRM announced that anyone 'disrupting peace' would be shot;[77] the main opposition candidate, Kizza Besigye, was arrested and detained multiple times;[78] and the NRM again ran election ads featuring skulls from the 1980s NRA war against the Obote regime.

The NRM District Registrar stated that the ads were meant to remind the 'country that poor choice in the coming election can take the country back to war'.[79] Kayihura described the crime preventers as 'a reserve of the army' and implied the possibility of arming them with rifles. Specifically, he contextualized this comment in the NRM's people's war, when 'they fought terrorism in the government after 1981' – linking rationale for the crime preventers to the political agenda of the NRM.[80] Rumours circulated that crime preventers would guard polling stations, monitor voting and arrest anyone who caused disruption. Many politicians, journalists and members of civil society called them government 'militia' and 'crime promoters',[81] noting that at times these self-identified volunteers used their newfound roles to extract for personal gain.

However, in addition to raising fears of intimidation or potential electoral or post-electoral violence, crime preventers also constituted a new structure to distribute government resources and implant hope of future benefits. Notably, the Crime Preventer programme recruited *en masse* a group that the regime needed to placate – unemployed and underemployed young men. This population might otherwise have supported the political opposition, whether at the ballot box or in street protests.

Patronage distributed via the Crime Preventer programme took a variety of forms: crime preventers gained part-time work associated with the elections, some were given gifts including T-shirts, bicycles and motorcycles. Representatives in the National Crime Preventer Forum explained that the programme helped connect crime preventers with government programmes and services such as HIV screenings and microfinance opportunities.[82] After the elections, some crime preventers organized into groups that reportedly received contracts to provide catering for the police.[83]

At the same time, participating in the Crime Preventer programme was also framed as a social good, with government officials declaring that all citizens acted as crime preventers when they supported the police, for example by volunteering information. As one police officer explained, 'Crime preventers is voluntary, and it is the work of every Ugandan citizen. Their work is just to bring information.'[84] A Community Liaison Officer described crime preventers as apolitical youth, who merely sensitize the community about the law and share information with the police:

We decided that a greater number of crime preventers, cutting across schools and other institutions, will make it easier for people to embrace community policing. People know the solutions to their problems. Crime preventers are their children. In a village of 30 homesteads, we may have 30 crime preventers – that would be one per family. Crime preventers are informed about laws and can help sensitise people. They report lots of cases to the police, unlike those days when people did not report cases of murder, rape or defilement … now, they know that their son or grandson has trained with the police, and they report … Their job is just to inform police. The constitution is very clear, any person has the powers of arrest. If someone is about to commit or has committed an offense, you can arrest, but then you must hand over to police. It is the duty or responsibility of civilians [to arrest others] so long as they suspect someone is about to or has committed a crime.[85]

This effectively meant that sometimes crime preventers were framed as agents of the state and at other times as ordinary citizens, obscuring who was reporting on whom, and the role of the state in this arrangement. Crime preventers then could be driven by a logic of naked political power, of livelihoods or of civic-mindedness. Each of these different framings conferred different responsibilities and rights to crime preventers.

However, I found that when crime preventers sought to make a claim on the grounds of any given logic, state authorities would undermine it with another. For example, when some crime preventers tried to demand payment for participating in a political event, they were told that the programme was a volunteer effort for civic people. When those same crime preventers tried to take their complaints to the press, they were told that they had received special training, and were therefore cadres of the regime, and would face court martialling if they spoke with reporters. By redefining the jurisdiction relevant to crime preventers, the regime was able to limit their ability to claim benefits from the programme along different avenues.

Similarly, the programme helped fragment civic action among society more broadly. For example, the massive recruitment to the Crime Preventer programme reinforced a widely held perception that the NRM had eyes and ears everywhere, even in the most rural and remote parts of the country. In this way, the programme helped the regime in two ways: first, by taking a disaffected group – unemployed young men – and aligning their financial and livelihood interests with regime survival; and second, by using this diffuse and poorly defined group of citizens to give the sense that crime preventers were present everywhere, helping reinforce the perception of state presence during the electoral season.

The programme's design also reflects existing forms of political organization that themselves are shaped by legacies of colonialism and the NRM's history as a vanguardist liberation movement, both outsourcing governance responsibilities to citizens on the one hand, and blurring the line between citizen and state on the other.

The Crime Preventer programme is one important illustration of how institutionalized arbitrariness works – but similar dynamics can be seen across the various sectors of governance, and in different regions of the country.[86] Institutionalized arbitrariness is particularly pertinent to questions of autocratic adaptability because it helps illuminate how and why citizens might contribute to producing a state form in which they are both bound to participate but in which that participation has limited democratic promise.

Conclusion

This chapter has sought to situate unpredictability as an important element of the NRM's autocratic adaptability. In particular, it aimed to emphasize both the important role of unpredictability and perhaps more essentially, the extent to which its particular manifestations are historically constituted and contingent, rooted in legacies of political organization shaped by both colonial and liberation interventions. I have proposed that these moments in particular set Ugandan political organization on a pathway to favour highly fragmented sites of power layered with efforts to consolidate state control, in a context of a highly militarized political economy interfacing with ethnic and regional patronage networks.

The result is an approach to governance that implicates citizens in a project of self-rule at a local level, while bestowing some sense of democratic legitimacy upon the regime at a national level. The fuzziness of the line between citizen and state, and state and regime, creates an environment in which opposition to the regime can be narrated as an existential threat to the state. This helps explain why, despite broad-based participation, Uganda has not seen the emergence of democratic accountability or collective action, but rather the consolidation of an increasingly authoritarian and repressive state.

Notes

1   See the Introduction to this volume.
2   Rebecca Tapscott, *Arbitrary States: Social Control and Modern Authoritarianism in Museveni's Uganda* (Oxford: Oxford University Press, 2021).
3   Henni Alava, *Christianity, Politics and the Afterlives of War in Uganda: There Is Confusion* (London: Bloomsbury Publishing, 2022); Moses Khisa, 'The Making of the "Informal State" in Uganda', *Africa Development* 38, no. 1 & 2 (2013): 191–226.
4   Ben Jones, *Beyond the State in Rural Africa* (Edinburgh: Edinburgh University Press, 2009), 65, 85; Sverker Finnström, *Living with Bad Surroundings: War, History, and Everyday Moments in Northern Uganda* (Durham, NC: Duke University Press, 2008), 94–7; Rebecca Tapscott, 'The Government Has Long Hands: Institutionalized Arbitrariness and Local Security Initiatives in Northern Uganda', *Development and Change* 48, no. 2 (2017): 278–80.
5   Anna Macdonald, SJ Cooper-Knock and Julian Hopwood, '"Maybe we should take the legal ways": Citizen Engagement with Lower State Courts in Post-war Northern Uganda', *Law and Society Review* 56, no. 4 (2022): 509–31. Also See Kathryn Hendley, 'Legal Dualism as a Framework for Analyzing the Role of Law under Authoritarianism', *Annual Review of Law and Social Science* 18, no. 1 (2022): 211–26, on the need to consider law in the everyday to understand the functioning of legal authoritarianism today.
6   Elliott Green, 'Patronage, District Creation, and Reform in Uganda', *Studies in Comparative International Development* 45, no. 1 (2010): 86.
7   Tapscott, *Arbitrary States*.
8   A clear illustration of this is ongoing efforts to unify the political opposition in Uganda in the hopes of removing the NRM through electoral means. For instance, in 2018, Bobi Wine reportedly chastised Kizza Besigye, saying: 'You cannot participate in an election for four times and on the fifth time you come and say that democracy doesn't work ... We believe democracy works. A shaky win gives Museveni chance to steal the votes but we are going to give him a knockout.' See: Derrick Wandera, 'Bobi Wine or Besigye: Who Can Galvanise Opposition Unity?'

      Daily Monitor, Kampala (7 November 2021). https://www.monitor.co.ug/uganda/
      magazines/people-power/bobi-wine-or-besigye-who-can-galvanise-opposition-
      unity–3610996. I thank Moses Khisa for bringing this example to my attention.

9   Henni Alava, 'There Is Confusion': *The Politics of Silence, Fear and Hope in Catholic
      and Protestant Northern Uganda* (PhD Diss., University of Helsinki, 2017), 198;
      Susan Reynolds Whyte, 'Subjectivity and Subjunctivity: Hoping for Health in Eastern
      Uganda', in *Postcolonial Subjectivities in Africa*, ed. Pnina Werbner and Richard
      Werbner (London: Zed Books, 2002), 171–90.

10   Frederick Golooba-Mutebi and Sam Hickey, 'The Master of Institutional Multiplicity?
      The Shifting Politics of Regime Survival, State-Building and Democratisation in
      Museveni's Uganda', *Journal of Eastern African Studies* 10, no. 4 (2017): 601–18.

11   Ibid., 602.

12   Author interview with CLO, 30 January 2018.

13   Also See Rebecca Tapscott, 'Local Security and the (Un)Making of Public Authority
      in Gulu, Northern Uganda', *African Affairs* 116, no. 462 (2017): 39–59.

14   Anne Mette Kjær, 'Land Governance as Grey Zone: The Political Incentives of Land
      Reform Implementation in Africa', *Commonwealth & Comparative Politics* 55, no. 4
      (2017): 426–43.

15   Ibid., 427.

16   Mahmood Mamdani, *Citizen and Subject: Contemporary Africa and the Legacy of
      Late Colonialism* (Princeton: Princeton University Press, 1996), 3.

17   Ibid., 19.

18   Following Mamdani, I recognize the pejorative nature of terms such as civilized and
      traditional, but forego quotation marks after first usage for a less cumbersome read
      (Mamdani, *Citizen and Subject*, 7).

19   Beverly Gartrell, 'British Administrators, Colonial Chiefs, and the Comfort of
      Tradition: An Example from Uganda', *African Studies Review* 26, no. 1 (1983): 1–24;
      Onek C. Adyanga, *Modes of British Imperial Control of Africa: A Case Study of
      Uganda, c.1890–1990* (New Castle: Cambridge Scholars Publishing, 2011), 4.

20   Joshua Rubongoya, *Regime Hegemony in Museveni's Uganda: Pax Musevenica*
      (New York: Palgrave Macmillan, 2007), 19–22.

21   Elizabeth Laruni, *From the Village to Entebbe: The Acholi of Northern Uganda and the
      Politics of Identity, 1950–1985* (PhD Diss., History, University of Exeter, 2014), 89.

22   Ibid., 88.

23   Lauren Benton, 'Colonial Law and Cultural Difference: Jurisdictional Politics and the
      Formation of the Colonial State', *Comparative Studies in Society and History* 41, no. 3
      (1999): 564.

24   Ibid., 586.

25   Rubongoya, *Regime Hegemony*, 33.

26   Mamdani, *Citizen and Subject*, 20.

27   Ibid., 24.

28   See, e.g., Stefan Lindemann, 'Just Another Change of Guard? Broad-Based Politics
      and Civil War in Museveni's Uganda', *African Affairs* 110, no. 440 (2011): 387–416.

29   Yoweri Museveni, 'Why We Fought a Protracted People's War: At the Beginning of
      the War of Liberation-1981', in *Museveni's Greatest Speeches* (Kampala: Sest Holdings
      Ltd, 2009), 11.

30   Ibid., 1.

31   Ibid., 10.

32 Nelson Kasfir, 'Guerrillas and Civilian Participation: The National Resistance Army in Uganda, 1981–86', *The Journal of Modern African Studies* 43, no. 2 (2005): 271–96; Jeremy M. Weinstein, *Inside Rebellion: The Politics of Insurgent Violence* (Cambridge: Cambridge University Press, 2007).

33 Onek C. Adyanga, 'A Macabre Exhibit: Ugandan President Museveni's Public Display of the Luwero Triangle War's Human Remains', *Advances in Historical Studies* 4, no. 5 (2015): 389; Abigail Meert, 'Suffering, Consent, and Coercion in Uganda: The Luwero War, 1981–1986', *International Journal of African Historical Studies* 53, no. 3 (2020): 389–412.

34 Museveni, 'Why We Fought', 4, 6, 13.

35 Mamdani, *Citizen and Subject*, 200.

36 Adam Branch, *Displacing Human Rights: War and Intervention in Northern Uganda* (Oxford: Oxford University Press, 2011), 59–60.

37 Ibid., 60.

38 Per Tidemand, *The Resistance Councils in Uganda: A Study of Rural Politics and Popular Democracy in Africa* (PhD Diss., Roskilde University, 1994), 82.

39 Yoweri Museveni, *Sowing the Mustard Seed: The Struggle for Freedom and Democracy in Uganda*, ed. Elizabeth Kanyogonya and Kevin Shillington, First Edition (London: Macmillan, 1997), 189.

40 Mamdani, *Citizen and Subject*, 200.

41 Ibid., 208.

42 Tidemand notes that 'The formation of the RCs, organising the elections and giving out information about the functions of the RCs were carried out with very few resources. One presidentially appointed Special District Administrator and no more than some five to ten cadres would be in charge of a district with some 1000–2000 villages. The district administration would not even have a complete list of all villages. Only at the lower administrative levels like the sub county or the parish would the officials like the chiefs have the simplest information like the names of the villages and their very roughly estimated population. But the DA and the cadres operated from the district. Sugar happened to be in scarce supply in 1986–87 and its distribution was left to the RCs. Such a solution was not unknown in Uganda, but it definitely gave people an immediate incentive to form an RC: no RC no sugar!' Tidemand, *The Resistance Councils*, 95.

43 Ibid., 28, 95.

44 Frederick Golooba-Mutebi, 'Reassessing Popular Participation in Uganda', *Public Administration and Development* 24, no. 4 (2004): 296.

45 Sub-county chairman, cited in Ibid., 296.

46 Mamdani, *Citizen and Subject*, 215; Tidemand, *The Resistance Councils*, 81.

47 Mamdani, *Citizen and Subject*, 215–16.

48 Tidemand, *The Resistance Councils*, 95.

49 Author interviews and observations during fieldwork between 2014 and 2018.

50 Author interview, Gulu, 21 September 2015.

51 Tidemand, *The Resistance Councils*, 86.

52 Mahmood Mamdani, 'Uganda in Transition: Two Years of the NRA/NRM', *Third World Quarterly* 10, no. 3 (1988), 1176.

53 Sam Wilkins, 'Re-Electing the Local (Party) State: Village Chairpersons in NRM Uganda and the Lessons of Their 2018 Re-Election', *Unpublished Manuscript*, 2022.

54 Kasfir, 'Guerrillas and Civilian Participation', 274.

55　While I do not go into detail in this chapter, Obote and Amin also built and reinforced similar patterns of fragmentation and patronage through ethnic divisions and their use of the military.

56　John-Jean Barya, 'Performance of Workers and Youth Members of Parliament in Uganda 1995–2015' (Kampala: Friedrich Ebert Stiftung, 2017), 10; Fumihiko Saito, 'The Representation of the Disadvantaged: Women, Youth and Ethnic Minorities', in *Decentralization and Development Partnership: Lessons from Uganda*, ed. Fumihiko Saito (Tokyo: Springer Japan, 2003), 116.

57　Anna MacDonald, Arthur Owor and Rebecca Tapscott, 'Youth Politics in Uganda: Barriers to Youth Mobilization and the Bobi Wine Factor', *Working Paper*, n.d.

58　Author interview with Miria Matembe, 9 February 2018, Kampala.

59　Nicholas Awortwi and A.H.J. Helmsing, 'Behind the Façade of Bringing Services Closer to People the Proclaimed and Hidden Intentions of the Government of Uganda to Create Many New Local Government Districts', *Canadian Journal of African Studies* 48, no. 2 (2014): 297–314.

60　Pauline Bernard, 'The Politics of the Luweero Skulls: The Making of Memorial Heritage and Post- Revolutionary State Legitimacy over the Luweero Mass Graves in Uganda', *Journal of Eastern African Studies* 11, no. 1 (2017), 204.

61　Ibid.

62　Dan Wandera and Mudangha Kolyangha, 'Luweero Tells NRM to Stop Skulls Campaign Adverts', *Daily Monitor*, Kampala (11 February 2016). http://www.monitor.co.ug/SpecialReports/Elections/Luweero-tells-NRM-to-stop-skulls-campaign-adverts/-/859108/3071996/-/13e74dt/-/index.html.

63　Frederic Musisi, 'Museveni: Why I Entrusted Naads Programme with Army', *Daily Monitor*, Kampala (16 June 2014). https://www.monitor.co.ug/News/National/Museveni–Why-I-entrusted–Naads-programme-with-army/688334-2349720-1guvia/index.html.

64　Ibid.

65　Sally Hayden, 'Uganda's "Locust Commander" Leads the Battle against a New Enemy', *The Guardian* (26 February 2020). https://www.theguardian.com/global-development/2020/feb/26/ugandas-locust-commander-leads-the-battle-against-a-new-enemy; James Nkuubi, 'When Guns Govern Public Health: Examining the Implications of the Militarised COVID-19 Pandemic Response for Democratisation and Human Rights in Uganda', *African Human Rights Law Journal* 20, no. 2 (2020): 607–39.

66　See Also Rubongoya, *Regime Hegemony*, 64 on how mchakamchaka programmes were initiated during the 'Bush War' as a way to provide peasants the tools to resist government tyranny and serving as the basis to build early legitimacy for the NRA/M.

67　For further details on my findings, see Rebecca Tapscott, 'Where the Wild Things Are Not: Crime Preventers and the 2016 Ugandan Elections', *Journal of Eastern African Studies* 10, no. 4 (2016): 693–712.

68　Bruce Baker, 'Multi-Choice Policing in Uganda', *Policing and Society: An International Journal of Research and Policy* 15, no. 1 (2005): 30.

69　'Crime "Preventers" or Just Another Militia Group?' *Daily Monitor*, Kampala (22 August 2015). https://www.monitor.co.ug/uganda/magazines/people-power/crime-preventers-or-just-another-militia-group–1621740.

70　Baker, 'Multi-Choice Policing', 30.

71　Ibid.

72   Author interview with Chairman of Community Policing Forum, 6 October 2014.

73   Baker, 'Multi-Choice Policing', 31.

74   Edris Kiggundu, 'How Kayihura Became Museveni's Point Man', *The Observer* (5 May 2017). https://observer.ug/news/headlines/52732-how-kayihura-became-museveni-s-point-man

75   Daily Monitor, 'Crime "Preventers" or Just Another Militia Group'.

76   Conor Gaffey, 'Who Are Uganda's Crime Preventers?', *Newsweek* (14 January 2016). http://www.newsweek.com/who-are-ugandas-crime-preventers-415704.

77   Nelson Wesonga, 'Lumumba Shoot-to-Kill Threat Sparks Outrage', *Daily Monitor*, Kampala (13 January 2016). http://allafrica.com/stories/201602012356.html.

78   Tendai Marima, 'Uganda Elections: Besigye Detained by Police Again', *Aljazeera* (23 February 2016). http://www.aljazeera.com/news/2016/02/uganda-elections-besigye-home-detention-160223055948991.html.

79   Wandera and Kolyangha, 'Luweero Tells NRM'.

80   A few days after making the remarks and they were widely covered in the media as plans to arm crime preventers to ensure an electoral win for the NRM, Kayihura insisted he had been quoted out of context. The full speech, transcribed by Police Spokesman Fred Enanga, was reprinted in the New Vision. Kayihura suggests arming crime preventers in the context of 'empower[ing] people to fight crime in the government ... they fought terrorism in the government after 1981, where some patriots went to the bush. This was by mobilizing people to fight the government which had the support of the most powerful countries in the world and removed it after five years' Vision reporter, 'Kayihura Clarifies on Crime Preventers Reports', New Vision (28 January 2016). https://www.newvision.co.ug/news/1415755/kayihura-clarifies-crime-preventers-reports.

81   Author interviews and observations in Uganda in 2015 and 2016.

82   Author interview with Regional Police Commissioner, 6 November 2015; Author interview with Crime Preventer, 4 February 2016.

83   Author interview with crime preventer, 16 February 2018.

84   Author interview with police officer, 19 October 2015.

85   Author interview with CLO, 14 November 2015.

86   Tapscott, *Arbitrary States*, 151–87.

Part Three

Institutions and coalition politics

9

Between change and continuity in the ruling coalition[1]

Moses Khisa

President Museveni sworn-in for a sixth (elected) term in May 2022, putting him on course to rule Uganda for forty uninterrupted years by 2026. According to a keen analyst with close connections to State House, the new cabinet named in June 2022, was the most shocking line – up of ministers in Museveni's three and a half decade-long rule.[2] Shocking for the personnel both picked and dropped. A woman vice-president, a woman prime minister and many relatively young unknowns. Only a few members of the old guard from the National Resistance Army (NRA) cradle were drafted into the new line-up, which sits at the apex of the executive branch.

Before this much-anticipated and long-awaited cabinet announcement, Museveni had successfully wrestled the position of speaker of parliament, Uganda's third most powerful job, from long-standing ruling party cadre, Rebecca Kadaga. Instead of Kadaga – who spiritedly fought to keep the job – Museveni went for a relatively recent convert to the ruling party, Jacob Oulanyah,[3] former member of the Uganda People's Congress (UPC) – Uganda's independence political party – who unfortunately passed away less than a year into the job.[4] After coming second best in an acrimonious race to head the legislature, Kadaga was defeated, deflated and at the mercy of Museveni who in turn drafted her back into cabinet where she previously served during the 1990s.

As head of the legislature Kadaga held the number three position in government for a decade, and was equally number three in the hierarchy of the ruling NRM as second national vice chairperson, only to be demoted to the lowly portfolio of minister for East African Affairs. Both the calibre of the cabinet line-up and the booting of Kadaga for Oulanyah reflected broader reassignments in Museveni's ruling coalition in the wake of the January 2021 general elections with parallels to previous electoral cycles. Museveni's cabinet appointments depend, at least in part, on the ruling party's electoral performance, both presidential and in parliamentary races, and Museveni's own power calculus at the national and subnational levels.

Thus, going by official presidential results – rejected by the opposition – Museveni and the NRM substantially underperformed not just in the heretofore-traditional bastion of Buganda but also in Kadaga's backyard of Busoga. By contrast, in northern Uganda, where Oulanyah had emerged the biggest political name and power broker, the region gradually come around to electorally be in Museveni's corner after decades of war and voting against him in successive elections in 1996, 2001 and 2006.

In line with the electoral outlook and overall political support for the incumbent, since 1986, the vice president was always either from Buganda or Busoga.[5] In fact, at one point, individuals from Buganda and Busoga held the top four positions after the president, that is, the vice president, speaker, deputy speaker and prime minister.[6] By contrast, following the 2021 elections, individuals from regions other than Buganda and Busoga took those four top positions. The vice-president from Teso, a northeast sub-region which, much like the north, for long rebelled violently and voted vigorously against Museveni. Likewise, the speaker is from the same region as the vice president, deputy speaker and prime minister both from the west. In addition, the chief justice is from northern Uganda. Hence, of the top four positions in the government apparatus, individuals from the north and northeast of the country occupy three, a rather dramatic change and a reflection of the shift in regional political balance of power.

The above snapshot is instructive for several reasons. First, cabinet represents the core and most prized layer of Uganda's civilian state power or, at a minimum, carries high symbolic value in the realm of power sharing. Second, the way Museveni constitutes his cabinet is representative of regional and religious balancing, demographic, generational and gendered considerations. Third, this balancing tends to track with electoral dynamics, which are shaped by both national and subnational political imperatives.

How has Uganda's ruling coalition changed overtime in line with Museveni's power calculations and survival strategies? Specifically, how has the nature of the ruling coalition affected electoral fortunes of Museveni and the NRM during successive election cycles, and in turn how do election-results shape coalition realignments? This chapter takes a close look at the evolution of Museveni's ruling coalition as it intersects particularly with the country's electoral landscape.

The concept of a ruling coalition as used in this chapter refers to the structure and make-up, or the line-up and distribution of key positions in the governing apparatus, primarily in the two core branches of government that are vested with everyday authority and power, that is, the executive and the legislative branches. Museveni has built his rule on two primary and crucial pillars: force and finance, i.e. coercive power and material spoils. In this schema, the armed forces are the repository of the former and the latter is reflected in the distribution of patronage through public sector positions, educational scholarships at home and abroad, handouts and even outright bribery. The ruling coalition combines management of elites through distribution of patronage chiefly by way of appointments to political offices, on the one hand, and ensuring proper management and the tight guarding of military might, on the other.

Argument and theoretical overview

As a necessity, authoritarian regimes have to rule through a coalition of one form or the other. This is a widely shared conclusion in the comparative politics literature on authoritarianism.[7] The size, structure and composition of ruling coalitions vary considerably and may include a range of actors,[8] but the principle is for the most part the same – authoritarian rule is unsustainable without allies and alliances to shore it up, credible partners to pump up legitimacy and power brokers to assuage possible popular discontent. This is especially necessary where autocrats can be credibly threatened with removal from office by either internal or external forces, from within the governing core or from outside the ruling establishment. Threats to the incumbent ruler can either be by the popular force of the masses or the narrow conspiracy of elites.[9] The latter looms large with military elites as the primary source of threat, thus requiring measures to 'coup-proof' to guard against coups d'etat.[10] Yet successful coup-proofing can in turn trigger civil war.[11]

Coalition dynamics under authoritarian rule are obviously different from coalition-governments in parliamentary democracies, as has long been the case in many European countries. In the latter, governments form at least in part through bargains and negotiations by different parties in situations where no one party has significant majority-support to govern on its own. In authoritarian settings, by contrast, an altogether different set of imperatives and motivations inform coalitions, largely centred on regime survival and legitimation. At issue is the fact that unlike in democracies, authoritarian regimes inherently face severe legitimacy problems, thus an overarching need to reach different constituencies, interest groups and power brokers to buy legitimacy and mitigate credible threats and keep a hold on power.[12]

Authoritarian ruling coalitions are a reflection of the overall structure of politics in a country and the competing interests the incumbent party and president have to contend with. That is, the ruling coalition mirrors the ensemble of social forces, interest groups and political alignments. Ruling coalitions strive to match up to and meet the balance of power between the incumbent, on the hand, and the challengers, on the other. Also, coalitions speak to the terrain of power contestations, whether built on specific ideological contests or driven by a fluid and flirting environment of particularistic pulls and pushes for access to the spoils of power.

For example, in a political system and social milieu characterized by fragmentation and the fracturing of political actors and social constituencies, of intense centrifugal forces, there is likely to be a ruling coalition that is fragile, unstable and precarious. By contrast, where there is more social cohesion, issue-based contests and more unified political groups, a stronger ideological predisposition and a more appealing governing agenda, the ruling coalition will likely be stable, better structured and predictable for the long-term.

A general observation it is plausible to argue that the strand and structure of politics at a specific time, and the broader existing political system seen at the macro level, drive the form, shape and substance of a ruling coalition. This is because the ruling coalition essentially aims to balance-out societal dynamics and political contests in the system, writ large. A ruling coalition emerges from the balance of political forces and the overarching composition of the political landscape. In other words, seen at a micro level, strategic calculations and immediate political considerations of the ruling group inform the shape, size, quality and calibre of the ruling coalition.

There is a logical overlap and convergence between structural forces and agential calculations, which means that ruling coalitions are not random or haphazard, rather they are deliberately shaped, constructed and produced. A combination of structural conditions and strategic calculations feed into the making of ruling coalitions in authoritarian settings.[13] For example, it matters whether opposition groups wield substantial and credible social power and the extent to which the incumbent feels vulnerable from the inside or out.[14] This and other factors influence an incumbent's moves in building a ruling coalition with the aim of obviating or at a minimum mitigating the dangers posed by challengers.[15] Here, electoral politics comes into play in shaping choices, calculations and decisions, as the literature on authoritarian institutions has underscored.[16]

Appointment of opposition figures to cabinet positions can have the net impact of fragmenting and weakening the opposition, making the latter unable to mount an effective challenge in general elections.[17] An incumbent can grant positions of power to different individuals and give access to opportunities, including patronage largesse, prospectively with an eye to the next election or retrospectively as rewards for contributions in past elections. In all, macro and micro level dynamics, both structural and agential considerations, inform the making and outlook of ruling coalitions. Since he came to power, both structure and agency have combined to shape Museveni's ruling coalition in Uganda in ways that display both change and continuity.

Change and continuity in Museveni's ruling coalition

Museveni's ruling coalition has evolved and transformed because of factors and forces both internal and external to the NRM, the stresses and strains of the political systems over time. In this respect there have been fundamental shifts in the nature and structure of Uganda's ruling coalition that are worth laying out here in order to set the stage for subsequent empirical discussion. Changes in the nature and form of the ruling coalition have happened in tandem with two major phases of the ruling regime, which can be further broken down into four time periods.

The first phase of Museveni's regime was the period from 1986 to 2006 with two time periods, first, from 1986 to the conclusion of the constitution-making process in 1995 and second, from 1996 to 2004. The former was the period of broad-based government and initial experimenting with the governance principles mapped out by the NRA rebels while still in the 'bush'. The latter period was the high point of consolidating the so-called no-party, 'Movement' rule and Museveni's tightening of his grip on power. The end of this phase in 2004 marked the final collapse of political engagement that had been built around a reform programme aimed at deepening democratic government. While the phase ended with a return to multiparty politics, there was simultaneous removal of presidential term limits, the former deployed as a bargaining chip for the latter, a move that greatly imperilled prospects for democratization. From then on, the calibre and content of the ruling coalition changed fundamentally in form and substance.

The second phase, also with two time periods, was from 2006 to 2021. The first period the initial experiment with the reintroduction of multiparty politics and the 2006 general elections. This period started in the immediate aftermath of a major assault on the 1995 Constitution that included the removal of presidential term limits, thus denting the elite consensus embodied in that instrument. A notable feature of this period was that Museveni attempted and partially succeeded in wooing back into the ruling coalition veteran NRM figures who had fallen out with him over the controversial removal of term limits in 2005. The most prominent among those returned to the NRM fold was Eriya Kategaya, for long considered the number two to Museveni in the power hierarchy of the ruling party, reappointed to cabinet after the 2006 elections.[18] Kategeya openly opposed the removal of presidential term limits; in turn, Museveni sacked him from Cabinet.[19] He had a short-lived association with the newly formed FDC opposition party in 2005.

It was also during this time that Museveni diversified his internal coalition pool by bringing in younger members of the NRM as he gradually started phasing out the old guard. He took similar measures in the military where starting in the mid-2000s a young cadre was on the ascendency best epitomized by Museveni's own son, General Muhoozi Kainerugaba, who rose from the commissioned rank of 2nd Lieutenant to a one-star General within a decade.[20]

The second time period of this second phase started with the 2011 elections and ran up to the 2021 elections. This period brought a deepening of contentious and confrontational politics, brazen patronage and blatant clientelist manoeuvres and with the use of money far more pronounced.[21] The 2011 elections also marked a big turning point in the balance of power between Museveni and the opposition. On the one hand, Museveni learnt that through finance and properly deployed force, he could maintain a hold on power. While finance and force had been key determinants in previous elections, it was in 2011 that money was used in the most brazen manner which triggered runaway inflation and street protests.[22]

The opposition, on the other hand, especially the main opposition candidate, Kizza Besigye, concluded that competing with Museveni in an election process where he wields overwhelming influence is nothing more than escorting him to victory. Thus, Besigye and a section of the opposition adopted a new form and repertoire of struggle dubbed 'defiance', which sought to force Museveni out of power through civic protest and popular street pressure.[23]

By taking the tack of defiance, Besigye and his followers had more or less abandoned the course of formal and institutionalized political engagement, turning instead to contentious and confrontational politics. This has had a significant bearing on the trends and trajectory of Uganda's politics and the ruling coalition over the past decade. Since 2011, Uganda's politics has deteriorated on a rapid downward spiral. The 2017 removal of the age limit provision from the constitution and a marked growth in militant youth opposition under the 'People Power' movement of Robert Kyagulanyi accentuated the precarious state of Ugandan politics. The electoral landscape became more fractured; violent and fraught with repression by the state, on the one hand, and spirited resistance by the opposition, on the other. Ruling party primary elections, for example, became a do or die affair in some parts of the country characterized by turf wars, factional struggles and fights for subnational territorial political control.[24]

Since at least 2005, Museveni's ruling coalition has taken on quite distinct features compared to the first phase of NRM rule as outlined above. In one sense, the composition of the ruling coalition during the first phase was based on a considerable degree of principled co-optation and a genuine quest for inclusivity in forging a government of national unity in a country scarred by civil war. This was a state/nation-rebuilding coalition even though it simultaneously served the purposes of regime legitimation and power consolidation for Museveni. However, in the main, it also sought to serve the purpose of enhancing political stability and state reconstruction.

By contrast, the ruling coalition of the last two decades, the 2000s and 2010s, has been much more about personal power calculations and regime survival by appearing to appease different constituencies for purposes of retaining power. This is a presidential and regime-survival coalition. During the first phase of Museveni's rule, particularly between 1986 and 1996, coalition arrangements took the form of principled partnership and involved credible and competent players. By contrast, in the years since 2006, the ruling coalition is far more transactional. If competency was a key consideration in the first phase, sycophancy became an overriding influence in the second phase of Museveni's ruling coalition.

In the early years of NRM rule, there was some commitment to ideas and relative openness to debating a range of issues. The notion of 'liberation struggle' had provided the basis for propagating a moral and ideological mission for the country. Persuasion rather than crass coercion and intimidation played key roles in appealing to and winning over political opponents. In particular, the military elite sought to project a different, somewhat intellectual image to mark a contrast with previous military actors seen as illiterate and unintellectual. Through the national leadership institute at Kyankwanzi, there was an attempt to convert followers and to nurture cadres of the 'Movement'. This thinking and modus operandi also informed the composition and calibre of the ruling coalition: built more on persuasion and projection of a superior set of ideas centring on the Museveni-led 'liberation struggle'. This contrasts sharply with the subsequent coalition iterations based largely on clientelism, patronage, outright and brutal force as well as renting support.[25]

One last note on the contrasting features of the ruling coalitions in the two phases is the rate of turnover. The first phase coalition was relatively stable and durable. It had continuity in personnel; the coalition since 2005 has been unstable with a very high turnover of personnel, particularly in parliament and cabinet.[26]

The dynamics of Museveni's ruling coalition: Structure and agency in practice

After close to four decades of uninterrupted rule, President Museveni has to contend with waning legitimacy. This is in part due to the sheer longevity of his reign, but also because of the ever-growing rustiness of his regime of rule, including glaring government inefficiencies and incompetence in a country facing enormous socio-economic demands. The less democratic and more diminished Museveni's legitimacy has come to appear, the more there is an overriding necessity for him to maintain a coalition of disparate actors and representatives of divergent constituencies in his government. This is a regime-survival coalition. While this necessity has always been a critical component of Museveni's rule and NRM politics since 1986, which started under the rubric of 'broad-base' politics,[27] since the mid-2000s it became more pressing to have a coalition that balances different interests and demands but one that, most importantly, enables Museveni to remain at the helm.

Given the multiplicity and plurality of interests that attend Uganda's socio-political landscape, and considering the country's history of fierce power contestation, often resulting in violent conflicts, managing a ruling coalition is fraught with numerous contradictions and controversies. For example, Museveni has appointed into the executive branch individuals of questionable credentials alongside competent and credible members.

At another level, for most of Museveni's rule there has been a notably skewed ethnic and regional representation in government positions, which is then balanced out with a targeted single but prominent appointment of, say, a vice president or prime minister intended to appease certain critical constituencies like the central region and the Catholic faithful. This juggling game gets messier as the political landscape becomes more contested, or even outrightly contentious and deeply uncertain, which in a feedback loop shapes and influences the nature, quality and calibre of the ruling coalition. These contradictory postures reflect, and are reflective, of Uganda's overall political landscape today, and display a range of perverse characteristics including extreme clientelism and factional struggles for access to state resources.[28]

Above all, however, the most important driver of politics of coalition and contestation, factional struggle and uncertainty, which all contribute to shaping the ruling coalition, is the unresolved question of presidential succession. Museveni remains firmly focused on ruling for life with no apparent plan of managing a transition to another leader within the NRM party. It has become increasingly unlikely that Museveni will leave power peacefully or at any rate in an orderly manner anytime in the near future. The controversial removal of the presidential age-limit provision from the constitution in December 2017, done in a most chaotic manner on the floor of parliament,[29] was only the latest statement of Museveni's determination to rule for life.[30] With presidential term limits scrapped from the constitution back in 2005, the age limit provision, capped at seventy-five in the 1995 constitution, was the very last constitutional redoubt against Museveni's continued stay at the helm.

Museveni's life-presidency project has at least two key driving factors. First, a deeply held and somewhat exaggerated messianic mission not just for Uganda but for Africa too. Museveni sees himself as a liberator and saviour, and has for long held a somewhat narcissistic belief that only he has an all-round and accurate grasp of not just Uganda's but Africa's problems. He believes only he has the skills, competences and grand vision to oversee the transformation of the country and continent. In the words of a former minister, Museveni 'still believes himself to be the all-knowing, all-powerful, all-conquering "Ssabalwanyi" (the chief fighter) and "Ssabagabe" (King of Kings)'.[31] Underlying his trans-historical and extraterritorial saviour ambitions, his Rwanda counterpart, Paul Kagame noted in a media interview, 'Museveni has a flaw of thinking that everyone must bow to him whether he's wrong or right. He actually thinks he has that right, that this region is his'.[32]

If the first *rationale* for Museveni's life-presidency project – that of a saviour on a grand mission to liberate Africa and Uganda – sounds somewhat illusory, the second driver of his determination to rule for life is fundamentally existential, it is real and practical: the trap of power. The longer Museveni has stayed on, the more it has become difficult for him to contemplate life outside State House and the more impractical it increasingly looks for him to negotiate a befitting and viable exit. For most of his adult life, Museveni has known and done only two jobs. First, as a specialist in violence who spent time studying, internalizing and implementing the use of violence to capture state power and change society. Second, as a welder of vast, in fact unlimited, presidential power, which he has exercised for close to four decades of uninterrupted rule. In other words, for most of his life Museveni has lived a life of giving orders and issuing commands, first as leader of a rebel group and later as head of state in a highly patrimonial regime of rule. He has presided over the distribution of patronage and dispensing punishment; he has overseen the use of law and the coercive arsenal of the state for his personal benefit and as a tool of repression against his opponents.

Museveni has engaged in those two occupations – as a specialist in violence (successful rebel commander) and long-surviving authoritarian president – for a period spanning half a century. Now of advanced age and somewhat doused in power, it is rather jarring for him to contemplate life as an ordinary citizen where he is not in charge of managing and commanding the distribution of resources and the issuance of sanctions. It is unnerving for him to imagine a life where he is not giving directives and overseeing a mass clientele that routinely seeks his favours. What is more, the 'trap of power' and the reluctance to exit is also undergirded by the need to remain shielded from legal scrutiny and possible prosecution once out of power given all the violations, abuses and potential crimes committed under his long rule. Of course, the situation is not made any better by the emergence of an international regime of criminal law, which does not treat out-of-office dictators with much favour as was the case in the past.

To understand Museveni's different strategies of keeping power, which entail maintaining a coalition that balances out different interests, it is important to underscore these overarching drivers for pressing on with ruling for life and ensuring that even within an environment of relatively competitive elections, he remains unassailable. The imperatives for survival and ruling for life interact directly with how Museveni's ruling coalition is shaped, constituted and reproduced.

Evolution of the NRM system and its ruling coalition

The NRM regime has considerably evolved and changed since 1986, both as a system of rule and as a ruling coalition. The structure and tenor of the governing system have transformed, the same way the ruling coalition has undergone significant transformation in both form and substance, in the credibility and credentials of individuals as well as in the overall quality of the sum total. Internal contradictions within the ruling establishment itself, the party and the president, but also the external forces challenging the status quo have shifted as to play critical roles in shaping the evolution and change in both the ruling system and governing coalition. One thing though has remained constant; President Museveni's rule over and control of the coalition.

Internally, among other changes, the NRM regime and party have experienced a significant generational shift due in part to the mere passage of time. While Museveni has remained a permanent fixture and kept around with him some of the old guard, a demographic drift has nonetheless exacted itself on the political landscape and impacted the calculations of power. The demographic dynamic has meant the need to balance between the old guard, who are now far fewer in number, and the new Turks; that is, between the veterans of the 'liberation struggle' and the neophytes struggling to take control.

The issue of generational tension has played out quite instructively within Museveni's own family.[33] According to credible sources with knowledge of dynamics inside Museveni's family, there are tensions between Museveni, his brother Salim Saleh and son-in-law, Odrek Rwabwogo, on the one hand, pitted against first-son Muhoozi Kainerugaba and the first lady, on the other.[34] Museveni has on occasion reportedly rebuked his son for making decisions and taking actions on sensitive security issues without consulting him as commander-in-chief.[35]

The 2017 constitutional amendment to remove the age-limit provision set off internal disquiet within the ruling coalition and played a role in reassembling the coalition after beating the amendment hurdle and navigating the 2021 elections. In the run up to the constitution amendment exercise in parliament, for example, Odrek Rwabwogo openly called for debating succession within the NRM and directed a thinly veiled indictment at his father-in-law, emphasizing the need for political transition.[36] Through the editorial/opinion pages of the government owned *New Vision* newspaper,[37] under the title 'Are strongmen a hindrance or facilitator to institutional growth, successful political transition?', Mr Rwabwogo wrote:

Unlike Singapore, Uganda (1986), Rwanda (1994) and Ethiopia (1991) perhaps provide a good case study of how strongmen in various ways first grew, then progressively retarded, and in some cases replaced and eventually became the very institutions they meant to build.[38]

This overt and blunt criticism of Museveni drew a fast and fierce reaction from one of Museveni's aides, David K. Mafabi, who accused Rwabwogo of fomenting 'ideological confusion'.[39] Interestingly, Mafabi published his rejoinder in the independent *Daily Monitor* and not the government owned *New Vision,* the former a paper Museveni publically chides and calls the 'enemy' paper.

Outside the ruling party's factional struggles and presidential in-house fissures, Uganda's overall political landscape has shifted in at least two interrelated ways. First, in the structural composition of opposition parties and personnel, and second with respect to the underlying nature of the threats the ruling regimes faces from opposition political actors. With regards to the latter, for example, one key change since the mid-2000s has been the near end of armed insurgency throughout the country, which means Museveni has in past decade or so been dealing with purely civil opposition that often manifests in different forms including street protests and riots along with the more structured processes of the five-year election cycle and the terrain of 'controlling consent'.[40]

Regarding the first aspect, of the changing composition of opposition forces, also since the mid-2000s Uganda's opposition politics entered a decidedly contentious phase of defiance characterized by confrontation rather than constructive engagement.[41] The 2011 Walk-to-Work protest movement led by Kizza Besigye, was the first major manifestation of this new form of struggle against Museveni, happening outside the established spaces and structures of the extant political system. Besigye's opposition approach marked a notable departure from the political engagements of the 1990s and 2000s especially after the 2016 elections when the defiance strand of struggle intensified with the new torchbearer being the youthful popstar-cum-politician, Robert Ssentamu Kyagulanyi, also known as Bobi Wine, under the banner of the 'People Power' movement starting in 2018. Kyagulanyi's youthful fervour brought out an increased supply of young foot soldiers, renewed street militancy and popular pressure against Museveni's tenure, although in the main his campaign remained anchored and couched in Besigye's politics of defiance.[42]

Under the impetus of the defiance campaign, during the 2010s Uganda's political landscape became far more polarized, radicalized and fiercely contested. The constitutional order and consensus embodied in the 1995 Constitution was largely shredded, giving way to violent confrontations especially during election campaign-time. In late-2020, security forces killed more than fifty people on the streets of Kampala,[43] a repeat of previous election violence in campaign seasons (see Anders Sjogren's chapter in this volume). Electoral violence has intensified in the past cycles including within the ruling party's primary elections, a product of ruling coalition factional struggles.[44]

The emergence of Kyagulanyi's NUP as the main opposition party in parliament, and NUP's routing of the NRM in its traditional strongholds of Buganda and Busoga, wrought a discomfiture on the electoral landscape. NUP's unexpected performance at the polls rattled the status quo and shook Museveni's political calculus, thus, his ruling coalition had to change in the face of these new opposition challenges. As with previous elections, the 2021 elections played a significant role in Museveni's coalition-calculus.

Presidential survival, the 2021 elections and coalition realignment

The dynamics of the 2021 elections and their impact on Museveni's ruling coalition were closely tied to the processes of removing the presidential age-limit from the constitution, which started in earnest shortly after Museveni started his 2016–21 term. This controversial move to allow Museveni stand for president again came through in December 2017. Initially, there was uncertainty surrounding how to push through with the constitutional change. The amendment was generally unpopular with the public and MPs met disapproval from their constituents while purporting to consult.[45]

Given the overall environment, Museveni had to shuffle the cards of his coalition to clear hurdles particularly in parliament to fight the battle for yet another critical turn in Uganda's political trajectory. Here, a relatively young crop of legislators, who were more of 'outsiders' to NRM, took the lead in doing Museveni's bidding with an eye on possible rewards through appointments to cabinet. In the past, Museveni relied on the old guard and the experienced in his ruling coalition armour to navigate legal and constitutional hurdles. However, with many of these old guard actors such as former Prime Minister Amama Mbabazi now out of favour or Ruhakana Rugunda lacking the needed political combativeness, Museveni turned to the young and relative outsiders who brought with them new zeal, aggressiveness and determination to appease the master. Museveni's choice to go with the young and unknown, but loyal and suited for the moment, to push through changing the constitution in parliament was later to be replicated in picking cabinet after the 2021 elections.

Unsurprisingly, after securing the seal and stamp on the deal to amend the constitution, some of the MPs at the forefront of handling the amendment process and delivering on the ultimate goal of removal of the age-limit were rewarded with cabinet appointments in a reshuffle in December 2017 less than two years into Museveni's term of office. Those rewarded included Rafael Magyezi (the main sponsor of the amendment bill) and Judith Nabakoba, a new member of Museveni's frontline political apparatchiks in parliament. In line with a well-established practice of Museveni's appointments, and in keeping with 'big tent' politics,[46] some of the ministers who were dropped in the 2017 reshuffle were appointed presidential advisors to add to a bloated list that has become difficult to keep track of. This reshuffle was done with an eye on the next general elections. Museveni needed to embolden the young Turks in the NRM ranks while keeping around some among the Old Guard by giving the latter alternative appointments such as presidential advisors.

As it turned out, because overall public opinion appeared to have been decidedly against amending the Constitution to remove the age-limit provision,[47] many of the MPs at the forefront of the constitutional amendments came up against a hostile political terrain going into the 2021 elections. Many lost their seats. In fact, the main actor, MP and Minister Raphael Magyezi, opted not to run for re-election perhaps gauging the mood among his constituents and concluding he was unlikely to get re-elected.[48] Godfrey Kiwanda, the then state minister for Tourism and a vocal advocate of the age-limit amendment, was among those who withdrew from seeking re-election.[49] Other overzealous supporters of the age-limit removal like MP Simeo Nsubuga lost in the NRM primaries and opted to run as an independent in the general elections in which he lost too in what became a sweep of NRM incumbents in Buganda.[50]

Successive parliamentary elections in Uganda tend to result in a fairly high turnover, so it is difficult to determine the extent to which sentiments against the age-limit removal may have played a role in the 2021 elections. However, the issue arguably contributed to the NRM's massive losses in parliamentary races in Buganda and Busoga, and Museveni's official loss on the presidential count in these two heretofore NRM electoral strongholds. What was quite clear was that removal of the age-limit provided a new mobilizing issue and a rallying agenda for renewed opposition to Museveni.[51] The age-limit controversy contributed to the momentum that in part produced the 'People Power' movement and the Bobi Wine 'phenomenon'. The other major issue was the land question, which remains an intractable problem and one that may well form the next major source of social conflict in Uganda.

In all, going into 2021 the opposition drew on the unpopular removal of the age-limit provision to build momentum against Museveni especially by appealing to the young and urban-based, the latter the opposition's historical base but which needed renewed mobilization. Bobi Wine seized on this momentum along with the social base of militant and ghetto young Ugandans, to pile pressure on Museveni albeit in a contest where the outcome was always a foregone conclusion considering that the incumbent has a firm grip on the electoral processes and full force of the state.

Opposition struggles against Museveni's rule in the past decade have generally moved to the city and the urban spaces as the primary spaces of confrontation and contestation. In this respect they presented a somewhat unconventional front characterized by youth militancy. Being able to mobilize and tap into the enormous energy and the daring predisposition of unemployed youths willing to be the suppliers of 'street-soldiers' is both unnerving and daunting for Museveni. Thus, he had to find ways of countering and curtailing this renewed front, started by Besigye during to the Walk-to-Work protests in 2011 and carried forward by Bobi Wine starting in 2018.

This new front of opposition carried with it potentially more combustible fuel of the 'Bobi Wine phenomenon' powered by two core social sources – urban youth militancy and the ghetto community. These two draw their drive and zeal from the clamour for a livelihood in an environment of hopelessness. With Bobi Wine commanding the frontlines, drawing on his popstar status and successful music career both of which endeared him to the urban, ghetto youth, this situation was bound to produce an enthusiastic following and a heightened, albeit not entirely new, political nightmare for Museveni.

Never to take any threat lightly or to underestimate his opponents, as 2021 drew closer Museveni took the fight against Bobi Wine to the latter's professional turf, in the music world and among musicians, and to his primary social base – the ghetto. The first crucial step was to stop Bobi Wine from using the music stage to market himself and propagate his agenda for challenging Museveni and changing the status quo.

In response, the government told Bobi Wine to separate 'Hon Kyagulanyi', the MP, from 'Mr. Bobi Wine', the musician. It expressly banned his musical shows, and swiftly deployed police and the military against any attempt to hold them.[52] This move not only denied Bobi Wine a platform for his political movement, it also denied him and other musicians associated with him income from live musical performances.[53] But stopping Bobi Wine from performing alone was not enough to counter the Bobi Wine phenomenon.

To penetrate his network and demobilize his following, Museveni had to bring into his fold individuals from Bobi Wine's professional circles and social terrain. Thus, in October 2019 Museveni appointed musician Catherine Kusasira as Presidential Advisor on Kampala affairs and Mark Bugembe aka 'Buchaman' Presidential Advisor for the ghetto.[54] The latter previously held the number two position in the 'Firebase Crew' with Bobi Wine as the principal and the self-appointed 'Ghetto President'. The appointment of Bugembe as a Presidential Advisor was intended to shore up Museveni's presence among Kampala's ghetto space but also cut into Bobi Wine's hold on the ghetto social group. This was as much about campaign optics and symbolism as anything substantive.

Although not given any formal positions, two other individuals on the musical front who had been on board with Museveni since at least the 2011 elections became even more critical in countering the Bobi Wine threat: Moses Ssali aka Bebe Cool and Balaam Barugahare. Bebe Cool is son of former prominent politician and long-serving Local Government Minister, Bidandi Ssali, who fell out with Museveni over the 2005 removal of presidential term limits. Bebe Cool has as big a music profile as Bobi Wine. In fact, he considers himself, and his fans agree, that he has a bigger music name and pedigree than Bobi Wine's. He has been an outspoken supporter of Museveni even after his father, Bidandi, became a key regime critic and opponent of Museveni, running against the incumbent for president in 2011. On his part, Balaam has been a leading promoter and events manager in the entertainment industry with a big network of clients and collaborators.

Both Balaam and Bebe Cool took on active roles in pushing back the 'Bobi Wine phenomenon', the former throwing around cash in music and ghetto circles while the latter was on the offensive especially in the media going against Bobi Wine and rooting for Museveni. These two became prominent players especially in the elections campaign season. Thus, in the light of the new front of political threat posed by an unconventional entrant onto the scene who came with a popstar profile and appealing to a ghetto social base, going into the 2021 elections Museveni and his handlers had to match the new front-of-threat by aggressively penetrating the music industry.

In one sense, these overtures and outreach actions bespoke of how far Museveni was willing to go to secure his hold on power, but in another they underscored his pragmatism and agility in staying ahead of the game so as not to leave anything to chance. Since he came to power, Museveni has mastered the practice of never taking any chances and of not underestimating his challengers. From the outset he took the threat posed by Bobi Wine very seriously, and took proactive measures that included reaching out to one of Bobi Wine's ostensible social base – the ghetto – through presidential appointments and financial largesse. It did not matter if the appointments actually came with real power or held any substantive consequence; the symbolism alone did matter and made a big difference in the broader scheme of things.

Indeed, recognizing the power and potency of the music arena, its appeal and resonance in a country of majority young people, during the 2016 campaign season Museveni had tried to tap into Uganda's legion of music celebrities, wooing a group of top musicians into what became known as the 'tubonge nawe' (we are with you) group. He made promises of financial largesse to the group at a campaign performance held at Speak Resort, Munyonyo.[55]

What is more, within this political performativity and theatrics of embracing popstar status and seeking to appeal to the youthful segment of Uganda's voters, Museveni put out a hit of his own in the 2010/11 election cycle dubbed '*do you want another rap*', although he was criticized, and even sued, for appropriating an Ankole folk chant.[56] To keep up with this effort of appealing to the young and appearing 'cool', Museveni's handlers also created for him and popularized a stage name 'Sevo' derived from Museveni, as part of a broader strategy of exciting and appealing to ghetto youth and the slang-loving sections of young Ugandans.

The disruptions in Uganda's political landscape during the 2000s and 2010s, particularly the role of a demographic shift and the turn to politics of defiance at the same time that Museveni had to tinker with the constitution to cling to power, became critical to Museveni's power calculus and how to sustain a viable ruling coalition. The 2021 elections marked a significant turning power in coalition politics as reflected in the cabinet that Museveni appointed subsequent to the elections.

The 2021 elections and the surprise cabinet

The 2021 elections campaign season rattled Museveni, arguably, far more than any previous electoral contest in part because he faced a different type of opposition threat but also the unprecedented environment that brought together several new factors and forces. First, the atmosphere generated by the Covid-19 pandemic presented a state of uncertainty even though Museveni was able to instrumentalize the fight against the novel virus. Second, the 'Bobi Wine phenomenon' posed a somewhat different (albeit not entirely new) threat given that the main opposition challenger was not a traditional politician, nor a former Museveni insider, but rather a popstar with a big celebrity profile.

Third, for the very first time there was inordinate external media focus on the elections, with especially the Western media obsessing about a popstar who was out to oust a dictator, garnering a great deal of bad press for Museveni. Fourth, according to someone with inside knowledge,[57] from internal NRM polling, in the months leading to the January 2021 elections Museveni's poll numbers were quite bad; NRM polling data apparently showed Museveni unpopular and unable to obtain majority votes in the first round of voting short of rigging. Fifth, there was an upsurge in militancy and a determination to oppose Museveni's re-election from especially urban youths in part driven by social media mobilizing and unprecedented diaspora engagement in support of Bobi Wine.

Last, and most important was the election result itself. Despite state repression including deadly shootings in Kampala in November 2020 targeting protests against Bobi Wine's arrest, financial resources that the opposition could not match and the possibility of rigging, Museveni nevertheless officially lost the popular vote in central Uganda and parts of the east. Worse, in Buganda, the NRM lost the majority of parliamentary seats to Bobi Wine's NUP. In a post-election address after the electoral commission officially declared him president-elect, Museveni slammed Bobi Wine's victory in what was heretofore his stronghold of Buganda. 'Instead of people looking to solve the social economic issues of the people', a visibly angry Museveni asserted in a live televised address, 'they now bring back sectarianism. Like you saw the voting, for instance, in Buganda.'[58]

Going into the 2021 elections, veteran challenger, Dr Kizza Besigye, decided that it was futile to run against Museveni in an election the incumbent exercised unlimited powers and latitude to twist the outcome in his favour. Thus, Besigye opted out. In came Bobi Wine who occupied the front opposition seat as main the challenger to

Museveni. In the circumstances, it was inconceivable at the time that Bobi Wine would mount a serious challenge and place Museveni on the back foot, which he did, in the end actually scoring a symbolic victory of officially defeating Museveni in Buganda/ central region. The icing on the cake was Bobi Wine party's sweep of parliamentary seats in Buganda that handed his NUP party the status of lead opposition party in parliament. The election results, and the overall political landscape before and after the elections, came to have a bearing on the form and substance of Museveni's new cabinet announced in June 2021.[59]

Museveni's exasperation with Buganda, as noted above, was vividly reflected in the new cabinet line-up he announced in June following his swearing-in on 12 May 2021. The most noticeable feature of the new cabinet was the absence of a Muganda at the top of the executive pyramid of authority, no Vice President or Prime Minister and, in the very least, no deputy Prime Minister. In the past, Buganda always 'ate big' in Museveni's cabinets. Not this time.

The most senior surviving Muganda at the top of the ruling coalition now is Moses Kigongo, the NRM Vice Chairman, a position that accords him largely symbolic power and almost no say in the actual exercise of executive authority. Buganda's decisive switch from NRM to NUP appears to have extremely rattled Museveni. Given the centrality of Buganda in Ugandan politics,[60] and considering that Museveni had always viewed Buganda as a critical constituency in his governing juggernaut, not naming a Muganda figure to the top echelons of government was unprecedented. With no Muganda at the helm of the judiciary branch, we would have expected Museveni to get one at the top of the legislature or the executive if not both. He did not.

But arguably, the most shocking aspect of Museveni's post-2021 election cabinet lineup was not so much the individuals he did not pick as those he did. After booting Speaker Rebecca Kadaga from the powerful position of Speaker in favour of a relatively new convert, Jacob Oulanyah, the expectation would have been that Kadaga gets the Vice President or at least the slot of Prime Minister.[61] On her part, Kadaga had publicly denounced the prospect of becoming Vice President, insisting there was no power in the office compared to being Speaker.[62] A last ditch meeting of the NRM Central Executive Committee to persuade her to drop out of the race for speaker came to naught. The CEC then picked Museveni's preferred candidate, Oulanyah, as the NRM official candidate to run for Speaker.[63] Unfazed, Kadaga defied the party position of endorsing Oulanyah. She went on to run for Speaker as an 'independent candidate' with support from a combination of NRM and opposition MPs.[64] In the end though, she was resoundingly defeated, and in a post-election speech Museveni boastfully revealed how he had worked the phone the night before and persuaded many NRM MPs to defect from Kadaga to Oulanyah.[65]

Following the race for Speaker, the next anticipated big news over which there was so much media and public speculation, between May and June 2021, was the announcement of a new cabinet line-up. Would Museveni name Kadaga Vice President, a position the latter had denigrated, in fact denounced? If he did, would she accept it? Perhaps wanting to send a strong message that no one can challenge or defy him and remain unscathed, Museveni relegated Kadaga to the distant and obscure position of deputy Prime Minister and Minister for East African Affairs. Politically humbled, and perhaps bruised by her dramatic loss in the race for Speaker, Kadaga quietly took up this third-rate cabinet appointment where she has to answer to a much junior and low profile Prime Minister.

Museveni has a knack for not wanting to be predicted or second-guessed. In early June, the *Daily Monitor* newspaper published what it claimed was a leaked cabinet lineup with some unexpected names including that of Vice President, Finance and Foreign Affairs ministers.[66] According to a senior editor at *Daily Monitor*, the leaked list was authentic but once published, Museveni had to change personnel on his final list in some areas to maintain his tradition of being unpredictable.[67]

A few days after the leaked list appeared, Museveni announced the cabinet with a shocking slate of names, many different from those leaked to the *Daily Monitor*. He picked Robinah Nabbanja as Prime Minister and Jessica Alupo as Vice President, both political lightweights with no gravitas to be in the running for Uganda's topmost office – the presidency.[68]

In so doing, Museveni underscored his resolve to continue being fully in charge and giving no signals that he might stepdown in the near future. According to one perceptive observer of Uganda politics, it signalled that Museveni had no immediate plans of starting a transition to a future president.[69] Museveni's post-2021 elections cabinet was 'a pointer to whether a transition was in the offing or not. As it turned out, reading the faces and names in this cabinet one could clearly see that a transition is still so far away'.[70]

There are several features of the post-2021 elections cabinet worth underlining. First, the total number of ministers increased from seventy-nine to eighty-three. Raising the number of ministerial slots is in line with previous trends when the size of cabinet increases following elections, pointing to the need to create openings for rewarding or placating specific constituencies or interest groups. Secondly, there was a relatively high turnover of cabinet membership, much higher than previous rounds of such appointments. Only about half of the previous ministers returned to the new line-up. Museveni named thirty-five new individuals (about 43 per cent), many of whom were total unknowns on the national political scene. Five had been in Cabinet before, lost elections and were dropped but returned to office after winning their MP races in the January 2021 elections.[71]

The third noticeable feature of this cabinet, and indeed the broader ruling coalition, is the shift away from Museveni's old guard and 'bush war' comrades to a crop that is both relatively inexperienced and young. When it was named in 2021, the average age of the cabinet members was about forty-six years for a president who was officially seventy-seven. What is more, the core members of the 1986 crew that remain on the table are only a handful: Tom Butime, Kahinda Otafire and Jim Muhwezi, the latter brought in only to replace another 1986 figure, Elly Tumwine, as Security Minister. By appointing relatively young political novices, and locking out possible contenders for the president, Museveni effectively made it impossible for the NRM and the country to mull a transition from within.[72] In all, it appears that Museveni went for loyalty: 'He called them fishermen in an unveiled attack on intellectuals'.[73]

Lastly, regional balancing has always been a key component of Museveni's Cabinet appointments. There was a pronounced change in the pattern of regional distribution, which underlined shifts in the political terrain and particularly the impact of the 2021 elections. Museveni has always made appointments with an eye on regional distribution in tandem with his electoral support but also the perceived overall political significance of each of Uganda's four major regions – central, east, north and west.

Up to until the 2021 elections, the central (Buganda) and western regions tended to take larger shares of cabinet slots. However, in the cabinet named after these elections, for the first time since 1986 Buganda took the smallest share at thirteen slots out of eighty-one compared to the west's twenty-six, and the east following closely at twenty-five. The north – which previously always got the least share – received seventeen slots, more than Buganda's. Yet this actually represented a consistent trend in Museveni's ruling coalition where the allotment of positions, especially cabinet appointments, tracks with official or perceived political support for the president and his party. The 'rewards' for the north apparently come out of Museveni's appreciation of the region's shift in its political support towards him and the NRM.[74] For long a time, and as war raged in that part of the country, most of the north and northwest regions consistently voted against the NRM and Museveni in successive elections. In turn, Museveni would give the lower shares of cabinet slots to these regions compared to the central and west.

Conclusion

What do the above outlined shifts in the nature and calibre of the ruling coalition mean for politics in Uganda? Normatively speaking, there is a dearth of principled and progressive voices in the ruling coalition who can drive the country in the direction of better government and especially propel a peaceful transition from Museveni's rule. As Museveni has become captive to his own lust for power and hostage to different actors lining up to extract rents for personal aggrandisement, there are few voices, if any, at the table to speak candidly and courageously about the state of affairs in the country, and who can face Museveni forcefully. This contrasts with the ruling coalition during the first phase of the NRM, which had a few independent-minded and progressive figures like the late Eriya Kategeya, Miria Matembe, Amanya Mushega, Matthew Rukikaire, Kintu Musoke and Bidandi Ssali, to mention but these few, who had the gravitas to articulate alternative ideas and contradict the chief at the top.[75]

The change in the calibre of the ruling coalition has implications for electioneering processes and in turn, elections have an impact on the dynamics of the ruling coalition. First, because personal power calculations and access to state patronage inform the quest for public office, running for political office has taken on a fierce and highly-monetized orientation. This has made elections extremely costly for individuals. There are high levels of election violence and shambolic internal selection processes, starting with the NRM primaries. Campaign finance, combined with outright force and violence, have become the key determinants of presidential and parliamentary election outcomes. Secondly, elections are now a key medium for entry into the ruling coalition, thus turnover in parliamentary elections has a direct impact on turnover in Cabinet. One is likely to lose their place in cabinet after losing an election, although there are some who whether the storm and get a place in the cabinet lineup.[76]

In addition to the marked rise in election campaign costs, the growth in transactional politics means that the overall price and cost of keeping Museveni and the NRM regime in power have grown tremendously. A coalition that is bereft of principles and persuasion is inherently costly to maintain, but also the system of rule and the size of the public sector has become so expansive and bloated, making it much more expensive to run. At a personal level, as he has stayed for so long and feels more and more insecure, Museveni is compelled to pay, literally, for his legitimacy.

All this adds up to arguably the most important implication: the likely fate and future of presidential succession in Uganda. Museveni has practically outlasted all his peers and original allies at the onset of his rule in 1986. He tactfully and skilfully kept the question of succession off the table by successfully making himself a permanent president. Yet, one way or the other, his rule will end, and going by the quality and calibre of the current ruling coalition, the end to Museveni's rule will likely proceed violently or spark violent confrontations. Already, there have been flashes of fissures and possible factional struggles around Museveni, for example concerning his son as heir apparent, that point to the future succession battles being, at a minimum, politically chaotic if not entirely violent.

Notes

1   An earlier version of this chapter appeared as Moses Khisa, 'Uganda's Ruling Coalition and the 2021 Elections: Change, Continuity and Contestation,' *Journal of Eastern African Studies* 17, 1–2 (2023): 325–343. Doi.org/10.1080/17531055.2023.2 246761. I thank the publisher, Taylor and Francis for the permission to use material from that article.

2   Interview with a veteran journalist 12 June 2021, Kampala.

3   Job Bwire, 'Jacob Oulanyah Voted Speaker of 11th Parliament', *Daily Monitor*, Kampala (24 May 2021). https://www.monitor.co.ug/uganda/news/national/jacob-oulanyah-voted-speaker-of-11th-parliament-3412358

4   Job Bwire, 'Speaker Jacob Oulanyah Dies in Seattle', *Daily Monitor*, Kampala (20 March 2022). https://www.monitor.co.ug/uganda/news/national/speaker-jacob-oulanyah-dies-in-seattle-3754188

5   These were: Samson Kisekka (Buganda), Specioza Kazibwe (Busoga), Gilbert Bukenya (Buganda) and Edward Ssekandi (Buganda).

6   In the 2000s, the vice president was Bukenya (Buganda), the speaker Ssekandi (Buganda), deputy speaker Kadaga (Busoga) and prime minister Apollo Nsibambi (Buganda).

7   See, for example, Brownlee, *Authoritarianism in an Age of Democratization* (Cambridge: Cambridge University Press, 2007); Gandhi, *Political Institutions under Dictatorship* (Cambridge: Cambridge University Press, 2008); Svolik, *The Politics of*

Authoritarian Rule (Cambridge: Cambridge University Press, 2012); Sean L. Yom, *From Resilience to Revolution: How Foreign Interventions Destabilize the Middle East* (Cambridge: Columbia University Press, 2015); Matt Buehler and Mehdi Ayari, 'The Autocrat's Advisors: Opening the Black Box of Ruling Coalitions in Tunisia's Authoritarian Regime', *Political Research Quarterly* 71, no. 2 (2018): 330–346; Barbara Geddes, Joseph George Wright, Joseph Wright and Erica Frantz, *How Dictatorships Work: Power, Personalization, and Collapse* (Cambridge: Cambridge University Press, 2018).

8   Buehler and Ayari, 'The Autocrat's Advisors', 330.

9   Svolik, *The Politics of Authoritarian*, 55; Geddes et al., *How Dictatorships Work*, 65.

10   Sabastiano Rwengabo, 'Regime Stability in Post-1986 Uganda: Counting the Benefits of Coup – Proofing', *Armed Forces & Society* 39, no. 3 (2013): 531–59.

11   Philip Roessler, *Ethnic Politics and State Power in Africa: The Logic of the Coup-Civil War Trap* (Cambridge: Cambridge University Press, 2016).

12   Buehler and Ayari, 'The Autocrat's Advisors', 331.

13   Anne Mette Kjær and Mesharch W. Katusiimeh, 'Nomination Violence in Uganda's National Resistance Movement', *African Affairs* 120, no. 479 (2021): 179.

14   Svolik, *The Politics of Authoritarian*, 68.

15   Ibid., 65.

16   For example, Magaloni, *Voting for Autocracy*; Brownlee, *Authoritarianism in An.*

17   Arriola et al., 'Democratic Subversion', 1359.

18   Charles Mwanguhya, 'Kategaya Turns Up for Cabinet Vetting', *URN*, Kampala (26 May 2006). https://ugandaradionetwork.net/story/kategaya-turns-up-for-cabinet-vetting?districtId=0

19   Eriya Kategaya, *Impassioned for Freedom* (Kampala: Wavah Books, 2006).

20   Emmanuel Mutaizibwa, 'How Muhoozi Rise Was Known in 1997', *The Observer*, Kampala (29 August 2012). https://www.observer.ug/news/headlines/20646–how-muhoozi-rise-was-known-in-1997

21   Moses Khisa, 'Shrinking Democratic Space? Crisis of Consensus and Contentious Politics in Uganda', *Commonwealth & Comparative Politics* 57, no. 3 (2019): 345.

22   Svein-Erik Helle and Lise Rakner, 'Grabbing an Election: Abuse of State Resources in the 2011 Elections in Uganda', in *Corruption, Grabbing and Development: Real World Challenges*, ed. Tina Søreide and Aled Williams (Cheltenham, UK: Edward Elgar Publishing, 2013).

23   Sam Wilkins, Richard Vokes and Moses Khisa, 'Briefing: Contextualizing the Bobi Wine Factor in Uganda's 2021 Elections', *African Affairs* 120, no. 481 (2021): 629–643.

24   Kjaer and Katusiimeh, 'Nomination Violence', 183.

25   Anna Reuss and Kristof Titeca, 'When Revolutionaries Grow Old: The Museveni Babies and the Slow Death of the Liberation', *Third World Quarterly* 38, no. 10 (2017): 2347–66.

26   Parliamentary turnover was more than 60 per cent for the 2011 and 2016 election and likely higher for the 2021 elections given that the NRM suffered massive loses in central Uganda. See Agather Atuhaire, '200 MPs Kicked Out', *The Independent* (6 March 2016). https://www.independent.co.ug/200-mps-kicked/. In 2021, only two members of cabinet were part of cabinet in 1986 and more than half were newcomers to the ruling establishment.

27   Khisa, 'Inclusive Co-optation and Political Corruption in Museveni's Uganda', in *Political Corruption in Africa: Extraction and Power Preservation*, ed. Inge Amundsen (Cheltenham, UK: Edward Elgar Publishing, 2019), 98.

28 Kjaer and Katusiimeh, 'Nomination Violence', 184.
29 Elias Biryabarema and James Akena, 'Lawmakers Brawl in Uganda Parliament for Second Day Over Presidential Age Limit', *Reuters* (27 September 2017). https://www.reuters.com/article/us-uganda-politics/lawmakers-brawl-in-uganda-parliament-for-second-day-over-presidential-age-limit-idUSKCN1C21VI (accessed 14 January 2022).
30 Khisa, 'Shrinking Democratic Space', 353.
31 Miria K. Matembe, *The Struggle for Freedom and Democracy Betrayed* (Kampala: Self-Publication, 2019), 26.
32 Patrick Smith, Parselelo Kantai, Nicholas Norbrook, 'How Kagame and Museveni Became the Best of Frenemies', *The Africa Report* (4 October 2019). https://www.theafricareport.com/18087/kagame-and-museveni-the-best-of-frenemies/ (accessed 29 June 2021).
33 Haggai Matsiko, 'Divided State House', *The Independent* (10 April 2017). https://www.independent.co.ug/cover-story-divided-state-house/3/ (accessed 30 July 2021).
34 Multiple interviews, May-June 2021, Kampala.
35 Interview with a senior journalist, Kampala, 14 June 2021.
36 Baker Batte Lule, 'Rwabwogo Attack Rekindles Museveni Succession Debate', *The Observer* (3 March 2017). https://observer.ug/news/headlines/51572-rwabwogo-attack-rekindles-museveni-succession-debate.html#comment-2643 (accessed 30 July 2021).
37 This was quite surprising because the *New Vision* for the most part maintains an editorial posture of not publishing articles critical of Museveni and his family.
38 Odrek Rwabwogo, 'Are Strongmen a Hindrance or Facilitator to Institutional Growth, Successful Political Transition?' *New Vision* (13 February 2017) (not published online).
39 K. David Mafabi, 'Of Ideology Experts and Ideological Confusion', *Daily Monitor* Kampala (24 February 2017). https://allafrica.com/stories/201702240043.html (accessed 30 July 2021).
40 J. Oloka-Onyango and Josephine Ahikire, *Controlling Consent: Uganda's 2016 Elections* (Trenton, NJ: Africa World Press, 2017).
41 Wilkins et al., 'Briefing: Contextualising the Bobi', 633–5.
42 Ibid., 636.
43 'Deadly Protests in Uganda after Bobi Wine is Arrested Again', *Aljazeera* (18 November 2020). https://www.aljazeera.com/news/2020/11/18/bobi-wine-uganda-opposition-presidential-candidate-arrested
44 Kjaer and Katusiimeh, 'Nomination Violence'.
45 '85% of Ugandans Opposed to the Age Limit Amendment – Survey', *The Observer*, Kampala (9 December 2017). https://observer.ug/news/headlines/56340-85-of-ugandans-opposed-to-age-limit-amendment-survey.html
46 See Vokes, 'Primaries, Patronage and Political', 661.
47 The Observer, '85% of Ugandans Opposed'.
48 The Independent, 'I Am Taking a Rest from Elective Politics – Magyezi', *URN*, Kampala (2 August 2020). https://www.independent.co.ug/i-am-taking-a-rest-from-elective-politics-magyezi/
49 'Kiwanda Joins 3 Cabinet Colleague out of MP Race', *Daily Monitor*, Kampala (28 August 2020). https://www.monitor.co.ug/uganda/news/national/kiwanda-joins-3-cabinet-colleagues-out-of-mp-race-1929358

50   'Brutality on Bobi Wine Cost us in Buganda – Defeated Ministers', *The Observer*, Kampala (22 January 2021). https://observer.ug/news/headlines/68206-brutality-on-bobi-cost-us-in-buganda-defeated-ministers

51   Wilkins et al., 'Briefing: Contextualising the Bobi', 636.

52   'Bobi Wine Banned from Performing at Music Shows', *Daily Monitor*, Kampala (18 October 2017). https://www.monitor.co.ug/uganda/news/national/bobi-wine-banned-from-performing-at-music-shows-1722518.

53   Julian Friesinger, 'Patronage, Repression, and Co-optation: Bobi Wine and the Political Economy of Activist Musicians in Uganda', *Africa Spectrum* 56, no. 2 (2021): 137.

54   Ibid., p.139.

55   'Museveni Campaign Song by Ugandan Stars, Cash Hand-out, Divide Uganda's Music Industry', *The East African* (31 October 2015). https://www.theeastafrican.co.ke/tea/news/east-africa/museveni-campaign-song-by-ugandan-stars-cash-hand-out-divide-uganda-s-music-industry–1342254

56   Barry Malone, 'Uganda President Draws Fire for Copyrighting "Rap"', *Reuters* (7 December 2010). https://www.reuters.com/article/us-uganda-idUSTRE6B64M420101207

57   Interview with a senior journalist, 15 June 2021, Kampala.

58   https://www.youtube.com/watch?v=ir9HyPs_lus

59   Morris Kiruga, 'Uganda Elections: Museveni Wins, Bobi Wine the Rising Power in Parliament', *The Africa Report* (17 January 2021). https://www.theafricareport.com/59593/uganda-elections-museveni-wins-bobi-wine-the-new-power-in-parliament/

60   Phares Mukasa Mutibwa, *The Buganda Factor in Uganda Politics* (Kampala: Fountain Publishers, 2008.)

61   This was what Museveni did with Kadaga's predecessor, Edward Ssekandi, who went from Speaker to Vice President. Ssekandi fell out of favour after losing his parliamentary seat in the January 2021 elections, making it easy for Museveni to dispense with him. He was dropped as Vice President. The natural replacement would have been Kadaga, moving from Speaker to Vice President as had happened with Ssekandi but also because Kadaga is the third most senior NRM party leader and would not be expected to hold any position below that of Speaker or Vice President.

62   Misairi Thembo Kahungu, 'Kadaga Rules Out Vice President Job', *Daily Monitor*, Kampala (29 March 2021). https://www.monitor.co.ug/uganda/news/national/speaker-kadaga-rules-out-vice-presidency-job-3340404

63   'NRM CEC Drops Kadaga, Endorses Oulanyah for Speakership race', *Daily Monitor* (23 May 2021). https://www.monitor.co.ug/uganda/news/national/nrm-cec-drops-kadaga-endorses-oulanyah-for-speakership-race-3411244

64   Quite ironic for the NRM's third top leader to contest an election as an 'independent' running against an official party candidate. Thus the race for Speaker was between two NRM candidates.

65   'Museveni Reveals How Kadaga Was Edged Out', *The Independent* (25 May 2021). https://www.independent.co.ug/museveni-reveals-how-kadaga-was-edged-out/ (accessed 7 November 2021).

66   Yasiin Mugerwa, 'New Cabinet List Leaks', *Daily Monitor* (8 June 2021). https://www.monitor.co.ug/uganda/news/national/new-cabinet-list-leaks-3429992 (accessed 31 October 2021).

67 Interview with a senior editor for *Daily Monitor*, Kampala, 11 June 2021.
68 Phone interview with a senior investigative reporter and editor for *NTV-Uganda*, 24 September 2021.
69 Interview with a veteran journalist and businessperson, Kampala, 11 June 2021.
70 Email Interview with a senior editor for *Daily Monitor*, 29 October 2021.
71 These include the new Vice President and a few veterans of the NRA bush war – such as retired Major General Jim Muhwezi and retired Colonel Tom Butime.
72 Op Cite note 66.
73 Personal communication with a veteran journalist and former senior editor for *Daily Monitor*, 29 October 2021.
74 Ibid.
75 In fact in 2005, Kategaya, Matembe and Bidandi were sacked from cabinet after they openly opposed the removal of presidential term limits. In her book, *The Struggle for Freedom and Democracy Betrayed*, Matembe recounts many incidents in which she confronted the president and strongly disagreed with his positions on issues like corruption, rule of law and accountability.
76 For example, after the 2021 elections, Ruth Nankabirwa, John Chrysostom Muyingo, Judith Nabakoba and Evelyn Anite, among others, lost their MP seats but were reappointed to cabinet for a variety of reasons.

10

Autocratization by elections

Anders Sjögren

The swearing in of Yoweri Museveni as President of Uganda on 12 May 2021 constituted the beginning of his sixth elected term in office. It also put an end to yet another general election characterized by a tumultuous process followed by a predictable outcome. Just like elections before it, the campaigns before the poll were marked by partisan administration, violence against the opposition, and heated contestation. And once again, official but disputed results secured Museveni another five years in power and his NRM party an overwhelming majority in parliament. Despite defiant challenges to Museveni posed by Kizza Besigye, and most recently Bobi Wine, over the course of two decades, Uganda had by the early 2020s settled into a stable hegemonic electoral autocracy where elections by and large are an instrumental and reliable mechanism for reproducing power for Museveni and the NRM.

Such hegemonic domination is not given; it is created. Nor is its evolution linear: it is dynamically linked to resistance against it. The interplay between power and resistance is both expressed and intensified by electoral dynamics. Multi-party elections in authoritarian settings always contain a degree of uncertainty by aggregating mobilization. For instance, even though Uganda's return to multi-party politics in 2005 was preceded by two decades of an effective ban on opposition parties and accompanied by the removal of presidential term limits, the 2006 presidential elections turned out to be surprisingly challenging to Museveni because of Besigye's sudden return from exile and his capacity to reignite grievances.

However, just as opposition actors mobilize to increase the uncertainty of electoral outcomes, autocrats seek to minimize it by shaping playing fields to their advantage. Such struggles over electoral regulation and outcome extend over time; autocrats learn from experience and adapt in order to strengthen domination and have extensive and powerful resources and networks at their disposal. Drawing on existing scholarship on multi-party elections in authoritarian systems, this chapter analyses how elections have contributed to the consolidation and deepening of authoritarian rule in Uganda under Museveni. For that purpose, the chapter assesses the argument that a key source of autocratic longevity is government capacity to adapt different aspects of formal and informal electoral management to stabilize the uncertainty of competitive politics at low levels.

President Museveni has made use of elections to entrench his rule under two political regimes, characterized by very different conditions in terms of managing uncertainty. The chapter examines the trajectory of general elections with an emphasis on presidential ones since the re-introduction of political pluralism, but stretching back to the no-party era by covering the 1996 and 2001 elections which in different ways shaped multi-party politics. The former of those elections constituted the high-water mark of legitimation and consolidated control during the no-party period, assets that were carried over into multi-party competition, while the latter election posed challenges to Museveni and NRM hegemony that contributed significantly both to the shift to multi-party politics and to shaping electoral regulation in that era.

In relation to the overall theme and argument of this book, the chapter addresses the evolution of electoral regulation as a crucial instance of autocratic adaptability and resilience through institutional manipulation. Apart from the transition to multi-party elections, a particularly important aspect of institutional manipulation is of course the twin tampering with restrictions on executive power through the removal of the term and age limits in 2005 and 2017, respectively. More specifically the chapter investigates how the institutional management and manoeuvring of electoral regulation induced by the President and the ruling party has evolved in relation to opposition resistance and repeated calls for electoral reform.

The chapter proceeds with a review of the literature on multi-party elections in authoritarian contexts, focusing on the factors that shape how and when elections stabilize autocratic rule. Based on existing research, it deploys an argument about evolving government capacity to manage regime-challenging activity and institutionalize predictability. The chapter then assesses the period covering the six general elections held under Museveni's rule with special attention to key features of and important turning points in the arrangement of electoral rules and practices. Under the no-party system with its ban on political party activity, the reduction of uncertainty was part and parcel of the political regime.

The empirical part of the chapter begins by briefly revisiting this period, as it produced the conditions and foundation for incumbent domination during subsequent multi-party politics. The no-party elections to Resistance Councils in 1989 and to the Constituent Assembly in 1994 offered Museveni good opportunities to build and broaden a governing coalition and create internal and external legitimacy. This trajectory of carefully guided and guarded elections producing low uncertainty and extensive rewards culminated with the 1995 constitution and the 1996 general elections. Subsequent elections, with the 2001 election as a turning point, were all marked by deeper divisions and more intense challenges to Museveni, creating greater uncertainty and, beyond securing extended control of state power, less added benefits as a result of negative reactions to extensive and visible manipulation and coercion.

This section concludes with an important caveat. All general election processes and results under the NRM, and especially since 2001, have been disputed. In 2001, 2006 and 2016 losing candidates in presidential elections went to court to challenge the results, and in 2001 and 2006, the Supreme Court in its rulings was divided down the middle. This chapter recognizes the questionable quality of Ugandan election results, and throughout the results referred to are the officially declared ones, which are not necessarily assumed to be reliable and valid but are the only ones available.

Elections in autocracies

Electoral autocracies – authoritarian political systems with democratic trappings such as elections – have since the end of the Cold War become increasingly common, and the dynamics of multi-party elections under authoritarianism is correspondingly subject to extensive and growing scholarly examination. Existing research shows that while autocratic elections are always manipulated by incumbents, the extent to which such manipulation is efficient differs widely. In some contexts, elections are tightly fought and genuinely uncertain and are potential mechanisms for regime change. In others however, the outcome is predictable and elections mainly serve as tools for reinforcing domination.[1]

How and why do elections contribute to the consolidation and deepening of authoritarian rule? Research emphasizing the regime-entrenching effects of autocratic elections has theorized and documented the many mechanisms through which this occurs. The menu of manipulation with items that can be deployed during an electoral cycle is a long one.[2] A main factor highlighted by the literature is stabilization through co-optation. Elections provide opportunities for incumbents to make use of their privileged access to state resources. They can distribute spoils among elites to signal and effectuate the stability of ruling coalitions by ensuring collaboration and counteracting defections; evidently, ruling parties also frequently use public funds to create measures designed to reward loyal sections of the electorate and to divide, co-opt and punish opposition politicians, activists and supporters.[3]

Elections further function as information systems. Rulers can use electoral campaigns and results to send and receive communication about government and opposition strength and weakness at elite and popular levels. Such mapping of capacity and vulnerability underpins learning and facilitates adaptation, and may serve to reduce the risks of non-institutionalized change such as coups or rebellions. Finally, elections can offer opportunities to create and sustain legitimacy for rulers in relation to domestic and international constituencies.[4] To summarize, from this perspective autocratic elections constrain political contestation through the ways rulers shape and control an unlevelled playing field populated by loyal insiders and disempowered outsiders. In Sub-Saharan Africa a mechanism frequently utilized by incumbents to this end is to adapt legislation on executive term limits and other restrictions on presidential power;[5] this has happened twice in Uganda.[6]

However, while incumbent advantage is a given, the balance of power in the electoral arena is not uniform among electoral autocracies. Nor is it constant within cases over time. A rich literature has documented how autocratic elections are focal points of contestation.[7] Even though incumbents have sufficient means and opportunities to influence the structural and institutional parameters of contestation and subvert genuine competition in a great number of ways, opposition parties and civil society groups can raise challenges that to a varying extent deepen the uncertainty built into every electoral contest.[8]

When can opposition groups turn autocratic elections into opportunities for change? The political opposition in electoral autocracies face incumbents that are willing and able to demobilize dissent and thus need to overcome major coordination and collective action challenges. Research points to the importance of financial resources and organizational capacity which may underpin and reproduce much-needed sustained opposition unity.[9] Such assets may help to transform sporadic expressions of grievances into systematic government – challenging mobilization and politicization. A strong opposition can more forcefully contest elections and dispute electoral frameworks. However, the presence of political opposition parties or coalitions with convincing competitive capacity raises the electoral stakes and prompts governments to intensify their demobilization efforts using legislation, administration, money, technology and violence.

Observations of differences among electoral autocracies in terms of the extent of ruling-party political dominance and electoral competitiveness has led to the analytical distinction between competitive and hegemonic variants.[10] Uganda is arguably a case of hegemonic electoral authoritarianism. What explains stable hegemonic electoral domination? Recent scholarly contributions point to its development over time, and more precisely to increasing government capacity to institutionalize low and easily manageable levels of electoral uncertainty. The uncertainty always brought about by elections tends to be more threatening during the early stages of electoral competition, as witnessed in the case of Uganda's 2006 elections.[11] The main challenge for autocrats in relation to multi-party elections is thus to master their regulation in order to promote stabilization, using combinations of coercion, co-optation and legitimation.

Existing research thus tells us that the ability of autocrats to use elections in order to consolidate power is, as can be expected, conditioned by the level of sustained resistance that opposition forces in political parties and social movements can raise. Where incumbents face weak opposition contenders, elections offer rulers rich opportunities and resources for not only retaining but also expanding and consolidating power through co-optation, information and legitimation. Where opposition forces are better organized and less vulnerable to manipulation, elections are more challenging and complicated for officeholders. They are a necessary mechanism for holding on to power, but bring greater uncertainty and require more efforts and resources, including monetary and coercive ones, to win. Under more competitive circumstances, therefore, autocratic rulers will need to intensify their efforts to minimize electoral uncertainty and maintain an unlevelled playing field through the interconnected processes of calibrating the manipulation of electoral regulation and demobilizing opposition groups.

The no-party elections era: From grassroot participation to contestation and coercion

Having captured state power following a civil war and in the wake of two decades of institutional and economic decay, the NRM found itself in a politically weak and insecure position. It possessed military strength but lacked significant political clout. In addition, politicians and military leaders who were overthrown in 1986 or in the coup of 1985 created rebel groups to fight the new NRM government. To address challenges to its authority, the NRM simultaneously restricted and accommodated contending political forces through what was presented as broad-based politics, supposedly in marked contrast to what the NRM condemned as the 'sectarian' political party competition of the past.[12] At the elite level, rival political and military forces were incorporated through pacts, as discussed in other chapters in this book. At the local level, the Resistance Councils (RCs) – village structures created during the war – were turned into mechanisms of political participation and representation. These different expressions of incorporation were key components of what was to constitute NRM's 'no-party' model of democracy.[13]

While direct elections took place at the village or RC 1 level during 1988, the NRM rejected proposals to extend this practice to higher levels, where elections were to remain indirect.[14] However, having stayed in power unelected for close to three years, the new government needed to anchor and broaden its base and legitimize its rule without risking losing power. For that purpose, local and national elections were held in February 1989.[15] The elections were assessed to have been by and large fair but severely restricted: there was no freedom to campaign, to organize for competition, or to debate issues.[16] Only at the RC 1 level were elections direct, meaning that the expanded National Resistance Council (NRC) parliament was elected indirectly. The uncertainty of the outcome was thus minimized by election rules that ensured NRM a parliamentary majority through appointed members and guaranteed Museveni's continuation as president.[17] This laid the foundation for Museveni's control over the legislature which he has maintained ever since. Over successive parliamentary elections, much effort has been geared towards deepening the NRM grip on the legislature using a wide range of actions, including gerrymandering through the creation of new districts and parliamentary constituencies, thereby manufacturing and maintaining a parliamentary super-majority.

Despite their democratic shortcomings, the 1989 elections aided to reinforce the NRM's claims to promoting political participation and accountability – but they also served to strengthen executive power within the NRC through the creation of the National Executive Committee. Later the same year the NRC made use of its powers by voting to extend the NRM's interim period of government by another five years.[18] This extension turned out to be longer. In 1992, the Constitutional Commission presented its report and draft for a new constitution, one of the most controversial proposals of which was that the no-party or 'Movement' system should continue for five years after the promulgation of the new constitution, followed by a referendum.[19] This met fierce rebuke from the old parties, UPC and DP, who regarded this as a breach of earlier agreements about a transition to multi-party politics. For this and other reasons, the elections to the Constituent Assembly (CA) in 1994 were intensely politicized – '[e]thnic, religious, regional and party factors combined to make the CA elections a referendum to some degree on the NRM government'.[20]

At the close of the CA debates, the Constitutional Commission's (and NRM's) proposal held sway, and no-party politics was enshrined in the 1995 Constitution and renamed the 'Movement political system' as an alternative to multiparty, which was to be subject to a referendum after five years. Political parties could exist but not campaign, and any activity that might interfere with the Movement system was expressly banned through Article 269.[21] All candidates in every election had to run for office on individual merit. On its part, the NRM recast itself as a constituent part of the movement as opposed to being a political party. In essence, the constitutional and legal framework suspended any meaningful political party activity and created immense possibilities for the NRM to extend and expand its political domination through and beyond elections.

The constitution and associated legislation thus established the formal structures of the 'Movement-state' and gave Museveni's rule legal and institutional anchoring. The next step was to underwrite this with legitimacy derived from popular support. The presidential and parliamentary elections of 1996 provided the obvious opportunity for simultaneous electoral legitimation of Museveni, the NRM and the Movement political system. NRM-affiliated candidates were elected as individuals but could still have their victories associated with the party despite public and official denials that the NRM was in fact a political party. Although the framework disallowed party-based organizing, many contenders were, just like with the CA elections, either associated with or members of opposition parties or the NRM.

As a result of the conflicts in the CA over the issue of political pluralism, DP left the government, and in 1996 its party leader Paul Ssemogerere stood against Museveni for the presidency. As Ssemogerere during the campaigns became associated with Obote, his support remained in parts of the north and east but dwindled in central and the west. Museveni on the other hand drew on incumbency advantages, including state financial, administrative and security resources to win a landslide victory receiving 75 per cent of the votes.[22]

In hindsight, the 1995 constitution and the 1996 elections proved to be the zenith of Museveni's legitimate control. The years that followed witnessed emerging discontent with the rise of corruption and regime repression. The Movement system was increasingly criticized as a one-party system in disguise.[23] A key manifestation of this development was the Movement Act of 1997, which created structures that were in essence those of a political party,[24] and also incorporated state and societal entities into the movement.[25] The Act represented the legal expression of the gradual de facto fusion of Movement, state and NRM structures. Another event that cemented the Movement system was the constitutionally anchored referendum on political systems in 2000. Opposition parties condemned the exercise as illegitimate and arranged a boycott. A majority voted for retaining the Movement system. However, turnout was low, suggesting evidence of Museveni's waning legitimacy.[26]

Criticisms of growing political intolerance and corruption were sporadically voiced by individuals, but it was difficult to channel them into organized dissent in the no-party context. The decisive change to this came with Kizza Besigye's candidature for president in the 2001 elections. With that challenge from a former senior member of the regime, Museveni faced an insider who shared three important bases of power, that is, the NRM, the military and the south-western as region of origin, and who represented discontent within all three and beyond them. He was also able to rally opposition forces, gaining the support of sections of the DP, UPC and independents. As the 2001 elections were held under the Movement system, Besigye and his followers all ran as independents, with campaigns organized by the small Elect Kizza Besigye Task Force. Museveni on the other hand relied on the extensive and partisan deployment of state power, not least through coercive state institutions, to stay ahead and beat the uncertainties of the electoral processes. Official as well as informal security agencies targeted opposition activists and supporters with severe intimidation, harassment and open violence.[27] Museveni officially won the elections by a big margin – 69 per cent against Besigye's 28 – but the democratic credentials of the president and the Movement system were seriously dented by electoral irregularities and state-based violence.

Some of the weightiest critical assessments of the elections came from the third branch of government: the judiciary. Besigye lodged an election petition with the Supreme Court to nullify the election due to illegal practices by Museveni in cahoots with the Electoral Commission (EC), the members of which were appointed directly by the president. While a divided Court upheld the result by three to two verdict, the ruling concurred with the petitioner (Besigye) that due to shortcomings of the EC the elections were marred by serious mismanagement, administrative incompetence and state-sanctioned violence.[28]

Following widespread criticism of the EC, the commissioners were dismissed in mid-2002 and a new body appointed later that year. Concerns caused by the unparalleled level of election-related violence in which a vast number of mostly opposition affiliated individuals were injured, abducted and detained and seventeen people killed, also generated responses. A parliamentary select committee report documented extensive and organized targeting of the opposition, planned and exercised by numerous state security agencies alongside state-authorized informal militias.[29] However, the report was never tabled for debate.[30]

The extreme violence meted out against activists and supporters of Besigye needs to be understood in the broader context of the deteriorating ability of the Movement system to manage contradictions and to contain disagreements. Ever since the CA-debates, political differences had produced factions within the NRM, and during the late 1990s differences were reinforced by increased corruption and intolerance.[31] Besigye's candidature brought into the open and amplified such differences. The experiences of 2001 set off a process of rethinking among the NRM leadership, and after two years of various commissions, in March 2003 the National Executive Committee resolved that Uganda should open up for multi-party politics.[32]

The change of political system was however part of a political package deal: the two-term limit for the presidency was proposed to be lifted.[33] Term limits had been introduced with the 1995 constitution as a safeguard against executive overstay and excesses, and Museveni had in public consistently promised to abide by it.[34] In fact he had clearly stated in his 2001 re-election manifesto that he was seeking his second and last term as president to complete the process of professionalizing the army. But in a move that inverted the 1995 constitutional compromise, the competitive uncertainty introduced by the change to multi-party politics was thus counteracted by the simultaneous lifting of term limits. After much public controversy, accusations of coercion and bribery, and a series of different attempts to legally effectuate the change, parliament in July 2005 voted to revoke article 105(2) and thereby abolish presidential term limits. The president assented to the Bill shortly thereafter.[35] The shift to multi-party politics was formally sealed with an undramatic referendum in 2005, in which all relevant actors backed the change – though some in the opposition regarded the referendum itself as unnecessary and illegitimate.[36]

The lifting of term limits had enormous political consequences. Some institutional changes are of the kind and magnitude that they fundamentally restructure the content and time horizons of expectations for everyone. In Uganda, the removal of term limits constituted such a change. While reducing uncertainty for Museveni, it re-introduced uncertainty for the country regarding a problem that had haunted Uganda: how to institutionalize the peaceful transition of executive power and change of government, and how to de-personalize the different organs of the state, especially the judiciary and the legislature. By removing the main regulatory mechanism for this, the term limit removal also set off a process of legal and constitutional de-institutionalization. It set Uganda on a path of life-presidency and uncertainty over when and how change from Museveni's long rule would happen.

The first decade of multi-party elections, 2006–16: Deepening autocracy

The first three multi-party elections in 2006, 2011 and 2016 were conducted within the same general and disputed framework where the incumbent exercised full control over the state's coercive and financial resources with an electoral management body that lacked independence. The three electoral cycles followed a similar pattern, beginning with the aftermath of the preceding elections and the disputes that had surrounded them. Condemnation of irregularities voiced by a wide range of actors, including foreign election observers and the Supreme Court, set off demands for electoral reforms that were in turn neglected or dismissed by the government, and so Uganda entered another round of elections regulated by the same disputed institutions and lopsided rules. The period however witnessed some variation in Museveni's strategies for domination. This section traces the trajectory of domination and resistance in relation to the regulatory and competitive dimensions of electoral politics during the first decade of multi-party politics.

The opposition's demands for electoral reforms before 2006 were based on its two main grievances with the 2001 elections: the extensive violence meted out against opposition activists and supporters and the perceived partisanship of the EC, issues also raised in the Supreme Court ruling on the 2001 petition and recommended by the Court to be addressed in a set of reforms. Momentarily united as the G6, the opposition demanded that the EC be transformed and that the military and security forces be reconstituted and removed from electoral management before the 2006 elections,[37] demands that the government refused to agree to.

The opposition was thus not able to improve its position by way of legal reform. Furthermore, efforts to unite the various opposition parties under one electoral umbrella failed due to disagreement over who should be the flagbearer. When Besigye returned from exile in October 2005 he was widely regarded as the obvious choice, but after he was arrested a few weeks later, some of the other parties argued that this effectively ruled him out.[38] The historical parties, DP and UPC, were also keen to try to revive their former status after two decades in limbo and opted to field their own presidential candidates.

The amendment of presidential term limits had, from the government's point of view, counteracted the setbacks brought by the concession to opposition demands for multi-party politics. The unreformed parts of the electoral framework and a disunited opposition added to the enormous incumbency advantages President Museveni and the NRM enjoyed going into the campaigns for the 2006 elections. Yet, in the context of the new multiparty dispensation, uncertainty still remained over the strength of Besigye's candidacy and the competitive capacity of the FDC. Following Besigye's triumphant return to Uganda he was soon arrested and charged with treason, concealment of treason and rape (accusations from which he was eventually acquitted) and spent most of the campaign period in prison or in court.[39] Besigye insisted he was innocent and all charges against him were politically motivated. His FDC party stuck with him. Indeed, he was eventually nominated as a presidential candidate from prison, subsequently granted bail and had to divide his time between the campaign trail and attending court hearings or reporting to court per the bail conditions.

Despite these far-reaching and heavy-handed efforts to contain Besigye before and during the campaigns, he was able to put up a strong challenge and officially received 37 per cent of the votes against Museveni's 59 – up by almost ten per cent from the previous elections. FDC performed less well in the parliamentary race and gained a mere 37 seats out of 309 or 12 per cent; this difference in opposition appeal between the presidential and the parliamentary contests would be repeated in subsequent elections. Again, Besigye challenged the election results in the Supreme Court, which, just like in 2001, in its ruling acknowledged numerous violations of the law and recommended a raft of electoral reforms, but still ruled (in another narrow four to three verdict) to uphold Museveni's victory.[40]

The 2006 elections thus tested President Museveni who encountered the relative uncertainties of his first multi-party challenge and faced a competitive and, given Besigye's surprise return, unexpected contender. Despite strongly orchestrated advantages, with some of the main elements of the regulatory framework – the partisan role of the EC and the security forces[41] – intact from the no-party era, Museveni needed to deploy a range of resources for securing domination. While documented overt violence by the security forces was not as extensive as in 2001,[42] it was still at a high level, and indirect violence through intimidation was rife and occurring against the overall background of increasing militarization in the exercise of state power.[43] The elections were declared by many observers to have fallen far below international standards, assessments which together with the critical parts of the Supreme Court ruling contributed to undercut Museveni's legitimacy.[44]

The clear and consistent critique of the management of the 2006 elections formed the basis for renewed opposition efforts towards electoral reform ahead of 2011. In 2009, the once more temporarily united opposition, this time under the Inter-Party Cooperation (IPC) umbrella and joined by a section of civil society networks, reiterated its previous demands for changes along with a call to reinstate presidential term limits.

Again, the government dismissed the need for any major changes. While parliament eventually passed a few minor administrative changes, the structure and orientation of the EC remained unreformed.[45]

The 2011 electoral contest played out slightly differently compared to the two preceding ones. While militarism remained a structurally anchored and crucial foundation of the NRM state,[46] and the campaigns were marked by sporadic attacks on opposition supporters and activists as well as heavy deployment of security agencies on Election Day, the 2011 elections by and large contained relatively little state-organized violent repression.[47] Instead, the defining feature of the campaigns was the vast amount of money and state resources used by the NRM.[48] These resources were distributed widely through reactivated and extended patronage networks across the country. While the use of state resources had always been a component of Museveni's election campaigns, the 2011 elections took this to new heights and placed this strategy at centre stage.

The government's change in strategic emphasis of domination techniques from coercion to large-scale clientelist co-optation allowed for a more productive use of electoral opportunities. Particularly noteworthy in this regard were the ambitious and successful efforts of Museveni and the NRM to capture the Teso and Acholi sub-regions from opposition control. The creation of a broader regional electoral base can be read as a way to counteract the uncertainty that surrounded voting patterns in Buganda in the wake of the fall-out between Museveni and Mengo, culminating in the Kayunga riots in 2009.[49]

For obvious reasons, the opposition could not match the resources available to the NRM side. And when Museveni's campaign emphasis shifted towards incorporation through expenditure and promises of development, Besigye's defiant mode of politics worked less well. Apart from being resource-constrained, the opposition also once again suffered from inter-party divisions, intra-party factionalism and a consistent message. Besigye's share of the presidential votes, officially, fell to 26 per cent, and FDC got 34 out or 375 seats, or 9 per cent of the final tally.

Unlike after the two proceeding elections, Besigye did not lodge a petition in 2011, having declared after the 2006 presidential election petition decision that he would not return to the Supreme Court. Instead, opposition discontent was to be expressed in a different way – the court of public opinion and on the streets. Two months after the elections, a loosely organized movement, 'Walk-to-Work', emerged initially to protest against the high inflation and spikes in costs of living, unofficially blamed on excessive spending during the election season. Soon, the protest movement was spearheaded by Besigye.

The 'Walk-to-Work' protests did not address electoral politics, but the defiance exhibited by Besigye together with the participation in the marches by all opposition parties and many civil society groups expressed general political grievances. The government responded with considerable repression.[50] While the protests did not accomplish their stated aims, 'Walk-to-Work' and other social movement-based protest actions during the year that followed the elections made it clear that even though the government appeared to have improved its skills in dealing with electoral uncertainty, extra-parliamentary mobilization could provide at least a temporary outlet for dissent.

The general dialectics of protest and repression affected the more specific contestation over electoral reforms ahead of 2016. Partly as a response to the protests of 2011, but also reflecting a broader pattern of deepening intolerance and increasing repression, parliament in 2013 passed the Public Order Management Bill which immediately thereafter was signed into law as the Public Order Management Act (POMA). It serves to restrict public gatherings, and was widely assumed – and later evident – that its implementation would target opposition parties and critical civil society groups.[51]

These events suggested that not only was the government unlikely to concede to calls for political liberalization and electoral reform; it was seemingly intent on further narrowing the scope for dissent. This generated a raft of initiatives among opposition parties and civil society organizations, which eventually culminated in the campaign for 'free and fair elections'. While this was the most ambitious and comprehensive effort to promote electoral reforms thus far, the government eventually ignored all its substantive proposals.[52] Yet again, Uganda entered an election (in 2016) that was to be conducted within an unreformed and thoroughly criticized framework.

As the 2016 elections drew closer, Museveni's way of dealing with the opposition was again more confrontational. A number of factors indicated a more competitive and uncertain contest than in 2011. In 2015, former Prime Minister Amama Mbabazi declared that he would run for President, and later that year Kizza Besigye made a surprise return as FDC's presidential candidate after having left the position of party president a few years earlier. During the early stages of the campaign, Mbabazi was the main target of harassment, but as it gradually became evident that he did not pose as much threat as expected and that Besigye's confrontational approach once more energized opposition supporters, the latter was made the chief victim of persecution.[53] Yet again, the opposition unsuccessfully attempted to form a unified front with a joint presidential candidate under the 'The Democratic Alliance' (TDA). Another failed opposition attempt to create an electoral coalition made selective victimization easier for the government.[54]

The government's return to more extensive deployment of intimidation, harassment by formal and informal security agencies,[55] and overt violence as election management strategy was accompanied by the even more excessive use of financial and other resources than in 2011,[56] as well as efforts to block information.[57] Election day was marred by serious administrative irregularities. Unsurprisingly Museveni was declared winner with 61 per cent of the votes against Besigye's 35. The full-scale approach to securing Museveni's election victory was sealed during the post-election period as the government placed Besigye under house arrest for more than forty days. Museveni stayed in power, but his reputation was severely tarnished; the election observers' assessments of the 2016 elections were even more condemning than past ones.[58]

2017–21: Consolidating hegemonic electoral autocracy

Following Museveni's inauguration in 2016, many analysts predicted that his next target would be to remove the only remaining institutional mechanism that prevented him from staying in office indefinitely: the presidential age limit of seventy-five. Museveni would be seventy-six at the time of the 2021 elections, thus ineligible to run for president. When, after a period of hushed talks and staged initiatives, the proposal was raised, it was also a foregone conclusion that he would succeed. While the amendment proposal was unpopular among most sections of society, it did not, unlike the removal of term limits, meet much resistance from within the NRM, but mainly from the opposition. When the motion was to be presented to parliament in September 2017, the opposition had organized demonstrations ahead and planned a countermotion. This was not to be: the military Special Forces and the police entered parliament and violently removed a great number of opposition parliamentarians from the debating chamber.[59] This led to repeated unrest throughout the country during the following months. In December 2017, the Bill was passed and assented to, and following appeals based on arguments about the unconstitutionality of the process, the Supreme Court in April 2019 ruled to uphold the law and to validate the law-making process.

The age limit removal, from its conception to the Supreme Court ruling, illustrated how the long-term trajectory towards the personalization and autocratization of power in Uganda had reached its logical conclusion. Other developments after the 2016 elections further underlined how Museveni exercised his powers to quell dissent without inhibition. In November, security agencies carried out extra-judicial killings on a massive scale at the palace of the king of the Rwenzururu in the western town of Kasese. The stated motive was to disarm palace guards, but the massacre occurred within a context of tension as the region had voted overwhelmingly in favour of the political opposition in the just-concluded elections.[60] Civil society organizations and individual activists critical of government were systematically harassed and many organizations shut down.[61] And when a group of members of parliament campaigned for the independent contender against the NRM candidate in the Arua Municipality by-election in August 2018, several of them were brutalized and arrested.[62]

The most well-known of these MPs was Robert Kyagulanyi, more famous as Bobi Wine. The arrest and alleged torture of Bobi Wine set off street protests in Kampala and generated international campaigns for his release.[63] From his election in 2017 onwards, much attention around Uganda's opposition politics centred on Bobi Wine and his 'People Power' movement. Riding on a wave of discontent with Museveni's rule in general and specific unpopular instances of it such as the social media tax and the removal of the age limit, Bobi Wine drew on Besigye's defiant political approach and tapped into and eventually overtook Besigye's constituencies.[64] And when in August 2020 it became clear that Bobi Wine would contest for the presidency and that Besigye would not, the former also inherited much of the repressive treatment previously reserved for Besigye.

As with previous elections, the 2016 contest had produced recommendations for reforms to level the playing field, voiced to little effect by the opposition, civil society groups and the Supreme Court. The reforms passed by parliament in mid-2020 were of little significance.[65] The 2021 elections thus took place in the same unreformed context, but one in which long existing formal and informal constraints on opposition campaigning were further enforced by the emergency measures taken to contain the Covid-19 pandemic. Predictably, the restrictions on public meetings were selectively applied: while Museveni's campaign proceeded largely without interference, security forces consistently disrupted opposition rallies, and especially those of Bobi Wine and his National Unity Platform (NUP).[66] And when Bobi Wine was arrested in November 2020 for having broken pandemic-related laws, massive protests erupted in Kampala and many other urban centres. At least 54 people were killed by security agencies, more than 300 were injured, and more than a thousand were arrested,[67] placing the 2021 elections as the most violent in Uganda's history.

The official results of the January 14 elections unsurprisingly declared Museveni winner with 58.4 per cent against Bobi Wine's 34.1 per cent; NUP also captured 57 seats in the 529-member parliament. Of particular importance was Bobi Wine's and NUP's unexpectedly strong performance in Buganda and Busoga regions, long-standing electoral strongholds for Museveni and the NRM. The results were rejected by the opposition, and Bobi Wine filed a petition which he later withdrew, citing bias of the court.[68] The repressive mark that the elections left also characterized the period that followed. A vast number of opposition, and in particular NUP, activists and supporters have gone missing, or been confirmed as detained and tortured.[69] While Museveni has always relied on a combination of foundations and techniques of control, including persuasion, co-optation, coercion and violence,[70] the latter years have been marked by a more pronounced reliance on increasing and intensifying repression.

Conclusions

This chapter has documented the many and shifting ways in which elections have been used to consolidate authoritarian rule for Yoweri Museveni. It confirms the findings of previous research that stress the regime-entrenching role of autocratic elections through co-optation, legitimation, and coercion. Museveni has adeptly made use of elections to dispense patronage and to renew and extend such networks, to map the strengths and weaknesses of the NRM and the opposition, to justify his continued rule, and to demonstrate his determination to remain in power by force.

The relative significance of these dimensions of electoral manipulation have however shifted over time. From an incumbent's point of view, elections can be anything from a constraining requirement to a productive resource: from being the formal and necessary mechanism for retaining power to providing opportunities for expanding and deepening domination between and beyond the contests. Elections during the first decade of NRM-rule by and large functioned as multipliers of domination: not only did they extend and stabilize Museveni's rule, but they also consolidated and legitimized the NRM-state and regime. As discontent grew and politics became more competitive from the late 1990s on, elections confronted the government with starker choices and trade-offs between control and consent. As the means deployed to handle electoral uncertainty became more visibly authoritarian, legitimacy was gradually undercut and resistance grew, which in turn was met by intensified coercion and co-optation.[71]

Much significant research has over the years documented the fine-grained mechanisms and complex patterns that shape Ugandan elections across localities and levels.[72] Together these studies have produced indispensable knowledge about the nuances of electoral politics in Uganda. This chapter has applied a different approach: it has taken a step back in order to provide a birds' eye view of presidential elections under Museveni, and by doing so assessing the role of elections as a form of institutional manipulation to promote autocratic adaptability and longevity. From this perspective, there is a distinct shift in composition of the main components of domination, from a relatively higher degree of consent during the early years to the naked coercion and crude co-optation that has marked most of the multi-party era.

Uganda's recent political trajectory may usefully be situated in a wider context: it has corresponded with global trends of autocratization from the early 2010s onwards. The country also effectively illustrates these tendencies. Indeed, Uganda's overall electoral trajectory under Museveni, as examined in this chapter, is a textbook example of how, in electoral autocracies, elections can be used to enable and further authoritarian consolidation.

Notes

1   Michael Bernhard, Amanda B. Edgell and Staffan I. Lindberg, 'Institutionalising Electoral Uncertainty and Authoritarian Regime Survival', *European Journal of Political Research*, 59, no. 2 (2020): 465–87; Valerie J. Bunce and Sharon L. Wolchik, *Defeating Authoritarian Leaders in Post-Communist Countries* (Cambridge: Cambridge University Press, 2011); Daniella Donno, 'Elections and Democratization in Authoritarian Regimes', *American Journal of Political Science* 57, no. 3 (2013): 703–16; Stephan Haggard and Robert R. Kaufman, *Dictators and Democrats: Masses, Elites and Regime Change* (Princeton, NJ: Princeton University Press, 2016); Carl Henrik Knutsen, Håvard Mokleiv Nygård and Tore Wig, 'Autocratic Elections: Stabilizing Tool or Force for Change?' *World Politics* 69, no. 1 (2017): 98–143; Philip G. Roessler and Marc M. Howard, 'Post-Cold War Political Regimes. When Do Elections Matter?', in *Democratization by Elections. A New Mode of Transition*, ed. Staffan I. Lindberg (Baltimore: The Johns Hopkins University Press, 2009): 101–27; Andreas Schedler, *The Politics of Uncertainty. Sustaining and Subverting Electoral Authoritarianism* (Oxford: Oxford University Press, 2013).
2   Andreas Schedler, 'Elections without Democracy: The Menu of Manipulation', *Journal of Democracy* 13, no. 2 (2002): 36–50.
3   Thomas Ambrosio, 'Constructing a Framework of Authoritarian Diffusion: Concepts, Dynamics, and Future Research', *International Studies Perspectives* 11, no. 4 (2010): 375–92; Jennifer Gandhi and Ellen Lust-Okar, 'Elections under Authoritarianism', *Annual Review of Political Science* 12 (2009): 403–22; Jennifer Gandhi and Adam Przeworski, 'Authoritarian Institutions and the Survival of Autocrats', *Comparative Political Studies* 40, no. 11 (2007): 1297–301; Stephen G. F. Hall and Thomas Ambrosio, 'Authoritarian Learning: A Conceptual Overview', *East European Politics* 33, no. 2 (2017): 143–61; Knutsen et al., 'Autocratic Elections'; Ellen Lust-Okar, 'Legislative Elections in Hegemonic Authoritarian Regimes: Competitive Clientelism and Resistance to Democratization', in *Democratization by Elections. A New Mode of Transition*, 226–45.
4   Gandhi and Lust-Okar 'Elections under authoritarianism'; Knutsen et al., 'Autocratic Elections'.
5   Alexander Baturo and Robert Elgie, eds., *The Politics of Presidential Term Limits* (Oxford: Oxford University Press, 2019); Andrea Cassani, 'Autocratisation by Term Limits Manipulation in Sub-Saharan Africa', *Africa Spectrum* 55, no. 3 (2021): 228–50;

Christof Hartmann, 'Authoritarian Origins of Term Limit Trajectories in Africa', *Democratization* 22, no. 1 (2022): 57–73.

6   Nic Cheeseman, 'Should I Stay or Should I go? Term Limits, Elections, and Political Change in Kenya, Uganda, and Zambia', in *The Politics of Presidential Term Limits*, ed. Alexander Baturo and Robert Elgie (Oxford: Oxford University Press, 2019), 333.

7   Emily Beaulieu, *Electoral Protest and Democracy in the Developing World* (Cambridge: Cambridge University Press, 2014); Dawn Brancati, *Democracy Protests. Origins, Features, and Significance* (Cambridge: Cambridge University Press, 2016); Bunce and Wolchik, 'Defeating Authoritarian Leaders'; Haggard and Kaufman, *Dictators and Democrats*; Schedler, *The Politics of Uncertainty*; Guillermo Trejo 'The Ballot and the Street: An Electoral Theory of Social Protest in Autocracies', *Perspectives on Politics*, 12, no. 2 (2014): 332–52; Joshua A. Tucker, 'Enough! Electoral Fraud, Collective Action Problems, and Post-communist Colored Revolutions', *Perspectives on Politics*, 5, no. 3 (2007): 535–51.

8   Schedler, *The Politics of Uncertainty*.

9   Leonardo Arriola, *Multi-Ethnic Coalitions in Africa. Business Financing of Opposition Election Campaigns* (Cambridge: Cambridge University Press, 2012); Bernhard et al., 'Institutionalising Electoral Uncertainty'; Bunce and Wolchik, 'Defeating Authoritarian Leaders'; Donno, 'Elections and Democratization'; Haggard and Kaufman, 'Dictators and Democrats'; Marc Morjé Howard and Philip G. Roessler, 'Liberalizing Electoral Outcomes in Competitive Authoritarian Regimes', *American Journal of Political Science*, 50, no. 2 (2006): 365–81; Adrienne LeBas, *From Protest to Parties: Party-Building and Democratization in Africa* (Cambridge: Cambridge University Press, 2011); Elvin Ong, 'Electoral Manipulation, Opposition Power, and Institutional Change: Contesting for Electoral Reform in Singapore, Malaysia, and Cambodia', *Electoral Studies* 54 (2018): 159–71; Schedler, *The Politics of Uncertainty*.

10 Bernhard et al., 'Institutionalising Electoral Uncertainty'; Donno, 'Elections and Democratization'; Yonatan L. Morse, 'From Single-Party to Electoral Authoritarian Regimes. The Institutional Origins of Competitiveness in Post-Cold War Africa', *Comparative Politics* 48, no. 1 (2015): 126–51; Roessler and Howard, 'Post-Cold war'; Schedler, *The Politics of Uncertainty*.

11 Bernhard et al., 'Institutionalising Electoral Uncertainty'.

12 Nelson Kasfir, '"No-Party Democracy" in Uganda', *Journal of Democracy* 9, no. 2 (1998): 49–61, 50.

13 Kasfir, Ibid., examines the shifting content and meaning of the model.

14 Ibid., 55.

15 Nelson Kasfir, 'The Ugandan Elections of 1989: Power, Populism and Democratization', in *Changing Uganda. The Dilemmas of Structural Adjustment and Revolutionary Change*, ed. Holger B. Hansen and Michael Twaddle (Kampala: Fountain Publishers, 1991), 247–78.

16 Ibid., 273.

17 Ibid., 249–50.

18 Ibid., 274.

19 Nelson Kasfir, 'Uganda Politics and the Constituent Assembly Elections of March 1994', in *From Chaos to Order: The Politics of Constitution-Making in Uganda*, ed. Holger B. Hansen and Michael Twaddle (Kampala: Fountain Publishers, 1995), 148–79.

20 Ibid., 150.

21   Sabiti Makara, 'Deepening Democracy through Multipartyism: The Bumpy Road
      to Uganda's 2011 Elections', *Africa Spectrum* 45, no. 2 (2010): 81–94, 82; Aili Mari
      Tripp, 'The Politics of Constitution Making in Uganda', in *Framing the State in Times
      of Transition*, ed. Laurel E. Miller (Washington, DC: United States Institute for Peace,
      2010), 158–75, 167–8.

22   Sabiti Makara, Geoffrey B. Tukahebwa and Foster E. Byarugaba, eds., *Voting for
      Democracy in Uganda: Issues in Recent Elections* (Kampala: LDC Publishers, 2003);
      William Muhumuza, 'Money and Power in Uganda's 1996 Elections', *African Journal
      of Political Science* 2, no. 1 (1997): 168–79.

23   Human Rights Watch, *Hostile to Democracy* (New York: Human Rights Watch,
      1999).

24   Erica Bussey, 'Constitutional Dialogue in Uganda', *Journal of African Law* 49, no. 1
      (2005): 1–23, 3.

25   Joe Oloka-Onyango, 'New Wine or New Bottles? Movement Politics and One-
      Partyism in Uganda', in *No- Party Democracy in Uganda. Myths and Realities*, ed.
      Justus Mugaju and Joe Oloka-Onyango (Kampala: Fountain publishers, 2000), 40–59,
      56–7.

26   Michael Bratton and Gina Lambright, 'Uganda's Referendum 2000: The Silent
      Boycott?' *African Affairs* 100 (2001): 429–52.

27   Anders Sjögren, 'Wielding the Stick Again: The Rise and Fall and Rise of State
      Violence during Presidential Elections in Uganda', in *Violence in African Elections,
      Between Democracy and Big Man Politics*, ed., Mimmi Söderberg Kovacs and Jesper
      Bjarnesen (London: Zed Books, 2018): 47–66, 53.

28   Sabiti Makara, Lise Rakner and Sabastiano Rwengabo, 'Administering the 2006
      Multiparty Elections: The Role of the Electoral Commission', in *Electoral Democracy
      in Uganda. Understanding Institutional Processes and Outcomes of the 2006 Multiparty
      Elections*, ed. Julius Kiiza, Sabiti Makara and Lise Rakner (Kampala: Fountain
      Publishers, 2008), 90–118, 96; Jude Murison, 'Judicial Politics: Election Petitions
      and Electoral Fraud in Uganda', *Journal of Eastern African Studies* 7, no. 3 (2013):
      492–508, 496–7.

29   Uganda Parliamentary Select Committee, *Report of the Parliamentary Committee on
      Election Violence* (Kampala: Parliament of Uganda, 2002), chapter 7.

30   Sabiti Makara, 'Managing Elections in a Multiparty Political Dispensation: The Role
      of the Electoral Commission in Uganda's 2011 Elections', in *Elections in a Hybrid
      Regime: Revisiting the 2011 Ugandan Polls*, ed. Sandrine Perrot, Sabiti Makara,
      Jérôme Lafargue and Marie-Aude Fouéré (Kampala: Fountain Publishers, 2014),
      110–37, 115.

31   Sabiti Makara, Lise Rakner and Lars Svåsand, 'Turnaround: The National Resistance
      Movement and the Reintroduction of a Multiparty System in Uganda', *International
      Political Science Review* 30, no. 2 (2009): 185–204, 190–2.

32   Makara et al., 'Turnaround', 186.

33   Cheeseman, 'Should I Stay'.

34   Clare Pamela Atoo, George Okiror and Arne Tostensen, 'Changing the Rules of
      the Political Game', in *Electoral Democracy in Uganda*, 27; Cheeseman, 'Should I
      Stay', 319.

35   Atoo et al., 'Changing the Rules', 29–32.

36   Makara et al., 'Turnaround', 195.

37   Charles Mwanguhya, 'Parties Threaten to Boycott 2006 Polls', *Daily Monitor*, 9
      September 2009.

38 Nicole A. Beardsworth, *Electoral Coalition-Building among Opposition Parties in Zimbabwe, Zambia and Uganda from 2000 to 2017* (PhD diss., University of Warwick, 2018), 82–3.

39 Sjögren, 'The Rise and Fall'.

40 Murison, 'Judicial Politics'.

41 Human Rights Watch, *In Hope and Fear: Uganda's Presidential and Parliamentary Polls* (New York, NY: Human Rights Watch, 2006).

42 Alexander Kibandama, 'The Security Question in the 2006 Presidential and Parliamentary Elections', in *Electoral Democracy in Uganda*, 134–49.

43 Sjögren, 'The Rise and Fall'.

44 COG, *Uganda Presidential and Parliamentary Elections, 23 February 2006* (London: Commonwealth Observer Group (COG), Commonwealth Secretariat, 2006); EU-EOM, *Uganda: Presidential and Parliamentary Elections 23 February 2006* (Brussels: European Union Election Observation Mission (EU- EOM) 2006).

45 Makara, 'Managing Elections', 117–18.

46 Jude Kagoro, 'Competitive Authoritarianism in Uganda: The Not So Hidden Hand of the Military', *Zeitschrift für Vergleichende Politikwissenschaft* 10, no. 1 (2016): 155–72; Anders Sjögren, *Between Militarism and Technocratic Governance: State Formation in Contemporary Uganda* (Kampala: Fountain Publishers, 2013).

47 Ryan Gibb, 'Presidential and Parliamentary Elections in Uganda, February 18, 2011', *Electoral Studies* 31, no. 2 (2012): 458–61; Angelo Izama and Michael Wilkerson, 'Uganda: Museveni's Triumph and Weakness', *Journal of Democracy* 22, no. 3 (2011): 64–78; Sandrine Perrot, Jérôme Lafargue and Sabiti Makara, 'Introduction: Looking Back at the 2011 Multiparty Elections in Uganda', in *Elections in a Hybrid Regime: Revisiting the 2011 Ugandan Polls*, ed. Sandrine Perrot, Sabiti Makara, Jérôme Lafargue and Marie-Aude Fouéré (Kampala: Fountain Publishers, 2014), 1–34; Sjögren, 'The Rise and Fall'.

48 Svein-Erik Helle and Lise Rakner, 'Grabbing an Election: Abuse of State Resources in the 2011 Elections in Uganda', in *Corruption, Grabbing and Development: Real World Challenges*, ed. Tina Søreide and Aled Williams (Cheltenham and Northampton, MA: Edward Elgar Publishing, 2014), 161–71.

49 Frederick Golooba-Mutebi and Anders Sjögren, 'From Rural Rebellions to Urban Riots: Political Competition and Changing Patterns of Violent Political Revolt in Uganda', *Commonwealth & Comparative Politics* 55, no. 1 (2017): 22–40; Izama and Wilkerson, 'Uganda'.

50 Golooba-Mutebi and Sjögren, 'From Rural Rebellions'.

51 Kagoro, 'Competitive Authoritarianism'. Section 8 of the Act which gave sweeping powers to the Inspector General of the Police was declared illegal and unconstitutional by the Constitutional Court in 2020.

52 Maria Nassali, 'A Political Coming of Age for Ugandan NGOs? The Campaign for Free and Fair Elections', in *Controlling Consent: Uganda's 2016 Elections*, ed. J. Oloka-Onyango and Josephine Ahikire (Trenton, NJ: Africa World Press, 2017), 279–301; Anders Sjögren, 'Civil Society and Contested Elections in Electoral Autocracies: Dissent and Caution in Uganda's 2016 Elections', *Journal of Civil Society* 18, no. 3 (2022): 307–25.

53 Sjögren, 'The Rise and Fall'.

54 Beardsworth, *Election Coalition–Building*.

55   Human Rights Watch, 'Uganda: Suspend "Crime Preventers"' https://www.hrw.org/news/2016/01/13/uganda-suspend-crime-preventers (New York: Human Rights Watch, 2016).

56   ACFIM, *Analytical Case Study on Flow of Budget Funds and Expenditure during the Election Period. Final Report* (Kampala: Alliance for Campaign Finance Monitoring, ACFIM, 2016).

57   Human Rights Watch, *'Keep the People Uninformed': Pre-election Threats to Free Expression and Association in Uganda* (New York, NY: Human Rights Watch, 2016).

58   COG, *Uganda General Elections, 18 February 2016* (London: Commonwealth Observer Group (COG), Commonwealth Secretariat, 2016); EU-EOM, *Uganda: Final Report Presidential, Parliamentary and Local Council Elections 18 February 2016* (Brussels: European Union Election Observation Mission (EU-EOM, 2016).

59   Ivan Ashaba and Shingirai Taodzera, 'Uganda', in *Political Chronicles of the African Great Lakes Region 2018*, ed. Filip Reyntjens (Antwerp: University of Antwerp Press, 2019): 91–117, 94.

60   Gerald Bareebe and Ivan Ashaba, 'Uganda', in *Political Chronicles of the African Great Lakes Region 2017*, ed. Filip Reyntjens (Antwerp: University of Antwerp Press, 2018), 89–111, 107–10.

61   Rita Abrahamsen and Gerald Bareebe, 'Uganda's Fraudulent Election', *Journal of Democracy* 32, no. 2 (2021): 90–10, 96–7; Moses Khisa, 'Shrinking Democratic Space? Crisis of Consensus and Contentious Politics in Uganda', *Commonwealth and Comparative Politics* 57, no. 3 (2019): 343–62, 348.

62   Ashaba and Taodzera, 'Uganda', 112.

63   Ibid., 112–13.

64   Sam Wilkins, Richard Vokes and Moses Khisa, 'Briefing: Contextualising the Bobi Wine Factor in Uganda's 2021 Elections', *African Affairs* 120, no. 481 (2021): 629–43, 636–7.

65   Martha Bakwesegha, 'Uganda Elections 2021', *Rift Valley Institute Briefing Paper* (January 2021), 3.

66   Abrahamsen and Bareebe, 'Uganda's Fraudulent Election', 93; Williams et al., 'Briefing', 639.

67   Abrahamsen and Bareebe, 'Uganda's Fraudulent Election', 93; Bakwesegha, 'Uganda's Election', 5; Wilkins et al., 'Briefing', 639.

68   Wilkins et al., 'Briefing', 13.

69   Ivan Ashaba and Karolina Werner, 'Uganda', in *Political Chronicles of the African Great Lakes Region 2021*, ed. Filip Reyntjens (Antwerp: University of Antwerp Press, 2022): 97–107, 105–9.

70   Frederick Golooba-Mutebi and Sam Hickey, 'The Master of Institutional Multiplicity? The Shifting Politics of Regime Survival, State-Building and Democratisation in Museveni's Uganda', *Journal of Eastern African Studies*, 10, no. 4 (2016): 601–18.

71   Oloka-Onyango and Ahikire, *Controlling Consent*.

72   Among a vast literature, see the collected volumes by Kizza et al., *Electoral Democracy*; Makara et al., *Voting for Democracy*; Oloka-Onyango and Ahikire, *Controlling Consent*; Perrot et al., *Elections in a Hybrid Regime*.

11

From 'movement' to multiparty:
The state and the role of political parties

Frederick Golooba-Mutebi and Mesharch W. Katusiimeh

This chapter examines the role of political parties as agents of democracy in Uganda. The chapter analyses the fate of parties during two decades of no-party politics and the subsequent return to multiparty politics starting in 2005. We argue that the plight and status of political parties has been integral to the survival of the National Resistance Movement (NRM) and President Museveni and the manner in which he and the ruling party have dominated Ugandan politics over the past nearly four decades. So fundamental are political parties to the operation of modern politics and government that their role and significance are often taken for granted.

In this chapter, we question whether political parties have lived up to the theoretical expectations of building democratic governments in Africa. Basing on case study evidence from Uganda, we attempt to bridge the gap between theory and reality by offering a realistic assessment of the prospects of party politics as a path towards, and political parties as agents of, democratization.[1]

This chapter charts the evolution of multi-partyism in Uganda and, focusing in particular on the NRM period in power, examines why, despite enjoying much vocal support from the general public, political parties continue to be ineffectual political actors and unable to successfully counter NRM rule. We argue that the challenges political parties face have undermined their effectiveness and confined them to issues that do not fundamentally challenge or affect the status quo, thus inadvertently aiding the continuation of Museveni's rule and its deleterious effects. The chapter aims to contribute to our understanding of the relationship between parties, democracy and the durability of authoritarianism.

Even if there is scepticism about the viability of liberal democracy in the African context, increasingly scholars have affirmed the importance of political parties for democratization and good governance.[2] It is widely believed that a thriving multiparty dispensation can widen democracy by promoting pluralism, and embedding its values and institutions within society at large, not simply at the narrow political level.

However, political parties face many challenges that undermine their aspirations and roles. In Uganda, this has confined them to focusing on issues that do not fundamentally challenge or affect the status quo. The first part of this chapter provides a general introduction, while the second looks at the key concepts as applied to the study of political parties and democracy. The third part takes up the experiences of political parties in Uganda and the challenges they have faced under the NRM government. In the last section, we provide some concluding reflections.

Political parties and democracy

Political parties constitute an important element of modern government. Before the emergence of political parties, governments were organized in cliques, factions or blocs. By definition, a political party is a group of people banded together for the purpose of seeking to win elective public office.[3] Uganda's *Political Parties and Organizations Act* (2020 as amended) defines a political party as '*a political organization the objects of which include the influencing of the political process or sponsoring a political agenda, whether or not it also seeks to sponsor or offer a platform to a candidate for election to a political office or to participate in the governance of Uganda at any level*'. Generally, a political party is a group of people who share a common conception of how and why state power should be organized and exercised. The contesting of the elective public offices is crucial, because it signifies the difference between parties and other social groups which do not seek to contest for political power or to occupy elective office. In this way, parties differ from all other political groups in society because they seek to influence government policy and undertake responsibilities for actually implementing such policies.

Although there continues to be controversy about the most desirable form of democracy,[4] in modern times democracy – usually qualified as liberal democracy – is a system of government based on a number of accepted principles.[5] They include: periodic elections which are free and fair and based on universal adult suffrage; respect for human rights, including freedom of speech, freedom of association and freedom of assembly; constitutionalism and rule of law and an independent judiciary; separation of powers between the organs of government; political accountability and transparency; existence of a civil society which is autonomous from the state; the mass media, that is television, radio, newspapers, are not monopolized by the government and have, within certain limits freedom to criticize government.

In addition to these elements of democracy, it is expected that entry and recruitment to positions of political power is relatively open and competition for power is transparent (not secretive) and based on established and accepted forms of procedure. Most importantly, it is assumed that there is a genuine and unfettered competition for power based on political groups. In other words, there is more than one party and the parties are able to compete freely with each other for political power.

It is generally agreed that political parties perform some very useful functions in the functioning of modern government. Several scholars highlight the functions of political parties.[6] First is political education. Parties achieve political education by highlighting the problems of society, outlining alternative approaches to possible solutions. Second is the aggregation of interests. In trying to work out a common platform on an election issue the party necessarily brings together the political interests and views of a large number of people thereby giving weight to each of the separate views or interests. Parties transform a multitude of specific demands into more manageable packages of proposals. Parties select, reduce and combine interests. They act as a filter between society and state, deciding which demands to allow through their net.

Third is the articulation of interests. Once the party has evolved a common programme on the basis of the interests of its members,[7] it mounts a campaign of education to sell its programme to the electorate. Through the use of various media, the party helps to give expression to political and social interests that would otherwise have remained private ideas, views or interests of specific individuals. Fourth is to act as a school or training ground for political leaders. Parties are a major source of recruitment of people into political and governmental leadership positions.

Fifth is provision of the choice of government. Parties provide citizens with alternative programmes for the governing of society, and therefore, make the choice of a government easier. Sixth is the identification of good and bad leaders – as a result of the close connection between governmental and party leadership, political parties also provide society with a ready means of identifying and rewarding successful leaders by a renewal of their mandate, while punishing incompetent ones by voting them out of office. Finally, political parties still serve as a point of reference for many supporters and voters, giving people a key to interpreting an otherwise complicated political world. To what extent have parties in Uganda played these roles during NRM rule?

Political parties, political transition and the NRM government

To understand contemporary party politics in Uganda, one has to look back at the country's history since parties first emerged as key political players. The first political party to be formed in Uganda was the Uganda National Congress (UNC) in 1952. UNC was led by Ignatius Musazi who was very influential in the Uganda African Farmers Union (UAFU). Prior to the establishment of the UNC, an organization of clan leaders, the Bataka Movement, together with the UAFU were influential in pressuring the colonial government for economic reforms in the 1940s. The leaderships of both pressure groups were subsequently influential in the formation of the UNC. However, by the time of independence, due to divisions related to ethnicity and religion, the UNC had collapsed. The collapse led to the emergence of separate political parties, among which were: the Democratic Party (DP) and the Uganda People's Congress (UPC).

Uganda has had only eight general elections since independence: 1962, 1980, 1996, 2001, 2006, 2011, 2016 and 2021. Six were conducted on the basis of multi-party competition (1962, 1980, 2006, 2011, 2016 and 2021). The major political parties that contested the 1962 elections were the DP and the UPC. These elections were marred by conflicts inspired by religious differences and arguments over the position of the King of Buganda *vis-à-vis* elected local politicians, and how the people of Buganda were going to be represented in the national legislature.[7] The conflicts and arguments resulted in the establishment of the Kabaka Yekka movement/political grouping that allied with UPC to form the first government of independent Uganda.

Multi-partyism did not last long after independence. In 1969, only seven years later, the Uganda People's Congress (UPC) government proscribed all rival parties as well as other organized interest groups and actors on the political scene, the Uganda National Union and the Uganda Farmers' Voice. Between the coup of 1971 which toppled the Obote government and the 1979 war which overthrew Idi Amin's military government, political parties went underground and reappeared shortly before the 1980 general elections. The elections which were conducted amidst state-instigated violence and intimidation of the opponents of the Obote-led UPC, involved four political parties: UPC, DP, the Conservative Party and the Uganda Patriotic Movement (UPM).

The 1980 elections were widely perceived as rigged in favour of the UPC at the expense of DP. A section of the leadership of UPM reacted by declaring war on the new government under Milton Obote, back in office for the second time. Along with other guerrilla groups, the former UPM now reconstituted as the National Resistance Army (NRA) fought the Obote government from 1981 to 1985. Unable to defeat the different rebel groups fighting in central Uganda and quite close to the seat of power, especially the NRA, Obote's army toppled the government in July 1985 and ushered in a military junta which was in turn overthrown by the NRA rebels in January 1986.

Ostensibly driven by a desire to reunite the country after years of political upheaval, the NRM subsequently established a broad-based government into which it invited individual members of other political groups but not representatives of parties. In fact one of the first major actions of Museveni's NRM government was to suspend activities of political parties under Legal Notice Number One of 1986. A provisional parliament, the National Resistance Council (NRC) was established, initially comprising appointed and later indirectly elected members.

A Constitutional Commission was appointed to gather views from the public about a proposed new constitution which would replace the 1967 Republican Constitution. Country-wide public consultations led to an elected Constituent Assembly (CA) whose role was to debate the findings of the Constitutional Commission and make a new constitution. In 1995 a new constitution was promulgated. It entrenched the 'Movement' as an alternative political system and maintained the suspension of political party activity. This happened against the wishes of what was by then a significant minority which was actively agitating for the restoration of multi-partism but which had little sympathy from the general public. The international community was also at the time still besotted with Museveni and the NRM and was generally supportive of the 'Movement' idea.[8] The promulgation of the new constitution opened the way for the first general elections in well over a decade, which were held in 1996 for president, parliament and local government leaders. It was also the very first time a president was elected through a direct ballot on the basis of universal adult suffrage.

The intellectual argument behind the proscription of multi-party politics was that Ugandan (and African) society was still backward and unable to function within a multi-party system without the influence of ethnic and religious affiliation. Its corollary was that such a society needed to be nurtured into maturity, for example by cultivating a large middle-class shorn of ethnic and religious bigotry, before multi-partism could be reintroduced. Coupled with the prolonged turmoil the country had hitherto experienced under one-party and military dictatorships and the havoc it had wreaked on economic and social structures, this argument was sufficiently powerful to convince large numbers of Ugandans fatigued by war and violence to support the idea of a break from political party activity. Also easily convinced was the international community which was eager to see the country stabilize and leave its ugly past behind.

It was against this background that the 1996 and 2001 elections were conducted under the so-called no-party 'Movement System'. Although preceded by quarrelsome and somewhat violent campaigns, the 1996 elections were perceived both inside the country and by external observers as generally peaceful and reflective of popular opinion. However, in 2001 the campaign-related violence and malpractices which preceded the elections were such that the losing candidate against President Museveni, Dr Kizza Besigye, petitioned the Supreme Court seeking to annul the election results. The Court ruled 5–0 that there had been widespread irregularities and non-compliance with provisions of the law, but ruled 3–2 against nullifying the results. The majority opinion of the Court contended that the malpractices had not been sufficient to have affected the outcome substantially.

The experience of the 1996 and 2001 elections ultimately undermined a key justification for suspending party activity: the argument that political parties, through their appeal to ethnic and religious sectarianism, had been responsible for fomenting political violence in the past. As it turned out, there was widespread state-instigated and perpetuated electoral violence even when political parties were no longer active. To continue the suspension of political party activity eventually became untenable especially with mounting external pressure from western donors as well as internal activism from pro-multiparty actors.

While support for continued prohibition of political-party activity was arguably logical and justified at the time the NRM seized power, the real intentions of the NRM leadership, which were to weaken the parties, and the devastating impact the enforced inactivity had on their capacity to organize and vie for power, became clear only after opposition to Museveni and the NRM started to grow and people began to agitate for the right to associate outside the 'Movement' system.[9] It was then that it became clear, also, that by supporting the NRM's curtailment of political-party activity, Ugandans and the international community had helped perpetuate Uganda's historically poor record on freedom of association.

The above developments represented a key phase in cementing Museveni's rule and providing a firm grounding for his long stay in power. For many years, whenever parties attempting to defy the prohibition of political party activity were harassed by the security forces, many local and foreign observers viewed such harassment as justified, and as a law-and-order matter, given that the law was clear on what they could and could not do. The long-term negative impact on the parties' development and the implications for their capacity to play the role of holding the government to account in future, were disregarded.

Prohibiting political parties from sponsoring candidates or campaigning for candidates vying for parliamentary elections meant that parties did not have formal representation in the legislature. Neither did they develop opportunities for grooming new leaders at the national level. However, some known members and supporters of political parties were elected to parliament on a 'no-party' platform. While in some cases they would have been elected on their individual merit as required by the law at the time, it was widely known that others were elected largely because of their affiliation with parties and avowed commitment to the principle of multiparty politics. This was partly because they usually expressed the known positions of their parties on various matters and were therefore seen as de facto representatives of those organizations. The party affiliation of a number of MPs was made more evident by the formation of party caucuses in parliament, even as far back as during the time of the CA, when the National Caucus for Democracy (NCD) stood for pluralism as opposed to the 'Movement' system.

The formation of caucuses and their apparent success at aggregating the collective positions of subscribers to multi-party politics which hitherto the Movement Secretariat had opposed eventually spurred the NRM into forming its own caucus in the CA and later in the Sixth Parliament. These developments demonstrated that, despite pretence to the contrary, the so-called 'Movement' system, was actually a party like the others, with insiders and outsiders. This was underscored in a landmark ruling by the Constitutional Court when the constitutionality of the 'Movement' system was challenged by members of the opposition Democratic Party led by its president, Paul Kawanga Ssemogerere. The NRM's adoption of the caucus idea from the parties stemmed from what was clearly their continued significance on the national political scene and their capacity, through their caucuses, to mount a spirited and sometimes effective challenge against the government in parliament, official restrictions notwithstanding.[10] For example, the DP and UPC had a long history and deep roots in society, dating from the pre-independence period, and enjoyed remarkable, if at the time mainly silent, support from their traditional supporters.

Until 1996 when Museveni was popularly, although controversially, elected for the first time under the 'Movement' system he had installed, he had ruled for ten years unelected and largely as a de facto military ruler. By the time of the 2001 elections, divisions in the Movement government had emerged. In 1999, Dr Kizza Besigye an insider and one of the 1986 war heroes issued a statement accusing the NRM government of undemocratic tendencies. Besigye's critique riled President Museveni who sought to have him prosecuted under military law, given he was a military officer at the time. He was saved by intervention by elders from his home district of Rukungiri and was retired from the army.

Besigye went on to challenge President Museveni in the 2001 elections, marking the first major split in the NRM and 'Movement' establishment. After the elections, this split in the NRM led to the coalescing of supporters of political parties and some disillusioned Movementists to form a loose grouping which they named 'Reform Agenda' and joined the ranks of those agitating for return to multiparty politics. The opposition to restrictions on parties was at its highest since 1986. The parliamentary elections which followed the presidential race were also marred by intimidation by the military, other security agencies and civilian agents of the state, of 'opposition' candidates.[11] Multi-partyists were therefore not contesting simply against a party disguised as a 'system', but against the state itself. By this time, however, local and international tolerance for the NRM's state-supported dominance and the government's determination to maintain its monopoly had to an extent worn thin. In 2005, a shift to multiparty politics was concluded by way of a national referendum and constitutional amendment.

Rebirth of multiparty politics

The decision to free parties and revert to multi-party politics stemmed from a number of considerations within the NRM itself, and pressure bearing on the government from several external quarters to bring 'Movement' politics to an end.[12] Among the sources of pressure was the donor community most of whose members had hitherto been staunch Museveni and NRM supporters and largely unsympathetic towards advocates of multi-partyism. Within the NRM, the key source of pressure and support for the lifting of restrictions on parties were dissenters from the mainstream view which favoured their retention.[13] Among them was, unsurprisingly, President Museveni and his coterie of inner-circle supporters.[14]

Although ideologically they were still opposed to the restoration of multi-party politics, President Museveni and a select group of close confidants saw in the pressure to restore multi-party politics a chance to pursue a clandestine scheme to amend the constitution and remove the article that imposed limits on the number of terms an individual could serve as president. Hence the appointment of the 'Ssempebwa Commission'. Consequently, as the debate about whether or not to restore multi-party politics captured the public's imagination, the question of whether or not to lift term limits from the constitution was smuggled onto the national agenda. It became a handy bargaining chip of sorts. Museveni's supporters were urging him to stand for another term in office, even as they knew that the constitution imposed a two-term limit on individuals serving as president.

By the close of 2005, Museveni had secured his coveted prize of unlimited terms, while political parties had won the freedom to organize and to canvass freely for support. It was victory for multipartyists but a bargaining chip for Museveni to remain eligible as a presidential candidate indefinitely barring the age-limit cap set at seventy-five, a hurdle that was removed in 2017 to pave way for Museveni's eligibility in the most recent elections in 2021.

President Museveni in particular made no secret of his continuing distaste for multi-party politics when he attributed the restoration of party politics to 'donor pressure', and to the need to get rid of those within the Movement who were dissatisfied, not to his own convictions.[15] His distaste for party competition was not entirely unrelated to what some of his closest associates characterize as a pathological fear of competition and defeat.[16]

When in August 2005, presidential term limits were lifted from the constitution through a majority vote (220 against 53) in parliament, amidst charges of bribery and intimidation of MPs by the executive, the question whether or not to free political parties from restrictions or retain the 'Movement' system was put to a referendum, also in August 2005. The referendum was opposed by some in the NRM who did not see its justification, given both the political party advocates and the NRM leadership had agreed to the return to multi-party politics from 2003. Political party leaders and their supporters boycotted the referendum as they had done with the one in 2000 which re-enacted the suspension of party activity.

The parties' strongly held position against the referendum was that freedom of association should not be subjected to a vote. When the referendum took place, turn-out was low, between 18 and 48 per cent. However, the majority (92.44 per cent) voted for multi-party politics to be reintroduced.[17] Political parties, including the successor to the Movement, the National Resistance Movement Organisation (NRM-O), had already began registering or applying to do so.[18] Nonetheless, although legally free to hold rallies, before the referendum parties were still subject to arbitrary harassment by the police and other security agencies. From time to time they disrupted their activities while allowing members and supporters of the NRM to hold public events unhindered.

Even after restrictions were fully lifted under the law, in reality political parties continued to contend with harassment from the police, security agencies and other agents of the state at national and especially local levels. In addition to public rallies suffering deliberate disruption, the police often withhold permission for them to be held. Meanwhile the law requires parties only to inform the police of impending rallies and their venues, not to seek permission to hold them.[19] It is not unusual for their leaders or cadres to be denied access to radio and TV stations in and outside the capital, Kampala. Meanwhile the activities of the ruling NRM and its agents are neither obstructed nor disrupted.

More importantly, the NRM remains fused with the state in significant ways, including having some of its officials in government employment with their salaries and allowances paid by the state rather than the party.[20] These officials routinely take advantage of their appointments in government to make use of state resources for party purposes, including campaigning for NRM candidates during presidential and parliamentary elections. Also, there have been reports of money being taken out of the accounts of ministries and spent on the activities of the party.[21] Even State House, the president's official residence, is routinely used to host large party meetings in total disregard of public opinion. To crown it all, members of the armed forces also divert army resources and time to activities that are intended to further the interests of the ruling party. Despite the official return to multi-party politics, therefore, the political playing field remains heavily skewed in favour of the NRM.

Impact of the suspension of political activity on political parties

The impact twenty years of enforced inactivity had on the parties in existence at the time was immense. As a starting point, the specific restrictions the law imposed on them must be revisited. Party activities were confined to their headquarters in Kampala. If they held events outside the capital, they had to be indoors. Even then, they had to secure approval of the police working alongside a range of local-level officials making up local security committees. Few meetings could take place given the litany of conditions to be fulfilled, obstruction by officials, and a perennial lack of resources.

Barred from opening branches and engaging with upcountry members on an on-going basis, parties were rendered incapable of renewing memberships through fresh recruitment exercises. Nor could they revive their local structures and networks which had broken down during the Obote II regime and the civil war of the first half of the 1980s, both of which rendered the normal practicing of party politics impossible. Then there was the restriction pertaining to sponsoring candidates for elections. A party prevented from competing for power, a key reason why parties emerge and grow, cannot hope to attract potential members seeking to build political careers. People seeking to join politics in pursuit of political careers were therefore more likely to seek to join the NRM with all the advantages it enjoyed. Parties could only count on veteran members to seek election, albeit on the basis of individual merit as the law required. Only in that way could their interests be represented.

Parties were prohibited from holding delegates conferences, the only mechanism through which they could hold elections and, if necessary, change leaders. This meant that, regardless of the quality of their leaders and of the leaders' services to the parties over the twenty-year period, they could not be removed. This brewed animosity and infighting as factions bickered over the need to change leadership, which was impossible without convening a proper delegates' conference. With key party organs not functioning partly because of the disarray in which members were left following the suspension of party activity, the question of formulating, defining and refining ideologies, core values or policy positions could not arise.

Hence, when the parties were eventually freed, they generally descended into internecine wars as members fought over positions and power rather than over policy or matters of principle or ideological importance. This has remained a lasting legacy long after the formal return to multiparty politics in 2005. Prevented from functioning as proper parties outside the period of elections, their capacity to compete effectively against the ruling party is severely limited. Coupled with the numerous restrictions imposed on them during periods of presidential and parliamentary polls, the term 'election parties' is a misnomer.

For a long time, at the grassroots people were still stuck in the mind-set of the previous no-party (individual-merit) politics which was replaced by the current multiparty system in 2005. For many people, support for a particular candidate running for any office was not necessarily linked to party membership. Rather, candidates were judged on their own personal merit, such as their potential for delivering the services deemed beneficial to the community or what they could offer voters in terms of material or financial incentives. For people who make decisions in this kind of way, ideological considerations do not matter when it comes to deciding who to elect. It would suggest that individual candidates for election matter more than the parties to which they belong and ostensibly represent in an election and when in office. It matters not which party espouses what ideology; people make decisions on the basis of evaluation of the personal bonafides of particular candidates or even peer influence (the bandwagon effect). This is another lasting legacy of the 'Movement' or no-party politics. It has negatively impacted the strength, presence and place of political parties and contributed indirectly to the perpetuation of Museveni's rule.

During the years that political parties spent under restriction, the NRM took advantage of the absence of competition to build and consolidate its position. In this it benefitted a great deal from the absorption into the government and eventually into its own ranks, of prominent and experienced members and leaders of the political parties which it had co-opted into the government in 1986. Also, the NRM became dominant because of the advantages of incumbency and the unlimited access it had to state resources as a result.

Meanwhile, the free haemorrhage of talent from opposition political parties deprived them of the human resources necessary to build and sustain them as credible and worthy competitors for power. The restrictions against holding public meetings severely constrained their capacity to recruit new members and to keep them motivated to remain in the party to serve the purpose partly of injecting new blood in their leaderships.

The impact of all this could be seen in intra-party demographics, whereby many of the party leaders were for many years past retirement age, having been active since before independence. The consequence of this in some parties was the explosion of intra-party conflicts pitting the old guard against so-called young Turks. When the young Turks eventually took over the reins of power, their lack of leadership skills and experience was evident in the difficulties they encountered in their efforts to unite parties which had been torn apart by internal conflicts. This has been the case in the two main and oldest political parties – the DP and UPC.

While restrictions against opening offices outside Kampala constrained the capacity of parties to keep in touch with their old members before 2005, currently it is the lack of resources coupled with obstruction by state operatives that prevents this. The lack of contact with supporters and activists outside the capital has deprived the parties of much-needed financial resources which in the past they received as subscription or registration fees and which played an important role in helping them to manage their affairs. It has also rendered difficult the task of building structures and recruiting new members from the countryside.

Another consequence of two decades of enforced inactivity was diminished access to resources and a decline in the capacity to mobilize them. In the past, UPC and DP to some extent depended on membership subscriptions. Over the twenty-year period of stagnation, memberships lapsed and were never renewed. This lowered significantly the levels of income that parties could get from this crucial source. Worse still, potential individual donors feared making donations, lest they be accused of collaborating with 'anti-government elements', which is what political parties had become. Apparently, some people who have donated money to opposition parties have suffered repercussions, including forcing their businesses into bankruptcy or losing their public sector jobs.[22]

Also, having rendered parties redundant, the restrictions meant that they could not devise resource mobilization strategies and devise mechanisms through which they could be implemented. Their difficulties were compounded by the unrestricted access the NRM had to state resources through its fusion with the state. It was a contest of the extremely unequal. The difficulties faced by their older counterparts did not spare the new parties when they emerged starting in 2005. A brief examination of the scale of difficulties all opposition parties face in connection with resource mobilization shows the extent to which they are constrained.[23]

With the exception of the UPC which receives some funding from its own Milton Obote Foundation, parties are generally and mainly financed through donations from well-wishers in Uganda and outside the country, including Ugandans in the diaspora and foreign parties and their foundations. Other financial resources come from member contributions. These can be in the form of purchases of membership cards which, although entailing small amounts of money with cards costing no more than Uganda shillings 1,000 in most cases, bring in only small amounts, because there are few card-carrying members. There are also parties which depend largely on a small number of backers, among them, their own leaders. For example, as president of DP, John Ssebaana Kizito used his ample wealth to finance many of its activities.

Why opposition political parties are ineffective actors

Despite the existence of all the necessary legislation to guide the working of a multi-party political system in Uganda, there are still misgivings about the behaviour of the NRM government when it comes to political tolerance and respect for divergent actors especially parties. This is one of the main obstacles to the flouring of multi-party politics. For instance, President Museveni is fond of hurling insults at opposition leaders and their aspirations in a bid to undermine their credibility and, as a result, their ability to garner support and take a realistic shot at power. Opposition party supporters and their leaders have been constantly harassed, arrested and detained. The harsh treatment is meant to instil fear in their members and supporters and to obstruct their activities so that others who might aspire to oppose the government are effectively dissuaded from doing so. If the state were truly in support of multi-party politics, the opposition would not face such harassment. This lack of tolerance and respect for alternative views is one reason why the government has been so resolute in its efforts to obstruct the activities of opposition parties in order to keep them weak.

President Museveni has used the army and police to suppress the opposition, money and state patronage to recruit support, engineer defections from opposition groups to the NRM, reward loyalty, and pay off actual and potential opponents. After a long time of resisting Museveni's attempts, sections of the DP and UPC, or at a minimum their official leaderships, finally succumbed to the NRM's advances by negotiating so called 'cooperation agreements' – the UPC doing so ahead of the 2016 elections after which party member and MP Betty Amongi, also wife to disputed party president Jimmy Akena, was appointed to Museveni's cabinet.[24] More recently, in July 2022, DP president Norbert Mao signed a 'cooperation agreement' with NRM and was appointed Minister of Justice and Constitutional Affairs.[25]

In Uganda today, the decision to join or support a political party is not entirely devoid of strategizing for employment. It is widely believed that once one belongs to the party in power, they will have privileged access to job opportunities that tend to be closed off to outsiders. This belief is hardly mistaken given the NRM's fusion with the state. The fusion enables its leadership to reward party supporters with jobs in a wide range of areas, a point President Museveni routinely emphasizes.[26] For people looking for an easy way to power, fame, influence and wealth, the NRM, by virtue of being in power, has become the party of choice.

For people seeking to embark on political careers, the choice of which party to join is informed by considerations of its relative strength *vis-à-vis* other parties, and also its popularity which serves as a pointer to how easy or difficult it may be for its candidates to win elections. Consequently, people are inclined to join a party (in this case the NRM) which they judge to have the greatest potential to win elections or to enable them to win should they consider running for parliament, for example. In a country with high rates of unemployment and where politicians earn among the highest salaries and allowances and are therefore some of the wealthiest people, the attraction of becoming a councillor or Member of Parliament is very strong.

The NRM's long stay in power has generated a general perception by members of the public that there is no credible potential alternative among opposition parties. It is arguable that few Ugandans actually support the NRM because of its values or aspirations. It is not so much out of conviction. Rather, for many, the attraction of the NRM is linked to the belief that 'better the devil you know than the angel you don't'. Accordingly, the NRM is strong because the other parties are viewed as weak and disconnected from the public. It is not because of any intrinsic values the NRM espouses or its performance as the ruling party. On its own, without the power of the state, the NRM is not a solid and sound institution.

In the main, opposition political parties have found it difficult to recruit members. Even if they had well-laid-out formal mobilization strategies, they face a key constraint in the lack of financial and human resources. Of no less significance is the obstructive behaviour of the police and security agencies generally which deny opposition parties permission to hold rallies or which disrupt their gatherings as and when they choose. Owing to these constraints, opposition party candidates resort to informal mobilization strategies whenever a chance presents itself. It could be during public functions such as wedding and engagement ceremonies, burials, last funeral rites, religious functions etc.

However, the NRM enjoys the advantage of having access to state resources. That plus the total freedom it enjoys from police harassment translates into great capacity for mobilization. In addition, the NRM takes advantage of opportunities provided by so-called ideological training in different parts of the country, including at the National Leadership Institute (NALI) at Kyankwanzi, to recruit members and supporters. All this allows the party to reach out to people in ways opposition parties cannot.

Observers attribute frequent internal wrangles and factional breakaways afflicting political parties to the NRM and Museveni's actions that seek to weaken the opposition. Hence, the NRM has employed a strategy of compromising and co-opting opposition party leaders, which causes confusion in the affected parties, leading to internal conflicts and disharmony. The upheaval in parties underscores a failure by their leaderships to build cohesive organizations and muster the institutional capacity to challenge the NRM.[27] This, however, has to be understood in the context of the overall political and security environment that is hostile to the free functioning of a multiparty system. Failure to build cohesion has undermined their development into organizations with credible chances of defeating the ruling party at the polls and winning power. Internal wrangles and breakaways, especially at national level, are signs of weakness which undermines the well-being of any party. Consequently, key opposition members have over the years been easily lured into joining the ruling NRM.[28]

Failed attempts at change and transformation

Different approaches have been used to bring parties together in inter-party dialogues to discuss issues that advance democracy and development in Uganda. However, suspicions among the larger and older political parties have undermined the effectiveness of dialogue as a mechanism for initiating much-needed change. Two cases demonstrate this. The first is the Inter Party Organisation for Dialogue (IPOD). The second are the opposition alliances. IPOD – which brings together all political parties with representation in parliament – was established courtesy of a three-year Memorandum of Understating in 2017, with fourteen objectives, including fostering and facilitating peaceful mitigation and resolution of conflict without resorting to undemocratic means such as violence.

IPOD decisions are made through its summit, the topmost organ that brings together the presidents of all member parties. However, its future remains uncertain as its facilitators and member political parties accuse the government of failing to implement its resolutions.[29] Among them was the failure to implement a resolution on increased funding of IPOD to stop dependence on donors.

Needless to say, tensions have arisen between the parties, leading to a loss of trust in IPOD. Disdain for the body escalated when FDC, JEEMA and UPC decided to boycott the third ordinary summit of leaders of IPOD-affiliated parties, chaired by President Yoweri Museveni on Friday 5 March 2021. Among other demands, the opposition parties wanted Mr Museveni to apologize to them for what they termed 'shameless abuse' of the Constitution and the rights of members of the opposition and the public.

At another level, opposition alliances are considered a potential solution to the weakness of individual parties and the fragmentation of the opposition in general under conditions of authoritarianism.[30] However, opposition alliances in Uganda are often formed shortly before elections and usually collapse even before they are tried and tested by the electorate. Indeed, in each and every general election cycle since independence, there have been attempts at forming political coalitions.[31] Unfortunately, each time they have either failed immediately, or collapsed soon after formation, or just after the elections. The 2015/16 coalition collapse was by the most instructive. Opposition party alliances during the NRM era have for the most part been ineffective and sometimes even counterproductive. There are many explanations for these coalition failures, ranging from inner-party struggles to contextual conditions.[32]

For instance, general elections took place in 1996, but under the so-called 'Movement' system, according to which political parties were banned from sponsoring candidates. Nevertheless, opposition political parties and organizations established the Inter-party Forces Cooperation (IPFC) led by veteran politician Paul Ssemwogerere, who had competed against Milton Obote for the nation's top job back in December 1980. An attempt at coalition was repeated in the 2011 elections via the Inter-Party Cooperation (IPC) led by Kizza Besigye. Both the IPFC and the IPC fronted a joint candidate for president but did not succeed in wrestling the presidency from President Museveni. In the case of the IPC, the DP snubbed the alliance as its president, Norbert Mao, contested in the 2011 elections, as did Jabeli Bidandi Ssali of the newly formed People's Progressive Party (PPP).

Before the 2016 elections, opposition parties and NRM factions of former Prime Minister, Amama Mbabazi, and former Vice President Gilbert Bukenya, attempted to form an electoral coalition known as The Democratic Alliance (TDA).[33] Negotiations took place between the notable contenders for a joint candidacy of the opposition. However, the parties failed to agree on a single candidate for president, between FDC's Kizza Besigye and Amama Mbabazi who had decamped from the NRM. A majority of opposition parties moved to nominate Mbabazi, but the FDC rejected his candidacy and the TDA alliance collapsed. The parties subsequently faced Museveni individually although a section of the opposition supported Mbabazi while the overwhelming anti-Museveni public mood went with Besigye as the most credible challenger to the incumbent. There were no attempts at coalition building in the run-up to the 2021 elections because parties were beset by feuds, acrimony, suspicion and numerous defections from one party to another.

Some scholars argue that Museveni has not used only the stick to undermine coalition formations, but also the carrot of political patronage.[34] Hence, the regime has created numerous politically inspired posts that are dangled in front of potential political opponents to co-opt them.[35] Such posts are used as sources of patronage to buy off dissidents and prevent any formidable opposition coalition from emerging. Most prominent opposition leaders – the latest being DP's Nobert Mao – are co-opted into these positions, thereby depriving the opposition of credible leaders and also denting the image of opposition leaders as unprincipled and amenable to compromise. This explains why the National Unity Platform (NUP), currently the biggest opposition party in parliament, led by Robert Kyagulanyi, popularly known as Bobi Wine, has to an extent become an ineffectual actor in the politics of Uganda.

Some analysts have claimed, not without justification, that the NRM government is a military government in civilian disguise.[36] There are indeed valid reasons for such claims. For from 1986 until 2004, President Museveni was a serving military officer, substantive minister of defence and Commander-in-Chief of the Armed Forces. Even after retiring from the army, he continues to go around the country, attending public meetings and rallies in military fatigues. This is especially in areas where the population is largely opposed to his government or where his popularity is not that high. The army now has a well-established reputation and record of supporting ruling-party positions, including the controversial lifting of term limits in 2005 where all army MPs, save for one abstainer, voted in favour of the motion. Also, serving military officers have a history of siding with the NRM during election campaigns, usually through hostile pronouncements and actions against opposition groups and their leaders, supporters and activists.

In recent times the former Commander of the Land Forces and now Senior Presidential Advisor on Special Operations, Gen Muhoozi Kainerugaba, who is President Museveni's son, was sued for allegedly engaging in political activities and pronouncements. Lawyer Gawaya Tegulle petitioned court challenging what he called the 'unconstitutional acts' by Gen Muhoozi, of engaging in political activities and pronouncements as he celebrated his 48th birthday in April 2022 despite being a serving army officer.[37] The plaint asserts that Article 208(2) of the Ugandan constitution states that the UPDF shall be non-partisan, national in character, patriotic, professional, disciplined, productive and subordinate to civilian authority.

The country has a long history of militarism that has cowed Ugandans.[38] In such a hostile environment, parties suffer and are not able to contribute much to strengthening democracy because most citizens are afraid to challenge the state due to historical reasons and current realities. More recently, there has been the systemic brutalizing of the opposition by members of the armed forces, police and intelligence agencies. Further, a culture of political apathy prevents many from active participation in politics on the opposition side.

Conclusion

Multi-party politics operates under a system in which there are multiple active political parties with ample space to play their rightful roles. This ensures a choice of organizations through which people can participate in politics, have their voices heard, and ensure that their aspirations are reflected in the decisions the government makes. Despite the existence and operation of political parties in Uganda, they have largely been and continue to be ineffectual political actors. This is largely because of the dilemmas and tribulations they face courtesy of the incumbent party leadership that professes to be democratic while ruling autocratically.

The tribulations include dealing with a sitting government whose leadership is determined to destroy them, and a strong perception by the population that they are not able to mount a successful challenge to the party in power. There is deeply held apathy and resignation against opposition parties while the NRM enjoys a sense of invincibility.

These factors have combined to facilitating the continuation of Museveni's autocratic rule which is built on using state assets and resources to ensure that the ruling party remains dominant. What all this implies is that multi-party politics in Uganda has not been conducive to the emergence and growth of democracy. For countries in similar conditions as Uganda, the prospects of evolving into a vibrant multiparty democracy depend on whether the ruling party and the leadership in charge deem it necessary to preside over the creation of conditions that allow and enable their rivals to play their rightful roles within an appropriately regulated environment. Also, this chapter highlights the need for focused research into the impact of regime longevity on party development and prospects for transforming an authoritarian dispensation into a progressive and democratic one more generally.

Notes

1   While political parties can be agents of democratization, it is not obvious that 'multiparty' politics can be.
2   George M. Bob-Milliar, 'Activism of Political Parties in Africa', in *Oxford Research Encyclopaedia of Politics* (Oxford: Oxford University Press, 2019).
3   Andrew Heywood, *Politics* (London: Palgrave, 2019).
4   Issa G. Shivji, 'The Democracy Debate in Africa: Tanzania', *Review of African Political Economy* 18, no. 50 (1991): 79–91.

5   Sabiti Makara, 'The Challenge of Building Strong Political Parties for Democratic Governance in Uganda: Does Multiparty Politics have a Future'? *Les Cahiers d'Afrique de l'Est / The East African Review* 41 (2009): 43–80.

6   Russell J. Dalton, David M. Farrell and Ian McAllister, *Political Parties and Democratic Linkage: How Parties Organize Democracy* (Oxford: Oxford University Press, 2011).

7   The latter argument was over whether Members of Parliament from Buganda region could be elected directly by the population, or indirectly by the Lukiiko, the kingdom's own legislature. Under instructions from their powerful monarchy, most Baganda boycotted the elections which were won by the Catholic-dominated Democratic Party whose leadership had defied the royalist view that MPs be elected by the Lukiiko.

8   The constitution provided for three political systems: the movement system, the multi-party system and any other democratic and representative system (Article 69), and for regular referenda to decide what system to adopt. Following the adoption of one system, others would be held in abeyance for the duration. The first referendum held in 2000 and boycotted by political parties, endorsed the continuation of the 'Movement' system.

9   For a detailed study of the impact of the nearly two-decade suspension of political party activity on political parties, see Giovanni Carbone, *No-Party Democracy? Ugandan Politics in Comparative Perspective* (Boulder, CO and London: Lynne Rienner Publishers, 2008).

10 See, for example, J. Oloka-Onyango, 'New Wine or New Bottles? Movement Politics and One-partyism in Uganda', in *No-Party Democracy in Uganda: Myths and Realities*, ed. Justus Mujaju and J. Oloka-Onyango (Kampala: Fountain Publishers, 2000).

11 Government of Uganda, *Report of the Select Committee on Election Violence and Other Related Matters* (Kampala, 2002).

12 Eriya Tukahirwe Kategaya, *Impassioned for Freedom* (Kampala: Wavah Books, 2006).

13 The pressure from within the Movement camp had actually started way back in 1994, in the Constituent Assembly. Three army representatives, among them Kiiza Besigye (who late became an opposition activist and four-time presidential candidate, also former president of opposition FDC party), Lt. Colonel Sserwanga Lwanga, and Major-General (now Retired General) David Tinyefuza had pushed for an early relaxation of the stranglehold on parties, only to be slapped down by the Movement political machine.

14 In 2002 the president appointed a task force to study the question of whether the country should continue being ruled under the Movement system, or whether restrictions on political parties should be lifted. The task force, comprising mainly known supporters of Museveni and his government, recommended the continuation of the Movement system. A veteran politician, and until recently a committed Museveni supporter, however, wrote a minority report arguing for the freeing of parties. The latter argument won the day.

15 Muniini Mulera, 'Museveni Hasn't Changed Heart, Only Strategy', *Daily Monitor*, Kampala (23 February 2003).

16 The Observer, 'Why Museveni Fears NRM Vote', Kampala (16 February 2014). https://observer.ug/component/content/article?id=30192:-why-museveni-fears-nrm-vote

17 See https://www.electionguide.org/elections/id/14/

18   The NRM-O was the first party ever to register in Uganda's history, as before 2003 parties were not required to register.

19   The issue of police "permission" for public rallies and other political events, has long been a contentious one. Indeed, the relevant provision of the Police Act was challenged in the courts of law in the case of *Muwanga Kivumbi v. The Attorney General*. Although the court declared the section unconstitutional, the ruling was simply ignored and compounded by the enactment of the notorious Public Order and Management Act (POMA). But in 2020 the Constitutional Court struck down Section 8 of POMA that had smuggled back the provision in the Police Act requiring permission to hold activities like political rallies.

20   Several senior party officials are ministers, ambassadors and, according to the press, security operatives.

21   Conversations with senior civil servants over several years.

22   Reports which are difficult to substantiate claim that members of the business community who were seen or believed to support the opposition, became the targets of punitive taxes and cancellation or denial of government contracts. Whether by coincidence or not, it is also true that a sizeable number of opposition-leaning members of the business community have lost their businesses through bankruptcy and indebtedness. Those in government employment often lost their jobs (interviews with several opposition personalities).

23   Information on party funding comes from Leni Wild and Fred Golooba-Mutebi, 'Review of International Assistance to Political Party and Party System Development: Case Study Report, Uganda', Overseas Development Institute (August 2010). The paper details the different ways through which parties in Uganda manage to secure funding to run their offices and (try to) perform their other functions. Here we exclude important sources of funding such as the donor-funded Deepening Democracy Programme and others which have injected large amounts of money into parties, but whose money is tied to specific activities and is not available for use as they see fit.

24   Sulaiman Kakaire, 'Museveni Cabinet Job Splits Obote Family', *The Observer*, Kampala (10 June 2016). https://observer.ug/news-headlines/44707-museveni-cabinet-job-splits-obote-family.

25   The Independent, 'Deal: Mao Signs Cooperation Agreement with Museveni', Kampala (21 July 2022). https://www.independent.co.ug/mao-signs-cooperation-agreement-with-museveni/

26   See, for example, Eriasa Mukiibi Sserunjogi and Dicta Asiimwe, 'We Don't Want Your Jobs: Why Party Losers are Defying Museveni', *The Independent*, Kampala (1–7 October 2010). https://www.independent.co.ug/dont-want-nrm-jobs/.

27   Moses Khisa and Sabastiano Rwengabo, 'Beyond Legal Reform in Understanding Opposition Underperformance', in *Controlling Consent: Uganda's 2016 Elections*, ed. J. Oloka-Onyango and Josephine Ahikire (Trenton, NJ: Africa World Press, 2017).

28   As happened ahead of the 2011 elections. See Daily Monitor, 'Top UPC Chiefs Cross to NRM', Kampala (1 November 2010). https://www.monitor.co.ug/uganda/special-reports/elections/top-upc-chiefs-cross-to-nrm-1480868

29   The Independent, 'NIMD, Politicians Question the Future of IPOD', Kampala (8 February 2022). https://www.independent.co.ug/nimd-politicians-question-the-future-of-ipod/

30   See Leonardo R. Arriola, *Multi-ethnic Coalitions in Africa: Business Financing of Opposition Election Campaigns* (Cambridge: Cambridge University Press, 2013).

31 Sallie Simba Kayunga, 'Unpacking the Politics of Opposition Political Party Partnerships: The Democratic Alliance (TDA)', in Controlling Consent.

32 Mwambutsya Ndebesa, 'Forging Political Coalitions in Uganda: A Difficult but Necessary Task in an Emerging Democracy', *Rosa Luxemburg Stiftung* (30 October 2021). https://www.rosalux.de/en/news/id/43268/forging-political-coalitions-in-uganda

33 Ibid.

34 Richard Vokes and Sam Wilkins, 'Party, Patronage and Coercion in the NRM'S 2016 Re-Election in Uganda: Imposed or Embedded?', *Journal of Eastern African Studies* 10, no. 4 (2016): 581–600.

35 Ndebesa, 'Forging Political Coalitions'.

36 Moses Khisa, 'Politicisation and Professionalisation: The Progress and Perils of Civil-Military Transformation in Museveni's Uganda', *Civil Wars* 22, no. 2–3 (2021): 304.

37 Faustin Mugabe, 'When Soldiers Were Accused of Making Political Statements', *Sunday Monitor*, Kampala (22 May 2022). https://www.monitor.co.ug/uganda/magazines/people-power/when-soldiers-were-accused-of-making-political-statements-3822834.

38 Amii Omara-Otunnu, 'The Currency of Militarism in Uganda', in *The Military and Militarism in Africa*, ed. Eboe Hutchful and Abdoulaye Bathily (Dakar: CODESRIA, 1998).

Conclusion: Uganda at political crossroads?

Moses Khisa and Sabastiano Rwengabo

This book has underscored that autocratization – the antithesis to democratization – evolves in the context of regular elections, constitutional and legal rules regulating the exercise of state power and where democratic institutions coexist with authoritarian practices. Rules-based orders or the mere existence of democratic institutions is not synonymous with democratic government or democratization for that matter. A system of rules and institutions, whether written or otherwise, does not necessarily translate into democratic governance.

Quite to the contrary, democratic institutions can be handy tools for autocratization. Rules can be manipulated, instrumentalized and abused or simply set aside in service of the narrow interests of regime elites. Rules and institutions can also be selectively applied to stifle opposition voices and groups, or they can be conveniently evoked, modified or manipulated to suit the interests of incumbent rulers. State structures can be hitched to patrimonial controls by the top elite actors, who stifle the independent operation of state institutions and curtail healthy state-society relations.

This book has critically analysed the Uganda case where the fusion between the ruling party, government and the state has served to entrench President Yoweri Museveni's long rule. As detailed in the preceding chapters, Museveni's autocratic reign has been legitimated through regular elections, inclusive co-optation, the establishment of a facade of democratic institutions and the maintenance of a semblance of the rule of law. He has also drawn heavily on the coercive arsenal of the state with the national army, police and other security agencies playing a pivotal role in the grand scheme of things. By successfully navigating his way to rule for so long and cultivate a system of rule built around him, Museveni has sowed the seeds of a future potential crisis and the persistence of wide-ranging uncertainty, indeed trepidation, over a viable system of governing the country.

At the start of the decade of the 2020s, Uganda sits at a precarious, if altogether dangerous, political crossroads. There is uncertainty over the present and future of the country's politics, economy and broader social relations especially intra, interethnic coexistence and the viability of the nation-state project. While Uganda faces similar socio-economic strains much of the world is wrestling with against the backdrop of a global pandemic and a raging violent conflict in Eastern Europe, a potentially explosive and uniquely domestic political atmosphere looms large. This potential crisis is at its core about a peaceful transition and how to forge a stable political order in the context of deepening autocratization, militarism and a growing militant agitation for change that could well go in the direction of violent confrontation between those in charge of state power and the forces pushing for end to the status quo.

Uganda's social situation is deeply worrying with latent inter-ethnic, intra-regional and inter-regional tensions; demographic pressures; communal and state-society contestations over land, water and other non-renewable resources. These varied yet converging social strains are compounded by climate change-induced conditions that imperil the material, ecological and environmental well-being for a country still facing pervasive poverty and dire material conditions for majority of citizens. On a very specific political front, there are no indications that President Museveni will relinquish power peacefully anytime in the near future, yet Uganda needs precisely a power transition in order to guarantee stability in politics as a prerequisite for any meaningful economic progress. The urgency for rapid economic transformation and expansion of economic opportunities cannot be overemphasized in a country of mounting social and demographic pressures as an overwhelmingly youth population closes in on the 50 million mark.

Over the past four decades, there has been one constant on the Ugandan socio-political scene: the now septuagenarian President Museveni. This book has focused on Museveni, for good reasons, considering the deep contours of his long rule and how under his presidency Uganda has gradually descended into a deeper autocratic system. At the same time, the book has also attempted to go beyond the man so as to understand the country's wider politics and society in the *pax-Musevenica* era.[1]

The key focus of the anthology is in understanding the making of a regime of rule that other scholars characterized as 'hybrid', revolving around Museveni and his inner circle,[2] but which in recent years has accelerated into a decidedly personalist, repressive system primarily focused on retaining power perpetually and at all costs. In the main, Museveni has acquired the status of an imperial president who presides over a state and government with a *modus vivendi* of a police state.[3] This process entailed the evolution of institutionalized arbitrariness in which Museveni's unchecked and unaccountable power is 'exercised in such a way that those affected cannot predict or understand how power is wielded and have no means of questioning or challenging it'.[4] How has this been possible and what are the different recipes?

The promise and peril of Museveni's politics

The promulgation of the 1995 constitution promised to place power in the hands of the people through a rule-based government, and a compact with Uganda's citizens exercising and expressing their consent on who should govern them and how. For the most part, the constitutional promise embedded in the 1995 constitution has since been usurped and the 'people's consent' has been heavily controlled.[5] Such control is manifest in a variety of ways including militarism, constitutional manipulation, the abuse of state institutions including parliament and the judiciary, the shrinking of civic and democratic space and sustained repression against the political opposition. The different chapters in this volume have cast the spotlight on these many facets of Museveni's rule, the making and unmaking of a revolutionary regime and how power pursuits and the agency of a range of actors, institutions and structural forces have placed Uganda in a political tempest.

While Uganda has witnessed tremendous changes, socially, demographically and economically, the country's politics in the main remains trapped in the same old postcolonial conundrum and the jinx of post-independence – viable statehood and accountable government. This includes the failure to establish a routinized and predictable system of change of leadership at the top and the fashioning of an elite pact that endures and assures long-term stability. In the absence of critical pillars of government accountability and broad civic empowerment, political institutions are beholden to big-man controls and coercion.

Given the developments underway in Uganda under Museveni, there are important contrasts to draw with immediate neighbours and the key East Africa Community (EAC) peers, Kenya and Tanzania, both of which have had periodic and quite predictable changes of leadership at the top. Even Burundi – for long beset with cycles of crises and bloody violence – witnessed an accelerated transfer of power to the newly-elected president Évariste Ndayishimiye on 18 June 2020 following the sudden death of President Pierre Nkurunziza. In that regard, Burundi seems to fair better than Uganda. Neighbouring and troubled Democratic Republic of Congo (DRC) witnessed a post-election, post-Mobutu change of leadership at the top, from Joseph Kabange Kabila to Félix Antoine Tshisekedi Tshilombo on 25 January 2019. That is not to say that these neighbouring countries have become immune to political crises; it is that they have experimented with a relatively peaceful change of top leadership, an opportunity promised but not delivered to Uganda since Museveni ascended power in 1986.

For much of the early years of his rule, Museveni received praise as a revolutionary, or at a minimum reformist, president.[6] In recent years, such acclamation has been replaced with a deep sense of trepidation and disappointment as NRM rule has become rusted, autocratic and repressive. Indeed, Uganda appears likely to join the trend of father-to-son presidential transitions witnessed on the African continent since the early 2000s.[7]

What has transpired in Uganda over the past four decades is not strictly reducible to Museveni. Nevertheless, he has been the single most important actor. He has incomparably shaped the country's political trajectory. Museveni has been far more consequential than whole institutions of state and government. He has exacted a deep and far-reaching imprint on the country, for good and bad. He has had a larger-than-life presence, wielding enormous power and control in the clientelist system analysed by Nelson Kasfir's chapter in this volume. Yet, despite his enormous role and unrivalled place in the annals of Ugandan history, there is more to be said about a much broader range of forces and structures driving the country's political development over and beyond the person of Museveni.

Uganda's socio-political and historical context may have shaped Museveni's politics and aided his ascendance to power, but in turn the country's governing infrastructure of the last four decades has had Museveni's ubiquitous and unmistakable imprint. Museveni is a product of Uganda's chequered post-independence politics, in the same vain he has played monumental roles in the making of Uganda especially since 1986. Throughout his long rule, Museveni has mostly had his way, although not always, successfully navigated a plethora of challenges and complications around his rule but also encountered obstacles and impediments he could not overcome. Yet no obstacle, including regime uncertainty, has heretofore imperilled his rule or significantly compromised his grip on the country.

This book has attempted to sketch out the contours and configurations that have created possibilities and impossibilities in the political circuit of rule superintended by Yoweri Museveni. His domination of Ugandan society and politics unfolded in ways that were decidedly unprecedented in the country's history. Indeed, Museveni has few parallels across the African continent. For one, he has outlived most of his Ugandan colleagues in the ruling party and his continental peers, writ large, with the exceptions of Theodore Obiang and Paul Biya. Museveni has impressively weathered storms and struggles against his rule at different times in the course of the decades of his stay at the helm. He has counterbalanced internal and external threats and opportunities, becoming a master of political survival, employing both deception and dexterity, coercion and co-optation.

Yet, as we show in this book, a broader, in fact comprehensive and compelling, account of Museveni's long rule and the autocratic deepening, now manifest in the different economic and political realms, must theoretically as well as empirically capture the bigger picture. Such an effort needs to cover a wider terrain that straddles a range of actors, institutions, structures and processes. That is, there is more to Museveni and his rule than just Museveni 'the man'.

President Museveni has not just outlasted his Ugandan colleagues with whom he captured power in 1986 and peers on the continent; his long rule has crossed generations. He has lived through profound cultural, technological and ecological transformations, domestically and internationally, and has been an active player in a great number of developments regionally and globally. These include, inter alia, the Global War on Terror (GWOT),[8] the revival of the EAC, the transformation of the Organisation of African Unity (OAU) into African Union (AU), 'Africa's World War' in the DRC and debates about reform of the United Nations especially the Security Council.

From the start, Museveni's rule was fundamentally built on militarism and coercive power, on the command of the means of violence, but the forces and structures that underpinned his ascendance to power in 1986 were quite different from the manifold dynamics and developments that are at play nearly forty years later. A lot has changed that places matters over and above the persona of Museveni as an individual ruler and his ruling regime. For better or worse, the Uganda of 1986 is not the one of four decades later. And yet, the two Ugandas have the same man at the helm: Museveni. This in itself is simply extraordinary and a pertinent empirical puzzle. Equally important, in fact arguably more important, is the huge implications that abound for the country, now and in the years ahead, as the stakes become higher and the political pressure piles.

The trajectory and travails of Musevenism

This book has framed Museveni's long rule in terms of autocratic adaptability, which suggests there is a thread (or sets of threads) that combine change and continuity, progress and retrogression, transformation but also stagnation. In the early years, Museveni was seen by especially Ugandans in central, southwest and parts of the east (south Uganda, broadly) and external allies as truly revolutionary and as representing a major departure from previously brutal post-independence leaderships and governments. A key feature of the Uganda before 1986, which Museveni highlighted as a rallying call, was the abuse of coercive state power with uniformed personnel engaging in egregious abuses and no robust accountability mechanisms to reign them in. The gun was used extensively against hapless civilians.

Museveni's 1986 declaration that Uganda was witnessing not just another change of guard but 'a fundamental change' gained significant traction and embrace from large sections of the Ugandan public desperate and hopeful for turning the corner to a Uganda where personal freedoms and respect for fundamental rights would become entrenched. Many Ugandans construed the promise and agenda of the NRM regime as placing the country on a new pedestal and progressive path. Fast forward to four decades later, Museveni no longer enjoys the extensive support and goodwill he once commanded from across much of the country (except the-then rebellious north and northeast).

Museveni initially built his rule around the solid support he garnered from the 'south' of Uganda during and after the war that brought him to power. This support was in part predicated on a northern foil ostensibly associated with the previous governments of Obote and Amin. Ugandans in central and southwest held grievances against these past governments, faulted for wrongs against civilians and political opponents using the state's coercive arsenal during the turbulent and troubled decades of the 1960s through to the 1980s but especially 1981–5 when the NRA and other rebel groups fought Obote's government.

In that regard, as analysed in Chapter 9 by Moses Khisa, it is instructive that the central region has recently turned politically 'rebellious' against Museveni, albeit through ballots and not bullets, while the north 'crossed' to the NRM starting with the 2011 elections. In a sense, the north and central have switched political sides, which is testimony to the tectonic shifts and challenges that Museveni has had to contend with in his long rule. It speaks to Museveni's autocratic adaptability in managing shifts in regional support in ways that serve his continued stay in power.

Museveni's long rule has entailed divergences and variations in its tenor, tone and texture and precisely why, as we argue in this book, he has been able to adapt to changing circumstances and conditions, to weather storms and negotiate complicated bends on a long and bumpy road. Dynamism has been at the core of the trajectory of Museveni's rule. Such dynamism has both a tinge of Museveni's agency and an element of contingency, structural forces and unintended occurrences. The changes and transformations at different stages and phases of Museveni's rule have to be understood with Museveni as the central figure, but a robust explanation also has to be situated within broader structural and systemic processes both in Uganda and beyond.[9]

The structure of Ugandan society has changed significantly over the past four decades, just as the political landscape has undergone tremendous transformations. Museveni has been adept and shrewd in charting a path to power and sustain a long and resilient tenure, but he also has been a beneficiary of other people's actions and inactions, of forces, structures and systems over which he has no direct control. For example, he skilfully engineered a prolonged (and arguably deleterious) twenty-year legal and constitutional suspension of political party-activities, which helped him consolidate his power and successfully fuse the NRM with the state (see Golooba-Mutebi and Katusiimeh's chapter, this volume). In the same vein, however, the historical negative role of parties in Uganda played into Museveni's favour and to the disadvantage of his opponents.[10]

Associated as they were with past negative attributes including sectarianism, divisions and violence, Museveni and the NRM convinced Ugandans of the necessity of proscribing activities of political parties. The long absence of active and engaged political parties coupled with a less-than-inspiring slate of individual opposition leadership did combine to inadvertently help Museveni's hand and stay at the helm.

The contours of wider regional and international geopolitics have changed and in ways that have shaped Uganda's domestic politics. Uganda has had an oversized role in the geopolitics of the Great Lakes region with Museveni as, by far, the most important actor in a volatile region precisely because he is the region's longest surviving ruler. He occupies the front-row seat on security matters in the region, and used his mastery of the region's security complexities to maintain leverage over especially Western benefactors. He has continuously made the case that he has unique and distinct qualities and competencies necessary for assuring security and stability in a troubled region.[11] This has been Museveni's stated raison d'être to both domestic and foreign audiences for his continued and indefinite stay at the helm.[12]

This book does not address the regional and international dimensions of Museveni's rule,[13] which is not to gainsay the role that external forces have played in the evolution and trajectory of his reign. Instead, the book has largely focused on how Museveni's rule has been shaped and conditioned by forces and factors internal to the country's social structure, political culture, institutional configurations and demographics.

In different ways, the chapters in this book have taken up a range of arguments and analyses that converge on what we consider to be the core themes around the pillars and drivers of Museveni's rule. We have summarized the crux of Museveni's long rule as autocratic adaptability to denote both the democratic deficiencies that deepened over the past decades but also the sheer resilience of his system of rule. Adaptability has limits; it cannot be in perpetuity. All long reigns have come to an end, one way or the other, and Museveni's rule too will certainly grind to a halt in the near future if for nothing else, at a minimum, for the random course of nature and biological inevitability. Needless to say, the implications of the end to Museveni's rule loom very large, indeed.

The stakes and fates of a post-Museveni Uganda

Countries that experience long-haul personalist rule, institutional muzzling and the fusion of ruling elites with governments and the state structure with ruling party are more likely to experience uncertain political futures than those where ruling elites – revolutionary or otherwise – allow for a change of guard, shifts in policy and the gradual protection of institutional autonomy. The future stability and security of Uganda are intricately tied to the ways and circumstances of Museveni's departure from state power given the paucity of institutional autonomy and capacity deliberately incubated over the long period of Museveni/NRM rule. The stakes have become higher the longer Museveni has held onto power and exacted an overriding influence on key processes of Uganda's political development and social order.

The bulk of uncertainty surrounding Uganda's politics today emanates from questions about *how* and *when* Museveni will leave power, who will succeed him, how political power in a post-Museveni era will be structured and exercised, whether the country will forge a stable future or lapse into instability akin to its dreaded past. It is not just that Museveni has ruled Uganda longer than the combined time of all previous eight governments before 1986, it is also that he has had such an imposing and unparalleled imprint on the country, making him quite inseparable from the state. His future departure holds enormous implications for what happens once he leaves the stage.

Museveni's imprint on Uganda has taken a variety of dimensions, but perhaps the most important has to do with the defence, security and stability of Uganda. On the security circuit, Museveni has created a somewhat self-serving narrative that consistently justifies his stay in power – the ostensible restoration of security of person and property compared to the supposed insecurity and lawlessness of the 1970s and '80s. At different times, especially during election campaigns, Museveni forcefully argues that the security and stability of Uganda would be jeopardized without him at the helm. In one sense, this can be interpreted as little more than self-serving blackmail. But in another light, there is a real possibility that Uganda could unravel in the absence of Museveni considering the personalized and fragmented manner of the coercive state apparatus that he has built and presided over, as analysed in the chapters by Bareebe, Rwengabo and Tapscott in this volume.

Uganda's current national security architecture and the law-and-order infrastructure are not set up to outlive Museveni and the immediate imperatives of regime survival that have informed security calculations and designs. Regime-survival imperatives and navigating an uncertain political environment have made the deepening of militarized rule a crucial component of Museveni's power calculus, as analysed by Sabastiano Rwengabo in this volume. Regime-survival is intricately tied to militarized rule. The state's coercive instruments are enmeshed in the incumbent's power and political-survival imperatives, and other actors invested in a continuation of the status quo are also beholden to this overarching logic. Given the uncertainty and militarism that undergird Uganda's political system, Museveni's departure will likely imperil the regime's coercive capacity, which is the stabilizing force of both state and society, a force that is acutely necessary for holding together a socially fragile society and economically weak polity.

Cohesion and convergence in the armed forces writ large are especially crucial to the maintenance of a sound and solid coercive state apparatus considering Uganda's history of instability and insecurity fuelled by divisions in the military and state intelligence apparatus. The two decades of instability and insecurity, 1960s to 1980s, which formed the primary stepping stone to Museveni's ascendance to power in 1986, had to do with the disharmony and disarray among the military, security and intelligence agencies. The July 1985 coup of the Okellos was infamously referred to as 'uncoordinated troop movements'.[14] Taking this lesson seriously, Museveni built his rule around tight command and control of the military apparatus and the militarization of governmental activities, themes ably explored by Bareebe and Rwengabo in this volume.[15] What remains entirely uncertain and a source of grave trepidation is whether that firm command control can remain in place post-Museveni.

How to navigate and negotiate the uses and abuses of military power will be squarely at the heart of any future transition of power, whether peaceful or violent, if viable change or possible implosion results from change at the top. This is especially because balancing the boat in the armed forces has become ever more precarious and delicate the longer Museveni has stayed on in power. There are newer forces taking shape particularly those pitting older factions against relatively younger individuals among the uniformed personnel. Of particular pertinence is the power and strength of groups aligned to the first son, Muhoozi Kainerugaba, who rapidly rose to the rank of full General and previously commanded the Special Forces and the Land Forces. He has recently taken an openly political posture of seeking to take over from the father. As initially point out by retired General David Sejusa in a 2013 dossier, the so-called 'Muhoozi Project'[16] affects not only the cohesion and patriotic ethos of the military and security services but sends worrisome signals in the country's overall body politic.[17]

What might happen, as different groups fight to keep ahead in the contest and scramble around presidential succession, remains difficult to foresee. However, the perils of an imposed father-to-son presidential transition are not hard to predict considering the experience of DRC, Togo and Chad, among others.[18] As a harbinger to what might lie ahead, the human rights situation appears to have worsened in recent years with security agencies and actors engaging in excesses at the behest of different factions including that of Muhoozi, which in April 2022 organized highly publicized 'birth-day' celebrations as Muhoozi seeks to build political popularity, all done contrary to UPDF rules.[19]

The disquiet and trepidation over Museveni's succession, as analysed in Khisa's chapter in this volume, have a lot to do with how the ruling coalition evolved and shifted over the past decades. In a sense, Museveni outran and outlasted almost all his peers and potential successors within the NRM, arguably the last credible contender being former Prime Minister and NRM Secretary General, Amama Mbabazi, whose bid to succeed Museveni fell by the wayside in 2016. This has created an environment in which Museveni is the sole actor with the gravitas and standing to authoritatively command the armed forces. In his absence, anything is possible – from a problematic father-to-son transition to raptures within the security services, to external intervention and general political crisis.

Museveni's security grip, which is the primary justification for his rule, is not only internal to Uganda; it has important regional dimensions. It is difficult to theoretically predict the extent to which a security implosion in Uganda would travel across the region for a country that has for long been the leading host of refugees from its neighbours (now in excess of 1.5 million). Uganda's military adventurism and interventionism across national borders, have served to stabilize as well as complicate not just national but also regional security. Thus, how Museveni's rule ends is likely to have enormous implications not just for the domestic political scene but also for contours and configurations of regional security.

Whatever the form and framework to the end of Museveni's reign – violent, peaceful, orderly or disorderly – Uganda will have to renegotiate a new political settlement for governing the polity in a viable and durable manner. The shattering of the minimum elite consensus embodied in the 1995 constitutional compromise has meant that over the last two decades, Uganda's politics has operated in a state of deep uncertainty. Contestations and defiant challenges to the status quo, from Kizza Besigye and 'Walk-to-Work' in 2011 to Bobi Wine and the 'People Power' Movement in 2019,[20] have unfolded dangerously towards political and security confrontation increasingly fuelled by an impatient and militant urban youth.

To avert descend into bloody violence, those commanding the security forces will have to exercise restraint and strike a consensus on how to manage challenges to Museveni but especially to whoever is at the centre of a post-Museveni government. Previous (and ongoing) challenges and contests against Museveni, and his determination to fight back, have eroded structured and principled political engagement, hollowing out of state institutions, and corroding trust, leaving Uganda's political landscape at once uninspiring to moderate voices but also patently repressive to hardened opposition activists.

Reforming and reimagining a new political system will require considerable national goodwill, broad consensus from key political actors and social institutions, and signalling hope and promise to an agitated young population. Refashioning a new political system and marshalling the necessary compromises for a stable and viable long-term political system will take statesmanship and political maturity among key actors. An elite pact and programme of reforming politics and economic management is critical for national reconciliation and recovery. Renegotiating a new viable Uganda will necessitate healing the painful wounds of war and scars of armed conflict especially in the north and northeast, bridging the north-south divide. This will aid the forging of a united republic based on shared national aspirations and political inclusivity, and reconfiguring power centres and loci in a manner that transcends Museveni's personalist rule.

With opposition actors currently deep in the trenches fighting to not only bring an end to Museveni's rule but also press for accountability and punishment for abuses of the era of NRM rule, the current rulers will undoubtedly need some assurances of protection against prosecution once out of power. This potential standoff between accountability and reconciliation is likely to be a stumbling block to negotiating a path forward for Uganda. Hence, there will be a need for (re)casting the spotlight on understanding the tribulations of revenge-driven politics.

As and when Uganda gets to the point of actually negotiating a transition away from Museveni's reign, finding a middle ground between accountability and closure, retribution and reconciliation, prosecution and protection, will be a critical part of the broader national compromise and compass necessary for moving the country forward. That Uganda can overcome Museveni's autocratic grip on the country is possible, but this will require outstanding leadership, innovative thinking, statesmanship and imaginative acumen on the part of key political and civic actors.

Concluding reflections

Museveni's long autocratic rule may well culminate in the kind of renewal and reformation that could give Uganda a new path forward for the country's political development and socio-economic transformation. It is impossible to predict the future, so all we have done in this chapter is to speculate about the possibilities ahead on the basis of what we know at the present. We have underscored the precarious political juncture and the uncertainty attendant to such a long reign as Museveni's, its rustiness and repressiveness but also its resilience and ability to replenish. This book as a whole has taken stock of the different ways that Museveni has perpetuated his rule but also the implications this has meant for Ugandan politics and society, writ large.

Further research and analysis can cast the spotlight on the factions and forces currently positioned to take charge of a future post-Museveni environment, be they in the military or civilian politics, their social bases and holding power. The role of external forces and actors, regional and international, not quite addressed in this book yet very important in getting a full understanding of Uganda's political road ahead, too deserves careful examination.

Last, since 2017 there has been a great deal of activism around the push for a national dialogue as a catalyst to peaceful change of leadership away from Museveni. We do not as yet know enough about the framework and viability of a negotiated transition through a broad national dialogue and what roles different actors are likely to play and to what end. This chapter has alluded to the possibilities of a new negotiated political settlement only as a normative statement and not an empirical analysis.

Notes

1   Joshua Rubongoya, *Regime Hegemony in Museveni's Uganda: Pax Musevenica* (New York: Palgrave Macmillan, 2007).

2   Aili Mari Tripp, *Museveni's Uganda: Paradoxes of Power in Hybrid Regime* (Boulder, CO: Lynne Rienner, 2010).

3   Rubongoya, *Regime Hegemony*, 4.

4   Rebecca Tapscott, *Arbitrary States: Social Control and Modern Authoritarianism in Museveni's Uganda* (Oxford: Oxford University Press, 2021), 6.

5   J. Oloka-Onyango and Josephine Ahikire, eds., *Controlling Consent: Uganda's 2016 Elections* (Trenton, NJ: Africa World Press, 2017).

6   Joe Oloka-Onyango, "'New-Breed" Leadership, Conflict, and Reconstruction in the Great Lakes Region of Africa: A Sociopolitical Biography of Uganda's Yoweri Kaguta Museveni', *Africa Today*, 50, no. 3 (2004): 29–52.

7   David Bilungule Bakamana, 'New Type of Democracy in Africa: Father-to-Son Presidential Transitions (Kings and Owners of Africa and Democratic Hereditary Presidents in Africa)', *Journal of African Interdisciplinary Studies* 5, no. 7 (2021): 4–25.

8   Jonathan Fisher, "'Some More Reliable than Others": Image Management, Donor Perceptions and the Global War on Terror in East African Diplomacy', *Journal of Modern African Studies* 15, no. 1 (2013): 1–31.

9   Jonathan Fisher, 'Managing Donor Perceptions: Contextualizing Uganda's 2007 Intervention in Somalia', *African Affairs* 111, no. 444 (2012): 404–23.

10   Lise Rakner Sabiiti-Makara and Lars Svasand, 'Turnaround: The National Resistance Movement and the Reintroduction of a Multiparty System in Uganda', *International Political Science Review* 30, no. 2 (2009): 185–204.

11   Filip Reyntjens, 'Path Dependence and Critical Junctures: Three Decades of Interstate Conflict in the African Great Lakes Region', *Conflict, Security & Development* 20, no. 6 (2020): 747–62.

12   Fisher, 'Managing Donor Perceptions'.

13   Except Tangri and Mwenda's chapter on relations with foreign business actors and aspects of Rwengabo's chapter that touch on regional military interventions.

14   Ian Katusiime, 'Museveni and Military Coups', *The Independent*, Kampala (13 September 2021). https://www.independent.co.ug/museveni-and-military-coups/

15   See Also Sabastiano Rwengabo 'Regime Stability in Post-1986 Uganda: Counting the benefits of Coup- Proofing', *Armed Forces & Society* 39, no. 3 (2013): 531–59; Moses Khisa, 'Politicisation and Professionalisation: The Progress and Perils of Civil-Military Transformation in Museveni's Uganda', *Civil Wars* 22, no. 2–3 (2020): 289–312.

16   Daily Monitor, 'Probe Assassination Claims, Says Tinyefuza', *Daily Monitor*, Kampala (6 May 2013). https://www.monitor.co.ug/uganda/news/national/probe-assasination-claims-says-tinyefuza-1542336

17   Daily Monitor, 'NRM Historicals Split on "Muhoozi Project"', *Daily Monitor*, Kampala (17 May 2013). https://www.monitor.co.ug/uganda/news/national/nrm-historicals-split-on-muhoozi-project-1543332

18   Bakamana, 'New Type of Democracy', 7–8; *BBC News*, 'Uganda's David Sejusa: "Oppose Museveni's Monarchy"', *BBC World Service* (18 June 2013). https://www.bbc.com/news/world-africa-22957712

19   The Citizen, 'Museveni's Son, Gen Muhoozi, Announces Interest in Uganda Presidency', *The Citizen*, Dar es Salaam (7 May 2022). https://www.thecitizen.co.tz/tanzania/news/east-africa-news/gen-muhoozi-politics-3808492

20   Sam Wilkins, Richard Vokes and Moses Khisa, 'Briefing: Contextualizing the Bobi Wine Factor in Uganda's 2021 Elections', *African Affairs* 120, no. 481 (2021): 629–43.

Index